NORTHERN COOKBOOK

NORTHERN COOKBOOK

Edited by

Eleanor A. Ellis

Original Illustrations by

James Simpkins

Hurtig Publishers, in co-operation with
Indian and Northern Affairs Canada
and the Canadian Government Publishing Centre,
Supply and Services Canada

Hurtig Publishers
10560–105 Street
Edmonton, Alberta

Co-published through
Publishing Centre
Supply and Services Canada
Catalogue No. R72-4667-1

ISBN 0-88830-178-2

Printed and bound in Canada
by John Deyell Company

CONTENTS

CHAPTER I   Basic Nutrition and Meal Planning, 1

CHAPTER II   Soups, Stuffings, Sauces, Appetizers and Dips, 19

CHAPTER III   Wild Game, 41

CHAPTER IV   Game Birds, 97

CHAPTER V   Fish and Sea Mammals, 121

CHAPTER VI   Eggs, Cereals and Beverages, 161

CHAPTER VII   Flour Mixtures: Bread, Cookies and Cakes, 171

CHAPTER VIII   Vegetables, Salads and Salad Dressings, 205

CHAPTER IX   Desserts, Jam, Jelly, Candy, Pastry and Pie, 245

CHAPTER X   Arctic Gourmet Recipes, 273

CHAPTER XI   Pointers from Pioneers, 293

CHAPTER XII   Hunting in the Northwest Territories
and a Summary of the Northwest Territories
Game Regulations, 315

APPENDIX   Calorie Values of Some Common Foods, 327
Standard Portions and Measures, 331
Substitution Values, 333

INDEX   335

PREFACE

The purpose of this book is to record facts about some of the wild game, game birds, fish, fruit, and vegetables available in Canada's north (which includes not only the Arctic and sub-Arctic, but the northern lake and forest regions of all the provinces), and to suggest methods by which these foods may be prepared and served. To include recipes for all of the indigenous foods would be a mammoth task, but I have tried to include enough to be representative of a cross-section of this vast land. Some basic information on nutrition and family meal planning has been included for the benefit of young homemakers, and I have drawn on the experience of those who pioneered the north for a section that offers advice to wilderness wives.

I would like to thank Don Simpson and Gordon Rancier for making it possible for me to edit this book, Diane Armstrong and Lois Klages for their helpful advice, Cathy Prindiville for research and typing, and Ferguson L. Short for smoothing the way.

Good recipes, like good books and good wine, often improve with age. I hope you will adopt these recipes as your own, and, over the years, share with us your suggestions for improving them.

ELEANOR A. ELLIS

Ottawa
1977

ACKNOWLEDGEMENTS

Many people assisted both directly and indirectly in compiling the material for this book. To those who contributed recipes; to those who tried and tested them; and to those who so generously shared their experiences and knowledge of the north; I offer my sincere and heartfelt thanks. If I have inadvertently omitted the name of any contributor, it has been because a good recipe can become the prize possession of many families, making it almost impossible to determine the originator.

Bertha Allen
Mavis and Ron Anderson
Phyl and Bill Applewhite
Diana Bacon
Mrs. Frank Bailey
Lydia Bartsch
Ernie Bennett
Beryl Bevington
Viola and Bill Bock
Lois Born
Marie Brown
Norm Burgess
Marion Burke
Dr. Gordon Butler
Ruth Butt
Canada Department of Agriculture
Kay Cardiff
Monah Carley
Angelo Casagrande
The Church of the Ascension
Heather Clayton
Olga Creelman
Ralph Currie
Harold Darkes
The Daughters of the Midnight Sun
Department of Fisheries of Canada
Department of National Health and Welfare
Julie DePass
Graham Douglas
Diane and Drew Craig
Betty and Bill Eades
Joyce Ellis
Rita and Roy Fewster
I. E. Fitzpatrick
Lynne Fujikawa
Scotty Gall
Mardy and Joe Gallagher
Gabriel Gély
Alice and Jerry Gill
Joan Gillespie
Peter Gillespie
Romeo Guay
Norah Herron
C. Hitz
Daisy Jensen
Verna Kirkness
Murielle Labonté
Jill Maddock
Diana Mansell's Grade Five Class at
   Hay River, N.W.T.

Frank McCall
Connie and Dusty Miller
Anna Milligan
Dr. J. E. Monagle
E. Rosalie Munroe
Peter Murdock
Hugh Macdonald
Ethel and Norm Macpherson
Eileen and Arnold McCallum
E. Berneice McFarlane
Jessie McVeigh
Lenore Newman
New York State College of Home Economics
Eileen Norman
Margaret Oldenburg
Dorothy and George O'Neill
R. J. "Bud" Orange
Helen Parker
Cherri Payne
Pennsylvania State University, College
   of Agriculture Extension Service
Barri Worthington Porter
Patricia Purl
Elsie Rancier
Kay Rawlings
Beverley Reid
Mrs. Wm. Ross
Suzanne Saint-Hilaire
Margaret Shugg
Dorothy Sinclair
Grace Spencer
Betty Stewart
Jean Stokey
Jack Taylor
Eileen Thrower
R. B. "Shorty" Tinling
Don Trent
United States Brewers Association Inc.
U.S. Department of Agriculture
University of Alaska Co-operative
   Extension Service
Utah State Agriculture College
   Extension Service
The Vancouver Sun (Edith Adams' Cottage
   Homemaker Service)
Marg Wickett
Joan Wilson Hunter
Didy Woolgar
Eleanor Zuk
and Bob, Dick, Wendy, Jane and Susan

To the people of the north

CHAPTER I

BASIC NUTRITION
and
MEAL PLANNING

We cannot live without food. We cannot be healthy unless we have the right kinds of food in the right amounts. Hunger pains tell us when our body needs food, and our instinct tells us we must eat. Unfortunately, our instinct does not tell us what kind of food to eat, or how much. The choice is up to us. It is important then, for us to be able to recognize the various types of foods, to understand their function in the body, to know how much of each is required to maintain good health, and to learn how best to prepare and serve the foods that are available to our families and to ourselves.

Many people have worked, studied and experimented to provide us with this information. We now have firm guidelines to follow for choosing the right kinds and the right amounts of food to keep us healthy. It is up to us to learn how to apply the guidelines to the food that is available, and to become good cooks. The residents of Canada's north are fortunate, because in addition to having most of the foods common to southern Canada in their stores and supermarkets, they also have access to many kinds of game animals, birds, fish, wild greens and berries that are not found "outside". By applying the guidelines for healthful eating to indigenous foods, infinite variety is possible and mealtime can be a happy, rewarding experience for the whole family.

Food is made up of materials called nutrients, and each nutrient performs a special function in the body. Not all foods contain the same number or kinds of nutrients, so in order to ensure that the body has enough of every kind, we need to eat a variety of foods. The names of the nutrients, their function in the body, and examples of foods which contain them are as follows:

Nutrient	Functions	Main Source
Proteins	To build and repair body tissues; to help us to GROW	meat, fish, fowl, eggs, cheese, milk.
Carbohydrates	To provide us with energy; to help us to GO.	sugar, starch, bread and flour mixtures, cereals, root vegetables such as potatoes and turnips
Fats	To provide us with energy; to conserve body warmth; to help us to GO.	butter, cream, fortified margarine, lard, shortening, oil, animal fat, nuts.
Minerals	To build strong bones, teeth and good red blood, healthy nerves and body organs; to regulate the body processes; to help us GROW and GLOW.	vegetables, whole grain cereals, eggs, milk, certain fruits (e.g. raisins).
Vitamins	To keep all parts of the body healthy; to regulate body processes; to help us GROW and GLOW.	fresh fruit and vegetables, meat (especially organ meats), milk, eggs, cheese.

In addition to the nutrients listed above, our bodies also need water and cellulose, or roughage to keep healthy. Water helps to regulate the temperature of the body, it is needed for digestion and for breathing and perspiring. It also helps our bones, muscles, kidneys and other organs to operate smoothly and efficiently, and we could not live long without it. Milk, fruits and fruit juices, soups, vegetables and beverages contribute to the body's supply of water.

Cellulose or roughage is the fibrous part of vegetables, fruits or cereals that cannot be digested, and it provides the bulk which is necessary for good digestion. It acts as an intestinal broom to sweep out the body wastes and prevent constipation.

2

To help us to choose the foods that will give our bodies the nutrients they need each day, the Nutrition Division of Health and Welfare Canada has prepared a Food Guide. Canada's Food Guide recommends that we eat 3 meals a day, and provides us with suggestions for healthful eating as follows:

Canada's Food Guide

Energy needs vary with age, sex, and activity. Eat a variety of foods from each group every day; foods selected according to the guide can supply 1,000 to 1,400 calories. For additional energy, increase the number and size of servings from the various food groups, or add other foods.

1. MILK AND MILK PRODUCTS—
   Children (up to eleven years). . . . . 2 to 3 servings
   Adolescents. . . . . 3 to 4 servings
   Pregnant and nursing women . . . . 3 to 4 servings
   Adults . . . . 2 servings

2. FRUITS AND VEGETABLES—4 to 5 servings. Choose a variety of both vegetables and fruits, cooked, raw, or their juices. Include at least two vegetables, preferably yellow or green.

3. BREAD AND CEREALS—3 to 5 servings. Whole-grain products are recommended.

4. MEAT AND ALTERNATES—2 servings. Choose lean meat, poultry, liver, or fish; eggs, cheese, peanut butter, dried peas, beans, or lentils may be used in place of meat.

Vitamin D: A supplement is recommended when milk is consumed that does not contain added vitamin D.

Approved by Health and Welfare Canada, 1977

While three meals a day are recommended for the family, this is not an absolute necessity for good health, and sometimes four or five smaller meals may suit an individual or a family better. Serving three meals each day, however, usually is more convenient for the person who prepares the meals, especially if there are school-age children in the family. If the three-meal pattern is followed, approximately one-third of the total food required for the day should be served at each meal. Following is an example of how this may be done.

Basic Meal Pattern for a Day:
  Breakfast—
    Citrus fruit or fruit juice with Vitamin C
    Whole grain cereal with milk
    Other protein food, such as fish, bacon or eggs
    Bread or enriched bannock with butter or fortified margarine
    Beverage (milk for children)

Dinner—

> Meat, fish or fowl
> Potatoes
> At least one other vegetable
> Bread or bannock
> Fruit or berries
> Beverage (milk for children)

Supper or Lunch—

> Cheese, egg, or meat alternates
> Vegetable
> Bread or bannock with butter or fortified margarine
> Dessert
> Beverage (milk for children)

Vitamin C

Fresh fruits and vegetables may not always be available in the north, and if dried fruits and vegetables must be used for prolonged periods of time there may be a shortage of Vitamin C which could lead to scurvy. If fresh citrus fruits: oranges, grapefruit or lemons, are not available, make sure the family get their Vitamin C by one of the following methods:

1. Use canned vitaminized fruit juices—juices such as apple, grape, grapefruit, pineapple, tomato or orange juice that contain Vitamin C.

2. Use concentrated frozen, or powdered citrus fruits or tomato juice, mixing them according to directions on the tin or package.

3. Use wild greens and berries that are rich in Vitamin C as much as possible. Sourdock, fireweed shoots, willow greens, scurvy grass, lambs quarters, rose hips, strawberries, raspberries, blueberries or cloudberries are satisfactory sources of Vitamin C.

4. Use soya or mung bean sprouts (purchase seed beans, as the dried beans sold in grocery stores will not sprout).
Spread the beans on newspaper on a pan or cookie sheet. Keep them in a dark place and water them several times a day. They will sprout in about three days. Use the sprouts, either cooked or in salads, when they are about three or four inches long. To prevent molding, add one-half teaspoon of chlorinated lime to a gallon of the water used for soaking the beans, but be sure to rinse the sprouts well before using them.
5. If none of these sources of Vitamin C are available, ascorbic acid tablets may be obtained from the drug store, nursing station or lay dispenser as the case may be.

Cereals

Cereals are inexpensive and a good source of the carbohydrates needed for energy. If whole grain cereals, which contain the seed or endorsperm of the kernel of grain, are used, the cereal also supplies some vitamins, minerals and protein. Rolled oats, oatmeal, cracked wheat, barley and rye cereals are excellent when cooked, and in most places, ready-to-serve whole grain breakfast cereals are also available.

Vegetables

The vegetables chosen may be fresh, canned, frozen or dried. Dried vegetables available now do not require long soaking or long cooking, and provide pleasant variety to the meal. In most cases directions and proportions for preparing them will be on the package, but generally one portion of dried vegetables will yield three to four portions when reconstituted. Once reconstituted, they may be substituted in most of the recipes calling for fresh vegetables. The dried vegetables most easily prepared are onions, potatoes, red and green peppers, parsley, cabbage, carrots, greens, herbs and sweet potatoes.

Fruit

The fruit chosen may also be fresh, frozen, canned or dried. Good quality dried fruits include apples, pears, peaches, prunes, apricots, raisins, currants, dates and figs. Except for their Vitamin C content, they have about the same food value as canned fruits and when properly prepared will be colorful, plump, juicy and not too sweet or leathery. Avoid long soaking and overcooking. One pound of dried fruit will yield about two quarts of stewed fruit. Soak the fruit in just enough lukewarm water to cover it for about one hour. For stewed fruit, bring the fruit and the water to a boil and let it simmer gently for 5 to 10 minutes or until tender. (Prunes will take about 30 minutes). For making pies or puddings, drain the fruit after soaking it for an hour, and use it as fresh fruit.

Fresh fruits and vegetables should be stored in a cool dark place and will keep well for several months if there is not too much fluctuation in temperature. If they should become frozen accidentally, keep them frozen until you are ready to use them and cook them without pre-thawing. Frozen oranges, grapefruit or lemons may be coated with ice to prevent drying. When you are ready to use them, thaw them slowly in a pan of cold water, then eat them as soon as the frost comes out. Never re-freeze them.

Meat and Meat Alternates

Beef, veal, lamb, pork, wild game, game birds, fish and sea mammals, or organ meats such as kidney, liver, heart, tongue may be used. Eggs, (chicken, duck or goose eggs) may also be used. Cheese and dried beans, peas or peanut butter, which also provide protein, may be substituted occasionally for a meat dish. When using dried eggs, add 3 tablespoons of lukewarm water to 1 tablespoon of egg powder to equal 1 whole egg. Better results are usually obtained if the eggs are reconstituted 2 or 3 hours ahead of the time they are to be used. Add ⅛ teaspoon of baking powder to the reconstituted egg for improved leavening action.

Milk

Milk should be used as the beverage for children if they are to get as much calcium and other minerals as their growing bones and teeth require. Milk powder may be reconstituted by adding water according to the directions on the package, usually 4 parts of water to one part of milk powder. If this is done ahead of time and chilled, the beverage is delicious. Evaporated milk diluted half and half with water may also be used. Sweetened condensed milk is more expensive and adds more sugar than is usually required in the diet. Powdered buttermilk may also be reconstituted and used satisfactorily both as a beverage and in baking.

Bread

Vary the breads served to the family. White, whole wheat or rye bread, bannock, raisin bannock, enriched bannock, tea biscuits, muffins, popovers, french toast, pancakes, sourdough bread and muffins are just a few of the many types that may be served.

How Much Food Do We Need?

Food provides us with the energy (called calories) which we need in order to carry on our daily activities. The number of calories which a person requires, including the energy needed to keep us breathing, to keep our heart beating and to keep our body processes functioning, depends on many things. For example, a person who works hard seal hunting or fishing or mining will need more calories than a person who sits at a desk all day long. A mother who looks after the house and cooks the meals and makes the clothes will need more calories than a baby lying in a basket. The number of calories required by the body depends on the physical activity, the age, size, sex, state of health, the climate (it takes more energy to live in a cold country than a hot one!) the temperature and the temperament of the person involved. If we eat food that provides us with more calories than we can burn up in our daily activities, we get fat. Conversely, if we don't eat enough food, we burn up our own body fat and tissues to get the calories required and we get thin. It is important to eat just the right amount of food needed to keep us healthy.

At the back of this book are tables which give the number of calories in average servings of some of the foods we commonly eat. If you find you are getting fat, change your eating habits by choosing foods that give fewer calories per serving (but always remember to follow Canada's Food Guide in choosing the types of foods to eat in any one day).

Meal Planning

Choosing the foods for your family to eat, from the five basic food groups as outlined in Canada's Food Guide, can be an interesting and rewarding experience. In some families, the only time the whole family can be together is at mealtime, and if the homemaker can make mealtime a happy occasion she will be well rewarded for the extra time spent on planning and preparing the food. There are several points to consider when deciding on the kinds of food to serve the family:

1. Try to choose foods that all members of the family can eat, although you may have to make some substitutions for the very young children.

2. Choose foods according to the season, particularly fruits and vegetables, as fresh fruits and vegetables generally have a better flavour. Use berries and home grown vegetables or wild greens whenever possible.

3. Consider the equipment that is available and choose foods that can be prepared with the utensils and facilities that are in your kitchen.

4. Use the facilities to their best advantage in order to prevent waste. For example, if you have an oven, and decide to have a roast for dinner, cook vegetables around the roast or in a casserole in the oven, and serve a baked pudding for dessert.

5. Plan your meal so that you have time to prepare it properly and have all the foods cooked and ready to serve at the same time.

6. Choose foods that will appear attractive when served together. Try to have variety in the colour, flavour, texture, temperature and form of the foods.

7. Don't repeat the same food twice in one meal, for example, rice for a vegetable and rice pudding for dessert.

8. Whenever possible, use foods that are available locally, rather than ones that have to be shipped in. Seal liver is just as tasty as calves liver when properly prepared.

9. Introduce a new food along with a family favorite, and keep the servings small the first time the new food is served.

Following are some suggestions for meals for the family, based on Canada's Food Guide. The largest meal of the day is called dinner, and it may be served either at noon or in the evening, depending on which time suits the family best. If dinner is served at noon, the evening meal is called supper. If dinner is served in the evening, the noon meal is called lunch.

Breakfasts

Canned Orange Juice
Bannock (made with milk
    and egg powder)
Jam or Peanut Butter
Milk for the children
Tea or Coffee

Stewed Prunes
Red River Cereal with Milk and Sugar
Enriched Bannock
Jam or Peanut Butter
Milk for the children
Tea or Coffee

Cranberry and Rose Hip Juice
Oatmeal with Milk and Sugar
Bannock or Toast with Jam
Milk for the children
Tea or Coffee

Mandarin Orange Sections
Bran Flakes with Milk and Sugar
Pancakes with Syrup
Milk for the children
Tea or Coffee

Vitaminized Apple Juice
Shredded Wheat with Milk and Sugar
Scrambled Eggs on Toast or Bannock
Milk for the children
Tea or Coffee

Grapefruit Juice
Sunny Boy Cereal with Milk and Sugar
French Toast or Bannock
Milk for the children
Tea or Coffee

Tomato Juice
Boiled Fish
Oatmeal Cookies with Raisins
Milk for the children
Tea or Coffee

Vitaminized Grape Juice
Oatmeal Porridge with Milk and Sugar
Moosemeat Hamburger on a Bun
    or Bannock
Milk for the children
Tea or Coffee

Dinners

Caribou Pot Roast with Vegetables
Carrot Sticks
Bannock or Bread
Applesauce and Cookies
Milk—Tea—Coffee

Baked Stuffed Arctic Char
Rice with Mushrooms
Buttered Peas
Fireweed Shoots with French Dressing
Charlie Pudding
Milk—Tea—Coffee

Cold Sliced Caribou
Scalloped Potatoes, Baked Squash
Bannock or Bread
Orange Vanilla Pudding
Milk—Tea—Coffee

Pan-Fried Liver with Onions
Baked Potatoes, Green Beans
Canned Tomato Casserole
Saskatoon Berry Pie
Milk—Tea—Coffee

Baked Stuffed Seal Heart
Roasted Canned Potatoes
Creamed Corn Casserole
Cranberry Crumble
Milk—Tea—Coffee

Reindeer Head Soup with Vegetables
Bannock or Buns
Blueberry Pie
Milk—Tea—Coffee

Roast Ptarmigan and Gravy
Mashed Potatoes
Turnip Balls in Parsley Butter
Cabbage and Pineapple Salad
Apple Betty
Milk—Tea—Coffee

Whale Pot Roast with Vegetables
Bannock or Buns
Ice Cream—Chocolate Cake
Milk—Tea—Coffee

Lunches or Suppers

Vegetable Soup
Peanut Butter and Jelly Sandwiches
Peach Crisp
Milk—Tea—Coffee

Boston Baked Beans
Brown Bread
Mixed Fruit Salad
Cocoa

Macaroni and Cheese
Cabbage and Cranberry Salad
Bannock or Bread
Canned Plums
Milk—Tea—Coffee

Spaghetti and Tomato Casserole
Bread Sticks
Green Salad
Apple Pudding
Milk—Tea—Coffee

Tuna Fish Casserole
Creamed Carrots and Peas
Biscuits with Jam
Milk—Tea—Coffee

Split Pea Soup
Baked Eggs with Cheese
Bean Salad
Lemon Jello
Milk—Tea—Coffee

Cream of Tomato Soup
Toasted Cheese Sandwiches
Pickles
Baked Rice with Raisins
Milk—Tea—Coffee

Creamed Fish on Toast or Bannock
Jellied Fruit Salad
  with Dream Whip
Milk—Tea—Coffee

Purchasing Food

Every homemaker is aware of how the rising costs of food can wreck the family budget, but there are many things that can be done to keep food costs down. With a little extra effort and wise planning the family can be well fed without extravagance.

1. Before going to the store, decide on the meals you are going to serve the family for the next few days (or, preferably, a week).

2. Check the supplies you have on hand, and make a list of the foods and the amounts you need to buy.

3. Buy according to the foods you have listed and buy only those foods. Impulse buying, while nice for the storekeeper, can play havoc with the food budget.

4. Read the labels on canned and packaged goods. The label tells what you are buying and how much it costs. Compare the cost per serving of two or more types of the same food and buy the most economical one.

5. Buy by the grade when possible. Many Canadian foods are graded according to quality. For example, the grades of canned fruit and canned vegetables are Fancy, Choice, Standard and Substandard. Fancy grade fruit is perfect in appearance with clear syrup. Standard grade fruit is not as attractive in appearance but the food value and the flavour is exactly the same and it costs much less than the Fancy grade.
A booklet describing the grades of Canadian foods called "Buy by Grade", Publication Number 305, may be obtained free of charge from the Information Division of the Canada Department of Agriculture, Ottawa.

6. Buy foods in as large a size as possible, as larger quantities are usually cheaper in price. Only do this, however, if you have enough room so the foods can be properly stored without spoiling.

7. Do not buy cans of food that are bulged, as this sometimes indicates that the food inside has spoiled.

8. Buy fresh foods as soon as they come into the store if you can afford them, but do not buy fresh foods if the price is too high. Canned, dried and frozen foods are often just as nourishing as fresh foods and may cost considerably less.

9. Be sure you have purchased all the food you need for your family's meals before you spend money on pop, gum, chocolate bars and "extras".

Ways to Keep Food Costs Down (from the Nutrition Division, Department of National Health and Welfare).

1. Use tested recipes and measure accurately.

2. Learn how to regulate your oven to have it at the right temperature.

3. Do not waste food. Avoid unnecessary left-overs by preparing foods in the amounts needed.

4. Check ice-box frequently to make sure all left-overs are used.

5. Save drippings for cooking other foods.

6. Watch your toaster and oven. Burnt foods are a waste.

7. Substitute vegetables for fruits in your meals if vegetables are more plentiful or if you cannot afford to buy two fruits each day.

8. Although you need to serve a vitamin C food every day, it does not have to be orange or grapefruit or other fruit containing vitamin C.
It could be:

potato	baked or boiled in skin
cabbage, turnip or cauliflower	large servings properly cooked or raw if possible

Remember that vitamin C is destroyed by heat and exposure to air.
Therefore, keep vitamin C foods in a cool place.
Keep canned foods containing vitamin C well covered and cool.

9. Know the appetites of members of your family and make the servings proportionate.

To Save Fuel

1. Serve raw vegetables frequently whenever possible.
2. Serve raw fruits for dessert whenever possible.
3. Cook two or more vegetables in the same pot; time the cooking periods accurately.
4. Serve dried fruits sometimes without cooking. Soaking is all that is needed in some cases.
5. Cook vegetables only until done, not too soft.
6. Reduce heat once food has reached boiling temperature; a gentle boil will still continue.
7. When oven is heated, use it to make several dishes baked in oven.
8. If double boiler is being used, the two sections can serve as cooking dishes.

To Save on Milk

1. Buy all or part of the milk as fluid skim milk or as skim milk powder.
2. If milk or cream sours, use it in cooking or baking.

To Save on Fruit

1. Select firm fruit, free of bruises.
2. Buy fruits in season.
3. Can or preserve berries and fruits when they are in season, or at the time of year when they are cheapest and most plentiful.
4. Use canned fruits when fresh fruits are not available or are too expensive.
5. Pick the brand, grade and size which best suits your needs and pocketbook.
6. Compare prices of citrus fruit juice, vitaminized apple juice, and tomato juice. Sometimes frozen orange juice is an inexpensive buy.
7. Know whether small or large tins of fruit juices are the best buy for your family.
8. Remember to serve dried fruits. They are available the year around and some are quite inexpensive.

11

To Save on Vegetables

1. Buy fresh vegetables when in season.
2. Use as much of your vegetables as possible—beet tops as a vegetable, outer leaves of lettuce and cabbage in soup, salad or sandwiches.
3. Canned vegetables have good food value and may be more economical than fresh ones.
4. Select the grade, brand and size of canned vegetables best suited to your needs and money available.
5. Reheat vegetables if necessary; do not re-cook them.
6. Frozen vegetables have no waste and may be an economical buy.
7. Use a small amount of boiling water when boiling fresh vegetables. Cook quickly, only until tender crisp, with the cover on, and serve immediately.
8. Have a vegetable garden if possible. Store and can your own vegetables.
9. Store vegetables carefully in a cool, dark place to retain food value. If you have no proper storage place, buy only in small quantities.
10. Cook vegetables with skins on, whenever possible, or peel skins thinly.
11. Use raw, baked, steamed or carefully boiled vegetables for good colour, flavour and food value.

To Save on Bread and Cereals

1. Consider cost, time of preparation, flavour and texture when deciding whether to bake at home or to buy bakery goods or ready-to-bake products. For large families especially, home baking is a real economy.
2. Buy whole grain and enriched cereals and breads. They are more nutritious than refined ones.
3. Breads with raisins or other foods added bring variety to the diet but are more expensive than plain bread.
4. Prepared cereals are usually more expensive than uncooked cereals.
5. Buy cereals in bulk or large packages if your family can use them before they spoil or if you can store them well.

To Save on Meat, Fish, Eggs and Cheese

1. Use local fish, meat and fowl whenever possible, especially if you can catch or kill it yourself.
2. Consider the amount of wastage such as bone and fat when buying meat. You need to buy more when there is much bone.
3. Buy cheaper cuts of meat. They are just as nutritious as the more expensive cuts but should be prepared very carefully by long, slow, moist cooking.
4. Serve fish, eggs, a cheese dish or baked beans occasionally instead of using meat each day for dinner. They are good substitutes for meat, nutritionally speaking, and are usually cheaper.

5. Extend meat by adding skim milk powder, breadcrumbs or cereals to meat loaves, patties or casseroles.

6. Canned meats may be money-savers. Compare their cost per serving with fresh meat.

7. Use bones, gravy, outer leaves of vegetables, meat scraps, ham water, to make soups.

8. Cook with Grade B eggs or egg powder. They are just as good as Grade A and less expensive.

9. Cook eggs at a moderate temperature. High heat toughens them.

10. Fancy and processed cheeses are usually more expensive than cheddar.

To Save on Vitamin D

1. Preparations containing other minerals and vitamins in addition to vitamin D are more expensive than ones containing only D.

2. It is wasteful to take amounts in excess of what is needed; i.e. 400 International Units. Therefore, if a capsule, tablet or recommended dosage gives more than the amount needed, it is an extravagant buy.

To Save on Extra Food

1. Make your own pickles, relishes, etc. Often it is extras such as these which greatly increase food costs. Remember that generally speaking they are not the most nutritious foods; when money is a consideration they should be kept to a minimum.

2. Do not buy candy, pop or gum until you have bought all the food your family needs for their regular meals.

Explanation of Some Cooking Terms Found in the Recipes

Bake   To cook food in the oven at the temperature given in the recipe.

Beat   To make a mixture very smooth by whipping it with over and under movements with a big spoon or a beater. The air is carried to the bottom of the bowl and back up to the top.

Boil   To cook food in boiling water or other liquid that is bubbling and steaming.

Blend   To mix two or more ingredients so that they are mixed well together (combined).

Brown   To bake, fry, or toast a food until the outside (surface) is brown.

Chill   To place food in a cold place (refrigerator or outside) until the food is cold.

Chop   To cut food into small pieces.

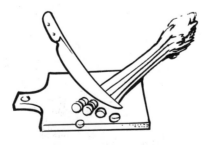

Combine   To mix or blend two or more ingredients.

Cook over hot water   To place the pan of food over another pan containing hot water (double boiler) to cook the food.

Cook in a pan of hot water   To place a dish of food, for example, custard in a shallow pan containing a small amount of water. Both pans are placed in the oven to cook the food.

Cream   To make a mixture soft and smooth by rubbing the ingredients (margarine or margarine and sugar) with a spoon against the sides of the bowl.

Cut in   To chop (distribute) shortening into flour using two knives or a pastry blender (the shortening is in little lumps, it is not smooth).

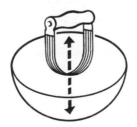

15

Dot   To put small bits of substance, usually fat, on top of a food.

Dice   To cut food (meat or vegetable) into small cubes.

Dissolve   To make a dry substance like sugar go into solution in a liquid.

Drain   To pour off liquid from food.

Fry   To cook food in hot fat in a heavy frying pan on the top of the stove.

Fold   To cut down through the mixture, across the bottom, up and across the top; turning the bowl after each stroke.

Knead   To press dough with the palms of the hands, turning the dough slightly as it is pushed (kneading bread).

Let Stand To leave the food in a bowl or pan for the length of time the recipe says.

Melt   To change a solid food to a liquid by heating it.

Mix   To combine ingredients, usually by stirring.

Remove from the Heat   To take the pan of food off the stove.

Roast   To bake (usually meat) in an oven.

Scald   To heat liquid (milk) on the top of the stove until little bubbles gather around the edges of the pan.

Season   To add salt, pepper or other ingredients to make the food taste better.

Shortening   Fats, like butter or margarine or lard.

Sift   To put dry ingredients through a sieve.

Simmer   To cook food slowly in water or other liquid which is just below the boiling point (water should not be boiling).

Slice   To cut food into thin flat pieces (slices).

Sprinkle   To cover the surface (outside) of the food with particles of an ingredient.

Stew   To simmer food in liquid.

Stir   To mix ingredients with a circular motion, around and around the bowl, with a spoon or fork.

Whip   To beat the ingredients very fast with an egg beater or wire whip.

CHAPTER II

SOUPS, STUFFINGS
SAUCES
APPETIZERS and DIPS

Soup can be light and clear to tempt an appetite, or it can be a heartwarming, soul satisfying meal in itself. It can furnish pleasant warmth at the start of a light lunch or it can be a main dish that will appease the lusty appetite of those who toil long hours in the biting cold of an Arctic winter. Regardless of its type or purpose, however, it must be well seasoned and generally speaking it must be served piping hot.

There are two main types of soups—those made with meat stock, and those made without meat stock. Meat stock is simply water that meat is boiled in, and an acceptable meat stock can be made quickly by dissolving bouillon cubes in hot water. The type of meat stock that conjures up visions of warm kitchens which abound with love and laughter though, is made by putting soup bones (crack large bones with an axe or hammer), and meat trimmings in a big pot, adding salt and enough cold water to cover, bringing them slowly to a boil and then letting them simmer for four to five hours on the back of the stove. Vegetables (fresh or dried) and rice or barley, may be added if desired to make a thick soup stock, or the soup may be strained, cooled and skimmed of fat to make a cleared soup stock. Whichever you prefer, you have a tasty base for endless variations.

SOUPS

Soups made without meat stock are cream soups, chowders and those made from vegetable stock. Quite often a thin cream sauce serves as the base for these soups, to which is added vegetables and seasonings as desired.

Soup Stock

2 pounds meat and bone
2 quarts (10 cups) cold water
1 medium onion, diced
½ cup diced carrots
2 stalks celery, including leaves
1 tablespoon dried parsley
4 whole cloves
1 bay leaf
¼ teaspoon marjoram
¼ teaspoon thyme
1 tablespoon salt
½ teaspoon black pepper

1. Cover the meat and bones with cold water in a large pot on top of the stove.
2. Slowly bring to a boil, then reduce the heat and let it simmer for 2 or 3 hours.
3. Add vegetables and seasonings and cook for 1 hour longer. Remove bones, gristle and skin, and strain if desired.
4. Let cool. Remove fat. Store in a clean covered jar in a cool place.

Brown Soup Stock

3 pounds bone and meat of elk
  or deer
¼ cup bacon fat
3 quarts cold water
½ cup celery
½ cup carrots
½ cup onions
1 tablespoon salt
2 sprigs parsley
5 whole cloves
1-2 bay leaves

1. Wipe meat with a clean damp cloth.
2. Cut meat from bones.
3. Melt fat in heavy fry pan and brown meat on all sides.
4. Place bones and browned meat in a large pot and cover with cold water.
5. Add remaining ingredients.
6. Cover, bring to a boil on top of the stove, then reduce heat and simmer 3½ to 4 hours.
7. Strain, chill, remove the fat which collects on the surface of the stock and strain again. (Other seasonings such as thyme or marjoram may be used).
8. Store the liquid in a clean covered container in a refrigerator and use within 3 days.
9. Pick out the meat from the strainer for use in any casserole or curry dish which calls for cooked meat.

Cabbage Soup

4 cups soup stock
4 tablespoons butter
1 large onion, sliced thinly
1 cup shredded turnip
2 cups shredded cabbage
½ teaspoon salt
¼ teaspoon pepper
½ cup commercial sour cream
   (if desired)
   Paprika (if desired)

1. Melt butter in a heavy saucepan on top of the stove.

2. Add thinly sliced onion and let simmer until onion is translucent but not brown.

3. Add shredded turnip and cabbage and heat for 3 minutes, stirring constantly.

4. Add soup stock, salt and pepper. Bring to a boil, reduce heat and simmer for 15 minutes.

5. Serve hot. Float a spoonful of sour cream and a dash of paprika on top if desired. Serves 4-6.

Onion Soup

4 tablespoons butter
6 medium onions, sliced thinly
1 teaspoon flour
½ teaspoon dry mustard
¼ teaspoon garlic salt
4 cups soup stock
¼ cup sauterne or dry white wine
½ teaspoon salt
¼ teaspoon pepper
1 teaspoon Worcestershire sauce
4 slices French bread *or* hard
   roll cut ½ inch thick
½ cup grated Parmesan Cheese

1. Melt butter in a heavy saucepan on top of the stove.

2. Peel the onions under water, then drain and slice thinly.

3. Lightly brown the sliced onions in the melted butter.

4. Mix flour, mustard and garlic salt together. Add to the butter-onion mixture and stir until smooth.

5. Add soup stock, wine, seasonings and 2 tablespoons grated Parmesan cheese, stirring until smooth.

6. Bring to a boil, reduce heat, cover and let simmer for 15 minutes until onions are tender.

7. Sprinkle slices of French bread or roll with grated Parmesan cheese and toast lightly in the oven or under the broiler.

8. Serve one slice cheese toast in each bowl of soup. Pass additional grated Parmesan if desired. Serves 4-6.

Vegetable Soup

4 cups soup stock
1 cup diced meat, cooked *or* uncooked
2 cups diced vegetables, fresh canned *or* dried
1 tablespoon rice *or* barley
½ teaspoon salt (if desired)

1. Combine all ingredients.
2. Simmer until meat and vegetables are tender.
3. Season to taste. Serve hot. Serves 4-6.

Clear Tomato Soup

2½ cups canned tomatoes
2 cups water
1 tablespoon chopped onion
4 cloves
1 bay leaf
2 teaspoons sugar
1 teaspoon salt
¼ teaspoon pepper
3 tablespoons flour
2 tablespoons butter

1. Melt the butter and blend in the 3 tablespoons flour.
2. Combine the tomatoes, water and onion and stir into the flour mixture until well blended.
3. Add the cloves, bay leaf and sugar, and let simmer for about 20 minutes.
4. Strain the soup through a sieve, reheat, season to taste and serve. Serves 4-6.

Navy Bean Soup

2 cups navy beans
1 ham bone *or* ½ pound salt pork
3 quarts water
1 tablespoon minced onion
½ teaspoon celery salt
⅛ teaspoon pepper
¼ teaspoon dry mustard
4 tablespoons flour
4 tablespoons melted butter

1. Soak the beans in cold water overnight.
2. Drain the beans and add them to 3 quarts water with the ham bone or salt pork. Bring to a boil, reduce heat and simmer until beans are tender.
3. When the beans are tender remove from liquid and press through a sieve.
4. Remove the ham bone or pork and return the bean puree to the liquid. Add the onion.
5. Blend the melted butter and flour, salt, pepper and mustard and stir into the soup.
6. Bring to a boil and cook for 5 minutes.
7. Serve hot with bread sticks.

Variations
Less water may be used and the liquid made up by adding milk at the last.

Court Bouillon

½ cup vinegar
1 tablespoon salt
1 stalk celery
¼ cup sliced onion
¼ cup sliced carrots
¼ teaspoon thyme
½ teaspoon peppercorns
1 bay leaf
1 teaspoon finely chopped parsley
1 quart (5 cups) boiling water

1. Combine all the ingredients in saucepan. Cover and boil for 10 minutes.
2. Drain the liquid from the vegetables and use with your favorite recipe.

Quick Carrot Soup

2 tablespoons grated onion
2 tablespoons fat
2 tablespoons flour
2 cups water
1 cup grated raw carrots
½ teaspoon salt
¼ teaspoon pepper
1 can milk
2 tablespoons butter

1. Cook the grated onion in 2 tablespoons fat for a few minutes.
2. Stir in 2 tablespoons flour.
3. Add the water, stirring well, then put in the grated raw carrots.
4. Season with salt and pepper and cook about 10 minutes or until the carrots are tender.
5. Add the milk and butter, reheat and serve.

Chicken Gumbo

½ cup diced raw ham
½ cup diced chicken
3 tablespoons fat
1 medium onion, minced
6 cups boiling water
3 chicken bouillon cubes
¼ teaspoon pepper
  Dash of cayenne
  Dash of thyme
1 bay leaf
3 tomatoes
½ cup sliced okra pods
2 tablespoons raw rice

1. Melt the butter or lard in a large pot. Add the ham and chicken and brown. When nicely browned add the minced onion and brown slightly.

2. Add the water, bouillon cubes, pepper, cayenne, thyme and bay leaf. Cover and bring to a boil, then reduce heat and simmer for 30 minutes.

3. Peel the tomatoes and remove most of the seeds. Chop the tomatoes and add to the soup.

4. Add the sliced okra pods and rice and continue to cook for another 30 minutes.

5. Remove the bay leaf and serve. Serves 6-8.

Clam Soup

2 quarts clams
2 cups hot water
1 pint milk
2 cups cracker crumbs
½ teaspoon salt
2 eggs
2 tablespoons butter, melted

1. Wash and clean the clams, scrubbing the shells thoroughly.

2. Place the clams in the hot water and bring to a boil, letting them boil until the clams clear from the shells. Remove the clams and the shells.

3. Add the milk to the broth.

4. Roll the cracker crumbs, not too fine, and add them to the broth and milk. Season with salt and bring to a boil. Boil for 3 minutes.

5. Beat the eggs until light and creamy and add the melted butter, then add slowly to the broth, stirring constantly.

6. Put the clams back into the broth, heat through and serve immediately.

Oyster Stew

1 pint oysters and their liquor
¼ cup butter
1 quart (5 cups) milk, scalded
1½ teaspoons salt
⅛ teaspoon pepper
⅛ teaspoon nutmeg (optional)

1. Melt the butter in heavy saucepan and add the oysters and liquor.

2. Simmer until the edges of the oysters begin to curl. This will take only about 3 minutes.

3. Skim off most of the scum which forms on top of the liquid.

4. Scald the milk and add oysters and seasonings, stirring constantly. Serve immediately with crackers. Serves 6.

Positanese Fish Soup

1 cup leftover fish, plus fish liquid
   or pan drippings
3 tablespoons oil
2 small chopped onions
1 sliced leek
1 minced clove garlic
   Tiny red pepper pod (optional)
   Salt and pepper to taste
¼ teaspoon saffron
1 bay leaf
1 tablespoon chopped parsley
3 chopped tomatoes
3 large diced potatoes
2½ cups water
   Garlic-rubbed toast

1. Heat oil.
2. Add onions, leek, garlic and red pepper and cook until onions soften.
3. Add salt, pepper, saffron, bay leaf, parsley, and tomatoes.
4. Bring to boil, simmer 5 minutes.
5. Add potatoes, fish liquid and/or drippings, if any, and water.
6. Simmer until potatoes are tender—about 20 minutes.
7. Remove red pepper.
8. Add boned and flaked fish and bring to boil.
9. Serve with garlic-rubbed toast. Serves 2-3.

Salmon Bisque

1 can (15½ oz.) salmon
¼ cup chopped onion
¼ cup diced celery
¼ cup butter *or* fat
1 teaspoon salt
3 tablespoons flour
3 cups liquid (salmon liquid plus milk to make 3 cups)
1 cup tomato juice
2 tablespoons chopped parsley

1. Drain and flake the salmon, saving the liquid.
2. Melt the butter or fat in heavy pot and cook the onions and celery until tender.
3. Stir in the flour and salt, blending well.
4. Add the 3 cups liquid slowly, stirring constantly and cook until thickened.
5. Pour in the tomato juice, stirring until blended, then add the flaked salmon. Serve hot, garnished with chopped parsley.

Mongole Soup

1 can tomatoes
1 can peas
1 medium onion, chopped
1 teaspoon sugar
½ teaspoon salt
¼ teaspoon pepper
½ teaspoon soda
2 tablespoons flour
2 tablespoons butter
½ cup milk

1. Combine the tomatoes, peas, onion, sugar, salt and pepper and cook for 10 minutes.
2. Mash the peas and tomatoes or put them through a sieve, then return them to the liquid.
3. Add the soda, then make a white sauce of the flour, melted butter and milk and add this to the soup. Reheat and serve hot.

Variations
The canned condensed tomato and pea soups may be used, thus eliminating the need to mash or put through a sieve.

Cream of Peanut Butter Soup

1 cup peanut butter
1 tablespoon flour
½ teaspoon salt
¼ teaspoon pepper
1 quart milk
1 tablespoon onion juice

1. Cream the peanut butter and add the flour, salt, pepper and onion juice.
2. Scald the milk and add slowly to the peanut butter mixture, stirring well.
3. Reheat the soup but do not boil. Serve hot.

Cream of Potato Soup

1½ cups stock
1½ cups mashed potatoes
1 teaspoon finely minced onion
½ teaspoon salt
⅛ teaspoon pepper
¼ teaspoon celery salt
3 cups milk
3 tablespoons fat, melted
3 tablespoons flour
Green onions

1. Combine the mashed potatoes and stock together, blending well. Put through sieve to remove any lumps.
2. Add the minced onion, salt, pepper and celery salt and heat thoroughly.
3. Make a sauce of 3 cups milk, 3 tablespoons fat and 3 tablespoons flour.
4. Add the sauce to the potato-stock mixture, stirring until well blended. Heat and serve hot. Top the soup dish with rings of green onions.

Puree of Split Peas

2 cups split peas
2 medium onions, chopped
5 medium potatoes, quartered
1 can cream of celery soup
1 cup light cream
Hard boiled eggs, sliced
Salt and pepper to taste

1. Wash the peas and soak in cold water overnight.
2. Drain the peas and put in large pot with the quartered potatoes and chopped onion. Add enough water just to cover.
3. Bring to a boil and simmer for 1 hour.
4. Put the cooked peas and potatoes through a sieve, then add the celery soup and cream.
5. Season with salt and pepper and reheat but do not boil. Serve hot and top the soup with slices of hard boiled eggs.

Cream of Tomato Soup

2 cups canned tomatoes
2 tablespoons chopped celery
2 tablespoons chopped onion
½ teaspoon salt
4 tablespoons butter
4 tablespoons flour
½ teaspoon salt
2 cups milk

1. Combine the tomatoes, celery, onion and salt and simmer for about 20 minutes.
2. Melt the butter, then add the flour and salt stirring until smooth, then add the milk gradually, stirring constantly. Cook until thickened to a thin sauce.
3. Strain the cooked tomato-vegetable mixture and pour into the cream sauce very slowly, stirring continually. If done slowly the mixture will not curdle.
4. Reheat but do not boil, and serve immediately. Serves 4-6.

STUFFINGS

Bread Stuffing for Baked Fish

1 cup bread crumbs
¼ teaspoon salt
¼ teaspoon pepper
2 tablespoons dried onion flakes
1 tablespoon chopped parsley
2 tablespoons melted butter

1. Mix the seasonings with bread crumbs.
2. Add the melted butter and toss lightly.

Note

If a more moist stuffing is desired, add a little milk or an egg.

Cheese Stuffing for Baked Fish

1 cup finely chopped onion
¼ cup butter *or* other fat
2 cups soft bread crumbs
½ cup grated cheese
2 tablespoons chopped parsley
2 teaspoons dry mustard
1 teaspoon salt
⅛ teaspoon pepper

1. Cook onion in butter until tender.
2. Combine soft bread crumbs, grated cheese, parsley, mustard, salt and pepper.
3. Add the onions and toss lightly.

Tarragon Dressing

½ cup diced onion
1 cup diced celery
½ teaspoon tarragon
½ cup butter
1 tablespoon salt
10 cups soft bread crumbs

1. Cook onion, celery and tarragon in butter until onion and celery are tender.
2. Add salt to bread crumbs.
3. Combine all ingredients and mix thoroughly.
4. This quantity will stuff a 9 pound fish.

Cranberry Stuffing

1 cup cranberries
½ cup chopped celery
¼ cup chopped onion
3 tablespoons sugar
3 tablespoons butter *or* other fat
1 cup soft bread crumbs
1 teaspoon grated orange rind
½ teaspoon salt
⅛ teaspoon pepper
½ teaspoon marjoram

1. Cook cranberries, celery, onion and sugar in fat until fruit is cooked (1 to 2 minutes).
2. Combine fruit mixture with bread crumbs.
3. Add orange rind and seasonings and toss lightly.

Fruit Stuffing for Goose

3 cups bread, coarsely chopped
½ cup butter
1 cup chopped apples
½ cup chopped nuts
½ cup raisins
½ teaspoon salt
¼ teaspoon pepper
1 tablespoon orange juice
    or lemon juice

1. Melt the butter and pour over coarsely chopped bread crumbs or cubes.
2. Add the apples, nuts, raisins, salt, pepper and juice, tossing lightly.

Nut and Raisin Stuffing

3 cups soft bread crumbs
¼ cup butter *or* other fat, melted
2 cups boiling water
½ cup seedless raisins
¾ cup chopped walnuts
1 egg, beaten
1 teaspoon salt
⅛ teaspoon pepper
½ teaspoon marjoram

1. Sprinkle crumbs with melted butter and toss until mixed.
2. Pour boiling water over raisins and let stand for 5 minutes.
3. Drain raisins and dry on paper towel.
4. Mix together raisins, nuts, beaten egg, salt, pepper and marjoram.
5. Toss with buttered bread crumbs.

Partridge Pineapple Stuffing

4 cups dried bread, cut in
   ½ inch cubes
¾ cup finely chopped celery
¾ cup pineapple wedges
½ cup chopped bacon
¼ cup green pepper, chopped
   Pinch of cayenne
1 teaspoon paprika
½ teaspoon salt
¼ cup butter
2 eggs, slightly beaten

1. Combine bread, celery, pineapple, green pepper and seasonings.
2. Cook the chopped bacon until lightly crisped, add to bread.
3. Melt the butter, remove from heat, stir in the slightly beaten eggs and add to the bread mixture, tossing lightly.

Potato Stuffing

4 cups hot mashed potatoes
2 oz salt pork, minced *or*
   2 thick slices bacon, cut up
3 cups fine bread crumbs
1 cup minced *or* chopped onion
½ teaspoon salt
¼ teaspoon pepper

1. Sauté the salt pork or bacon in heavy fry pan for 5 minutes.
2. Add the onion and sauté for another 10 minutes, mixing constantly.
3. Toss this mixture lightly into the bread crumbs.
4. Add the potatoes and mix lightly, then add salt and pepper.

Rice and Mushroom Stuffing

½ cup melted butter
1 cup chopped onion
2 cups diced celery
1 cup drained mushrooms
3 cups cooked rice
1 teaspoon salt
¼ teaspoon pepper
½ teaspoon marjoram
¼ teaspoon thyme

1. Melt butter in heavy fry pan then add onion, celery and mushrooms and sauté till onions are translucent but not browned.
2. Add butter and vegetables to cooked rice and seasonings and mix well.

Rice Stuffing

3 cups cooked rice
1 teaspoon finely minced onion
Chicken stock *or* bouillon to moisten
1 teaspoon minced celery
1 teaspoon minced parsley
1 teaspoon minced bacon
½ cup mushrooms, finely chopped

1. Combine cooked rice, onion and chicken stock, then add the celery and parsley.
2. Cook the minced bacon until lightly browned, then add the chopped mushrooms and sauté lightly.
3. Add the bacon and mushrooms to the rice mixture and toss to form a fluffy mixture.

Egg Rice Stuffing

½ cup rice
1 quart boiling water
1 tablespoon butter
½ pound mushrooms, finely chopped
½ teaspoon sage
Pinch of thyme
½ teaspoon salt
¼ teaspoon pepper
1 egg yolk, beaten

1. Cook rice in boiling water until tender, about 25 minutes. Drain and rinse.
2. Melt 1 tablespoon butter in heavy fry pan and sauté the mushrooms until lightly browned.
3. Add them to the cooked rice, then add the beaten egg, sage, thyme, salt and pepper, tossing the ingredients lightly together.

Wild Rice Stuffing for Duck

½ cup wild rice
1 quart boiling water
½ pound sliced mushrooms
2 tablespoons fat
½ teaspoon sage
2 egg yolks
½ teaspoon salt
¼ teaspoon pepper

1. Cook the rice in the boiling water until tender, about 20 minutes.
2. Drain and rinse.
3. Heat 2 tablespoons fat in heavy fry pan and sauté the sliced mushrooms.
4. Add the mushrooms to the drained rice, with salt, pepper, sage and slightly beaten egg yolks. Blend well.

SAUCES

Basic White Sauce

Thin White Sauce

1 tablespoon butter
1 tablespoon flour
1 cup milk
  Seasoning to taste

Medium White Sauce

2 tablespoons butter
2 tablespoons flour
1 cup milk
  Seasoning to taste

1. Melt butter in a heavy saucepan on top of the stove.
2. Add flour and seasonings and stir until well mixed and bubbly. Be careful not to scorch the ingredients.
3. Remove from heat, then add the cold liquid, stirring constantly.
4. Return sauce to heat and bring to a boil, stirring constantly. When mixture comes to a boil, reduce the heat and continue cooking for 7 minutes until there is no taste of raw starch.

Quick White Sauce

1 tin condensed cream of mushroom, cream of chicken *or* cream of celery soup
¼ cup milk *or* cream
2 tablespoons chopped parsley, fresh *or* dried
1 tablespoon onion flakes (optional)
1 tablespoon green pepper flakes (optional)
½ teaspoon salt
¼ teaspoon pepper

1. Mix the ingredients in top of double boiler and place over boiling water.
2. Cook, stirring constantly until smooth and hot.

Barbecue Sauce

½ cup catsup
½ cup water
4 tablespoons white wine vinegar
1 small chopped onion *or* 2 tablespoons onion flakes
2 tablespoons chopped green peppers, fresh *or* dried
1 tablespoon brown sugar
½ teaspoon salt
¼ teaspoon pepper
½ teaspoon dry mustard
¼ teaspoon garlic salt
1 tablespoon Worcestershire sauce

1. Mix ingredients in order given.
2. Heat to boiling, stirring constantly. Reduce heat and simmer for 10 minutes.
3. Use to baste barbecued chicken, hamburgers, pork chops or spareribs. Or pour over pan fried sausages and let simmer for 10 minutes.

Cantonese Sauce

½ cup beer
¼ cup dry mustard
½ teaspoon Accént
  (monosodium glutamate)
2 tablespoons soy sauce
1 cup apricot preserves
1 tablespoon lemon juice
1 teaspoon grated orange peel

1. Stir the beer into the dry mustard, then add the remaining ingredients.
2. Heat in double boiler over hot water.

Cheese Sauce

2 tablespoons butter
2 tablespoons flour
1 cup cold milk
½ teaspoon salt
¼ teaspoon pepper
½ cup grated cheese

1. Melt butter in a heavy saucepan on top of the stove.
2. Add flour and seasonings and stir until well mixed and bubbly. Be careful not to scorch the ingredients.
3. Remove from heat, then add the cold liquid, stirring constantly.
4. Return sauce to heat and bring to a boil, stirring constantly. Reduce heat, add grated cheese, cover and simmer for 7 minutes until cheese melts and there is no taste of raw starch.

Cocktail Sauce

1 tablespoon mayonnaise
3 tablespoons catsup
2 teaspoons lemon juice
1 teaspoon prepared horseradish
1 teaspoon prepared mustard
¼ teaspoon Worcestershire sauce
  Dash of Tabasco sauce

1. Combine all the ingredients, mix well and chill.
2. Serve with your favorite seafood, in lettuce lined glass or separately.

Creole Sauce

2 medium onions, sliced
1 clove garlic, chopped fine
1 tablespoon chopped parsley
3 tablespoons butter, margarine
  or oil
3½ cups tomato juice
¼ teaspoon Worcestershire sauce
  Salt and pepper to taste

1. Cook onions, garlic and parsley in fat or oil until onion is golden brown.
2. Add tomato juice and Worcestershire sauce and cook gently for 15 minutes.
3. Season with salt and pepper to taste.

Hollandaise Sauce no. 1

3 egg yolks
2 tablespoons lemon juice *or* vinegar
¼ teaspoon salt
⅓ cup butter, melted
¼ cup boiling water

1. Beat the egg yolks lightly. Add the salt and lemon juice or vinegar.
2. Stir in the melted butter, then add the hot water and blend well.
3. Place over hot water and cook, stirring continuously until thickened.
4. Store in a clean jar in refrigerator. Reheat when needed.

Hollandaise Sauce no. 2

3 tablespoons butter
2 egg yolks well beaten
½ teaspoon salt
¼ teaspoon pepper
¼ teaspoon paprika
2 tablespoons boiling water
1 tablespoon lemon juice

1. In the top of a double boiler, cream the butter and add the well beaten eggs.
2. Add seasonings and boiling water, then place over boiling water and cook until thick, stirring constantly.
3. Remove from heat, add lemon juice, stir well and serve at once over cooked cauliflower, broccoli, asparagus or fish.

Homemade Sour Cream

Wherever a recipe calls for sour cream and, at the moment, it is not available, try combining 1 tablespoon of white vinegar or lemon juice with 1 cup of evaporated canned milk. Let stand 30 minutes in warm temperature. Then place in refrigerator until needed.

Low-Bush Cranberry Sauce

3 cups sugar
½ cup water
4 cups cranberries

1. Wash berries.
2. Add sugar and water to berries and cook over low heat or simmer for 15 minutes.
3. Chill and serve with any meat dish.

   Variations
1. Reduce the sugar by ½ cup and the water by 2 tablespoons and add ½ cup honey.
2. Stir in ½ cup slivered blanched toasted almonds and ¼ cup slivered candied ginger; chill and serve with turkey.
3. Substitute ½ cup each citrus marmalade and corn syrup for 1 cup of sugar and reduce the water to ¼ cup.
4. Stir in 1 cup candied diced pears and ½ teaspoon grated lemon rind.

Mushroom Sauce

1 tablespoon flour
1 cup water
½ pound mushrooms
2 tablespoons lemon juice
   Salt and pepper
2 tablespoons butter, melted

1. Add flour to melted butter and stir until well blended.

2. Add the water and sliced mushrooms and cook until mushrooms are tender.

3. Add the lemon juice, season to taste, pour over meat and serve.

Hot Mustard for Ham

1 tablespoon dry mustard
1 teaspoon flour
1 teaspoon sugar
¼ teaspoon salt
   Few grains pepper
1 tablespoon vinegar *or* sweet pickle juice

1. Mix dry ingredients.

2. Add vinegar or pickle juice and stir till smooth.

3. Let stand 15 minutes before serving.

Parsley Sauce

2 tablespoons butter
2 tablespoons flour
1 cup cold milk
½ teaspoon salt
¼ teaspoon pepper
1 tablespoon chopped fresh *or* dried parsley

1. Melt butter in a heavy saucepan on top of stove.

2. Add flour and seasonings and stir until well mixed and bubbly. Be careful not to scorch the ingredients.

3. Remove from heat, then add the cold liquid, stirring constantly.

4. Return sauce to heat and bring to a boil, stirring constantly. Reduce heat, add chopped parsley, cover and simmer for 7 minutes.

Spiced Cranberry Sauce

1. To the basic sauce recipe, add ½ cup raisins and 1 teaspoon cinnamon. Serve with baked ham.

2. For serving with lamb, simmer with ¼ teaspoon curry powder. Add 2 teaspoons horseradish and ¼ cup french dressing and chill.

3. Add diced celery, cucumber and green pepper and a tablespoon of lemon juice. Chill and serve with any meat dish.

Maître d'Hôtel Butter

¼ cup butter
½ teaspoon salt
  Dash cayenne
1 teaspoon finely chopped parsley
¾ tablespoon lemon juice

1. Cream the butter and add salt, chopped parsley and cayenne.

2. Add the lemon juice slowly and blend well.

3. Chill the mixture, then shape into balls. Serve with meat or fish.

Marinade

⅔ cup vegetable oil
½ cup vinegar *or* white wine
½ teaspoon salt
¼ teaspoon pepper
½ teaspoon dry mustard
  Dash of Tabasco sauce

Meats and fowl are marinated or soaked for tenderizing, also for added flavour.

1. Combine all the ingredients and place in a sealer or covered jar.

2. Keep in a cool place.

Pepper Sauce

1 tablespoon butter
1 tablespoon flour
1 cup consommé *or* broth
2 sprigs thyme *or*
½ teaspoon powdered thyme
1 carrot, minced fine
1 onion, minced fine
1 stick celery, minced fine
1 bay leaf
  Grated rind of 1 lemon
  Dash of cayenne
  Salt and black pepper
½ cup red currant jelly
  or cranberry jelly

1. Put butter in saucepan, add flour and brown slowly, stirring constantly.

2. Slowly add the consommé or broth and bring to a boil.

3. Add thyme, carrot, onion, celery, bay leaf and grated lemon rind.

4. Simmer slowly for 30 minutes.

5. Add cayenne, salt and black pepper and simmer another 10 minutes.

6. Add jelly and return sauce to boiling point.

7. Serve hot with venison.

Raisin Sauce

½ cup raisins, scalded
½ cup brown sugar
½ cup fruit juice
2 tablespoons vinegar
½ teaspoon salt
¼ teaspoon pepper
1 teaspoon dry mustard

1. Wash and drain raisins, then pour boiling water over them, let stand 5 minutes, then drain well.
2. Mix sugar, fruit juice, vinegar and seasonings in a pot on top of the stove.
3. Add scalded raisins (chopped if desired) and bring to a boil, stirring constantly.
4. Reduce heat, cover and simmer gently for 10 minutes. Serve hot with ham, pork, bear or sausage.

Brown's Red Sauce

8 cups canned tomatoes
1 head celery, chopped
3 large onions, chopped
1 cup red and green pepper flakes
2 quarts vinegar
1 cup white sugar
1 tablespoon salt
½ teaspoon cloves
1 teaspoon allspice
1 teaspoon cinnamon

1. Combine all the ingredients, except the cloves, allspice and cinnamon, in a large pot and bring to a boil.
2. Reduce heat and simmer for 3 or 4 hours.
3. When cooked, sweeten and salt to taste and add the cloves, allspice and cinnamon.
4. Pour into scalded jars, seal and store in cool place.

Sour Cream Caper Sauce

½ cup commercial sour cream
2 tablespoons catsup
½ cup mayonnaise
2 tablespoons finely chopped capers (drained)
1½ teaspoons finely chopped onion
¼ teaspoon salt
⅛ teaspoon pepper

Combine ingredients in order given and mix well. Makes about 1 cup.

Spanish Sauce

¼ cup butter
2 tablespoons chopped onion
2 tablespoons chopped green pepper
½ cup chopped celery
4 tablespoons flour
2 cups canned tomatoes, juice and pulp
½ teaspoon salt
¼ teaspoon pepper
1 tablespoon lemon juice *or* vinegar

1. Melt butter in a heavy pan on top of stove.
2. Add chopped onions, green pepper and celery and simmer until onions are translucent but not browned.
3. Add flour and mix well.
4. Add tomatoes, seasonings and lemon juice.
5. Bring to a boil, stirring constantly.
6. Reduce heat, cover and simmer for 7 minutes. Serve hot on omelets, breaded fish, pork chops, veal cutlets, etc.

Sweet and Sour Sauce

3 tablespoons butter
½ green pepper, thinly sliced *or*
2 tablespoons red and green
  pepper flakes
1 medium onion, sliced *or*
2 tablespoons onion flakes
1 tablespoon cornstarch
1 20 oz tin crushed pineapple
2 tablespoons white wine vinegar
  or sweet pickle juice
1 tablespoon soy sauce
½ teaspoon ground ginger

1. Melt butter in a heavy pot on top of stove.
2. Add green peppers and onions and simmer gently for 5 minutes.
3. Mix cornstarch with 1 tablespoon of pineapple juice, add to sauce.
4. Add crushed pineapple and remainder of juice, vinegar, soy sauce and ground ginger.
5. Heat to boiling, stirring constantly. Reduce heat, cover and simmer for 15 minutes.

Tartar Sauce

1 cup mayonnaise
1 tablespoon chopped, stuffed
  olives
1 tablespoon chopped, sweet
  cucumber pickles
1 chopped hard boiled egg
1 tablespoon chopped capers
1 teaspoon chopped parsley
1 tablespoon vinegar *or* lemon
  juice

1. Add all the other ingredients to the mayonnaise. Mix well.
2. Serve cold with fish.

Tomato Sauce

2 tablespoons butter *or* fat
2 tablespoons chopped onion
2 tablespoons flour
1 teaspoon sugar
1 teaspoon salt
⅛ teaspoon pepper
6 peppercorns
1 bay leaf
1 20 oz tin tomatoes

1. Heat butter or fat in heavy fry pan and cook the chopped onion until clear and tender.
2. Stir in the flour, sugar, salt and pepper and blend well with the onions.
3. Add the tomatoes, peppercorns and bay leaf and simmer about 5 minutes or until sauce is thickened.
4. Remove the peppercorns and bay leaf before serving.

Venison Sauce

1 glass currant jelly
2 tablespoons butter
2½ teaspoons chili sauce
½ teaspoon Worcestershire sauce

1. Melt the butter in small pot.
2. Add jelly, chili sauce and Worcestershire sauce.
3. Bring to boiling point over low heat, stirring constantly. Serve hot.

Note
Chokeberry, pincherry, cranberry or grape jelly may be used in place of currant jelly.

APPETIZERS and DIPS

Pear and Cream Cheese Hors-d'Oeuvres

1 28 oz can pears
½ tablespoon light cream *or* milk
1 6 oz package cream cheese
1 4½ oz can shrimps, chopped
   fine
1 teaspoon lemon juice
   Salt and pepper
   Pinch of paprika
   Stuffed olives

1. Drain the pear halves well.

2. Mix the cream cheese with the cream or milk to a smooth consistency and beat in the chopped shrimps, lemon juice and seasonings.

3. Spoon a little into the hollow of each pear half and grind a little fresh pepper on top.

4. Decorate with stuffed olives.

Party Crackers

Soda crackers
Ice water
Garlic salt
Paprika

1. Soak crackers in ice water until soft.

2. Drain, then cut from corner to corner to form triangles.

3. Place on greased cookie sheet and sprinkle with garlic salt and paprika.

4. Place in a medium oven 350°F. until crisp and brown.

5. Serve with your favourite dip.

Bread Sticks

4 tablespoons shortening
1½ tablespoons sugar
1 cup scalded milk
½ teaspoon salt
1 package yeast
¼ cup lukewarm water
1 egg, separated
3½ cups sifted flour
   Garlic salt
   Sesame seeds

1. Dissolve yeast in ¼ cup lukewarm water.

2. Cream shortening and sugar and add 1 cup scalded milk. Cool to lukewarm.

3. Add dissolved yeast and blend well.

4. Beat the egg white and stir into mixture.

5. Stir in the sifted flour, then knead the dough and let rise until double in bulk.

6. Roll the dough out on a floured board to about ¼ inch thick.

7. Brush with egg yolk and sprinkle with garlic salt and sesame seeds.

8. Cut in strips 3″ × ½″.

9. Place on greased cookie sheet 1 inch apart, cover and let rise until doubled.

10. Bake in hot oven 400° F. for 10 minutes

11. Reduce heat to 350° F. and bake until the sticks are dry and crisp.

TV Snacks

½ pound butter
¼ teaspoon celery salt
1 teaspoon garlic salt
1 teaspoon onion salt
½ teaspoon paprika
3 tablespoons Worcestershire sauce
12 cups of prepared cereals such as Cheerios, Shreddies or Corn Chex, thin pretzel sticks and peanuts, mixed together

1. Melt butter, add Worcestershire sauce and seasonings. Mix well.

2. Pour over mixture of cereals, pretzel sticks and peanuts in a large roaster. Toss lightly several times to coat the cereals.

3. Bake in a 275° F. oven for two hours. Store in airtight containers.

DIPS

Crab Dip

1 large tin crab meat
1 small onion, chopped *or*
2 tablespoons dried onion flakes
3 tablespoons catsup
2 teaspoons Worcestershire sauce
Mayonnaise

1. Shred the crab meat.

2. Add the chopped onion or dried onion flakes which have been soaked in ¼ cup hot water, then drained well.

3. Add the catsup, Worcestershire sauce and enough mayonnaise to give the desired consistency.

4. Mix well and chill.

Cheese and Onion Dip

2 cups sour cream *or* 2 cups evaporated milk and 2 tablespoons vinegar
1 cup cream cheese (softened)
1 teaspoon vinegar
2 teaspoons celery salt
1 cup chopped onions *or*
2 tablespoons dried onion flakes
1 teaspoon italian seasoning
2 tablespoons grated Parmesan cheese

1. If dried onion flakes are used, soak them in ¼ cup hot water for 15 minutes. Drain well.

2. Combine all ingredients and mix well.

3. Chill and serve with chips, crackers or bread sticks.

Daisy Jensen's Cheese Dip

1 8 oz package Philadelphia cream cheese
½ cup mayonnaise
¼ cup chili sauce
2 tablespoons grated onion
½ teaspoon salt
¼ teaspoon pepper

1. Cream the cheese, add mayonnaise and chili sauce and beat till light.

2. Add remaining ingredients, mix well and chill 2 hours before serving.

Shrimp Dip

1. Arrange chilled, cooked, cleaned shrimp (whole, or split if shrimp are plump) on plate or tray.
2. In center, place mayonnaise with prepared mustard, horseradish, chili sauce, catsup, chives, or curry powder added.
3. Have tiny bowl of toothpicks handy.

Shrimp Avocado Dip

1. With toothpick, secure a cube of avocado in center of each cooked cleaned shrimp.
2. Serve with bowl of sauce for dunking as for Shrimp Dip.

California Dip

1 package onion soup mix
1 pint sour cream

1. Blend soup mix and sour cream thoroughly.
2. Let chill 2 or 3 hours before serving.

Bob's Dip

1 cup catsup
1 teaspoon steak sauce
1 tablespoon Worcestershire sauce
2 tablespoons lemon juice, fresh, frozen *or* canned
1 teaspoon prepared horseradish
¼ teaspoon garlic salt
½ teaspoon onion salt *or*
1 tablespoon chopped onion
½ teaspoon dry mustard

1. Mix ingredients in order given. Chill 2-3 hours.

2. Serve as a dip for cold meats such as bologna chunks, sliced kubasa, summer sausage, etc., or cooked shrimp.

Variation

Add 1 cup chopped celery and serve over shrimp in lettuce cups for shrimp cocktail.

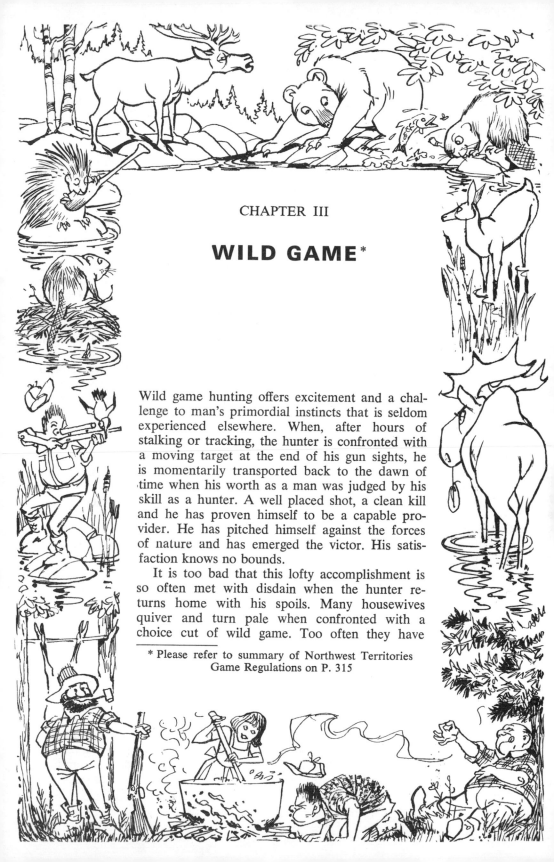

CHAPTER III

WILD GAME*

Wild game hunting offers excitement and a challenge to man's primordial instincts that is seldom experienced elsewhere. When, after hours of stalking or tracking, the hunter is confronted with a moving target at the end of his gun sights, he is momentarily transported back to the dawn of time when his worth as a man was judged by his skill as a hunter. A well placed shot, a clean kill and he has proven himself to be a capable provider. He has pitched himself against the forces of nature and has emerged the victor. His satisfaction knows no bounds.

It is too bad that this lofty accomplishment is so often met with disdain when the hunter returns home with his spoils. Many housewives quiver and turn pale when confronted with a choice cut of wild game. Too often they have

* Please refer to summary of Northwest Territories
Game Regulations on P. 315

learned through sad experience that it is almost inedible! But this reaction is not necessary. The flavour of the meat depends on the hunter's skill in caring for it under primitive conditions. Good marksmanship, correct field dressing, quick cooling of the carcass, and careful preparation and cooking can make wild game as delicious and as satisfying as any other protein food, and a worthy substitute for beef, pork, lamb or veal.

BIG GAME

Originally the term venison meant the meat of any animal or bird of the chase, but today it refers more specifically to the meat of antlered animals: antelope, caribou, deer, elk, moose and reindeer. The general directions for field dressing, skinning and cutting are similar for all. Most of the recipes which are given in this section are also interchangeable with any type of big game, and hunters and wives alike are urged to experiment until they find the ones that please them most.

Before going hunting, take time to study the general terrain around the camp. Position the camp in relation to prominent landmarks, hills or horizon. Observe trails and roads. Prearrange signals with others in the party—it may make the difference between success and tragedy. Check the equipment needed for hunting and handling the kill. Include a sharp knife for dressing, a light rope or nylon cord for trussing and dragging, compass, maps, matches in a waterproof case, emergency rations, large pliofilm bags (for the animal's heart and liver), black pepper to discourage flies, ravens or magpies, and, depending on the season, insect repellant. Be sure your gun is clean, of adequate calibre and sighted in with proper ammunition. Dress in conspicuous clothing appropriate for the weather, and be sure you have your license and game tag.

When you sight your animal, aim carefully, in the heart, lung or neck region. A neck or back-of-the-shoulder shot will ensure a quick kill and destroy the least meat. Approach the fallen animal cautiously, keeping the gun in position to fire if the animal is not dead. If the animal is still struggling kill it with a shot in the neck just under the ear, and then complete and fasten your big game tag to the carcass.

Bleeding

With modern high velocity ammunition, it may not be necessary to bleed the animal, but wild game is better when drained of blood. If there is any doubt about the amount of bleeding, place the animal with its head on a downhill slope. Insert a four to five inch knife blade at the top of the breast bone, with the point of the knife aimed toward the tail. Plunge it in to the hilt, tilting the blade downward toward the back bone, then withdraw it with a slight slicing motion. This should sever the carotid arteries where they join midway between the shoulders. Let the blood drain out by gravity, raising the rear portion of the animal to make certain that as much blood drains out as possible. Keep the cut open and free from clots. If the head is to be preserved for mounting, keep it as free of bloodstains as possible by pulling it back by the antlers, away from the flow of blood.

Field Dressing Big Game

Deer have musk glands on the hind legs, one on the inside of each leg, one on the outside. These are identified by the tufts of upraised hair growing in oval patches around them. They should be carefully removed from bucks and does before field dressing; avoid touching them with your hands or the meat will become tainted when you handle it later.

Dress the animal immediately. Roll it over on its back with the rump lower than the shoulders and spread the hind legs. Tie one hind foot to a tree if you are alone or if you have difficulty in keeping the animal in position. Make a cut along the centerline of the belly from the breastbone to the base of the tail. First, cut through hide, then through belly muscle. Avoid cutting into the paunch and intestines by holding them away from the knife with the free hand while guiding the knife with the other.

With a small sharp knife, cut around the anus and draw it into the body cavity so it comes free with the complete intestines. In doing this, avoid cutting or breaking the bladder. Loosen, then roll out the stomach and intestines. Save the liver. Cut around the edge of the diaphragm which separates the chest and stomach cavities, then reach forward to cut the windpipe and gullet ahead of the lungs. Pull the lungs and heart from the chest cavity and save the heart. Drain all excess blood from the body cavity by turning the carcass face down.

A clean cloth may be useful to clean your hands. If you had the misfortune to puncture the entrails with a bullet or your knife, wipe the body cavity as clean as possible or flush it with clean water and dry it with a cloth. Don't use water to wash out the body cavity unless the paunch or intestines are badly shot up.

Part of the satisfaction of the hunt comes from making a clean kill and in doing a neat job of field dressing. Veteran hunters may have variations in the steps of field dressing. The important points are to remove the internal organs immediately after the kill without contaminating the body cavity with dirt, hair or contents of the digestive tract and to drain all excess blood from the body cavity.

Back to Camp or Car

There are many methods of getting the animal out of the woods. If the distance is not too great and the ground is not too rough, the animal may be dragged over snow and leaves without ruining the hide for leather (but never drag it if it is possible to transport it any other way).

Tie a light rope or nylon cord to the base of the antlers, or around the neck of an antlerless deer. Take a half-hitch around the upper jaw and tie a short stick to the other end of the rope for a handle. Dragging is easier if the forefeet are crossed back of the animal's head and tied to keep the legs from hooking underbrush. With bucks, the feet can be crossed and hooked between the antlers.

At camp, or while waiting to transport the animal home, hang the carcass and cool it as quickly as possible. Hang it in the shade and prop the flanks open with sticks to permit air circulation in the body cavity. The air casehardens the surface and protects the exposed meat. The animal may be hung head up or head down, but if you intend to mount the head, hang it by the antlers to avoid bloodstains. Sprinkle the whole carcass with black pepper to help keep away the flies.

The hairs of most animals lie backward toward the rump. Therefore, if the animal is hung by its head the hairs will shed rain and snow instead of holding them, and blood will not collect in the chest cavity.

In the south, for many years it has been common practice to bring the animal home draped along the front fenders of a car. This practice is to be discouraged because heat from the engine will start meat spoilage. Tie the animal over the roof of the car, or put it in the trunk, even if it is necessary to quarter the animal to do so. Care should be taken to retain the tag and evidence of sex of the animal. In either case the carcass should be well covered to keep road-dust off and to keep the meat cool.

Skinning

With the animal hanging by its antlers start the skinning by cutting the hide around the neck. If the trophy is to be saved, make this cut at the shoulders. Cut along the inside of each leg from the cavity opening to the first joint and sever the shanks. When severing the shanks do not make the cut too high. The joint is about an inch and a half below the hock on the hind legs, and an inch below the knee on the fore legs. Except when skinning the legs, the knife is no longer needed. Proceed by pulling the hide down with one hand, and with a tightly clenched fist force the hide down from the carcass. This procedure will leave the hide free of flesh and there will be no holes from the knife.

The hide, if it is to be tanned, should be tacked out to dry as soon as possible. Tack it flesh side out with small nails to the side of a frame building. Start by tacking the neck first, then pull down at the tail until all the slack is taken up, and drive in two nails on each side of the tail. Next put a nail at each side of the belly and work both ways toward the neck and tail, putting a nail every four to six inches, Do not over stretch the hide; merely take up the slack.

Remove any excess flesh or tallow that may have clung to the hide. If the temperature is above freezing, rub the hide with a little table salt. In the Mackenzie Mountain Region a hide will dry in from 3 to 5 days. When sending the hide to the tanner, roll it up. Folding will cause the thin outer layer of the skin to crack. This will show up in the finished leather. Complete directions for home tanning of hides and for skinning and mounting a trophy head are available from Fish and Wildlife Officers or taxidermists.

Before cutting up the carcass it must be aged or ripened properly. Allow it to hang for 5 to 7 days in a well ventilated area, at a constant temperature between 35 and 40° F.

Cutting the Meat

If the carcass is to be placed in a home freezer or in locker storage, it may be more convenient to use the locker service of an experienced butcher for the cutting and wrapping. However, if this service is not available, or if you wish to gain experience by doing it yourself, the first step is to hang the carcass by the hocks with a spreader to keep the legs apart and saw the animal in half down the back bone. A common handsaw will be satisfactory. Take one half of the carcass at a time and cut it into pieces as indicated by the cutting lines on the following diagram. With a good sharp knife, a saw or a cleaver and a little care you can do a satisfactory job in your home.

Place the sides of venison, inside down, on a table and cut off the neck along line A − A. Then separate the forequarters from the hindquarters as shown by line B − B. Next, remove the legs by cutting close to and in front of the hip bone, along line C − C. Now, move forward to the shoulder and cut off the forelegs, starting between the fourth and fifth or fifth and sixth ribs and continuing along the line D − D.

Before cutting any further, remove any hairs and mutilated or bloody areas from the large cuts. If a particularly large area is affected by the shot, it can be saved by removing that portion immediately after the animal is dressed and placing it in a weak brine made by dissolving one-quarter pound of table salt in one gallon of water. The salt will draw out considerable blood within 24 to 48 hours and the meat will be suitable for boiling or grinding. Badly mutilated parts in the immediate bullet area make good dog food. The large cuts may now be cut into smaller pieces as illustrated on the diagram.

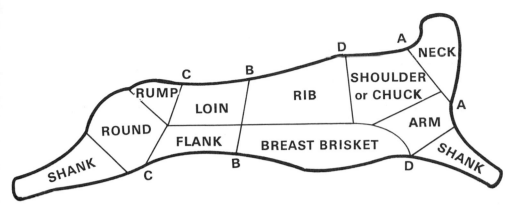

Cuts of Venison

Hind and Fore Shank—The shanks are used for soups or stews and ground for meat loaf and venison burgers.

Round—The round is usually tender and may be cut into steaks. If it is tough, it may be used for swiss steaks. When the leg is small, it may be roasted whole in an uncovered pan. Ground meat may also be made from the round to fry as meat patties or for using in a meat loaf.

Loin and Rib—This is tender meat, and is usually cut into sirloin and porterhouse, T-bone and rib steaks or may be boned and rolled for choice roasts.

Shoulder or Chuck—This meat may be tougher but it is very good for pot roasts or ground meat. It may also be used for corning or canning.

Rump—This is used for pot roast. If from a tender, young buck, it makes a very good uncovered oven roast. It may also be used for corning or canning.

Neck, Flank and Brisket—The neck is tender after the tendons are removed. It may be used as a stew or as ground meat, and believe it or not, it also makes good roasts. The flank and breast contain considerable meat. They may be ground for venison burgers, or used for soup or a stew. They are too good to waste.

Cooking of Venison

It should not be necessary to make any attempt to conceal the excellent flavour of venison, especially if the fat is trimmed from the meat, but remember that the fat must be replaced or the meat will be dry. This may be done by larding the meat with fat salt pork or thick slices of bacon, according to the following directions.

Larding of Venison

1. Cut the salt pork or bacon slices into strips ¼ inch wide and chill them until firm.
2. Thread a larding needle with a strip of pork and run the needle through the meat. Place the strips about every 2 inches throughout the roast.
3. If you do not have a larding needle, pierce the meat with a long thin knife or skewer and push the strips of chilled pork into the holes.
4. Wrap slices of fat salt pork or bacon around the meat and fasten them in place with toothpicks or string.

Cooking Methods

There are two general methods for cooking meat; by dry heat or by moist heat.

1. Dry Heat Methods:

   These are used for cooking the tender cuts of meat from the rib, loin and the top part of the round. The methods are:

   a. *Roasting*—cooking in an oven in an uncovered pan, with no liquid added. The meat may be seared first by having the oven very hot for the first 15 or 20 minutes, and then reducing the heat for the remainder of the cooking time. Tests have shown, however, that there is less shrinkage of the meat if it is cooked at a lower temperature for a longer period of time. Cooking at a lower temperature saves fuel, leaves the meat juicier, prevents the fat from spattering or burning and makes carving easier.

   b. *Broiling*—cooking the meat under (or over) direct heat or flame. The meat must be watched carefully to prevent burning and must be turned over to cook both sides.

   c. *Pan-Broiling*—cooking the meat in a heavy pan over high heat with no water, no lid, and only enough fat to prevent the meat from sticking.

   d. *Pan-Frying*—cooking the meat in a pan over moderate heat with fat added but no lid on the pan. Usually the fat is drained off as it accumulates. e.g. breaded chops, hamburgers, etc.

   e. *Deep Fat Frying*—meat is usually coated with egg and crumbs or a batter and immersed in hot fat.

2. Moist Heat Methods:

   These are used for cooking the tougher cuts of meat, such as the neck, shoulder or chuck, shanks, flank, plate or brisket and rump. This meat is tougher because it comes from the parts of the animal that receive the most exercise. The meat is usually very tasty, because exercise helps to develop the flavouring materials (called extractives) in the meat, and it has the same food value as tender meat. The problem then is to prepare it in such a way that its fine flavour may be enjoyed.

   Tough meat may be tenderized by grinding it, which cuts the tough fibres; by pounding it with a meat hammer or the side of a saucer, which also breaks down the tough fibres; by soaking or marinating it in an acid such as tomato juice or vinegar; or by using commercial tenderizers which contain enzymes that soften the tough fibres. If the meat is cooked slowly with moist heat, it should be both tender and delicious.

   a. *Braising*—Dredging the meat with flour, browning it in hot fat, then adding liquid, reducing the heat and simmering it in a pot with the lid on until it is tender.

   b. *Pot Roasting*—This is the same as braising, but the cut of meat is larger. It may be done in a roaster in the oven or in a heavy pot on top of the stove.

   c. *Stewing*—Cutting the meat in small cubes or pieces (1″ or 2″), and simmering it in liquid until it is tender. Vegetables are usually added for the last half hour of the cooking time and the liquid thickened with a flour and water paste.

d. *Boiling*—This is the same as stewing, but the meat is left in one large piece, covered with water, simmered until tender and then allowed to cool in the liquid. The meat is usually tasty, juicy and very little shrinkage occurs.

The recipes which follow have been developed specifically for wild game, but many of them may be used for preparing similar cuts of meat from the domestic animals, beef, pork, veal or lamb.

A few favourite recipes using beef and pork have been added to the end of this section, but do not hesitate to experiment and adapt any of these recipes to other cuts of meat. The truly great cooks are those who cook with imagination and flair.

Jerky

Jerky is a quick and practical way of preserving caribou, moose or other game meat. It can be carried along on trips to eat uncooked, or it can be cut into paper-thin slices and boiled, or added to a milk sauce and served on hot biscuits.

Sun Dried Jerky

Cut fresh meat into long thin strips, one inch wide. Rub strips with garlic or salt if desired. Dry in the sun as quickly as possible by hanging over a line. Do not let the strips touch. Store in a dry place in clean jars or sacks.

Cold Brined Jerky

Cut muscle meat lengthwise of the grain into strips an inch thick, about 1½ inches wide, and as long as you can make them. Put the strips into a wooden barrel or non-metallic container and cover with a sweet pickle or corning solution for three days. Hang the meat over a cord line or string to drip for 24 hours and continue to hang it in a room or other dry place. Keep the strips from touching each other and protect them from dirt and insects with a light cloth covering, if necessary. The jerky will continue to dry as long as it is exposed to air, therefore it should be taken down and put away in an air-tight container as soon as it is dried to your liking. A light smoke will add to the flavour and help preserve the meat.

Hot Brined Jerky

Hot brined jerky is made in much the same way, except that the meat is cut into finer strips like shoe-string potatoes, and salted in a hot brine. The hot solution is made by adding salt to boiling water until no more can be dissolved. Dip strips into the hot brine until they turn white, which will take about 5 minutes. Then string them up to dry and handle the same way as cold brined jerky.

Wild Game Marinade

1   bottle domestic red wine *or* Burgundy
¼ cup red *or* white wine vinegar
2   sliced carrots
3   large onions, sliced *or*
4   tablespoons dried onion flakes
6   chopped shallots (optional)
½ teaspoon whole black peppercorns *or*
¼ teaspoon black pepper
½ teaspoon whole cloves
½ teaspoon juniper berries
½ teaspoon thyme
1   tablespoon salt
3   sprigs parsley *or*
3   tablespoons dried parsley
1   bay leaf

1. Trim fat from meat, lard it with salt pork if necessary, and place in a glass, porcelain or enamel bowl.
2. Combine marinade ingredients. Mix well and pour over the meat.
3. Cover.
4. Refrigerate for 24 hours for small meat cuts or for 2 to 3 days for large cuts, turning the meat several times if the marinade does not completely cover it.
5. Remove the meat when ready, pat it dry and cook, following chosen recipe.

Bear

Hunting for bear in the Mackenzie Mountains of the Northwest Territories can provide even experienced hunters with many thrills. The wily and unpredictable grizzly bear is rated as one of the world's greatest hunting challenges. A wise hunter will accord it the respect it commands and hunt it with proper equipment—and extreme caution!

Meat from the Brown, Grizzly or Polar Bear is usually rich, tender and delicious, especially if the animal is under 3 years of age. Meat from older animals may need to be tenderized by placing it in a marinade for 24 hours, but many people prefer the flavour of bear meat unmasked by high seasonings.

Bears killed just before their hibernation period are fat from gorging on berries, roots or fish. The gamy flavour which some people find objectionable is concentrated in the fat, so the fat should be trimmed from the meat before cooking. Bear meat is not marbled with fat like top grade beef, so roasts and larger cuts of meat should be larded. The meat should always be cooked until it is well done to kill any trichinae that may be present. As with pork, there is danger from trichinosis if the meat is served pink and rare. Bear fat is excellent for pastry-making, provided it is rendered first (otherwise it will turn rancid even when frozen). To render bear fat, cut the suet and surface fat into cubes and heat it slowly in a heavy covered kettle, then strain it. Bring the liquid fat to a boil and simmer it for 10 minutes to sterilize it, then pour it into sterilized, air-tight containers. If the containers are sealed and stored in a cold place, the fat will remain sweet and edible for months.

Warning: Do not eat the liver of the polar bear. It has an excessively high content of Vitamin A, which if eaten, will produce a toxic reaction in the body and may cause death.

Barbecued Bear

3 pounds bear steak, cut in 2-inch cubes
1 slice salt pork, cut up
1 cup catsup
⅓ cup steak sauce
2 tablespoons tarragon vinegar
1 onion, diced
1 tablespoon lemon juice, (fresh, frozen, *or* canned)
1 teaspoon salt
1 tablespoon chili powder

1. Trim all fat from bear steak and cut in 2-inch cubes.

2. Sear meat on all sides with salt pork in a heavy fry pan.

3. Place meat in a casserole.

4. Add rest of ingredients to fry pan and bring to a boil, stirring constantly.

5. Pour sauce over meat in casserole.

6. Cover and bake for at least 2 hours in a 325° F. oven, stirring occasionally until meat is tender.

Pan Broiled Bear Steaks

4 bear steaks, sliced 1½ inches thick
1 cooking onion, sliced
½ cup vinegar
½ cup water
½ cup vegetable oil
1 tablespoon mixed pickling spice
1 tablespoon salt
1 tablespoon cooking fat *or* beef suet
  Salt and pepper

1. Trim all fat from the bear meat, wash well.

2. Place steaks in a glass or pottery bowl, add the onion, vinegar, oil, water, spices and salt and marinate for at least 24 hours in the refrigerator, turning occasionally.

3. Remove steaks, drain and pat dry.

4. Heat a heavy fry pan, and rub the pan with fat or suet.

5. Pan-broil the steaks, adding only enough fat to prevent sticking, and turning frequently until done. Season to taste with salt and pepper. Serves 4.

Roast Polar Bear

1   5-6 pound roast of bear
½   cup vinegar
1   tablespoon salt
4   cups water
3   strips thick sliced bacon *or*
     salt pork
1   large onion, quartered
3   tablespoons butter
1   teaspoon salt
¼   teaspoon pepper

1. Trim all fat from the roast. Wash well.

2. Soak meat for at least 2 hours in water, salt and vinegar. Remove and pat dry.

3. Place meat in a roaster, lay strips of bacon on top and place quarters of onion beside it.

4. Roast at 350° F. for about 3 hours.

5. 15 minutes before serving, remove bacon strips, coat top of roast with butter and sprinkle with salt and pepper.

6. Roast another 15 minutes and drizzle butter on top two or three times during this period. Serve hot. Serves 6-8.

Bear Stew à l'Espagnole

3   pounds bear meat
¼   cup vinegar
1   tablespoon salt
4   cups water
¼   cup shortening
1   medium onion, sliced
1   green pepper, chopped
1   clove garlic
½   cup chopped celery
1   7 oz can tomato paste
2   cups canned tomatoes
1   dash Tabasco sauce
½   teaspoon salt
¼   teaspoon pepper

1. Trim all fat from meat and wash meat well in cold water.

2. Cut into 1½ inch cubes and soak at least 15 minutes in 4 cups water to which has been added ¼ cup vinegar and 1 tablespoon salt. Drain and pat dry.

3. Melt shortening in a heavy fry pan, add bear meat and brown well on all sides.

4. Add onion, garlic and celery and simmer till onion becomes translucent.

5. Add remaining ingredients, mix well, cover and simmer for 30 minutes or until meat is tender. Serves 4-6.

Buffalo

Before the turn of the century, great herds of buffalo (or bison) roamed the Western Plains, and Indian and pioneer alike depended heavily on their meat for sustenance. Even when a greater variety of food became available, buffalo hunts were still organized on a grand scale. Because the killing was uncontrolled, the numbers of buffalo diminished rapidly. By the early 1920's only scattered remnants of the once magnificent herds remained, and it was obvious that drastic measures would have to be taken to prevent their extinction. The remaining buffalo were rounded up and placed in game sanctuaries at Wood Buffalo National Park, straddling the Alberta-Northwest Territories border and at Elk Island National Park, in northeastern Alberta.

The conservation measures proved to be effective and the buffalo have flourished on the succulent sweet grasses of the northern pastures. Although the once wild and thrilling buffalo hunt now belongs to Canada's storied past, modern game management methods have ensured that this taste thrill from the 19th century is still available for the dinner table of today.

Meat from buffalo under three years of age is tender, finegrained, and similar in taste to top grade beef, although slightly darker in colour. It may be cooked by any method suitable for similar cuts of beef. Meat from older animals may be lacking in fat and thus may need to be larded before cooking. The cooking time should be lengthened, and moist heat methods of cooking may be more successful than dry heat methods. The suet which surrounds the kidney is usually of excellent quality and may be satisfactorily used for larding. Always bring the meat to room temperature before preparing it to ensure maximum flavour.

Braised Sweetgrass Buffalo Steak Carbonade

6 buffalo round steaks,
   1 inch thick
   Salt, pepper and flour
3 tablespoons rendered buffalo
   kidney suet
2 cups sliced onions
1 tablespoon flour
1½ teaspoons vinegar
1 teaspoon salt
¼ teaspoon pepper
½ teaspoon brown sugar
1 bay leaf
¼ teaspoon thyme
1½ tablespoons minced parsley
½ teaspoon tomato paste
1½ cups beer

1. Rub steaks with salt and pepper, then dust with flour.

2. In a heavy pan, sear steaks on both sides in rendered kidney suet, then remove and place in large casserole.

3. Add onions to remaining suet and sauté until translucent.

4. Add remaining ingredients, then pour sauce over the meat in the casserole. Cover.

5. Cook at 350° F. for 3 hours, or until meat is tender. Serve with cottage style potatoes. Serves 6.

Northern Buffalo Paupiettes

4 Sweetgrass buffalo cutlets,
   ½ inch thick
½ cup onions, finely chopped
1½ cups dry red wine
4 strips bacon
4 tablespoons chopped onion
2 pickled cucumbers
4 tablespoons flour
1 cup beef stock
   Salt and pepper to taste

1. Wipe buffalo cutlets well with a damp cloth.

2. Place meat in a shallow pan, add ½ cup finely chopped onion and the dry red wine.

3. Marinate for 2 hours at room temperature, then remove and place flat on a board.

4. In a frying pan, sauté the bacon and 4 table-spoons of onion, divide in equal amounts and place on the cutlets.

5. Place half a cucumber pickle (sliced length-wise) across each cutlet and roll the cutlet around the pickle like a jelly roll. Fasten with a toothpick.

6. Dredge the rolls in flour then place them in a casserole.

7. Add the red wine from the marinade and 1 cup of beef stock. Cover.

8. Bake in a 350° F. oven until tender, then season to taste with salt and pepper.

9. Serve with unstrained sauce and hot rice. Serves 4.

51

Roast Prime Ribs of Sweetgrass Buffalo

Rib roast of buffalo
Salt
Pepper
Buffalo suet (if roast is lean)
Meat stock

1. Wipe roast well with a damp cloth.

2. Rub roast with salt and pepper, using ½ teaspoon salt for each pound of meat.

3. Put the meat, fat side up on a rack in a roaster.

4. If the meat is very lean, tie a flattened piece of buffalo suet over the top.

5. Insert a meat thermometer into the fleshy part of the roast, being careful not to touch the bone.

6. Place the meat in a 500° F. oven for 20-30 minutes, or until the meat is well seared, then reduce the heat quickly to 325° F. and roast until thermometer reads 140° F. for rare meat, 160° F. for medium meat and 170° F. for well done meat. If you do not have a thermometer, allow 18 minutes per pound (including searing time) for rare meat, 22 minutes per pound for medium or 27 minutes per pound for well done meat.

   Variation: Searing may be omitted if preferred. Place the roast in a 325° F. oven and roast 20 minutes per pound for rare meat, 24 minutes per pound for medium or 32 minutes per pound for well done meat.

7. Drain most of the fat from the roaster, and add meat stock or liquid to make pan gravy. Be sure to stir all the brown bits stuck to the bottom of the pan into the gravy.

8. Strain the gravy and serve hot in a sauce boat or with Yorkshire Pudding. (See page 192 for Yorkshire Pudding recipe.)

Chopped Sweetgrass Buffalo Cutlets

2 pounds ground buffalo meat
6 slices bread
1 cup red wine
1 cup water
4 tablespoons finely chopped onion
4 teaspoons salt
   dash freshly ground pepper
2 eggs slightly beaten
2 cups fine dry bread, cracker *or* corn flake crumbs
4 tablespoons rendered buffalo kidney suet
   English mustard

1. Trim the crusts from the bread, then soak the bread for 10 minutes in the wine and water.

2. Add the onion, salt and pepper and mix well.

3. Add ground buffalo meat and the eggs.

4. Mix and form into 12 flat cutlets.

5. Roll cutlets in crumbs and let the coating set for ½ hour.

6. Heat rendered suet in a heavy pan and pan fry the cutlets quickly until brown and crusty on both sides.

7. Serve piping hot with English mustard.

Caribou

Caribou are common in Canada's north and range over 750,000 square miles of treeless tundra and boreal forest. Depending on the locality, they may be called Arctic deer, tundra deer, tuktoo or tuktu, but the main subspecies in the north is the Barren-ground Caribou which is found all across the barren lands. There are three other common subspecies; the Woodland Caribou of the boreal forests south and west of the barren lands; the Peary Reindeer, smaller and lighter in colour, living on the Arctic islands; and Grant's Reindeer, found in the Mackenzie Mountains west of the Mackenzie Delta.

The annual trek of the caribou from their summer pasture on the tundra to their winter home on the edge of the treeline is followed with intense interest by all who make their living from the land. A variation of 50 to 100 miles in the route of the migrating animals could create severe hardship for those who depend on them for a portion of their year's meat supply. In addition to using the meat for food, the skin is used for clothing and bedding, the antlers and bones for tools and the sinews for thread.

During the summer the caribou feed on lichens, grasses, dwarf shrubs and flowering plants. In winter they eat mosses, lichens and twigs which they obtain by pawing through the snow or by using the brow tine of their antlers. Because of their diet and their leisurely roaming, the caribou's meat is tasty and tender, but it is inclined to be very lean and should be larded before cooking. (See larding of venison, page 45).

Standing Rib Roast of Caribou

1   6-pound rib roast of caribou
2   tablespoons cooking fat
½   teaspoon salt
¼   teaspoon pepper
2   tablespoons flour
1   large onion, quartered
1½ cups water

1. Wipe roast well with a damp cloth.

2. Rub fat over surface, then sprinkle with salt, pepper and flour.

3. Place in roaster, add cut onions and water. Cover.

4. Roast at 450° F. for 20 minutes, reduce heat to 350° F. and cook for 2 hours, or until desired degree of doneness is reached.

53

Hawaiian Caribou

1½ pounds caribou sirloin steak
1 tablespoon sugar
1 tablespoon powdered ginger
½ clove garlic, chopped fine
½ medium onion, chopped fine
¼ cup soy sauce
½ cup water
1 small tin crushed pineapple

1. Cut caribou steak into serving pieces.

2. Make a sauce of the ginger, garlic, onion, sugar, soy sauce and water. Add the crushed pineapple.

3. Pour the sauce over the meat and let stand 1 to 2 hours.

4. Spread the meat pieces out on a shallow pan and broil 3 to 5 minutes on each side. Serve immediately.

Caribou Hash With Eggs

2 cups finely cut cooked meat
3 cups finely cubed cooked potatoes
1 tablespoon finely chopped onion
1 teaspoon salt
½ teaspoon paprika
2 tablespoons fat
4 eggs

1. Combine meat, potatoes, onions, salt and paprika.

2. Melt the fat in a heavy fry pan and cook the meat mixture slowly, turning with a pancake turner to heat and brown slightly.

3. With a spoon make 4 hollows in the meat mixture and drop an egg into each hollow.

4. Cover the pan and cook slowly, about 10 minutes to set the eggs.

Barbecued Ribs of Caribou

3 pounds caribou ribs, cut in serving pieces
3 tablespoons cooking fat
1 cup catsup
1 cup water
2 tablespoons vinegar
1 tablespoon lemon juice (fresh, frozen *or* canned)
1 tablespoon Worcestershire sauce
1 tablespoon prepared mustard
3 tablespoons brown sugar
2 tablespoons onion flakes
1 teaspoon salt
¼ teaspoon pepper

1. Wash ribs in salted water and pat dry.

2. Melt fat in heavy fry pan, add ribs and sauté on all sides till lightly browned.

3. Place ribs in a greased casserole or baking dish.

4. Add rest of ingredients to fry pan and bring to a boil, stirring constantly, then pour over the ribs in the casserole.

5. Cover the casserole and bake in a 350° F. oven till meat is tender. Serves 4.

Braised Caribou

1   3-pound roast of caribou
2   thick slices salt pork *or* thick
      sliced bacon
3   tablespoons cooking fat
1   teaspoon salt
¼   teaspoon pepper
1   cup hot water
1   tablespoon lemon juice *or*
      vinegar
2   tablespoons dried onion flakes

1. Trim all fat off the roast, and wipe well with a clean damp cloth.

2. Lard the caribou meat as follows:
   Cut the salt pork or bacon into ¼-inch strips and chill thoroughly. Pierce the caribou meat with a sharp narrow knife or a skewer at 2-inch intervals and push the chilled strips of salt pork or bacon into the holes.

3. Rub the outside of the roast with cooking fat, then sprinkle with salt and pepper.

4. Brown the roast on all sides in a heavy pot on top of the stove.

5. Add the hot water, lemon juice or vinegar and the dried onion flakes. Cover.

6. Cook at low heat for about 2 hours either on top of the stove or in a 325° F. oven. Serve very hot. Serves 4-6.

Baked Stuffed Caribou Heart

1   caribou heart
1   cup fine bread crumbs
1   stalk celery, chopped
1   small onion, chopped
½   teaspoon poultry dressing
½   teaspoon salt
      Dash of pepper
4   tablespoons melted butter

1. Wipe heart with clean damp cloth, then soak overnight in salted water to cover.

2. Drain, then trim off blood vessels, fat and small thread-like cords. Wash heart thoroughly with cold water, drain and pat dry.

3. Fill cavity with stuffing of bread, celery, onion, poultry dressing, salt, pepper and butter.

4. Place on rack in roaster and pour 1 cup of water in bottom of roaster. Cover and bake in 325° F. oven for about 3 hours, or until tender.

Fresh Caribou Tongue

1   3-pound tongue
2   cups water
1   tablespoon salt
¼   teaspoon pepper
2   bay leaves
6   whole cloves
1   medium onion,
    quartered

1. Wash tongue thoroughly with water and brush.

2. Place clean tongue on rack in pot, add water, salt, pepper, bay leaves, cloves and onion.

3. Simmer about 3 – 3½ hours (or 1 hour per pound).

4. Plunge hot cooked tongue into cold water, then remove skin.

5. Strain liquid and pour over tongue. Slice and serve hot with Spanish Sauce.

Dall Sheep

The golden horns of this snow-white mountain dweller are one of the most sought-after game trophies in the world. This trophy unquestionably ranks first among North American game animals in the eyes of European sportsmen, and holds a similar position in the view of most American hunters, as it is the only known wild white sheep in existence.

In the rugged and picturesque Mackenzie Mountains of the Northwest Territories lies a large, virtually untouched mountain sheep range, grazed by the white Dall. There would appear to be an excellent chance that trophies ranking among the continent's best will come out of this area. The upland meadows 50 miles or more west of the Mackenzie River have experienced virtually no hunting pressure, even from trappers and other residents of settlements along the river, during the past 15 or 20 years. It takes from 11 to 13 years to produce an outstanding trophy head, and the Dall sheep population of the area now appears to be relatively stable with a high proportion of older animals. The area stretching roughly from the Mackenzie River to the Yukon Border, and from the Liard River north to the Peel River Game Preserve has been opened to residents of the Territories for sport hunting of trophy sheep.

The sheep weigh from 150 to 200 pounds when mature, and because they graze on the lichens and sweet grasses of the mountain meadows, their meat is tender and delicious. Like all lamb or mutton, it should be served either very hot or very cold.

Mackenzie Mountain Chops

6   Dall lamb chops, ¾-inch thick
2   tablespoons butter
    Salt and pepper
½   teaspoon marjoram
    Mint sauce

1. Rub the butter into the meat and season with salt and pepper.

2. Sprinkle the marjoram on the chops and place under the broiler.

3. Broil until well done, turning the chops often.

4. Serve hot with mint sauce.

Roast Stuffed Shoulder of Dall Lamb

4-5 pound shoulder of lamb
Salt and pepper
1 cup dry bread crumbs
2 tablespoons grated onion
1 teaspoon sage
½ teaspoon salt
¼ teaspoon pepper

1. Have the bone removed from the shoulder of meat.

2. Wipe the meat with a clean damp cloth and season with salt and pepper.

3. Make a stuffing of the bread crumbs, onions, sage, salt and pepper, and spread it between the two layers of meat. Sew the edges together.

4. Place fat side up in a roasting pan and roast in a 300° F. oven for about 3½ hours.

5. Slice and serve, sprinkled with minced fresh parsley or dried parsley flakes.

Roast Leg of Dall Lamb

1 leg of Dall lamb (3-4 pounds)
Cooking oil
Salt
1 cup cold water
4 small onions, whole
1 tablespoon butter

1. Wipe the meat with a damp cloth.

2. Rub the roast generously with cooking oil, then with salt, and place it in roasting pan with 1 cup cold water.

3. Place in a medium oven, 325° F. and roast about 3½ hours.

4. During the last hour of roasting add the onions and baste often, adding 1 tablespoon butter to the water, and adding more water if necessary.

5. Roast until well done. Serve very hot. The juices in the pan may be thickened if desired.

Golden Lamb Patties

2 pounds lean meat of mountain sheep
2 tablespoons grated onion
1 teaspoon salt
¼ teaspoon pepper
2 tablespoons butter

1. Wash the meat thoroughly and pat dry.

2. Put the meat through the food chopper twice.

3. Add the grated onion, salt and pepper to the ground meat and shape into patties.

4. Heat the butter in a heavy fry pan and fry the patties, turning to brown on both sides.
Serve with french fried potatoes and tossed green salad.

Elk and Deer

Elkburgers

2 pounds ground lean elk meat
¼ pound ground beef suet
1 cup moist bread crumbs
1 onion, diced
½ teaspoon salt
¼ teaspoon pepper
1 tablespoon catsup
4 tablespoons cooking fat

1. Mix all ingredients together except the fat, in the order given.
2. Shape into patties.
3. Melt fat in heavy fry pan and pan fry elkburgers till brown on one side. Turn burgers over and cook until no red remains on inside.
4. Serve on hot buttered buns. Serves 6.

Curried Game

3 pounds elk or deer meat, cooked and diced
¼ cup salad oil or shortening
1½ medium or
1 large onion, minced
3 stalks celery, chopped
2 large apples, minced
2 teaspoons curry powder
½ teaspoon salt
⅛ teaspoon pepper
¼ teaspoon ginger
1 dash of Tabasco sauce
½ tablespoon Worcestershire sauce
2 cups meat stock or bouillon
2 tablespoons flour
¼ cup cold water
1 cup top milk or coffee cream
1 egg yolk, well beaten
3 cups cooked rice prepared according to directions

1. Heat oil or shortening in a heavy pan on top of the stove.
2. Add onions, celery and apples and sauté until onions are translucent but not brown.
3. Stir in curry powder and simmer 5 minutes.
4. Add salt, pepper, ginger, Tabasco and Worcestershire sauce.
5. Add stock and cook 20 minutes.
6. Mix flour with cold water, then add to liquid and cook 7 minutes, stirring until thickened.
7. Remove from heat and allow to stand 1 hour.
8. Reheat, then add cooked diced meat, the cream and the egg yolk.
9. Heat just to boiling point, stirring constantly.
10. Serve immediately on hot fluffy rice. Serves 6-8.

Elk Meat Loaf

2 pounds ground elk meat
½ pound lean ground pork
1 onion, chopped
3 tablespoons dried parsley
3 tablespoons grated Parmesan cheese
1 teaspoon salt
¼ teaspoon pepper
½ teaspoon oregano
1 cup soft bread crumbs
2 cups milk
2 eggs, slightly beaten
4 strips bacon
1 cup tomato sauce or catsup

1. Mix all ingredients with exception of bacon and tomato sauce and press into a well greased loaf pan.
2. Overlap bacon strips on top of the meat and bake in a 350° F. oven for 45 minutes.
3. Remove bacon strips and pour tomato sauce or catsup over the top.
4. Bake another 20 – 30 minutes. Serves 6-8.

58

Elk Steak 'n Gravy

1   2½ to 3 pound elk round steak
1   medium onion
1   bell pepper
1   cup flour
2   teaspoons salt
1   teaspoon pepper
½   cup cooking oil
1   can cream of mushroom soup

1. Slice onion and bell pepper in rings and brown lightly in oil.

2. Remove from heat and drain.

3. Mix flour, salt and pepper and pound into well-trimmed (all fat and connective tissue removed) steak.

4. Brown on both sides in oil used for pepper and onions.

5. Pour off oil.

6. Place onion and pepper rings on top of steak and spread soup on top of all pieces.

7. Add water to almost cover meat and simmer 2 hours, adding water as needed to keep meat nearly submerged. Serves 6.

Elk Steak in Wine

3   pounds boneless elk steak
¼   cup flour
½   teaspoon salt
¼   teaspoon pepper
¼   cup butter
3   onions, sliced *or*
3   tablespoons onion flakes
1   green pepper sliced *or*
2   tablespoons red and green pepper flakes
1   cup canned mushrooms, drained
½   cup butter
2   cups canned tomatoes
½   cup red cooking wine *or* Burgundy

1. Trim fat from steak and wipe well with damp cloth.

2. Dredge steaks in seasoned flour.

3. Melt butter in heavy fry pan, add steak and sauté until lightly browned on both sides.

4. Remove steak and keep warm.

5. Melt remainder of butter in fry pan, add onions, pepper and mushrooms and cook at low heat until onions are translucent. Add canned tomatoes.

6. Return steaks to the sauce in the fry pan, cover and simmer for 15 minutes, or until steaks are tender, stirring occasionally.

7. Add wine and simmer another 2 or 3 minutes. Serve hot. Serves 6.

Frozen Deer Liver

1   deer liver
4   tablespoons butter
    Flour for dredging
    Salt and pepper

1. Soak liver for 2 hours in salted water, then drain and pat dry.

2. Quick freeze whole liver.

3. Slice frozen liver in thin slices, without thawing the whole liver.

4. Dredge each slice in seasoned flour.

5. Pan fry in butter over medium heat until tender.

English Brown Stew

1 pound elk *or* venison,
cut in 1-inch cubes
3 tablespoons flour
1 teaspoon salt
1 tablespoon fat
2½ cups boiling water
2 tablespoons chopped onion
½ clove garlic, chopped
1 teaspoon sugar
½ teaspoon paprika
½ tablespoon lemon juice
½ tablespoon Worcestershire
sauce
¼ cup tomato juice
½ cup pearl onions
¼ cup diced celery
½ cup diced carrots
1 cup cubed potatoes
2 tablespoons flour
½ cup cold water

1. Dredge the pieces of meat with flour and salt.

2. Heat the fat in a heavy pot and brown the meat on all sides.

3. Add boiling water, chopped onion, garlic, sugar, paprika, lemon juice, Worcestershire sauce and tomato juice to the meat. Cover tightly and simmer for 2 hours. Add more water if needed.

4. Add the pearl onions, celery, carrots and potatoes and continue cooking until vegetables are tender. Transfer meat and vegetables to a serving dish.

5. Thicken the gravy with a paste made from flour and cold water.

6. Pour the thickened gravy back over the meat and vegetables.
Serve hot. Serves 6.

Sweet and Sour Deer Ribs

3 pounds deer ribs, trimmed
and cut in 2-inch lengths
3 tablespoons melted fat
2 cups tomato juice
1 teaspoon salt
½ teaspoon dry mustard
¼ teaspoon *or* more, black pepper
3 tablespoons brown sugar
½ cup white vinegar
3 medium whole onions
3 tablespoons flour
½ cup cold water

1. Soak ribs in salted water overnight. Then drain well.

2. Melt fat in heavy fry pan on top of stove. Add ribs and brown well on all sides.

3. Transfer ribs to a roaster.

4. Mix tomato juice, salt, mustard, pepper, brown sugar and vinegar and pour over ribs in the roaster.

5. Roast in a hot oven at 400° F. for 15 minutes, turning ribs occasionally.

6. Add onions and reduce heat to 350° F. Cover and roast for 1 hour, or until meat is tender, stirring occasionally.

7. When meat is tender, transfer the ribs to a serving dish. Thicken the sauce with a paste made from the flour and water and cook a few minutes more on top of the stove, stirring constantly.

8. Pour sauce over the ribs in the serving dish. Serve with hot rice. Serves 6.

Lynx

The lynx is a shy, almost cowardly creature of the wilderness, seldom seen by hunters, but becoming ferocious if attacked. It may weigh up to forty pounds, but can travel quickly and easily over the deep snow, using its large furry paws as snowshoes. It is a nocturnal animal, sleeping during the day and hunting small game, game birds and their eggs by night. Like other felines, the lynx is fastidious and a clean eater.

Care should be taken in skinning the lynx to protect its deep silky fur. It should be "cased". Slit the skin on the inside of the hind legs from the paws to the vent, then work the skin off the legs, the rump and the tail. Tie the hind feet together over a hook or the limb of a tree and then work the skin off, inside out (like peeling off a sweater), using the knife as little as possible. When the forelegs are reached, they should be pushed back and worked out of the skin until the paws are completely skinned out. Take particular care when skinning around the eyes and lips. Scrape the pelt to remove any flesh and fat clinging to it, then wash with lukewarm water to remove all bloodstains. Place it on a stretcher, fur side in and let it dry until it can hold its shape. Then turn the fur side out, starting by folding in the nose and working the pelt inwards a little at a time. Replace the turned skin on the stretcher with the fur side out and let it dry thoroughly. Complete directions on preparing the pelts for marketing may be obtained from Fish and Wildlife Officers.

The meat of the lynx is white and very tender, and provides excellent eating, especially in the late fall and early winter when the animal is sleek and well fed.

Canadian Lynx Stew

2 pounds lynx meat
4 tablespoons fat
1 small onion, chopped
1 teaspoon salt
¼ teaspoon pepper
¼ teaspoon summer savory
¼ teaspoon oregano
4 potatoes, quartered
4 carrots, diced
½ cup celery, chopped
2 tablespoons flour
½ cup cold water
1 teaspoon Worcestershire sauce

1. Wash meat well, pat dry, and cut into 2-inch cubes.

2. Melt fat in heavy pot, add meat and cook until nicely browned.

3. Add onions and seasoning.

4. Cover with cold water, bring to a boil then reduce heat, place a lid on the pot and simmer for 1½ hours.

5. Add cut potatoes, carrots and celery and continue cooking for ½ hour or until meat and vegetables are tender.

6. Make a paste of the flour and water and add to the stew, stirring gently until thickened.

7. Just before serving add the Worcestershire sauce. Serve hot. Serves 4.

Moose

Moose range throughout the Great Slave Lake, Great Bear Lake, Mackenzie Valley and Mackenzie Mountain areas from the 60th parallel almost to the Arctic Ocean, as well as the southern part of the Keewatin District of the Northwest Territories.

They have for many years been an important part of the economy to the native northerner, who has used its meat for food, its hide for clothing and its bones and antlers for utensils. In addition, beautiful embroidery work has been created from the moose whiskers which are bleached, then dyed and used for thread.

Sport hunting for this majestic animal is open to residents of the Mackenzie Valley and Great Slave Lake Basin areas. (See pp. 320–323 for dates and zones.)

A moose may weigh from 800 to 1400 pounds, with some bulls being even larger. Its meat is the most coveted and sought-after of all the big game meats, and moose heart and moose liver are without equal for tenderness and flavour.

Broiled Mooseburgers

2 pounds minced moose meat
1½ tablespoons chopped green pepper
1½ tablespoons chopped onion
½ teaspoon salt
¼ teaspoon pepper
Bacon strips
Butter
1 can mushroom soup

1. Combine meat, chopped green pepper, chopped onion, salt and pepper.

2. Form meat into patties.

3. Encircle each patty with a strip bacon, fastening with toothpicks.

4. Dot surface of each meat patty with butter, then broil 6 minutes on each side 3 inches from flame.

5. Heat undiluted cream of mushroom soup and stir till smooth.

6. Serve hot over mooseburgers.

Braised Moose

1 4-pound moose roast
3 strips salt pork *or* thick sliced bacon
1 teaspoon salt
¼ teaspoon black pepper
½ teaspoon ground cinnamon
¼ teaspoon ground cloves
1 teaspoon dry mustard
4 tablespoons brown sugar
2½ cups water
½ cup white wine vinegar
2 tablespoons onion flakes
3 tablespoons flour
1 cup cranberry juice
1 cup milk

1. Remove all fat from the moose roast and wipe well with a clean damp cloth.
2. Lard the roast as follows:
   Cut salt pork or bacon into ¼-inch strips and chill thoroughly. Pierce the moose roast with a sharp knife or skewer at 2-inch intervals and insert the chilled strips of salt pork or bacon.
3. Place the roast in a glass, earthenware or porcelain bowl.
4. Mix the salt, pepper, cinnamon, cloves, mustard and brown sugar with the water and vinegar and pour over the moose (3 cups of sweet pickle juice may be used in place of the brown sugar, water and vinegar if desired).
5. Marinate the roast for 24 to 48 hours, turning it over frequently if the liquid does not completely cover it.
6. Remove the roast from the marinade and place it in a covered roaster in a 350° F. oven for approximately one hour.
7. Add onion flakes and cranberry juice and continue roasting until tender. (about 1 hour).
8. Transfer meat to a hot platter. Add flour to the pan drippings and stir until the flour has absorbed the fat.
9. Add the milk, stirring constantly, until gravy is desired thickness. Serve hot with the roast. Serves 6-8.

Moose Chili Con Carne

1 pound moose meat, ground
½ teaspoon salt
¼ teaspoon pepper
1 tablespoon flour
½ cup chopped onion *or*
4 tablespoons dried onion flakes
2 tablespoons fat
1 tablespoon Worcestershire sauce
4 cups canned tomatoes
1 10 oz can mushroom bits and pieces, drained
1 tablespoon chili powder
1 15 oz can red kidney beans

1. Sprinkle meat with flour, salt and pepper.
2. Melt fat in heavy fry pan.
3. Combine meat with onion, then brown it in hot fat.
4. Add remaining ingredients, reduce heat and simmer until meat is tender, about 45 minutes.
5. Serve hot with baking powder biscuits or buttered toast. Serves 6.

Marinated Moose

3 pounds moose stewing meat cut in 1½ inch cubes. (Use shoulder, neck *or* breast meat)
2 medium onions, sliced
1 carrot, sliced
2 stalks celery, chopped
1 clove garlic, crushed
1 teaspoon salt
10 peppercorns
5 juniper berries, crushed
1 tablespoon chopped parsley
1 bay leaf
Juice of 1 lemon
½ cup salad oil
16 oz beer *or* gingerale

1. Wash stew meat well in salted water. Remove any tough membranes or tendons. Drain.

2. Mix all ingredients in a large glass, crockery or earthenware bowl, add the meat, cover and let stand in a cool place or a refrigerator for 1 to 2 days, stirring occasionally.

3. Place meat and marinade in a large kettle and bring slowly to a boil.

4. Cover, reduce heat and simmer for 2 hours or until meat is tender.

5. Remove the meat and set aside.

6. Remove the bay leaf and discard.

7. Strain the liquid, forcing the vegetables through the strainer.

8. Return the liquid to the stove, bring it to a boil and thicken it if desired with a paste made from 2 tablespoons flour mixed with ½ cup cold water. Stir until smooth.

9. Add the meat and heat thoroughly. Serve hot. Serves 6-8.

Moosemeat Soup

2 pounds moose stew meat
2 tablespoons salt
1½ quarts cold water
5 carrots, cubed
1 bunch celery, cubed
2 cups tomatoes
2 medium potatoes, cubed
2 onions, cubed
½ teaspoon savory
1 bay leaf
Salt and pepper

1. Trim as much fat from meat as possible.

2. Soak meat in salted cold water for several hours, then drain.

3. Place meat in large pot and cover with cold water.

4. Bring to a boil, then simmer slowly for 2 hours, skimming occasionally.

5. Remove from heat and let the broth stand overnight in a cool place.

6. Next day remove the congealed fat from the surface, then add vegetables, savory and bay leaf, bring to a boil and simmer for 1½ – 2 hours.

7. Season to taste with salt and pepper. Remove bay leaf before serving.

Dorothy MacIntosh Moose Stew

3 pounds moose stew meat
   cut in 1½ inch cubes
4 tablespoons bacon drippings
2 medium onions, sliced
1 clove garlic
1 cup chopped celery
1 bay leaf
1 teaspoon salt
¼ teaspoon pepper
¼ teaspoon thyme
4 cups cold water
1 cup diced carrots
2 cups diced potatoes
1 cup diced turnip
1 tablespoon dried parsley
4 tablespoons flour
1 cup cold water

1. Trim fat, connective tissue or tendons from moose meat, wash in salted water, pat dry.

2. Melt bacon drippings in a heavy pot on top of stove.

3. Add the moose meat and brown well on all sides.

4. Add onions, garlic, celery, bay leaf, salt, pepper, thyme and 4 cups cold water. Cover.

5. Slowly bring stew to a boil, then reduce heat and let simmer for 2 hours.

6. Add carrots, potatoes, turnips and parsley and simmer for another hour, or until meat and vegetables are fork-tender.

7. Mix flour and water to a smooth paste, then add the thickening to the stew, stirring constantly.

8. Let cook for 7 minutes. Serve with thick slices of home made bread. Serves 6-8.

Savoury Moose Steaks

1½ pounds moose steak, 1 inch
   thick
1 tablespoon mustard
4 tablespoons cornstarch
½ teaspoon salt
⅛ teaspoon pepper
2 tablespoons fat
1 cup sliced onion
1 diced carrot
1½ cups canned tomatoes

1. Make ½ inch nicks around the edge of the steak with a sharp knife, about every two inches.

2. Mix mustard, cornstarch, salt and pepper and rub into steak on both sides.

3. Pound the steak on both sides with a meat hammer or the side of a saucer, rubbing in more of the mustard and cornstarch mixture as necessary.

4. Melt the fat in a heavy fry pan.

5. Sear the steak in the hot fat on both sides, then transfer to a greased casserole.

6. Cover with onions, carrots and tomatoes.

7. Cover and bake for 1½ hours in a 350° F. oven, or until meat is tender.

8. Serve hot with oven browned potatoes. Serves 4.

Jellied Moose Nose

1 upper jawbone of a moose
1 onion, sliced
1 clove garlic
1 tablespoon mixed pickling spice
1 teaspoon salt
½ teaspoon pepper
¼ cup vinegar

1. Cut the upper jaw bone of the moose just below the eyes.

2. Place in large kettle of scalding water and boil for 45 minutes.

3. Remove and chill in cold water.

4. Pull out all the hairs – these will have been loosened by boiling and should come out easily (like plucking a duck).

5. Wash thoroughly until no hairs remain.

6. Place the nose in a kettle and cover with fresh water.

7. Add onion, garlic, spices and vinegar.

8. Bring to a boil, then reduce heat and simmer until the meat is tender. Let cool overnight in the liquid.

9. When cool, take the meat out of the broth, and remove and discard the bones and cartilage. You will have two kinds of meat, white meat from the bulb of the nose and thin strips of dark meat from along the bones and jowls.

10. Slice the meat thinly and alternate layers of white and dark meat in a loaf pan.

11. Reheat the broth to boiling, then pour the broth over the meat in the loaf pan.

12. Let cool until jelly has set. Slice and serve cold.

Head Cheese

Head of moose, venison, caribou, reindeer or elk, plus heart, tongue and trimmings as desired
½ cup salt
1 gallon water

1. Clean the head by removing the eyes, ears, brains and all of the skin.

2. Trim off all fat.

3. Cut head into pieces and soak in brine made from ½ cup salt added to 1 gallon of water, for at least 6 hours (this draws out the blood).

4. Drain the pieces of head and rinse thoroughly in clean water.

5. Place in a large pot, add meat trimmings, cover with hot water, bring to a boil, then reduce the heat and let simmer until the meat can be removed from the bone.

6. Trim meat from the bones and chop fine. Weigh the meat on kitchen scales.

7. Strain the broth, then let it boil down until you have 4 cups of broth for each 3 pounds of chopped meat.

8. Add the chopped meat to the broth with the following spices for each 3 pounds of meat:
1 tablespoon salt, 1 teaspoon pepper, 1 tablespoon onion flakes (optional), 1 tablespoon dried red and green pepper flakes, 1 teaspoon ground allspice, ½ teaspoon ground cloves.

9. Heat the mixture, then let it simmer 15 minutes.

10. Pour into loaf pans or bowls, cover and chill till firm.

Note
If a firmer jelly is desired, add 1 tablespoon gelatin (softened in ¼ cup cold water) for each 2 cups of liquid.

Moose Mincemeat

2 pounds cooked moosemeat, put through meat grinder
1 quart apple cider *or*
4½ cups apple juice plus
½ cup vinegar
4 pounds chopped apples
2 pounds raisins
4 cups brown *or* white sugar
¾ pound chopped suet *or* butter
1 teaspoon mace
½ teaspoon cloves
½ teaspoon nutmeg
2 teaspoons salt
1½ teaspoons cinnamon

1. Mix all ingredients. Add enough cider to cover.

2. Bring to a boil, reduce heat and simmer gently until the fruit is tender, about 1 hour.

3. Put in scalded jars, seal and store in cool place. Makes about 4 quarts.

Stuffed Moose Heart

1 moose heart
1 cup fine bread crumbs
1 stalk celery, chopped
½ teaspoon salt
4 tablespoons melted butter
1 small onion, chopped
½ teaspoon sage
¼ teaspoon pepper
Flour, salt and pepper for dredging

1. Wipe heart with a damp cloth, soak overnight in salted water, then drain.
2. Mix stuffing ingredients in order given.
3. Drain the heart, hollow out the top and stuff with the sage stuffing, then close opening.
4. Dredge heart in flour, salt and pepper.
5. Dot with butter or dripping.
6. Place in a covered roaster and bake in a 325° F. oven until done, about 3 hours, basting occasionally.

Moose Sukiyaki

1½ pounds sirloin steak, cut in thin slices about 2 inches long, ½ inch wide
2 tablespoons salad oil
¼ cup sugar
¾ cup soy sauce
¼ cup mushroom stock
2 medium onions, sliced thin
1 green pepper, cut in thin slices
1 cup sliced celery, cut in 1½ inch strips
1 8 oz can mushrooms, sliced
1 can bamboo shoots, sliced thin
1 bunch green onions with tops, cut in 1 inch lengths

1. Heat 2 tablespoons salad oil in heavy fry pan. Add the meat and brown lightly.
2. Mix ¼ cup sugar, soy sauce and mushroom stock and add half of this to the meat.
3. Push the meat to one side of the pan and sauté the sliced onion, green pepper and celery, cooking for just a few minutes.
4. Stir the meat back into the onions, green pepper and celery. Add the remainder of the soy sauce liquid, bamboo shoots and mushrooms. Cook about 5 minutes.
5. Add the green onions and tops, cook one more minute. Stir well and serve immediately. Be careful not to over-cook the vegetables as they should be crispy. Serve with fluffy rice. Serves 6.

Moose Swiss Steak

1½ pounds moose round steak
¼ cup flour
½ teaspoon salt
¼ teaspoon pepper
4 tablespoons cooking fat
3 tablespoons onion flakes
1 teaspoon celery seed
2 cups canned tomatoes
2 tablespoons Worcestershire sauce
3 tablespoons flour
½ cup cold water

1. Trim all fat from moose steak and wipe with a clean damp cloth.
2. Dredge steak in seasoned flour.
3. Melt fat in heavy fry pan, add steak and brown on both sides, then remove and keep warm.
4. Add onion flakes, celery seed, canned tomatoes and Worcestershire sauce to fry pan and stir till well mixed with the drippings from the steak.
5. Add the steak, cover, and simmer until the steak is fork-tender, about 1½ hours.
6. Thicken the sauce with a paste made from the flour and water, stirring constantly while adding it to prevent lumping. Serves 4.

Reindeer Pot Roast With Vegetables

3 pound pot roast of reindeer
2 strips salt pork *or* thick sliced bacon
1 teaspoon salt
¼ teaspoon pepper
3 tablespoons dried onion flakes
2 cups water
1 bay leaf
4 potatoes, quartered *or*
1 tin canned potatoes
4 carrots, quartered *or*
1 tin canned carrots
1 tin canned peas
1 tablespoon dried parsley
3 tablespoons flour
1 cup water

1. Trim all fat from the roast, and wipe well with a clean damp cloth.
2. Lard the reindeer roast by piercing it with a sharp knife or skewer at 2 inch intervals and inserting chilled strips of salt pork or bacon.
3. Rub the roast well with salt and pepper.
4. Place meat in a roasting pan, add the water, onion flakes and bay leaf. (If you are going to use canned vegetables, use the liquid drained from the cans of vegetables in place of water).
5. Cover pan and roast at 350° F. until almost tender.
6. Add the vegetables and continue cooking until vegetables are tender and flavours have blended.
7. Remove pot roast and vegetables to a hot serving dish, discarding the bay leaf. Keep hot until serving time.
8. Thicken the gravy left in the pan by adding a paste made from flour and water, stirring constantly until thickened, and continue cooking for 7 minutes.
9. Pour gravy over the vegetables in the serving dish. Serves 4-6.

Roast Round of Reindeer

1 7 pound reindeer roast (upper round)
2 tablespoons flour
1 teaspoon salt
¼ teaspoon pepper
1 medium cooking onion, quartered
1 piece beef suet *or* salt pork

1. Wipe roast well with a clean damp cloth.
2. Rub roast with seasoned flour and place on a rack in a roaster.
3. Add cut onion. If roast is not fat, place a piece of suet or a slice of salt pork on top of the roast.
4. Cover and roast in a 325° F. oven until desired degree of doneness is reached (about 25 minutes per pound for rare, 30 minutes per pound for medium and 35 minutes per pound for well done). Serves 8-10. Serve hot with Pepper or Cranberry Sauce.

Reindeer Swiss Steak

3 pounds reindeer round steak cut 1 inch thick
4 tablespoons flour
1 teaspoon salt
¼ teaspoon pepper
2 tablespoons cooking fat or shortening
1 small onion, chopped
2 cups canned tomatoes
1 tablespoon red and green pepper flakes
1 tablespoon Worcestershire sauce

1. Trim fat from steak. Wipe well with a damp cloth and cut into serving portions.

2. Pound seasoned flour into both sides of each piece of steak, using a meat mallet, or the side of a saucer.

3. Melt fat in heavy fry pan, add steaks and brown on both sides.

4. Add sliced onion, tomatoes, pepper flakes and Worcestershire sauce, cover and simmer until tender, about 1½ to 2 hours, depending on the thickness of the steak.

Stuffed Rib Roast of Reindeer

1 6 pound rib roast of reindeer, boned
½ cup chopped suet
4 cups cranberries, chopped
1½ cups sugar
2 cups dry bread crumbs
1 small onion, chopped
1 teaspoon salt
¼ teaspoon pepper
½ teaspoon marjoram (optional)
4 tablespoons fat

1. Wash meat well, drain and pat dry.

2. In a heavy fry pan, cook suet until crisp, add chopped cranberries and sugar and cook. Stir until berries are clear.

3. Add bread crumbs, onion and seasonings to cranberry and suet mixture and mix well.

4. Spread stuffing on meat, roll up like jelly roll and tie with string.

5. Spread fat over roast, place in roaster, and roast in a 325° F. oven until done (about 20-25 minutes per pound).

Reindeer Goulash

1½ pounds reindeer stew meat
¼ cup flour
2 tablespoons fat
1 cup water
2 strips bacon, coarsely chopped
2 cups coarsely chopped onion
¼ teaspoon garlic powder
2 tablespoons brown sugar
1 tablespoon paprika
1 tablespoon Worcestershire sauce
½ teaspoon vinegar
2 teaspoons salt
¼ teaspoon pepper
Dash cayenne
¼ teaspoon mustard
1 tin tomatoes
5 cups cooked rice

1. Roll the pieces of meat in flour.

2. Heat fat in heavy pot and brown the meat, then add 1 cup water and simmer for about 1 hour.

3. Fry the bacon, then add the onions and cook until lightly browned. Stir in the garlic powder, brown sugar, paprika, Worcestershire sauce, vinegar, salt, pepper, cayenne and mustard.

4. Add this sauce and tomatoes to the meat in the pot, cover and cook slowly for another hour or until meat is tender. Serve with fluffy steamed rice. Serves 6.

Stuffed Reindeer Steak Rolls

1½ pounds reindeer round steak,
    cut ½ inch thick
6   slices bacon
1   dill pickle, sliced in sixths,
    lengthwise
1   small onion, finely chopped
4   tablespoons flour
½   teaspoon salt
¼   teaspoon pepper
3   tablespoons bacon fat *or*
    shortening
½   cup water
½   cup catsup
1   tablespoon Worcestershire
    sauce

1. Wipe steak with a clean damp cloth.

2. Cut steak into 6 strips, approximately 2 inches wide and 4 inches long.

3. Lay one slice of bacon lengthwise on each strip and sprinkle with finely chopped onion.

4. Place dill pickle crosswise on each strip, then roll each strip up carefully round the dill pickle and fasten with toothpicks.

5. Dredge each roll in the flour, season with the salt and pepper.

6. Melt the fat in a heavy fry pan and brown the steak rolls on all sides.

7. Add the water, catsup and Worcestershire sauce.

8. Cover and simmer until tender, about 1½ hours. Serves 6.

Note
Tomato soup or tomato juice may be used in place of catsup and water.

Venison Biscuit Roll

2   cups cooked venison, ground
½   cup brown gravy
½   teaspoon salt
¼   teaspoon pepper
1   small onion, minced *or*
1   tablespoon dried onion flakes
1   teaspoon dried parsley
2   cups flour
4   teaspoons regular baking
    powder
½   teaspoon salt
4   tablespoons fat
¾ to 1 cup milk

1. Combine cooked ground venison, gravy, salt, pepper, onion and parsley, adding more gravy if necessary to make it of spreading consistency.

2. Sift flour, baking powder and salt together in a bowl.

3. Cut in fat with a pastry blender or two knives until it is the size of small peas.

4. Add milk to make a soft dough.

5. Roll or pat dough in a rectangular shape ¼ inch thick.

6. Spread with venison mixture.

7. Roll up like a jelly roll and place, in the form of a circle, on a greased baking sheet.

8. Using kitchen scissors, slash through biscuit dough, cutting as for Swedish tea rings.

9. Bake 30 minutes in a hot oven at 400° F. until lightly browned. Serve with tomato sauce, catsup or sweet pickle relish. Serves 4-6.

Braised Venison in Sour Cream

2 pounds venison
¼ cup bacon fat
1 clove garlic
1 cup diced celery
1 cup diced carrots
½ cup minced onions
2 cups water
1 bay leaf
1 cup tart fruit juice (apple *or* grapefruit)
8 peppercorns
1 teaspoon salt
4 tablespoons butter
4 tablespoons flour
1 cup sour cream

1. Wipe meat with a clean damp cloth.

2. Cut venison in 2-inch pieces.

3. Melt bacon fat in heavy fry pan.

4. Add meat and garlic and sauté until brown on all sides.

5. Arrange meat in 2-quart casserole.

6. Put celery, carrots and onions in frying pan and cook 2 minutes in remaining bacon fat.

7. Add water, bay leaf, juice, peppercorns and salt to the vegetables and bring to a boil, stirring to get all the meat flavour from the pan drippings.

8. Pour mixture over the venison in the casserole and bake in a slow oven (325° F.) 30 to 60 minutes until the meat is tender.

9. Drain the liquid from the casserole and set aside.

10. Melt butter in fry pan, stir in flour, and when well blended, add the liquid from the casserole, stirring constantly until the mixture thickens and boils.

11. Add sour cream and more salt if necessary and mix well.

12. Bring to a boil, then pour over the meat and vegetables in the casserole. Remove bay leaf before serving.

13. Serve immediately with buttered noodles and peach, plum or currant jelly. Serves 6-8.

Roast Venison With Herbs

3 pound roast of venison
1 clove garlic
3 tablespoons salad *or* olive oil
1 sprig sweet marjoram *or*
½ teaspoon dried marjoram
1 teaspoon salt
½ teaspoon pepper

1. In a small bowl, grate the garlic clove into 3 tablespoons of salad or olive oil.

2. Add the finely minced sprig of sweet marjoram, or the ½ teaspoon of dried marjoram.

3. Let stand for 15 minutes before using.

4. Wipe the roast with a clean damp cloth.

5. Using a pastry brush, coat the roast on all sides with the oil mixture.

6. Sprinkle the salt and pepper on the roast and place it in uncovered roaster. Roast at 350° F. for 25 to 35 minutes per pound, depending on the degree of rareness desired. Serves 4-6.

Pan-Broiled Venison Steaks

6   venison steaks cut ½ to
    1 inch thick
½ teaspoon salt
¼ teaspoon pepper
¼ teaspoon charcoal seasoning
    (optional)

Marinade for Steak

¼ cup vinegar
2 tablespoons water
⅔ cup salad oil
1 teaspoon salt
½ teaspoon dry mustard
1 tablespoon catsup
1 tablespoon grated onion *or*
    dried onion flakes
½ teaspoon sugar
¼ teaspoon pepper
½ teaspoon paprika
¼ teaspoon garlic salt

1. Measure all marinade ingredients into a jar which has a close-fitting top.
2. Cover and shake vigorously or blend in electric mixer.
3. Place in large enamel, glass or earthenware bowl, add steaks and allow to stand for several hours or overnight in a cool place.
4. Remove steaks and drain well. Season steaks with salt, pepper and charcoal seasoning if desired.
5. Rub preheated heavy frying pan with a piece of fat.
6. Cook steaks quickly at high heat, turning every half minute until done. Do not over-cook. Add only enough fat to prevent meat from sticking to pan.
7. Serve sizzling hot. Serves 6.

Venison One-Dish Meal

1 cup rice
2 tablespoons fat
2 cups cooked venison,
    ground
2 small onions, cut fine
1½ cups canned tomatoes
2 cups canned corn
    Salt and pepper to taste

1. Cook rice in boiling salted water 20 minutes or until tender.
2. Drain rice.
3. Melt fat in a heavy fry pan.
4. Add onion and meat and cook 5 minutes, until lightly browned.
5. Combine all ingredients in a greased casserole.
6. Cover and bake in a 400° F. oven until heated through, about 30 minutes. Serves 4-6.

Venison Meat Loaf

2½ pounds ground venison
2 teaspoons salt
¼ teaspoon pepper
¾ cup dry bread crumbs
2 eggs, slightly beaten
¾ cup milk
½ small onion, chopped

1. Combine all ingredients and mix well.
2. Press into a greased loaf pan (9″×5″×3″).
3. Bake in a 350° F. oven for 2¼ hours.

Note
Beef suet or salt pork may be ground with the venison if it seems dry.

Venison Mincemeat

2 pounds lean venison (neck)
1 pound beef suet
6 pounds apples
2 pounds currants
2 pounds seedless raisins
½ pound citron
6 cups brown sugar
1 tablespoon allspice
¼ teaspoon ginger
1 tablespoon salt
2 teaspoons nutmeg
1 tablespoon cinnamon
1 teaspoon cloves
2 oranges
8 cups apple cider *or* grape juice

1. Bake venison in a covered roaster in a 350° F. oven for 40 minutes.
2. Cool and grind.
3. Mix with the chopped suet; pared, cored, and chopped apples, currants, raisins, and citron. Add sugar, spices, juice of two oranges, finely chopped rind of one orange, and the cider or grape juice.
4. Simmer in a large pot on top of the stove for 30 minutes.
5. Pack hot into clean jars, leaving 1 inch head space, seal, then loosen slightly and process in pressure canner 60 minutes for a pint jar and 70 minutes for a quart jar at 15 pounds pressure.
6. Remove from canner, complete the seal and store in a cool place. Makes about 8 quarts.

Braised Heart of Venison

1 venison heart
1 tablespoon salt
4 tablespoons flour
1 teaspoon salt
¼ teaspoon pepper
3 tablespoons bacon fat
  Water
1 cup diced carrots
1 cup diced celery
1 medium onion, sliced *or*
2 tablespoons dried onion flakes
2 tablespoons dried parsley

1. Wipe heart well with a damp cloth.
2. Soak overnight in enough water to cover, to which 1 tablespoon salt has been added.
3. Remove, drain and pat dry.
4. Slice heart crosswise in ½ inch slices and remove the tough white membrane.
5. Dredge the slices in seasoned flour.
6. Melt the bacon fat in a heavy fry pan and sauté the slices of heart, until lightly browned.
7. Add enough water to cover the meat, reduce heat, cover and let simmer for 1 hour, adding more water as required.
8. Add vegetables and more water if necessary, cover, and simmer until vegetables and meat are tender. Serves 4.

Venison Liver and Onions

1 venison liver, sliced
   Boiling water
4 tablespoons flour
½ teaspoon salt
¼ teaspoon pepper
4 tablespoons bacon fat
2 cups sliced onion
3 cups water

1. Pour boiling water over the sliced liver twice, then drain.
2. Dredge liver in seasoned flour.
3. Melt fat in a heavy fry pan.
4. Add liver and sauté till lightly browned.
5. Add 2 cups water, cover and allow to simmer slowly for 1 hour.
6. Remove liver and sauté 2 cups sliced onions until golden brown.
7. Replace liver, add 1 cup water, cover and simmer slowly for another half hour. Serves 4-6.

Spicy Venison Pot Roast

3 pound venison roast
4 tablespoons pork *or* beef fat
2 large onions, sliced
1 clove garlic
1 cup stock *or* water
2 bay leaves
2 tablespoons vinegar
1 tablespoon brown sugar
1 teaspoon salt
3 tablespoons catsup
½ cup raisins
   Buttered noodles

1. Trim fat from meat and discard. Wipe meat with a damp cloth.
2. Melt pork or beef fat in a heavy pot on top of the stove.
3. Brown meat on all sides.
4. Add onions and garlic; brown lightly.
5. Add liquid and bay leaves. Bring to a boil, then reduce heat.
6. Cover and simmer on low heat for one hour.
7. Add vinegar and brown sugar; continue cooking one hour longer.
8. Add salt, catsup and raisins and cook one-half hour longer, or until tender.
9. Place roast on serving platter; surround with buttered noodles and spoon on sauce. Serves 6.

Chili With Venison

1 pound ground venison
3 slices side pork *or*
   fresh seasoned sausage
1 onion
1 pint tomato juice
2 cups dried kidney beans
1½ teaspoons salt
¼ teaspoon pepper
1 teaspoon chili powder

1. Soak beans overnight in cold water.
2. Bring to a boil and simmer gently until tender, about 1½ hours.
3. Dice and brown side pork and onion.
4. Add ground venison and sear. Add tomato juice.
5. Season to taste with salt, pepper and chili powder.
6. Add to the beans and simmer for 30 minutes. Serves 4-6.

SMALL GAME

Beaver

The industrious beaver is the largest rodent on the North American Continent, and is found in all the waterways of the forested areas of the north. Its rich dark brown fur has long been prized by trappers and hunters, and the search for beaver pelts instigated much of the early exploration of the continent. Because of its contribution to the development of our Dominion, the beaver has been chosen as an emblem of Canada.

If the beaver pelt is to be prepared for market, care should be taken in skinning the animal. Lay the beaver on its back in a clean place and cut off the legs at the first joints. Then, with a sharp knife, slit the pelt, starting at the lower lip. Insert the knife in this slit and, with the sharp edge up, cut the pelt in a straight line down the chest and belly to the vent. Work out from this centre line cut and, with short strokes, separate the skin from the flesh. Carefully pull the legs through the skin, leaving four round holes in the pelt. Cut off the tail where it meets the fur. Skin carefully around the eyes and cut the ears close to the skull. Finish removing the pelt, taking as little flesh and fat with it as possible, then lay it on a flat surface, fur side down, and sponge off all blood marks with lukewarm water. Complete directions for stretching and cleaning the pelts are available from Fish and Wildlife Officers.

Beaver meat is dark red, fine grained, moist and tender, and when properly prepared, is similar in flavour to roast pork. Cut the head from the carcass and eviscerate the animal as follows: Make a cut through the thin layer of meat from the breast bone to the vent, encircling the vent, and being careful not to puncture the intestines. Lay the body cavity open, and remove the viscera by grasping them above the stomach and pulling down and out from the body cavity. Carefully cut out the tiny musk glands from under the skin on the inside of the legs and be sure to remove the castor gland under the belly near the tail. Trim off all the fat, then wash the carcass thoroughly with warm salted water.

Roast Beaver

1 beaver, skinned and cleaned
½ cup vinegar
1 tablespoon salt
2 teaspoons soda
1 medium onion, sliced
4 strips bacon *or* salt pork
½ teaspoon salt
¼ teaspoon pepper

1. Wash beaver thoroughly with salt water, then let soak overnight in enough cold water to cover. Add ½ cup vinegar and 1 tablespoon salt to the water.

2. The next day, remove the beaver from the brine, wash and cover with a solution of 2 teaspoons soda to 2 quarts water. Bring to a boil, reduce heat and simmer 10 minutes.

3. Drain, then place beaver in roasting pan. Cover with sliced onions and strips of bacon and season with salt and pepper.

4. Place lid on roaster and bake in 375° F. oven until tender. Serve with a tart jelly. Serves 4.

Sweet Pickled Beaver

1 beaver, skinned and cleaned
½ cup vinegar
1 tablespoon salt
2 teaspoons soda
2 tablespoons dry mustard
3 tablespoons mixed pickling
spice
1 teaspoon cinnamon
½ teaspoon ground cloves
½ cup brown sugar
½ cup dry white wine *or*
apple juice
1 cup pineapple juice
Juice and grated rind of 1
lemon

1. Wash beaver thoroughly with salt water, then let soak overnight in enough cold water to cover, adding ½ cup vinegar and 1 tablespoon salt to the water.

2. The next day, remove the beaver from the brine, wash and cover with a solution of 2 teaspoons soda to 2 quarts of water. Bring to a boil, reduce heat and simmer 10 minutes.

3. Drain and rinse the beaver, then place it in a clean pot. Add water just to cover. Sprinkle mixed pickling spice on top, bring to a boil, reduce heat and simmer 20 minutes.

4. Drain and rinse beaver, pat dry and place in roaster.

5. Mix mustard, spices, sugar, wine and fruit juices and spread over beaver.

6. Cover and roast at 325° F. until tender, basting frequently.

Beaver in Sour Cream

1 beaver, skinned and cleaned
½ cup vinegar
1 tablespoon salt
2 quarts water
2 teaspoons soda
½ cup flour
1 teaspoon salt
¼ teaspoon paprika
¼ cup butter
1 medium onion, sliced
½ cup water
1 cup sour cream

1. Soak beaver overnight in solution of ½ cup vinegar and 1 tablespoon salt in cold water to cover.

2. The next day, remove the beaver from the brine, wash and cover with solution of 2 teaspoons soda to 2 quarts of water. Bring to a boil, reduce heat and simmer 10 minutes.

3. Drain and rinse beaver and cut into serving pieces.

4. Dredge each piece of meat thoroughly in the seasoned flour.

5. Melt butter in heavy fry pan and brown the pieces of meat.

6. Transfer meat to a greased casserole, slice onions over top, add water, cover and bake at 325° F. until tender.

7. When meat is almost tender, add 1 cup sour cream to the casserole. Stir well and continue cooking until tender. Serves 4.

Fried Beaver Tail

2 beaver tails
½ cup vinegar
1 tablespoon salt
2 teaspoons soda
¼ cup flour
½ teaspoon salt
¼ teaspoon pepper
¼ cup butter
¼ cup sherry *or* cooking wine
1 teaspoon dry mustard
1 teaspoon sugar
¼ teaspoon garlic powder
1 tablespoon Worcestershire sauce

1. Skin beaver tails, clean thoroughly and wash well in solution of salt water. Let soak overnight in cold water to cover, adding ½ cup vinegar and 1 tablespoon salt to water.

2. The next day, remove from the brine, wash, then cover with solution of 2 teaspoons soda to 2 quarts of water. Bring to a boil, reduce heat and simmer 10 minutes. Drain

3. Dredge beaver tails in seasoned flour.

4. Melt butter in heavy fry pan and sauté tails at low heat until tender.

5. Mix wine with mustard, sugar, garlic powder and Worcestershire sauce.

6. Add to beaver tails and simmer gently for 10 minutes, basting frequently.

Muskrat

The muskrat is a prolific little animal, inhabiting the marshes, lakes and slow-moving streams of a large part of the continent. It has a coat of thick dense fur, with long glistening guard hairs, and has supplemented the income of trappers as far north as the delta of the Mackenzie River at the Arctic Ocean, three hundred miles beyond the Arctic Circle.

It is mainly herbivorous in its choice of food, so its flesh is sweet and palatable, similar to rabbit, although a little darker, and fine-grained. Because of this similarity it is called a marsh rabbit or marsh hare in some areas, and when properly prepared, is equally delicious roasted, broiled, braised or stewed.

The muskrat should be skinned as soon as possible after being trapped. Slit the skin on the inside of the hind legs from the paws to the vent and cut off both hind and fore paws and the tail. Then work the skin off inside out ("cased"), using the knife as little as possible, taking particular care when skinning around the eyes and lips. The skin should then be scraped with a dull knife to remove all flesh and fat, washed with lukewarm water to remove the blood, and placed fur side in on a wedge-shaped stretching board made of soft wood, to dry. Complete instructions for preparing the furs for market are obtainable from Fish and Wildlife Officers.

Remove the head from the carcass, then eviscerate the animal. Insert the knife blade, sharp edge up, at the tip of the breastbone. Cut through the thin meat over the belly down to, and encircling, the vent. Lay the body cavity open and remove the viscera by grasping them above the stomach, pulling down and out from the body cavity. Remove the heart and lungs, and wash the muskrat thoroughly with warm salted water. With a sharp knife, cut out the musk glands from inside the legs, the white tissuey skin, and all fat. Soak the meat for two or three hours in a weak brine solution (1 tablespoon salt to 1 quart of water) to draw out the blood, then drain and pat dry.

Smothered Muskrat and Onions

1 muskrat
1 tablespoon salt
1 quart water
1½ teaspoons salt
¼ teaspoon paprika
½ cup flour
3 tablespoons fat
3 large onions, sliced
1 cup sour cream

1. Skin and clean muskrat, remove fat, scent glands and the white tissue inside each leg.

2. Soak muskrat overnight in a weak brine solution of 1 tablespoon salt to 1 quart water. Drain, disjoint and cut up.

3. Put flour, salt and paprika in a paper bag. Add muskrat pieces and shake until each piece is well coated.

4. Melt fat in a heavy fry pan, add the muskrat pieces and sauté slowly until browned.

5. When meat is browned, cover with onions, sprinkle with salt and pour the cream over.

6. Cover fry pan tightly and simmer for 1 hour. Serves 4.

Fried Muskrat

1 muskrat
1 tablespoon salt
1 quart water
1 egg yolk
½ cup milk
1 teaspoon salt
½ cup flour
4 tablespoons cooking fat

1. Skin and clean muskrat, remove fat, scent glands and the white tissue inside each leg.

2. Soak muskrat overnight in a weak brine solution of 1 tablespoon salt to 1 quart water. Disjoint and cut muskrat into desired pieces.

3. Parboil for 20 minutes, drain and wipe with a damp cloth.

4. Make a smooth batter by beating the egg yolk and milk, then add salt and flour.

5. Heat the fat in a heavy fry pan.

6. Dip the meat in the batter then sauté in the hot fat until brown.

7. When brown, reduce the heat, cover and cook slowly for about 1½ hours. Serves 4.

Muskrat Meat Loaf

1½ pounds ground muskrat *or* other meat
2 eggs, beaten
⅓ cup dry bread crumbs
1 cup evaporated milk
1 small onion, minced *or* grated
¼ teaspoon thyme
1 teaspoon salt
¼ teaspoon pepper
1 teaspoon Worcestershire sauce
¼ cup catsup

1. Skin and clean muskrat, remove fat, scent glands and the white tissue inside each leg.

2. Soak overnight in a weak brine solution of 1 tablespoon salt to 1 quart water.

3. Cut meat from the bones with a sharp knife, then grind the meat.

4. Mix ground meat thoroughly with other ingredients.

5. Place in a greased loaf pan.

6. Place loaf pan in a shallow pan containing hot water.

7. Bake in a 350° F. oven for 1½ hours. Serves 6.

Rabbit

Rabbit is one of the most widely used of the small game animals. Most of the meat is white and comparable to chicken in taste and tenderness. Like other game animals, it should be field dressed as soon as possible after killing, and the method followed is the same as for cleaning and skinning muskrat or squirrel. If the skin is to be saved it should be skinned "cased", by slitting the skin on the inside of the hind legs from the feet to the anus, then peeling it off, inside out. The skin is thin and tears easily, so this must be done very carefully. If the skin is not going to be saved, it may be slit in the middle of the carcass and pulled both ways. Skin the legs to the lower joints and break them off. Pull the upper skin over the head and remove it with the head with a quick twist of the wrist. The skin on the back of the carcass is pulled down to the anus and tail and discarded with the entrails.

Be sure to remove any blood clots and shot, as well as any fur driven into the skin with the pellets. Wash well with lukewarm salted water, but there is no need to marinate it unless the animal is old and tough.

Rabbit Stew With Dumplings

1   rabbit
1½ teaspoons salt
1½ cups diced potatoes
1   cup diced carrots
1   medium onion, chopped
1   tablespoon fresh *or* dried
     parsley
1   teaspoon salt
¼   teaspoon pepper
3   tablespoons flour
¾   cup cold water

1. Skin and clean rabbit, wash thoroughly and cut into serving pieces.

2. Put rabbit into a pan large enough to hold the pieces without crowding. Add salt and enough cold water to cover the rabbit.

3. Cover pan, bring to a boil, then reduce heat and cook over low heat about 1 hour or until the meat is tender.

4. Strain the broth and set aside. With a sharp knife cut the rabbit meat from the bones and return the meat to the broth.

5. Add diced vegetables and seasonings to the broth. Simmer over low heat until vegetables are tender.

6. Mix flour into a paste with the cold water and add to the stew, stirring constantly to prevent lumping.

7. Make dumplings as follows:
   Sift ¾ cup of flour with 2 teaspoons baking powder and ½ teaspoon salt. Beat 1 egg slightly and add ⅓ cup milk. Add egg and milk to the dry ingredients stirring just enough to moisten them.

8. Drop dumpling mixture by spoonfuls on top of the boiling stew, spacing them so they will not run together during cooking.

9. Place heavy lid on top and cook for 15 minutes without lifting the lid. Serves 8.

Baked Stuffed Rabbit With Carrots

1 rabbit
2 large carrots, quartered
4 strips bacon *or* salt pork
1–2 cups hot water

Stuffing

4 average potatoes
2 tablespoons butter
1 teaspoon salt
½ teaspoon pepper
1 teaspoon dried summer savory
1 cup finely chopped celery

1. Skin and clean rabbit. Wash thoroughly with warm salted water.

2. Make dressing as follows:
   Mash potatoes to make 2 cups, add butter, salt, pepper, savory and celery. Fill body of rabbit with this stuffing and sew it up.

3. Place rabbit breast down on rack of baking pan, with legs folded under the body and fastened in this position with skewers.

4. Place quartered carrots beside it on the rack.

5. Fasten strips of bacon over the back of rabbit with toothpicks, to keep the flesh from drying out.

6. Place pan in a 400° F. oven for 10 minutes, then pour a cup or two of hot water over the meat and continue cooking until tender.

7. Remove the bacon for the last 10 minutes and let the rabbit brown. Serves 6.

Sweet-Sour Rabbit

1 small rabbit
  (about 2½ pounds)
¼ cup flour
½ teaspoon salt
¼ teaspoon pepper
2 tablespoons butter
1 cup pineapple juice
¼ cup vinegar
½ teaspoon salt
1 cup pineapple chunks
1 medium green pepper,
  chopped *or*
2 tablespoons dried pepper flakes
1½ tablespoons cornstarch
¼ cup sugar
½ cup water

1. Skin and clean rabbit, wash thoroughly and cut into serving pieces.

2. Put flour, salt and pepper in a paper bag, add the rabbit pieces and shake until well coated.

3. Heat butter in a heavy pan, and brown rabbit on all sides, over moderate heat.

4. Add pineapple juice, vinegar, and salt. Cover pan; cook over low heat 40 minutes or until meat is tender.

5. Add pineapple and green pepper; cook a few minutes longer.

6. Mix cornstarch and sugar, then add to the water.

7. Stir this mixture gradually into the liquid in the pan and cook slowly about 5 minutes. Serves 6.

Rabbit in Barbecue Sauce

1 rabbit (about 3 pounds)
4 tablespoons flour
½ teaspoon salt
¼ teaspoon pepper
4 tablespoons cooking fat *or* oil
  Barbecue sauce (see recipe below)

1. Skin and clean rabbit, wash thoroughly and cut in serving pieces.

2. Dredge rabbit in flour, salt and pepper.

3. Melt the fat in a heavy fry pan and brown rabbit on all sides over moderate heat (about 20 minutes).

4. Pour barbecue sauce over rabbit, cover and bake at 325° F. about 45 minutes, or until meat is tender.

5. Uncover pan and place under heated broiler for about 10 minutes, or until meat is brown. Be careful not to let it burn. Serves 6.

Barbecue Sauce

2 tablespoons brown sugar
1 tablespoon paprika
1 teaspoon salt
1 teaspoon dry mustard
¼ teaspoon chili powder
  Few grains cayenne pepper
2 tablespoons Worcestershire sauce
1 cup tomato juice
¼ cup chili sauce or catsup
¼ cup vinegar
½ cup chopped onion

Combine ingredients in order given and cook over low heat 15 minutes.

Rabbit à la Mode

1 rabbit
Water
Vinegar
1 onion
½ teaspoon salt
6 peppercorns
1 bay leaf
½ teaspoon salt
¼ teaspoon pepper
¼ cup flour for dredging
3 tablespoons fat
1 tablespoon flour
½ cup water
Sweet *or* sour cream

1. Skin and clean rabbit and cut into small pieces, place in stone crock or jar.

2. Cover with vinegar and water in equal parts.

3. Add onion, salt, peppercorns, and bay leaf.

4. Soak rabbit for 2 days, then remove meat, keeping the liquid.

5. Sprinkle meat with salt and pepper and dredge in flour.

6. Melt fat in heavy fry pan, brown the meat and then pour in vinegar water to the depth of ¼ inch.

7. Cover tightly and simmer until rabbit is tender. Do not boil at any time.

8. Remove rabbit from pot, add 1 tablespoon of flour to drippings then add sweet or sour cream until gravy is desired consistency. Serves 6.

French Fried Rabbit

2 small rabbits
1 tablespoon salt
Water to cover
1 pound shortening *or*
2 cups vegetable oil for frying
2 egg yolks, beaten
3 cups milk
1¼ cups flour
½ teaspoon salt
2 tablespoons baking powder

1. Skin, clean and wash rabbit thoroughly. Cut into serving pieces.

2. Boil in salted water until tender (approximately 35 minutes), then drain.

3. Make batter by adding sifted flour, salt and baking powder to the beaten egg and milk. Mix thoroughly until batter is consistency of cake batter.

4. Dip pieces of rabbit into the batter, then fry in deep fat fryer at 360° F. until golden brown.

5. Drain well and serve. Serves 4.

Rabbit Fricassée

1 rabbit
12 strips bacon
¼ cup flour
¼ cup butter or fat
½ teaspoon salt
¼ teaspoon pepper
1 cup milk
1 tablespoon onion juice

1. Skin and clean rabbit. Wash thoroughly. Cut into 6 pieces.

2. Fasten strips of bacon around each piece of rabbit by sewing them to the pieces of meat.

3. Dredge in flour. Melt ¼ cup butter in heavy fry pan and brown the rabbit pieces. Season with salt and pepper.

4. Add the milk to the pan very slowly, just enough to keep the meat from sticking. Cover and simmer until meat is tender.

5. Remove meat to serving dish and make gravy in the pan by adding more flour and water if necessary. Flavour with onion juice. Pour gravy over meat and serve hot. Serves 6.

Creamed Rabbit on Toast

2 tablespoons butter *or* margarine
2 tablespoons flour
2 cups milk (*or* milk plus rabbit broth)
½ teaspoon salt
¼ teaspoon pepper
2½ cups cut-up cooked rabbit meat
1 teaspoon grated onion
2 teaspoons lemon juice
4 slices hot buttered toast
1 hard-cooked egg, finely chopped

1. Melt butter in heavy pot and blend in the flour.

2. Add milk gradually and cook over very low heat, stirring constantly until smooth and thick.

3. Add salt and pepper.

4. Add rabbit meat and grated onion and heat thoroughly, stirring occasionally.

5. Add the lemon juice.

6. Serve on hot buttered toast with chopped egg on top. Serves 4.

Curried Rabbit

2 cups rabbit broth
¼ cup finely chopped onion
1 clove garlic, cut in half
1 teaspoon curry powder
¼ cup milk
⅓ cup sifted flour
2 cups coarsely cut cooked rabbit meat
½ teaspoon salt
¼ teaspoon pepper
1½ cups hot cooked rice (½ cup raw)

1. Bring the broth to a boil, add the onion, garlic, and curry powder. Cover and simmer 20 minutes.

2. Remove garlic.

3. Stir the milk into the flour.

4. Add a few tablespoons of the hot broth to the milk and flour, then stir the mixture into the rest of the broth.

5. Cook over low heat until thick and smooth, stirring constantly.

6. Add the cooked rabbit meat, salt and pepper.

7. Heat thoroughly and serve over rice. Serves 4.

Rabbit à la King

⅓ cup chopped celery
3 tablespoons finely chopped onion
3 tablespoons finely chopped green pepper
3 tablespoons sliced mushrooms
⅓ cup water
4 tablespoons butter *or* margarine
4 tablespoons sifted flour
2½ cups milk (part rabbit broth may be used)
½ teaspoon salt
¼ teaspoon pepper
2 cups coarsely cut cooked rabbit meat
4 slices hot buttered toast

1. Cook vegetables and mushrooms gently in the water in a covered pan until just tender (about 20 minutes). Drain, and save the liquid.
2. Melt butter or margarine; blend in the flour.
3. Add the vegetable liquid to the milk and pour gradually into the fat-flour mixture, stirring constantly.
4. Cook over low heat, stirring frequently, until thick and smooth.
5. Season with salt and pepper.
6. Add vegetables, mushrooms, and rabbit meat to the sauce and heat thoroughly. Serve on toast. Serves 4.

Baked Rabbit Hash

2 cups finely chopped, cooked rabbit meat
2 cups finely chopped raw potatoes
2 tablespoons chopped green peppers
¾ cup finely chopped onion
1½ teaspoons salt
¼ teaspoon pepper
½ cup rabbit broth (*or* water with 1 chicken bouillon cube)
¼ cup fine dry bread crumbs mixed with 2 tablespoons melted butter

1. Mix all ingredients except the buttered crumbs.
2. Pile lightly into a greased baking dish or pan.
3. Cover and bake at 350° F. (moderate oven) for about 40 minutes, until vegetables are tender.
4. Remove cover and sprinkle crumbs over the hash.
5. Bake uncovered 20 minutes longer to brown. Serves 4.

Rabbit Sandwich Spread

1 cup ground cooked rabbit meat
2 tablespoons finely chopped onion
2 tablespoons finely chopped green pepper
¼ cup finely chopped celery
¼ cup finely chopped sweet pickle *or* pickle relish
⅓ cup mayonnaise *or* other thick salad dressing
Salt to taste

1. Mix all ingredients well.
2. Keep cold and use within a week. Makes enough for 6 generous sandwiches.

Rabbit Pie

3 cups diced cooked rabbit meat
2 cups diced cooked vegetables
¼ cup butter *or* margarine
¼ cup chopped onion
½ cup chopped green pepper
¼ cup sifted flour
2 cups rabbit broth (*or* water with 4 chicken bouillon cubes)
½ teaspoon salt
¼ teaspoon pepper
   Pastry for a 10″ round

1. Heat butter or margarine in a large fry pan.
2. Add onion and green pepper and cook about 5 minutes over low heat.
3. Blend in the flour and cook until the mixture bubbles.
4. Pour in the broth gradually, stirring constantly.
5. Cook until thick and smooth, stirring frequently.
6. Add salt and pepper to taste.
7. Add meat and vegetables to the gravy and heat thoroughly.
8. Pour mixture into a baking dish.
9. Roll out the pastry and cut slits for steam to escape.
10. Fit the pastry to the top of the baking dish, crimping the edges of the crust.
11. Bake the pie at 425° F. for 15 to 20 minutes, or until the crust browns and sauce bubbles. Serves 6.

Jellied Rabbit Salad

1 envelope unflavored gelatin (1 tablespoon)
¼ cup cold water
1⅔ cups hot rabbit broth *or* water with 4 chicken bouillon cubes
½ teaspoon salt
1 teaspoon grated onion *or* onion juice
1½ tablespoons vinegar
1½ cups diced cooked rabbit
⅓ cup cooked peas
3 tablespoons finely chopped celery
1 hard-cooked egg, sliced
6 stuffed olives, sliced

1. Soften the gelatin in the cold water for a few minutes, then dissolve it in the hot broth.
2. Add salt, onion and vinegar.
3. Pour a layer of the gelatin mixture ¼ inch deep in the bottom of an oiled 3 or 4 cup loaf pan or mold, and cool until firm.
4. Let the rest of the gelatin mixture thicken but not set.
5. Press a design of the sliced egg and olives lightly in the firm gelatin in the pan.
6. Add the rabbit, peas, and celery to the thickened gelatin-broth mixture, and spoon it carefully over the sliced egg and olives.
7. Chill until firm.
8. Unmold on crisp greens and serve with chilled mayonnaise. Serves 4.

Rabbit-Ham Croquettes

2 tablespoons butter *or* margarine
2½ tablespoons flour
⅛ teaspoon dry mustard
¾ cup milk
1 teaspoon onion juice *or* grated onion
1⅓ cups chopped cooked rabbit meat
⅔ cup ground cooked ham
1 teaspoon chopped parsley
1 teaspoon chopped green pepper
1 beaten egg
3 cups fine dry bread crumbs
Fat *or* oil for deep fat frying

1. Melt butter or margarine and stir in the flour and mustard.

2. Cook until mixture bubbles.

3. Add the milk gradually, stirring constantly.

4. Add onion and cook over low heat until the sauce is thick and smooth, stirring occasionally.

5. Add the rabbit, ham, parsley, and green pepper. Cool.

6. If the mixture is very soft, chill it until it is firm enough to handle easily.

7. Shape into eight croquettes.

8. Dip them in the beaten egg, then roll them in the bread crumbs.

9. Heat the fat in a deep kettle to 360° F. or until a 1 inch cube of bread will brown in 60 seconds.

10. Fry the croquettes in the deep fat about 4 minutes, or until golden brown. Serves 4.

Ragoût of Arctic Hare

1 large arctic hare
4 tablespoons flour
½ teaspoon salt
¼ teaspoon pepper
¼ cup butter
Water
½ cup chopped celery
2 small onions, chopped
4 carrots, diced
6 potatoes, diced
½ teaspoon oregano
2 tablespoons flour
½ cup water

1. Skin and clean the hare, wash thoroughly and cut into serving pieces.

2. Put flour, salt and pepper in a paper bag, add the cut-up hare and shake until each piece is well coated.

3. Melt the butter in a heavy frying pan and brown the hare evenly on all sides.

4. Add the vegetables and oregano, and enough water to cover.

5. Simmer gently for one hour, or until meat and vegetables are tender.

6. Thicken the stew with a paste made of flour and water. Stir till smooth.

7. Cook 10 more minutes. Serves 6.

Arctic Hare

1 large arctic hare
1 onion
½ cup vinegar
  Water
¼ cup butter
1 small onion, chopped
½ cup chopped celery
2 cups bread crumbs
1 teaspoon poultry seasoning
½ teaspoon salt
¼ teaspoon pepper
½ cup melted butter for
  basting
2 tablespoons flour

1. Skin, clean and wash rabbit thoroughly.
2. Place rabbit in large kettle, add 1 onion cut in half, ½ cup vinegar and enough cold water to cover. Let stand 6 hours, then remove the rabbit and drain.
3. Melt the butter, add the chopped onion and celery and simmer till translucent. Add to the bread crumbs and seasoning and mix well.
4. Stuff the rabbit, sew up the opening and place rabbit on side in uncovered roaster.
5. Roast at 325° F. for 1½ hours or until tender, basting with melted butter every 10 minutes. When rabbit is half cooked, turn it over on other side.
6. Thicken pan drippings with the flour. Add water till gravy is desired consistency.
7. Pour gravy over rabbit before serving.

Squirrel

The noisy chattering and scolding of the squirrel is a familiar sound to hunters and trappers in forested areas from coast to coast. Although the value of the individual pelt is low, it helps to supplement the income of both part-time and professional trappers. The largest and finest quality Canadian squirrel pelts come from the Yukon, followed closely by those from the Peace River and Grande Prairie sections of Alberta, and from Northern Saskatchewan.

The procedure for skinning and cleaning the squirrel is similar to that outlined for muskrat, but the pelt should be "cased" with the fur out. Complete directions are available from Fish and Wildlife Officers.

The diet of the squirrel consists mainly of nuts, seeds and berries. The flesh is medium red in colour, is tender and has a truly delicious flavour. The slight gamey taste present in most wild game meats is almost absent in the squirrel. No soaking is necessary, and only the oldest and toughest animals require parboiling for tenderness. Be sure to remove the small waxy scent glands inside the forelegs, and wash thoroughly to remove all loose hair.

Broiled Squirrel

2 squirrels
1 teaspoon salt
⅛ teaspoon pepper
4 tablespoons melted butter
  for basting

1. Skin and clean squirrels. Wash thoroughly and pat dry.
2. Cut in half lengthwise and rub with salt and pepper.
3. Place halves on broiling rack and brush with fat.
4. Broil 6 inches from source of heat, 20 minutes on each side. Baste every few minutes with melted butter and drippings. Serves 4.

Brunswick Stew

3 squirrels
3 quarts water
¼ cup diced bacon
¼ teaspoon cayenne
1 teaspoon sugar
2 teaspoons salt
¼ teaspoon black pepper
1 cup chopped onion
2 cups canned tomatoes
2 cups diced potatoes
2 cups lima beans, fresh *or* frozen
2 cups corn, fresh *or* frozen
½ cup dry fine bread crumbs
2 tablespoons melted butter

1. Skin and clean squirrels. Remove waxy scent glands inside forelegs. Cut into serving pieces. Wash thoroughly.

2. Place squirrel pieces in a large kettle. Add water. Bring slowly to boil; reduce heat and simmer 1½ to 2 hours, or until meat is tender, skimming surface occasionally.

3. Remove meat from bones and return the meat to liquid.

4. Add bacon, cayenne, sugar, salt, pepper, onion, tomatoes, potatoes and lima beans.

5. Cook 1 hour.

6. Add corn and continue to cook 10 minutes.

7. Transfer to buttered casserole.

8. Add melted butter to bread crumbs, mix well then sprinkle on top of stew.

9. Bake 20 minutes at 375° F. till crumbs are golden brown. Serves 6.

Squirrel en Casserole With Biscuit Topping

2 squirrels
2 teaspoons salt
Water
3 tablespoons flour
½ tablespoon minced parsley
1 teaspoon salt
⅛ teaspoon pepper
½ cup fresh cut mushrooms
2 cups broth *or* milk
2 cups flour
4 teaspoons baking powder
½ teaspoon salt
¼ cup fat
⅔ cup milk

1. Skin and clean squirrels. Remove scent glands from inside forelegs. Wash thoroughly and cut into serving pieces.

2. Cover with salted water and simmer for 1 hour, until meat is tender.

3. Remove the squirrels. Using a sharp knife, cut the meat from the bones in large pieces.

4. Add flour, parsley, salt, pepper and mushrooms to the broth. Cook, stirring constantly until it thickens.

5. Add the meat and mix well. Pour into greased casserole.

6. Make the biscuits by sifting the flour, baking powder and salt together. Cut in the fat and add the milk. Stir only until dry ingredients are moistened. Roll out and cut in rounds.

7. Place biscuits on top of the stew in the casserole.

8. Bake in a 400° F. oven until biscuits are golden brown. Serves 4-6.

Roast Squirrel

2 squirrels
½ cup vegetable oil
¼ cup lemon juice *or* vinegar
2 cups dry fine bread crumbs
½ teaspoon salt
¼ teaspoon pepper
1 small onion, chopped
½ cup milk
½ cup melted butter for basting

1. Skin and clean squirrels. Remove waxy scent glands inside forelegs. Wash thoroughly.

2. Marinate for 2 or 3 hours in vegetable oil and lemon juice or vinegar, then drain.

3. Mix bread crumbs, salt, pepper and onion. Add milk just to moisten.

4. Stuff the squirrels with the bread crumb mixture and close the opening.

5. Place squirrels in uncovered roaster, brush with melted butter and roast at 325° F. for 1½ to 2 hours, until tender. Baste every 15 minutes with melted butter. Serves 4.

Squirrel Fricassée

1 squirrel
½ teaspoon salt
⅛ teaspoon pepper
½ cup flour
4 slices bacon, cut up
1 tablespoon diced onion
1½ teaspoons lemon juice
⅓ cup broth

1. Skin and clean squirrel, being sure to remove scent glands from forelegs. Wash thoroughly and cut squirrel into serving pieces.

2. Rub pieces with salt and pepper, then dredge with flour.

3. Cut up bacon and cook over low heat till crisp.

4. Add the squirrel and pan fry with the bacon for 20 minutes, until nicely browned.

5. Add diced onion, lemon juice and broth. Cover tightly and simmer for 2 hours.

Woodchuck or Groundhog

The woodchuck is a vegetarian, living on herbs, berries and sweet grasses. The meat is dark in colour but mild in flavour. If caught just before hibernation, the woodchuck will have an insulating layer of fat under the skin. This should be removed, along with the glands on the inside of the forelegs. No soaking is necessary but the meat from older animals should be parboiled before roasting or frying.

Fried Woodchuck

1 woodchuck
1 tablespoon salt
1 cup flour
4 tablespoons fat
½ teaspoon salt
¼ teaspoon pepper

1. Skin and clean woodchuck and cut into 6 or 7 pieces.

2. Put in pot, add salt and enough water to cover, and parboil for 1 hour.

3. Remove meat from the broth, and drain.

4. Dredge meat in flour, salt and pepper.

5. Melt fat in heavy fry pan and sauté woodchuck until nicely browned. Serves 6.

Woodchuck With Biscuits

1 woodchuck
1 tablespoon salt
¼ cup onion, chopped
¼ cup chopped green pepper *or*
1 tablespoon pepper flakes
½ tablespoon parsley, fresh
  or dried
⅛ teaspoon pepper
4½ tablespoons flour
½ cup cold water
3 cups broth

Biscuit Topping

1 cup flour
2 teaspoons baking powder
¼ teaspoon salt
2 tablespoons chilled fat
¼ cup milk (approximately)

1. Skin and clean woodchuck and cut into large pieces. Place in heavy pot, add 1 tablespoon salt and enough water to cover and parboil for 1 hour, or until meat is tender.

2. Strain and save the broth.

3. Remove meat from the bones in large pieces.

4. Add onion, green pepper, parsley, and pepper to the broth and bring to a boil.

5. Make a paste of the flour and water, then add it to the broth, stirring constantly until thick and smooth.

6. Add the meat to the broth mixture and stir thoroughly.

7. Pour into baking dish.

8. Top with biscuits made as follows:
Sift the flour, baking powder, and salt together. Cut in the fat. Add enough liquid to moisten the ingredients. Roll out quickly and cut into rounds with a cookie cutter.

9. Place biscuits on top of the meat in the casserole. Bake in a 400° F. oven for 20-30 minutes until biscuits are browned. Serves 6.

Woodchuck Meat Patties With Tomato Sauce

1 woodchuck
1 cup bread crumbs
¼ cup chopped onion
1 teaspoon salt
⅛ teaspoon pepper
2 eggs
4 tablespoons fat
1 cup catsup
¼ teaspoon Worcestershire sauce
½ cup water

1. Skin and clean woodchuck. With a sharp knife, cut the meat from the bones and grind.

2. Add ½ cup crumbs, onion, salt, pepper, one beaten egg, and 1 tablespoon melted fat. Mix thoroughly.

3. Shape into patties, then dip each pattie into the beaten egg, then into the rest of the crumbs.

4. Melt fat in heavy fry pan, add the patties and cook until golden brown. As each pattie is browned, place it in a greased casserole.

5. When all the patties have been browned, add the catsup and Worcestershire sauce and water to the pan drippings, heat to get all the bits from the pan, then pour over the patties in the casserole.

6. Bake in 325° F. oven for 1 hour. Serves 6.

MISCELLANEOUS MEAT RECIPES

Heather Clayton's Stuffed Wieners

1 can wieners (10 wieners)
4 servings instant mashed
potatoes, prepared according to
directions
2 tablespoons dried onion flakes
2 tablespoons chopped dried
parsley
½ teaspoon salt
¼ teaspoon pepper
2 tablespoons prepared mustard
½ cup grated cheddar cheese

1. Drain wieners, then pour boiling water over them and let stand 10 minutes.

2. Add boiling water to onion flakes and parsley, let stand 10 minutes, then drain.

3. Add onions, parsley, salt and pepper to mashed potatoes, mix well.

4. Make a lengthwise cut along the wieners and open them out. Spread the cut side with prepared mustard. Pile mashed potato mixture on each wiener, sprinkle with grated cheese.

5. Place wieners on cookie sheet and bake in a 350° F. oven for 15 minutes or until cheese melts. Serves 4.

Joan Wilson's Oven Baked Pork Chops

6 loin pork chops, thick cut
1 teaspoon onion salt
1 teaspoon garlic salt
1 teaspoon charcoal seasoning
1 teaspoon monosodium
glutamate

1. Wipe pork chops with a damp cloth; score fat.

2. Sprinkle the seasonings on the chops on both sides, rubbing in well. Place on rack of broiler pan or uncovered roaster in centre of oven.

3. Bake in 350° F. oven for 1 hour and 15 minutes, turning chops once during this period.

4. Serve hot with baked potatoes, sour cream dressing and tossed salad. Serves 4-6.

Ham Casserole

½ pound spaghetti
1 package frozen lima beans *or*
1 cup fresh cooked lima beans
6 slices cooked ham *or* thinly
sliced ham steaks
2 cups boiling water
2 bouillon cubes
1 can tomato paste
½ teaspon thyme *or* marjoram
½ cup grated cheddar cheese
¼ cup sherry (optional)

1. Cook the spaghetti in boiling water until tender, then drain and arrange half of it in the bottom of a large, shallow, greased casserole.

2. Spread the partially thawed Lima beans or the freshly cooked Lima beans over the spaghetti.

3. Place half the slices of ham over the beans, then repeat with a layer of spaghetti, a layer of beans and a layer of ham until all used.

4. Combine the seasoning, tomato paste, sherry, boiling water and bouillon cubes in saucepan and heat until the bouillon cubes are dissolved.

5. Pour the sauce over the spaghetti mixture to cover, using more water if needed.

6. Top with grated cheese and bake in 400° F. oven for 20-30 minutes.

Pork and Rice Casserole

3 pounds loin pork, cut in
   ¼ inch thick slices
2 medium onions, sliced
1 clove garlic
2 tablespoons salad oil
1 10 ounce tin beef gravy
3 tins whole mushrooms,
   and liquid
3 small onions, sliced
2 tablespoons salad oil
¾ teaspoon salt
¼ teaspoon pepper
4 tablespoons tomato juice *or*
   sauce
3 cups cooked rice
3 green peppers, sliced
2 tablespoons minced parsley

1. Sauté 2 medium onions sliced, and garlic clove in 2 tablespoons salad oil in heavy fry pan until lightly browned. Discard the garlic.

2. Add the gravy, mushrooms and juice, half the sliced onions and simmer about 1 hour. Remove from fry pan.

3. Heat 2 tablespoons salad oil in fry pan and sauté the pieces of pork sprinkled with salt and pepper. Remove from pan.

4. Stir a little tomato juice into fry pan to loosen meat particles and pour this into the sauce.

5. Arrange a layer of pork in bottom of casserole, then a layer of rice combined with half the sauce.

6. Place another layer of pork, the green peppers and remaining onions and sprinkle with salt. Pour the rest of the sauce over top, and sprinkle with the minced parsley.

7. Cover and place the casserole in the refrigerator overnight.

8. Leave cover on and bake in moderate oven 350° F. about 1½ hours.

Dick's Scalloped Beef Tenderloin

2 pounds beef tenderloin,
   thinly sliced
1 cup sliced mushrooms
2 green peppers, sliced
3 pimientos, sliced
5 finely chopped shallots
6 tablespoons butter
1 dried red chili pepper, crushed
2 tomatoes, peeled and diced
3 oz Madeira wine
1½ cups veal sauce, *or*
1 cup veal stock thickened with 2
   tablespoons flour
   Salt and pepper

1. Place 3 tablespoons butter in a heavy pot and heat slowly.

2. Sauté the shallots, mushrooms and green pepper until soft, then add the pimientos and chili pepper and cook a few more minutes.

3. Pour in the wine, veal sauce or stock and add the diced tomatoes. Let simmer for about 10 minutes.

4. Season the beef tenderloin with salt and pepper.

5. Heat the remaining butter in a heavy fry pan until very hot, then brown the slices of beef tenderloin lightly.

6. Place the browned meat in the simmering sauce and stir.

7. Add salt and pepper to taste, place mixture in a casserole and serve hot with hot biscuits and your favourite salad.

Beef Stroganoff

2 pounds stewing beef, cut in
  ½-inch cubes
½ cup butter
1 cup mushrooms (optional)
4 tablespoons dried onion flakes
1 tin tomato paste *or* soup
2 teaspoons salt
¼ teaspoon pepper
1 tablespoon Worcestershire
  sauce
1 tablespoon cornstarch
2 tablespoons cold water
1 cup sour cream *or*
1 cup evaporated milk and 1
  tablespoon vinegar

1. Heat butter in a heavy fry pan and brown pieces of meat on all sides.

2. Add mushrooms and cook slowly.

3. Soak onions in ½ cup boiling water for 15 minutes, drain well and add to meat mixture. Cook for 5 minutes.

4. Add tomato paste or soup, salt, pepper and Worcestershire sauce. Stir into meat mixture. Cover and simmer 1 hour.

5. Mix cornstarch and cold water and add to meat mixture. Cover and simmer for 10 minutes stirring frequently.

6. Just before serving, blend in sour cream. Serves 8.

Elsie Rancier's Beef Stroganoff

1½ pounds lean beef
3 tablespoons butter
1 cup sliced fresh mushrooms
1 large onion, sliced
2 tablespoons flour
2 cups beef consommé
2 tablespoons tomato paste
1 teaspoon dry mustard
3 tablespoons sherry
⅔ cup sour cream
½ teaspoon salt
¼ teaspoon pepper

1. Remove all fat and gristle from the meat and cut into strips 2½ inches x ¾ inch and about ½ inch thick.

2. Sprinkle the pieces of meat with salt and pepper and set aside for 2 hours at room temperature.

3. Melt 2 tablespoons butter in heavy fry pan and sauté the sliced mushrooms until tender (about 15 minutes). Remove from pan and set aside.

4. Sauté the sliced onion until lightly browned. Set aside.

5. Heat 1 tablespoon butter in fry pan and sear the pieces of beef, but leave rare. Remove and set aside.

6. To the fry pan, add 2 tablespoons flour and blend well, stirring to loosen any browned particles. Slowly add 2 cups consommé stirring until thickened and smooth.

7. To the gravy, add the sherry, tomato paste and dry mustard, blend well.

8. Add the browned meat, onions and mushrooms to the gravy and let simmer slowly for 20 minutes.

9. Just before serving add the sour cream and blend thoroughly. Serve with rice. Serves 4-6.

Steak in Foil

2 pounds round steak at least 1″ thick
½ package dehydrated onion soup mix *or*
2 tablespoons dehydrated onion flakes
½ cup canned mushrooms, drained
½ teaspoon salt
¼ teaspoon pepper
2 tablespoons water

1. Trim fat from the steak

2. Centre the steak on a large piece of aluminum foil. Sprinkle the remaining ingredients on it, then fold the foil over the steak, fastening it to make a leak-proof container.

3. Place on a cookie sheet in a 450° F. oven and bake for 1½ hours or until tender.
Serves 4-5.

Swiss Steak in Foil

2 pounds round steak, at least 1 inch thick
1 cup catsup
1 tablespoon Worcestershire sauce
½ teaspoon salt
¼ teaspoon pepper
½ teaspoon dry mustard
1 tablespoon sugar
1 large onion, sliced *or*
1 tablespoon dehydrated onion flakes
2 tablespoons lemon juice or vinegar

1. Trim fat from the steak.

2. Put ½ cup catsup in the centre of a large piece of aluminum foil, place the steak on it, then sprinkle the remaining ingredients on top.

3. Fold the foil over the steak, fastening it securely to make a leak-proof container.

4. Place the package on a cookie sheet in a 450° F. oven and bake for 1½ hours or until tender.
Serves 4-5.

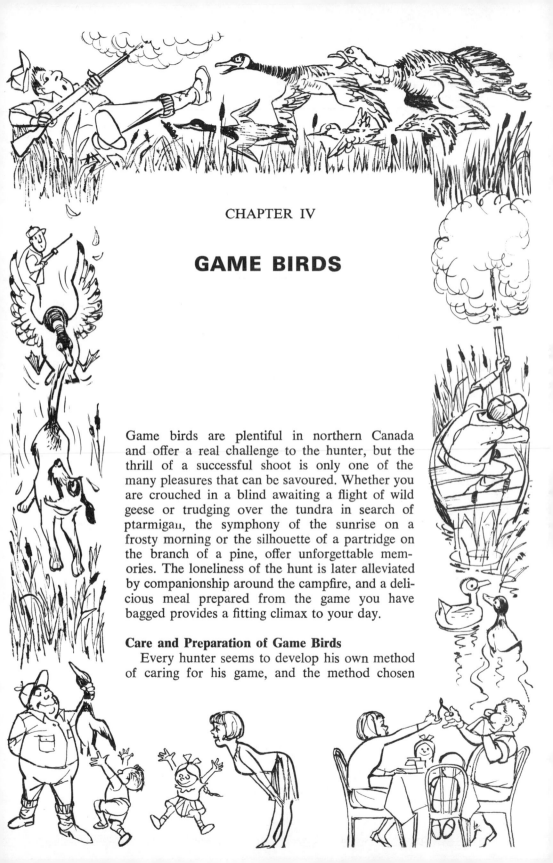

CHAPTER IV

GAME BIRDS

Game birds are plentiful in northern Canada and offer a real challenge to the hunter, but the thrill of a successful shoot is only one of the many pleasures that can be savoured. Whether you are crouched in a blind awaiting a flight of wild geese or trudging over the tundra in search of ptarmigan, the symphony of the sunrise on a frosty morning or the silhouette of a partridge on the branch of a pine, offer unforgettable memories. The loneliness of the hunt is later alleviated by companionship around the campfire, and a delicious meal prepared from the game you have bagged provides a fitting climax to your day.

Care and Preparation of Game Birds

Every hunter seems to develop his own method of caring for his game, and the method chosen will depend on the degree of wild game flavour that you prefer. Most hunters agree that game birds may be carried through the day without cleaning, but if the weather is warm, and the birds are to be kept more than one day without refrigeration, you may be wise to draw them as soon as possible after shooting. Pluck a narrow strip of feathers from the breast bone to the vent, and with a sharp knife, make a shallow cut along this line, encircling the vent. Cut just through the skin and the thin layer of meat, being careful not to puncture the intestines. Insert two or three fingers through this opening and reach as far up to the neck as possible, then rotate your hand to loosen all the organs, and bring the viscera out intact. Check to see if the lungs, which may be recognized by their bright red colour, are included, and if not, reach carefully up to the rib cage and loosen them. If the breast bone has been shattered by gunshot, remember that the tiny bones are razor-sharp and can cut careless fingers. Make a cut along the front of the neck and remove the crop and the windpipe. Separate and save the giblets, (the liver, the gizzard and the heart) and discard the remainder of the viscera. Wipe the inside of the cavity with grass, a clean cloth, or paper, then stuff it loosely with crumpled paper. Do not pluck the remainder of the feathers from the bird. Hang the birds in the shade, where air can circulate freely around them and let them hang until they have developed the degree of game flavour which you prefer.

Dry plucking of game birds, even though time-consuming, is the most satis-factory method of ensuring top flavour and quality of the meat, and the unbroken skin helps to keep the surface from drying out. The sooner the birds can be plucked after shooting, the easier the job will be and if the birds can be plucked in the woods or on the tundra before they are brought into the kitchen, more wives would welcome them! They are much less photogenic without their feathers, however, and if migratory game birds are transported, remember that one wing and the wing plumage must remain attached to the bird.

Pluck the feathers by pulling downwards on them in the direction in which they are growing, to avoid tearing the skin. Remove the feathers from the breast and back, and then to the first joint of the legs and wings. Chop off the remainder of the legs and wings and then chop off the head about one inch above the body. If any down or pin feathers remain, dip or coat the bird in melted paraffin, allow the paraffin to harden and then scrape it off using the blunt side of a table knife. If the bird was not drawn previously, do it now, then wash the bird well both inside and out with warm salted water. Cut out the oil sacs on either side of the backbone just above the tail. If the sacs are not removed they will impart a disagreeable flavour to the meat and will make the "pope's nose" which is really a delicious tid-bit, completely inedible.

If much time has elapsed since the bird was shot, the feathers may have to be loosened before they can be plucked. Dip the bird in scalding water repeatedly until the feathers are wet to their base. Then remove the feathers with gentle tugs. Do not grasp more than a few feathers at a time or the skin may tear. Examine the body carefully for shot damage, and remove any embedded shot or damaged flesh with a sharp knife. If the skin has been badly torn, it may be advisable to skin the bird. To do this, make a slash just through the skin over the breast with a sharp knife, then using the fingers, peel the skin back to the wing and leg sections on both sides. Cut the wings and legs off at the first joint from the body, then cut off the head and peel the remainder of the skin and feathers from the bird. Remove the viscera and wash the bird thoroughly with warm salted water.

To prevent the flesh from drying out during roasting, wrap the bird in a double thickness of greased tinfoil. Close the tinfoil securely, but allow room for the expansion of steam. If a crisp surface is desired, open the foil over the breast for the last 15 minutes of roasting. Pour melted fat over the breast, then sprinkle with salt, pepper and flour and roast uncovered till golden brown and crisp. This method works equally well regardless of whether the birds are skinned or plucked.

Wild Duck à l'Orange

2 wild ducks
¼ cup flour
½ teaspoon salt
¼ teaspoon pepper
1 tablespoon butter
2 cooking onions
2 squares foil
1 orange, juice and grated rind
1 teaspoon cinnamon
¼ teaspoon nutmeg
1 cup dry white wine

1. Pluck and draw ducks, wash thoroughly and pat dry.

2. Dredge ducks with flour, salt and pepper, then dot with butter.

3. Place an onion in the cavity, then wrap ducks individually in heavy foil. Seal well.

4. Place in medium oven (350° F.) for 60-90 minutes, depending on the size of the duck.

5. Combine orange juice and rind, cinnamon, nutmeg and wine and bring to a boil.

6. Five minutes before roasting time is up, peel back the foil from the duck breasts and baste with 2 tablespoons of the sauce.

7. When done, remove ducks from foil, place on serving dish and pour remainder of sauce over them. Serves 4.

Smothered Wild Duck

1 duck
1 teaspoon salt
¼ teaspoon pepper
½ cup flour
½ cup fat
1 cup milk

1. Cut cleaned duck into 6 or 7 pieces.

2. Season with salt and pepper and roll in flour.

3. Fry duck slowly in hot fat until brown on both sides, about 30 minutes, turning only once.

4. Add the milk, cover tightly and simmer slowly for 1 hour or until tender, or bake in slow oven at 325° F. until tender. Serves 2.

Barbecued Duck

2 large wild ducks
¼ cup lemon juice and grated rind
¼ cup vegetable oil
2 tablespoons minced onion
1 teaspoon Worcestershire sauce
1 crushed garlic clove or
¼ teaspoon garlic powder
1 tablespoon paprika
1 teaspoon salt
¼ teaspoon pepper

1. Clean and skin ducks and wash thoroughly.

2. Cut in serving pieces and place in a greased baking dish.

3. Combine lemon juice and rind, oil, onion and seasonings and pour over duck.

4. Cover and bake in a 350° F. oven for 1 hour, or until tender, basting at frequent intervals. Serves 6.

Purple-Plum Ducklings

2   5-6 pound ducklings, quartered
    Onion salt
    Garlic salt
4   oranges, halved crosswise
¼   cup butter *or* margarine
1   medium onion, chopped
1   17 ounce can purple plums
1   6 ounce can frozen lemonade,
    unreconstituted
⅓   cup chili sauce
¼   cup soy sauce
1   teaspoon Worcestersire sauce
1   teaspoon ginger
2   teaspoons prepared mustard
2   drops Tabasco sauce

1. Sprinkle duck quarters with onion and garlic salts.

2. Set each on an orange half on a trivet in a roasting pan, then roast them at 350° F. for 1½ hours.

3. While ducklings roast, melt butter in a large skillet, add onion and cook until tender; set aside.

4. Empty the can of plums, juice and all, into a food mill or strainer set over a bowl.

5. Pit plums and purée them.

6. Add purée to onion and blend in frozen lemonade, chili sauce, soy sauce, Worcestershire sauce, ginger, mustard and Tabasco sauce and simmer 15 minutes.

7. After quarters have been roasted 1½ hours, remove ducklings, oranges, and trivet from roasting pan; drain off fat.

8. Arrange ducklings and oranges side by side in pan.

9. Brush them with plum sauce and return to oven for 15 minutes. Then pour more sauce over them; return to oven.

10. Continue roasting, adding sauce every 10 minutes, until quarters are tender, oranges and ducklings glazed.

11. Arrange quarters and oranges on a large heated platter and serve with sauce. Serves 4.

Duck Fricassée

2 wild ducks
¼ cup flour
¼ cup butter
1 medium onion, minced
1 bay leaf
1 cup sliced mushrooms, fresh *or* canned
½ cup sliced green peppers
1 cup water
½ teaspoon salt
¼ teaspoon pepper

1. Clean and skin ducks, wash thoroughly, and cut into serving portions.

2. Dredge portions of duck in flour and season with salt and pepper.

3. Melt ¼ cup butter in a heavy frying pan, add the onion and bay leaf and brown the pieces of duck on all sides.

4. Transfer the pieces of duck to a greased casserole, and sauté the mushrooms and green peppers in the remaining fat in the frying pan for 3 minutes.

5. Add the mushrooms and green peppers to the duck in the casserole, add 1 cup of water, cover and bake until tender in a 350° F. oven. Serves 6.

Duckling with Onions

1 duckling, 4-5 pounds
3 tablespoons butter *or* margarine
2 cans (1 pound each) small white onions
1 tablespoon sugar
2 tablespoons flour
½ cup cold water
   Juice of 1 lemon
½ teaspoon salt
¼ teaspoon pepper
   Steamed rice

1. Heat 3 tablespoons butter in a dutch oven or heavy skillet and brown the duckling on all sides.

2. Drain the onions, reserving liquid.

3. Salt and pepper the duckling and place it in the dutch oven or a large casserole.

4. Add ¾ cup of the onion liquid; cover the casserole tightly and bake at 350° F. for 2 hours.

5. While the duckling is cooking, heat onions in butter, sprinkle lightly with sugar and toss them gently so they carmelize a bit.

6. When the duckling is tender, remove it to a hot platter.

7. Skim fat from the pan juices and thicken the juices with a little flour blended with water.

8. Add lemon juice, salt and pepper to the sauce and correct the seasoning.

9. Carve duckling into 4 portions, cover with the sauce and surround with the onions.

10. Serve with steamed rice.

Wild Goose Roast no. 1

1 young wild goose, 6-8
  pounds (dressed weight)
  Juice of 1 lemon
1 teaspoon salt
¼ teaspoon pepper
¼ cup butter
¼ cup chopped onion
1 cup chopped tart apple
1 cup chopped dried apricots
3 cups soft bread crumbs,
  made from day-old bread
½ teaspoon salt
⅛ teaspoon pepper
6 slices bacon
  Melted bacon fat

1. Wash cleaned goose thoroughly and pat dry.

2. Sprinkle goose inside and out with lemon juice, salt and pepper.

3. Melt butter in a large saucepan. Add onion and simmer until tender.

4. Stir in apple, apricots, bread crumbs, salt and pepper.

5. Spoon stuffing lightly into cavity. Close the opening.

6. Cover breast with bacon slices and cheesecloth soaked in melted bacon fat.

7. Place goose breast up on rack in roasting pan. Roast in preheated 325° F. oven for 25 to 30 minutes per pound, or until tender, basting frequently with bacon fat and drippings in pan. Serves 6.

Wild Goose Roast no. 2

1 10-12 lb. wild goose,
  cleaned and dressed
1 large apple, chopped
1 large onion, chopped
1 cup chopped celery

Stuffing

7 cups dry bread crumbs
3 cups chopped apple
1 cup scalded raisins
1 tablespoon sage
½ teaspoon salt

Seasonings

1 tablespoon flour
1 teaspoon salt
1 tablespoon sage
1 teaspoon paprika
1 teaspoon pepper

Mixture for Basting

1 cup clear apple juice
1 cup grapefruit juice
½ cup prune juice

1. Wash the cleaned goose thoroughly and pat dry.

2. Mix the chopped apple, onion and celery and place in the cavity. Let stand overnight in a covered roaster in a cool place.

3. Mix the bread crumbs, chopped apples, scalded raisins, sage and salt. Remove the apple, onion and celery mixture from the cavity of the goose and fill the cavity with the stuffing. Close the cavity.

4. Mix the flour, salt, sage, paprika and pepper and rub well into the outer skin of the goose. If any of the mixture is left over, sprinkle it over the breast.

5. Place the goose in an uncovered roaster and place in a 400° F. oven for 15 minutes.

6. Reduce heat to 325° F. and cook until tender, allowing 20 minutes per pound after the first half hour. Baste the goose with the mixed juices every 5 minutes during cooking.

Irish Roast Goose with Potato Stuffing

1 wild goose 8-10 lbs.
1 teaspoon salt
¼ teaspoon pepper

Stuffing

10 medium sized, boiled
   potatoes, riced
1 tablespoon butter
1 cup chopped onions
½ cup chopped celery
4 slices bread, crumbled
¼ pound ground salt pork
2 eggs, beaten
1 teaspoon poultry seasoning
1 teaspoon salt
¼ teaspoon pepper

1. Clean the goose, wash thoroughly and pat dry. Rub cavity and outside with salt and pepper mixture.

2. Stuffing: Boil the potatoes, drain and save the potato water for basting the goose. Rice the potatoes.

3. Melt butter in skillet and partially cook onions and celery, but do not brown. Add to riced potatoes, bread crumbs, salt pork, eggs, poultry seasoning, salt and pepper.

4. Stuff the goose with potato stuffing and close the cavity.

5. Roast in an uncovered roaster in a moderate oven 325° F. about 4 hours, or until tender, basting from time to time with potato water.

Canada Goose

1 wild goose
¼ cup salad oil
1 teaspoon salt
¼ teaspoon pepper
4 tablespoons flour
½ teaspoon tarragon
¼ teaspoon thyme
¼ pound salt pork *or*
6 strips bacon
1 cup melted butter
1 cup chicken broth
   Wineglass of claret, burgundy
   or sherry (optional)

1. Pluck and draw the goose, then wash with salt water, rinse and pat dry inside and out.

2. Stuff the cavity with your favourite stuffing, and sew it up.

3. Rub the surface of the bird with salad oil.

4. Mix the flour, salt, pepper, tarragon and thyme and dredge the bird. Sprinkle any remaining dredging mixture over the breast.

5. Lay the thick slice of salt pork or the bacon strips on the breast and tie in place with string.

6. Place the goose in an uncovered roaster and roast in a 325° F. oven until tender, allowing 30 minutes per pound roasting time.

7. Melt the butter in a small pot, add the chicken broth and wine or sherry if desired, and use it to baste the goose every 10 or 15 minutes during the cooking period.

8. Remove the salt pork or bacon for the last 15 minutes of cooking time to allow the breast to brown.

Fried Grouse and Onions

1 grouse (cut in pieces)
⅔ cup melted butter
½ teaspoon salt
¼ teaspoon pepper
½ cup thinly sliced onions
1 tablespoon flour
1½ cups milk

1. Skin and draw grouse, cut in serving pieces and soak overnight in a weak solution of salted water.

2. Drain well, then roll each piece in flour.

3. Heat butter in a heavy fry pan and sauté grouse pieces until golden brown and tender. Sprinkle with salt and pepper.

4. As each piece is cooked, take it from the pan and keep in a warm oven.

5. After the grouse is done, add the sliced onions to the fat in the pan and cook until translucent.

6. Stir in the flour and blend well.

7. Add the milk and bring to a boil, stirring constantly.

8. Arrange grouse on a hot platter and pour the onion sauce over it. Serves 2-3.

Grouse in Sherry

4 grouse
4 tablespoons flour
½ cup butter
1 cup chicken broth
1 onion sliced
2 tins condensed cream of mushroom soup
½ cup sherry
1 teaspoon salt
¼ teaspoon pepper

1. Cut off head, neck, feet and wings then skin and draw the grouse.

2. Split each grouse in half down the centre of the breastbone. Wash thoroughly and let dry.

3. Dredge the split halves of grouse in flour.

4. Melt butter in a heavy fry pan and brown the grouse well on all sides.

5. When golden brown, add the chicken broth and sliced onion, cover tightly and let simmer on low heat for 30 minutes.

6. Transfer the grouse to a greased baking dish.

7. Add the undiluted cream of mushroom soup, sherry, salt and pepper to the liquid in the fry-pan, heat and stir till smooth, then pour over the grouse in the baking dish.

8. Bake uncovered in a 325° oven for 15 minutes. Serves 4.

Roast Grouse

2 grouse
1 tablespoon vinegar
1 teaspoon salt
4 tablespoons butter
2 cups fine bread crumbs
1 tablespoon dried onion flakes
1 teaspoon red and green pepper flakes
1 teaspoon poultry seasoning
2 tablespoons butter
½ teaspoon salt
¼ teaspoon pepper

1. Pluck and draw grouse, wash well and soak overnight in cold water to which has been added 1 tablespoon of vinegar and 1 teaspoon salt.

2. Remove grouse and pat dry.

3. Melt 4 tablespoons butter and add to bread crumbs and seasonings.

4. Stuff cavities of grouse, then butter the outsides and sprinkle with salt and pepper.

5. Place in covered roaster in 350° F oven for approximately 1 hour, or until grouse is tender. Remove lid for last 10 minutes to brown the skin. Serves 4-5.

Braised Breast of Grouse

4 breasts of grouse
4 tablespoons butter
½ teaspoon salt
¼ teaspoon pepper
1½ cups cold water
1 small carrot, sliced
1 small onion, sliced
1 stalk celery
2 sprigs parsley
½ bay leaf
4 tablespoons butter
4 tablespoons flour
¾ cup canned tomatoes
1 teaspoon lemon juice
1 teaspoon minced parsley
½ cup sautéed mushrooms

1. Melt 4 tablespoons butter in heavy fry pan, add breasts of grouse and sauté until brown.

2. Season with salt and pepper, cover with water, add carrot, onion, celery, parsley and bay leaf.

3. Simmer until tender. Remove grouse and strain stock.

4. Melt 4 tablespoons butter in pan, add flour and blend. Add strained stock and tomatoes gradually, stirring constantly until smooth.

5. Add lemon juice, parsley and mushrooms and season to taste. Add grouse and reheat.

Partridge Stew

1 partridge
4 tablespoons butter
3 slices bacon
½ cabbage, chopped
4 onions, sliced
½ teaspoon salt
¼ teaspoon pepper
2 tablespoons parsley

1. Skin and draw partridge, wash thoroughly inside and out, pat dry.

2. Sauté partridge in butter in a deep fry pan until lightly browned, then tie the bacon around the bird with thread.

3. Put vegetables and seasonings in the pan used to sauté the partridge, then place bird on top of vegetables. Cover and cook slowly for 10 minutes. Do not let it burn.

4. Add 2 quarts of water and cook at low heat for 2 hours, stirring occasionally. Before serving, thicken stew with flour if desired.

5. Serve on hot buttered toast. Serves 4.

Partridge in Barbecue Sauce

2 partridges
1 cup tomato catsup
1 cup water
¼ cup Worcestershire sauce
¼ cup vinegar
1 lemon, juice and rind
3 tablespoons brown sugar
1 teaspoon dry mustard
1 teaspoon salt
½ teaspoon pepper
1 medium onion, chopped
1 teaspoon horseradish

1. Skin and draw partridge, wash thoroughly, split in half lengthwise, and place in large buttered casserole.

2. Mix the ingredients for the sauce in the order given and bring to a boil, stirring constantly.

3. Pour the sauce over the partridge in the casserole.

4. Bake in a 350° F. oven until tender, about 1½ hours, basting every 10 minutes. Serves 4.

Braised Partridge

4 partridges
4 tablespoons flour
1 teaspoon salt
¼ teaspoon pepper
4 tablespoons bacon fat or butter
1 can condensed cream of celery soup
½ cup milk
½ cup chopped onion
¼ teaspoon caraway seeds

1. Skin and draw partridge, wash thoroughly and pat dry.

2. Sprinkle partridge inside and out with salt, pepper and flour mixture.

3. Melt bacon fat or butter in a deep fry pan, add the partridge and brown well on all sides. Remove the partridge.

4. Add the milk, soup, onion and caraway seeds to the drippings in the fry pan, bring to boil, stirring constantly till smooth.

5. Add the partridge, cover and cook over low heat for 25 to 30 minutes, or until tender, basting frequently with the sauce in the pan. Serves 4.

Casserole of Partridge

2 partridges
½ cup flour
1 teaspoon salt
¼ teaspoon pepper
¼ cup butter
1 small onion, chopped
1 tin condensed cream of mushroom soup
1 cup water
½ teaspoon marjoram
1 pinch of thyme
½ cup sherry

1. Skin and draw partridge. Cut in serving pieces, wash thoroughly and drain.

2. Put flour, salt and pepper in a paper bag, add partridge pieces and shake until each piece is well coated.

3. Melt the butter in a heavy fry pan and brown the partridge pieces, then transfer them to a greased casserole.

4. Add the onion to the fry pan and cook at low heat for three minutes, then add the mushroom soup, water, marjoram, thyme and sherry and heat just to boiling point, stirring constantly.

5. Pour sauce over the partridge pieces in the casserole, cover, and bake in a 350° F. oven until partridge is tender, about 1½ hours. Serves 4.

106

Partridge Paprika

1 partridge
¼ cup soy sauce
¼ cup flour
1 tablespoon paprika
¼ cup butter
½ teaspoon onion salt

1. Skin and draw partridge, cut in serving pieces, wash thoroughly and drain.

2. Dip partridge pieces in soy sauce.

3. Put flour and paprika in a paper bag and add the partridge. Shake until each piece of partridge is well coated.

4. Melt butter in a heavy fry pan, then add the partridge. Brown well, then reduce the heat, sprinkle with onion salt, and cook over low heat until partridge is tender, about ½ hour. Serves 2.

Roast Partridge

4 partridges
4 strips bacon
1 teaspoon salt
¼ teaspoon pepper
1 cup slightly soured cream
4 slices hot buttered toast

1. Skin and draw partridge. Wash thoroughly and pat dry.

2. Rub partridge inside and out with salt and pepper.

3. Fasten long strips of bacon over partridge breasts and place in uncovered roaster. Roast at 350° F. for 30 minutes.

4. When partridge are a rich brown, pour the cream over them and let the cream bubble up in the pan for a minute.

5. Place each partridge on a slice of hot buttered toast, pour gravy over and serve hot. Serves 4.

Roast Stuffed Partridge

2 partridges
1 tablespoon vinegar (optional)
¼ cup butter
1 small onion chopped
1½ cups dry bread crumbs
½ teaspoon salt
¼ teaspoon pepper
½ teaspoon poultry seasoning
2 teaspoons butter
Salt and pepper
2 squares heavy foil

1. Pluck and draw partridge. Wash thoroughly.

2. Soak ½ hour in enough cold water to cover, add 1 tablespoon vinegar to the water to reduce the gamey flavour if desired.

3. Drain, wipe dry.

4. Melt ¼ cup butter in a small pot, add chopped onion and simmer till translucent.

5. Add butter and onion to bread crumbs and seasonings. Mix well.

6. Stuff birds lightly. Spread butter on the surface of the birds, sprinkle with salt and pepper.

7. Wrap birds individually in foil and bake in a roaster in a 375° F. oven for 1 hour, or until tender. Fold back foil from the breasts of the birds for the last 10 minutes to crisp the skin. Serves 4-5.

Partridge, Hunter's Style

4 partridges
Salt and pepper
4 cups shredded cabbage
4 slices cooked bacon, crumbled
16 large cabbage leaves
2 tablespoons butter
1 cup chicken broth
4 carrots, sliced
¼ teaspoon crushed thyme
¼ teaspoon crushed tarragon
1 teaspoon salt
¼ teaspoon pepper

1. Skin and draw partridge. Wash thoroughly and pat dry.

2. Sprinkle partridge inside and out with salt and pepper.

3. Combine shredded cabbage and crumbled bacon.

4. Spoon a fourth of the mixture into cavity of each bird.

5. Wrap each partridge with 4 cabbage leaves and fasten with string.

6. Place birds in a deep fry pan; add butter, chicken broth (canned or made with 1 chicken bouillon cube and 1 cup hot water) and remaining ingredients.

7. Bring liquid to boil. Reduce heat, cover and simmer 25 to 30 minutes or until tender.

8. Remove string and cabbage leaves. Serve with the sauce from the pan. Serves 4.

Partridge Pie

3 medium size partridges
  prepared and halved
Salt and pepper
⅛ cup minced parsley
¼ teaspoon sage
1 medium onion chopped
1 whole clove
⅛ lb. diced salt pork
1 tablespoon flour
1 tablespoon butter
1 cup diced potatoes
Pastry for 2-crust casserole

1. Put the birds in 1 pint of water and bring to boiling point.

2. Remove the scum, add salt, pepper, parsley, sage, onion, clove and salt pork.

3. Simmer until tender, being careful to keep the birds coverd with water. When the birds are done, thicken the liquid with the flour and let the gravy come to a boil. Add the butter, remove from the fire and cool.

4. Prepare your favourite pastry and put around the sides of a greased casserole, lay in some of the birds, then some potatoes, repeat until the dish is full.

5. Pour in the gravy, put on the top pastry, make hole in centre, and bake in hot oven 425° F. to 450° F. for 35 to 40 minutes until done.

Partridge With Sour Cream

1 partridge
4 tablespoons flour
½ teaspoon salt
¼ teaspoon pepper
1 teaspoon paprika
¼ cup butter
1 10 oz can condensed
  tomato soup
1 10 oz can mushroom bits
  and pieces
1 small onion, chopped
1 cup commercial sour cream

1. Skin and draw partridge, cut in serving pieces, wash thoroughly and pat dry.

2. Put flour, salt, pepper and paprika in a paper bag. Add the cut up partridge and shake until each piece is well coated.

3. Melt the butter in a deep fry pan and sauté the partridge until golden brown.

4. Remove the partridge pieces, add the tomato soup, the mushroom bits (and the liquid from the can), and the chopped onion. Stir till smooth and well blended.

5. Return the partridge pieces to the liquid, cover and simmer until partridge is tender, about 45 minutes, stirring occasionally.

6. Just before serving, add the sour cream, heat just to boiling and serve. Serves 4.

Partridge Baked in Sherry

2 partridges
4 tablespoons butter
1 small clove garlic, chopped
1 small onion, halved
1 tablespoon chopped celery
¼ teaspoon pepper
1 teaspoon salt
½ cup sherry

1. Remove breasts and thighs from 2 medium sized partridge, wash thoroughly and pat dry.

2. Melt 4 tablespoons butter in a heavy fry pan, add partridge, garlic and onion and cook until partridge is slightly browned.

3. Turn into roasting pan, add sherry, seasonings and chopped celery. Cover.

4. Bake 1½ hours in moderate oven until tender, baste frequently to prevent dryness. Serves 4.

Pheasant Pie

2 pheasants
1 bay leaf
1 stalk celery
6 peppercorns
1 tablespoon salt
½ cup butter
½ cup flour
1 cup light cream
⅛ teaspoon pepper
¼ teaspoon salt
1 can pearl onions, drained
1 small can sliced mushrooms, drained
1 package frozen peas
2 canned pimientos, sliced
1 10-inch round of pastry

1. Skin and draw pheasants, wash thoroughly.
2. Place pheasant in a large kettle and cover with water.
3. Add bay leaf, celery, peppercorns and 1 tablespoon salt. Bring to boil.
4. Cover, reduce heat and cook over low heat approximately 2½ hours, or until pheasant is tender.
5. Remove meat from bones in fairly large pieces and set aside. Strain broth.
6. Melt butter in a saucepan, add the flour and stir until blended.
7. Gradually add 2 cups of the broth, stirring constantly.
8. Add light cream, pepper and salt. Cook, stiring until thickened.
9. Arrange pheasant pieces, onions, mushrooms, peas and pimientos in a 2 quart casserole.
10. Add sauce, leaving at least 1-inch space at top.
11. Prepare pastry.
12. Cut pastry circle ½ inch larger than casserole and place over pheasant mixture, turning edge of pastry under and pressing to casserole with fork or spoon. Make a cut in the pastry to allow steam to escape.
13. Bake in preheated 425° F. oven 15 minutes, or until crust is golden brown. Serves 6.

Roast Pheasant

2 pheasants
2 whole carrots, cleaned
2 whole onions, cleaned
2 stalks celery
2 tablespoons butter
1 teaspoon salt
¼ teaspoon pepper

1. Pluck and draw pheasants. Wash thoroughly inside and out, pat dry.
2. Place a carrot, onion and a stalk of celery in each cavity.
3. Spread butter over surface of birds and sprinkle with salt and pepper.
4. Place in a covered roaster and bake in a 350° F. oven for 1½ hours, or until birds are tender. If birds seem very dry, add 1 cup boiling water to roaster.
5. Remove vegetables from cavity and discard before serving. Serves 4.

Curried Pheasant

2 pheasants
½ cup flour
4 tablespoons butter
2 medium onions, minced
1 teaspoon curry powder
2 tablespoons flour
3 cups chicken broth *or* bouillon
1 tart apple or stalk rhubarb
½ teaspoon salt

1. Skin and draw the pheasants, cut into serving pieces, wash thoroughly and drain well.

2. Melt butter in a heavy fry pan.

3. Dredge pheasant with flour, then sauté in hot fat until browned, removing each piece as it browns.

4. Cook onions in the same fat until translucent. Add the curry powder and the flour. Cook slightly stirring constantly. Add the broth and stir until mixture comes to a boil.

5. Replace the meat, add the apple or rhubarb and salt.

6. Cover and simmer for 1½ hours or until tender. Serves 4.

Faisant aux Choux (Pheasant with Cabbage)

1 pheasant
3 slices bacon *or* salt pork
1 medium onion, sliced
1 carrot, sliced
1 large cabbage, chopped
2 glasses white wine *or* apple juice

1. Skin and draw pheasant, wash thoroughly inside and out. Pat dry.

2. Pan fry the bacon in a heavy casserole or dutch oven, then remove it and add pheasant whole.

3. Brown the pheasant in the bacon fat, turning frequently to brown it on all sides.

4. Remove the pheasant, add the onions and carrots and cook until lightly browned.

5. Add the chopped cabbage and the wine or apple juice.

6. Bury the pheasant in the cabbage, cover and cook on top of stove for about 1 hour, until the pheasant is tender, (or cook in a 350° F. oven for 1½ hours.)

7. Remove pheasant to serving dish and arrange vegetables around it. Serves 2.

Southern Fried Pheasant

2 pheasants
2 eggs, beaten
1 cup fine cracker crumbs
1 teaspoon salt
¼ teaspoon pepper
½ cup butter
1½ cups rich milk *or* cream
½ cup sherry

1. Skin and draw pheasants. Cut in serving pieces, wash thoroughly and pat dry.

2. Melt butter in a heavy skillet.

3. Dip pheasant pieces in beaten egg, then in crumbs and sauté in butter until golden brown. Remove from pan and set aside.

4. When all the pheasant pieces have been browned, add the seasonings and milk to the pan drippings and stir till smooth.

5. Add the pheasant, cover and simmer over low heat until tender, stirring occasionally.

6. Just before serving, pour the sherry over the pheasant, bring to a boil and serve hot. Serves 4.

Pheasant With Mushroom Sauce

2 pheasants
4 tablespoons butter
½ teaspoon salt
¼ teaspoon pepper
½ teaspoon garlic salt
1 can condensed cream of mushroom soup
1 cup cream
½ cup sherry

1. Skin and draw pheasants. Cut into serving pieces, wash thoroughly and pat dry.

2. Melt butter in heavy fry pan and sauté pieces of pheasant until lightly browned. Remove pheasant and place in casserole.

3. Add seasonings, mushroom soup and cream to fry pan and bring to a boil, stirring constantly until smooth.

4. Pour sauce over the pheasant in casserole, cover and bake in 350° F. oven for one hour or until tender.

5. About 20 minutes before serving, add the sherry and mix well. Serves 4.

Roast Pigeon

4 pigeons
3 cups cooked wild rice
¼ cup butter
1 tablespoon minced onion
1 tablespoon minced celery
1 tablespoon crumbled cooked bacon
½ teaspoon salt
¼ teaspoon pepper
¼ cup melted butter
¼ cup hot water
¼ cup cranberry *or* red currant jelly

1. Pluck and draw pigeons. Wash thoroughly and pat dry.

2. Melt ¼ cup butter and add to the wild rice with the onion, celery, crumbled bacon and seasonings. Stuff pigeons lightly and close opening. Brush with melted butter.

3. Place pigeons in a greased casserole and bake at 450° F. for 10 minutes.

4. Melt ¼ cup butter, add hot water and jelly and stir till smooth.

5. Baste pigeons with jelly sauce, then cover and bake at 325° F. until tender. Baste every 5 minutes with the sauce. Serves 4.

Fried Prairie Chicken

2 prairie chickens
1 tablespoon vinegar
4 tablespoons flour
1 teaspoon salt
¼ teaspoon pepper
4 tablespoons butter
1 small cooking onion, sliced
1 cup milk

1. Remove breasts and thighs from 2 prairie chickens.

2. Wash well, and soak for 20 minutes in cold water to which a tablespoon of vinegar has been added, then drain well.

3. Mix flour, salt and pepper, place in a paper bag. Add the pieces of chicken, and shake thoroughly until all pieces are well dredged.

4. Melt the butter in a deep frying pan, then add the chicken pieces and brown well on all sides.

5. Reduce heat, slice the onion over the chicken. Cover and cook at low heat until tender.

6. Remove chicken to serving dish. Add milk to the pan drippings, heat and stir till smooth. Pour over the chicken in the serving dish. Serves 4.

Ginger Prairie Chicken

1 prairie chicken
¼ cup soy sauce
¼ cup flour
1 tablespoon ginger
¼ cup butter
½ teaspoon salt
¼ teaspoon pepper

1. Skin and draw prairie chicken. Cut in serving pieces, wash thoroughly.

2. Place chicken pieces in soy sauce, let drain.

3. Place flour and ginger in a paper bag, add the chicken and shake until each piece is well dredged with floured ginger.

4. Melt butter in heavy fry pan.

5. Add chicken pieces and sauté them slowly until well browned and tender.

6. Sprinkle with salt and pepper. Serve hot. Serves 4.

Prairie Chicken in Cream

1 prairie chicken
1 teaspoon salt
¼ teaspoon pepper
2 tablespoons flour
4 tablespoons butter
½ teaspoon thyme
1 cup heavy rich cream

1. Skin and draw prairie chicken, wash thoroughly and cut into serving portions.

2. Dredge pieces with salt, pepper and flour by shaking in a paper bag.

3. Melt the butter in a deep fry pan and brown chicken on all sides.

4. Sprinkle the thyme over the chicken.

5. Add 1 cup heavy cream, and sufficient water to cover.

6. Place lid on pan and simmer chicken until tender.

Roast Prairie Chicken

1 prairie chicken
¼ cup melted butter
2 cups cooked rice
1 teaspoon salt
1 teaspoon red and green pepper flakes
1 teaspoon dried parsley
1 tablespoon onion flakes
1 teaspoon marjoram
¼ teaspoon thyme
1 tablespoon butter
½ teaspoon salt
¼ teaspoon pepper
1 square of foil

1. Pluck prairie chicken, draw and wash thoroughly inside and out. Pat dry.

2. Melt butter and add to cooked rice, salt, pepper flakes, dried parsley, onion flakes, marjoram and thyme. Mix well.

3. Stuff prairie chicken. Close opening.

4. Spread butter over surface of chicken, sprinkle with salt and pepper.

5. Wrap chicken in foil, allowing room for expansion, but being careful to seal the foil.

6. Roast in a 375° F. oven for 1½ hours, or until the chicken is tender. Open the foil over the breast of the chicken for the last 10 minutes of roasting. Serves 4.

Roast Ptarmigan

1 ptarmigan
1 teaspoon salt
4 slices bacon
½ cup boiling water
¼ cup cooking oil
2 tablespoons flour

1. Pluck and draw ptarmigan, wash thoroughly, pat dry.

2. Rub cavity and outside with salt and fill with stuffing.

3. Do not sew opening together. Place slices of bacon on top of the bird, fasten with toothpicks and place on rack in roasting pan.

4. Pour boiling water into pan and bake in hot oven, 450° F., for 15 minutes, then reduce heat to 325° F. and bake 25 to 30 minutes longer, or until bird is tender.

5. Remove the bacon, brush the surface of the bird with cooking oil, dredge lightly with flour and bake 15 minutes longer, or until brown.

Stuffing for Ptarmigan

1½ cups dry bread crumbs
½ teaspoon salt
¼ teaspoon pepper
1 teaspoon poultry seasoning
1 onion, minced
¼ cup butter, melted

1. Mix bread crumbs, seasonings and onion.

2. Melt the butter slowly, add to the bread crumb mixture and toss lightly with a fork.

Breaded Breast of Ptarmigan

12 ptarmigan breasts
2 eggs, beaten
½ cup butter
½ cup fine bread crumbs
1 cup milk
1 medium onion
1 can cream of chicken or cream of mushroom soup
½ teaspoon salt
¼ teaspoon pepper

1. Slit skin over breast of ptarmigan and remove the breast sections with a sharp knife. Wash and pat dry.

2. Dip breasts in beaten eggs, then in the fine bread crumbs.

3. Melt ½ cup butter in a heavy fry pan, add the ptarmigan breasts and sauté until golden brown. As each breast is browned, transfer it to a buttered casserole.

4. When all breasts are browned, add the cup of milk to the drippings in the fry pan, heat and stir until all the bits from frying are loosened.

5. Slice the onion thinly and spread over the browned ptarmigan breasts in the casserole.

6. Add the milk and drippings from the fry pan, cover and bake 1 hour at 325° F.

7. Add the undiluted soup and continue baking another half hour, or until fork-tender. Serves 6.

Ptarmigan Stew with Dumplings

3 ptarmigan
3 tablespoons dried onion
3 tablespoons dried red and
  green pepper flakes
3 tablespoons pot barley
2 teaspoons salt
½ teaspoon pepper
3 tablespoons flour
1 cup cold water

1. Skin and draw the ptarmigan, wash and cut into serving pieces.

2. Put ptarmigan, onions, pepper flakes, barley, salt and pepper in a heavy pot.

3. Add cold water to cover, bring slowly to a boil, then reduce heat, cover and simmer for 2-3 hours.

4. Half an hour before serving, make a paste of the flour and water and add to the stew, stirring so that flour does not lump.

5. Fifteen minutes before serving make dumplings as follows:
Sift 1 cup flour with 1½ teaspoons baking powder and a pinch of salt. Cut in 4 tablespoons chilled beef fat or shortening. Add enough milk or water to make a soft dough. Drop by large spoonfuls on the top of the stew. Replace lid and do not remove until ready to serve. Serves 6.

Ptarmigan with Orange Rice

2 ptarmigan
2 cups cooked rice
¼ cup melted butter
½ cup chopped celery
1 small onion, chopped
  Grated rind of 1 orange
1 tablespoon butter
½ teaspoon poultry seasoning
½ teaspoon salt
¼ teaspoon pepper
1 cup orange juice

1. Pluck and draw ptarmigan, wash and pat dry.

2. Melt butter in a saucepan, add chopped celery and onion and sauté for 3 minutes.

3. Add cooked rice, grated orange rind and poultry seasoning and mix well.

4. Stuff the birds. Spread butter on breasts and sprinkle with salt and pepper. Place birds in uncovered roaster.

5. Bake in a 400° F. oven, basting the birds every 10 minutes with orange juice. Bake for approximately 45 minutes, or until birds are tender. Serves 4.

Fried Ptarmigan Breasts

6 ptarmigan breasts
⅓ cup bran
¾ cup flour
½ teaspoon salt
¼ teaspoon pepper
½ cup butter

1. Skin and draw ptarmigan and cut into serving pieces. Wash and drain.

2. Dredge in mixture of bran, flour and seasonings.

3. Melt butter in heavy fry pan and sauté ptarmigan slowly about 20 minutes or until tender. Serves 3.

Ptarmigan with Peaches and Cream

2   ptarmigan
¼   cup flour
1   teaspoon salt
½   teaspoon pepper
4   tablespoons butter
1   15-ounce tin of peaches
1   cup rich milk or cream

1. Skin and draw ptarmigan. Cut into serving pieces, wash thoroughly and drain.

2. Put flour, salt and pepper in a paper bag, add the ptarmigan and shake until pieces are well coated.

3. Melt the butter in a heavy fry pan, add the ptarmigan and sauté until golden brown on all sides.

4. Drain the peaches and add peach juice and milk to the ptarmigan. Simmer until ptarmigan is tender.

5. Serve hot, garnished with peaches. Serves 4.

Ptarmigan Pie

2   ptarmigan
3   medium potatoes, diced
3   carrots, diced
1   cup celery, chopped
1   tablespoon dried parsley flakes
1   tablespoon dried red and green
    pepper flakes
2   teaspoons salt
½   teaspoon pepper
3   tablespoons flour
1   cup cold water
1   cup canned peas
1   10-inch round of pastry

1. Skin and draw ptarmigan, wash thoroughly and cut into serving pieces.

2. Place ptarmigan in a heavy pot, cover with cold water, bring to a boil then reduce the heat and let the birds simmer for 1 hour.

3. Add the vegetables and seasonings and cook until vegetables are tender.

4. Make a paste of the flour and cold water and add it to the liquid, stirring so that the flour does not lump.

5. Add the canned peas, then transfer all to a greased baking dish.

6. Cover with pastry round, fastening it securely on the edges. Prick the surface of the pastry to allow the steam to escape.

7. Bake the pie in a 400° F. oven for 40 minutes until the pastry is nicely browned. Serves 6.

Quail in Wine Sauce

4   quail
¼   cup melted butter
1½ cups fine bread crumbs
1   small onion, chopped
¼   teaspoon marjoram
1   pinch of thyme
½   cup flour
1   teaspoon salt
¼   teaspoon pepper
2   tablespoons butter
1   cup dry white wine
½   cup water

1. Pluck and draw quail. Wash thoroughly, pat dry.

2. Melt the butter in a small pot, add the onion, bread crumbs, marjoram and thyme. Mix well and stuff the quail.

3. Butter the quail, then sprinkle with flour, salt and pepper. Place in greased casserole.

4. Pour wine and water over the quail, cover and bake at 325° F. until tender, basting occasionally with the wine. Serves 4.

Quail with Green Grapes

4 quail
¼ cup flour
½ teaspoon salt
¼ teaspoon pepper
¼ cup butter
½ cup water
½ cup seedless green grapes
2 tablespoons chopped hazelnuts
 or walnuts
1 tablespoon lemon juice
4 slices hot buttered toast

1. Pluck and draw quail, wash and pat dry.

2. Dredge inside and out with flour, salt and pepper.

3. Melt butter in a deep fry pan and brown quail on all sides.

4. Add water, and bring to a boil, then reduce heat, cover, and simmer 15 minutes until quail are tender.

5. Add grapes and cook 3 minutes.

6. Add lemon juice and chopped nuts.

7. Serve hot on buttered toast (1 quail per person). Pour sauce from pan on quail. Serves 4.

Quail in Toast Cups with Mushroom Sauce

4 quail
¼ cup flour
½ teaspoon salt
¼ teaspoon pepper
¼ cup butter
1 10-ounce tin mushroom pieces
2 tablespoons chopped parsley
 (fresh *or* dried)
4 buttered toast cups

1. Pluck and draw quail. Wash and pat dry.

2. Dredge inside and out with flour, salt and pepper.

3. Melt butter in a heavy fry pan and brown quail on all sides.

4. Drain mushrooms and sauté in pan with quail until lightly browned.

5. Add liquid drained from the mushrooms, and the 2 tablespoons chopped fresh or dried parsley.

6. Cover and cook over low heat for 20 minutes, or until quail is tender.

7. While quail is cooking, make the toast cups as follows:
   Slice crusty french bread in 2-inch slices, hollow out a place in the centre of each slice large enough to hold the quail. Butter lightly and toast in a 375° F. oven until golden brown.

8. Serve the quail in the toast cups. Pour a little sauce from the pan over each quail before serving. Serves 4.

Oven Broiled Woodcock

2 woodcock
½ teaspoon salt
¼ teaspoon pepper
¼ cup melted butter

1. Skin and draw woodcock, wash thoroughly.
2. Split birds in half lengthwise and flatten as for broiling with a blow of a cleaver. Sprinkle with salt and pepper.
3. Place birds in an uncovered roaster and pour melted butter over them.
4. Bake in oven at 450° F. for 5 minutes, then at 325° F. for 20-30 minutes, or until tender. Baste every 5 minutes with the melted butter in the pan. Serves 2.

Woodcock in Cream

4 woodcock
1 cup milk
¼ cup flour
½ teaspoon salt
¼ teaspoon pepper
¼ cup butter
1 small onion, thinly sliced
2 cups cream

1. Skin and draw woodcock. Wash thoroughly and cut into serving pieces.
2. Dip pieces of woodcock in milk.
3. Place flour, salt and pepper in a paper bag, add the pieces of woodcock and shake until each piece is well dredged with flour.
4. Melt butter in a heavy fry pan and sauté the pieces of woodcock until nicely browned.
5. Place woodcock pieces in a buttered casserole, spread thin slices of onion on top; then add cream just to cover.
6. Place lid on casserole and bake in a 350° F. oven until tender. Serves 4.

Broiled Woodcock

2 woodcock
1 teaspoon salt
¼ teaspoon pepper
4 slices bacon
¼ cup melted butter

1. Skin and clean woodcock, wash thoroughly.
2. Cut each bird in half lengthwise and flatten for broiling with a sharp rap of a cleaver.
3. Sprinkle salt and pepper over the birds and tie a piece of bacon around each half bird.
4. Preheat broiler. Place birds on broiler pan about 6 inches from the heat and broil each side 8 to 10 minutes, or until tender.
5. During the broiling, baste the birds frequently with melted butter. Serves 2.

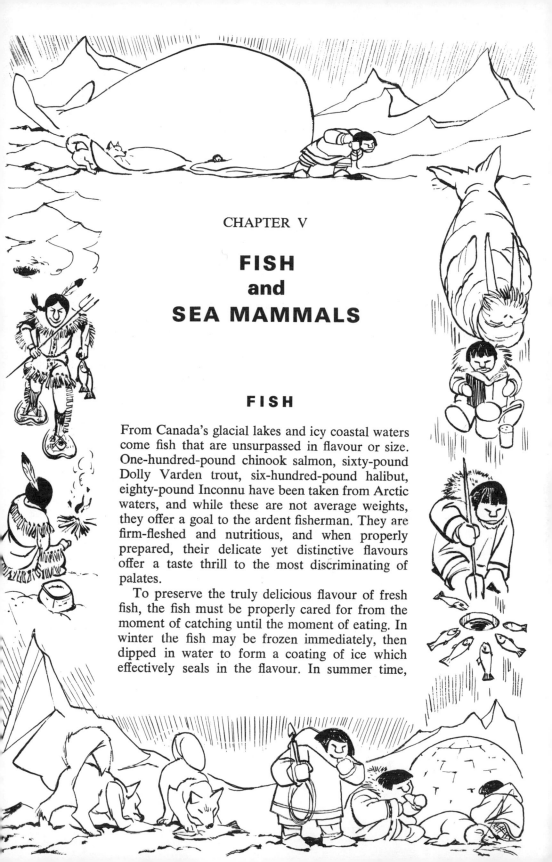

CHAPTER V

FISH
and
SEA MAMMALS

FISH

From Canada's glacial lakes and icy coastal waters come fish that are unsurpassed in flavour or size. One-hundred-pound chinook salmon, sixty-pound Dolly Varden trout, six-hundred-pound halibut, eighty-pound Inconnu have been taken from Arctic waters, and while these are not average weights, they offer a goal to the ardent fisherman. They are firm-fleshed and nutritious, and when properly prepared, their delicate yet distinctive flavours offer a taste thrill to the most discriminating of palates.

To preserve the truly delicious flavour of fresh fish, the fish must be properly cared for from the moment of catching until the moment of eating. In winter the fish may be frozen immediately, then dipped in water to form a coating of ice which effectively seals in the flavour. In summer time, however, extra precautions need to be taken. Keep the freshly caught fish in a covered box or can away from the sun's rays, clean them as quickly as possible, removing the gills as well as the entrails, and serve (or preserve) them at the first possible moment. Never let fish slosh around in the bottom of a boat, and never drag them in the water behind a motorboat unless you enjoy your fish flavoured with gasoline.

Fish is an excellent protein food, as shown in Canada's Food Guide, our pattern for meal planning. Fish protein is easily digested and for this reason fish may be included in diets for older people, invalids and young children.

The amount of fat varies greatly with the different kinds of fish. Lean fish, poached or baked without added fat, is a popular menu item for low calorie meals. The fat of fish is also easily digested. Some of the lean fish include cod, haddock, sole, ocean perch, freshwater perch, pike, pickerel, smelt and all shellfish. Halibut and whitefish are classed as moderate in fat while Alaska black cod, eel, herring, mackerel, salmon, shad, lake trout, tuna and turbot have a fairly high fat content.

In addition to protein and fat, fish supplies some minerals and vitamins. Fish contains iodine and is generally a good source of fluorine and phosphorus. Some calcium is added to our food when the softened bones of canned fish are used. Because the iron content of fish is low, iron must be supplied by other food, such as leafy green vegetables.

Fatty fish has a little vitamin A and is rich in vitamin D. Lean fish does not contain vitamin A or D in the flesh. Fish, like meat, is a good source of niacin and provides useful amounts of riboflavin as well.

Cuts of Fresh Fish

Whole or round fish

Whole or round fish are marketed just as taken from the water. To prepare for cooking, entrails, gills, fins, and scales should be removed. The head and tail may be left on if desired. Small fish, like smelts, and trout are frequently cooked with only the entrails removed. When purchasing whole fish, allow one serving per pound.

Dressed

Dressed fish have entrails and gills removed. To prepare for cooking, fins and scales should be removed. The head and tail may be left on if desired. When purchasing, allow one pound per serving.

Pan-Dressed

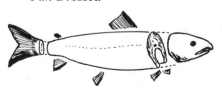

Pan-dresed fish have head, tail, fins, gills, entrails and scales removed. They are ready to cook as purchased. Very large fish are frequently cut into one-pound or two-pound pieces.

Steaks

Steaks are cross-section slices of large fish. They are ready to cook as purchased. Very large steaks may be divided by cutting through the backbone. Steaks are usually one-half to one inch thick. Allow one pound for two or three servings.

Fillets

Fillets are sides of fish cut lengthwise from the backbone. They should be practically boneless and very often the skin is removed. A fillet from one side of a fish is a single fillet. Two sides of a small fish (e.g. blue pickerel) with backbone removed and joined by the uncut skin form a butterfly fillet. Allow one pound of fillets for three servings.

Purchasing Fish

If you are buying fish for your family and want top quality, look for the following characteristics:

1. *Whole or Dressed Fish*
    a. mild characteristic odour but no strong or fishy odour.
    b. bright, full, clear eyes.
    c. bright red gills, free from slime.
    d. bright characteristic sheen on scales.
    e. tightly adhering scales.
    f. firm or rigid body.
    g. firm elastic flesh that does not separate easily from the bones or retain imprint of fingers when handled.

2. *Fillets and Steaks*
    a. mild characteristic odour but no strong or fishy odour.
    b. firm elastic flesh that does not separate easily from the bones or retain imprint of fingers when handled.
    c. fresh cut appearance with no trace of browning or drying out of the flesh.

3. *Frozen Fish*
    a. solidly frozen packages.
    b. wrapping material that is moisture-vapour-proof or a glaze of ice.
    c. tightly wrapped packages with little or no air space between fish and package.
    d. firm glossy flesh with no evidence of drying out.
    e. no discolouration or fading of flesh.
    f. no parched white areas indicating freezer burn.
    g. absence of frost and ice crystals when package is opened.

Preparation of Fish for Cooking

1. *To remove scales*

Hold the fish firmly by the tail with one hand. With the other hand, loosen the scales by pushing a dull knife or scaler against the skin at a 45° angle, working from the tail towards the head. If possible, do this under water, so the scales will not fly about. Scale each side, then the back. Wash and wipe dry.

2. *To remove the entrails*

Hold the fish by the tail. Insert a sharp knife at the vent, and slit the skin along the centre line of the belly to the gills. Cut the gill attachment under the throat to separate it from the head, then insert one or two fingers in the gill throat and pull gently but firmly downwards to remove the entrails. If done correctly, all the entrails can be removed intact. Cut around the vent to free the intestines. To remove the blood streak along the spine, draw the point of the knife along it, then plow out the blood with the thumbnail from one end to the other. Wash the entire inside with water and pat dry.

3. *To remove the head*

Cut across the base of the gills. If the backbone is large, cut through the flesh on each side of the backbone, then hold the fish head over the edge of the table and bend it backwards until backbone snaps. Cut through any remaining skin. The tail may be removed by the same method.
If you wish to leave the head and tail on when stuffing and baking a whole fish, you may remove the eyes with a small measuring spoon, then stuff the cavities with red or green cherries.

4. *To remove the fins*

Cut through the skin along both sides of the fins, then grasp the fins firmly and pull sharply towards the head to remove the root bones.

5. *To fillet a fish*

Lay the fish flat on the cutting board with its back nearest you and belly away from you. With a sharp knife, make a cut just under the head below the gill opening at a slight angle until the knife touches the backbone, twisting the knife so that the sharp edge is towards the tail. Using the backbone as a guide, cut all the flesh from the fish along the side with a slight sawing motion, easing the knife carefully over the rib bones. Stop the cut just before reaching the tail, then turn the freed fillet over so the skin side is down on the table, with the unsevered skin at the tail acting as a hinge. Grasp the tail and the attached skin and slide the knife between the meat and the skin at the tail end. Using a slight shoving motion, separate the skin from the meat, working from the tail end towards the wide end of the fillet. After it is well started, the meat will strip out easily from the skin, provided you work from the tail end forward. It will not strip out easily from the other end.
Turn the fish over and repeat the process to remove the fillet from the other side. Wash the fillets and pat dry.

124

Cooking Fish

Do not thaw frozen fish before cooking except when necessary for ease in handling, such as pan frying or stuffing a whole fish. Fish is juicier when cooked from the frozen state.

The flesh of fish is tender and contains little connective tissue and therefore does not require a long cooking period. Overcooking will dry and toughen it.

Serve fish immediately after cooking, while it is still piping hot, tender and juicy. The fish is cooked when:

1. The flesh loses its translucent appearance and becomes opaque.

2. The flesh flakes readily with a fork.

3. The flesh is easily pierced by a fork.

General Methods

A. *In the Oven*

Baking is a suitable method for cooking whole fish, steaks and fillets, both fresh and frozen.

To bake fish:

1. Measure the thickness of the fish or pieces of fish at the thickest part.

2. Season fish, place in a greased baking pan, and brush with melted fat or add a topping or sauce.

3. Bake in a very hot oven (450 to 500° F.) Allow 10 minutes cooking time per inch thickness. If fish is frozen, double the cooking time.

B. *In Aluminum Foil in the Oven*

The flavour and juices are sealed in by aluminum foil and the fish steams in its own liquid.

1. Measure thickness of fish or piece of fish. If a glazed fish is to be cooked, chip off as much ice glaze as possible. Season fish.

2. Wrap fish in an envelope of greased aluminum foil. Make double folds in the foil and pinch folds to make steam-tight.

3. Place package on baking sheet and bake in a hot oven (450° F.). Allow 10 minutes cooking time per inch thickness for fresh fish and 20 minutes cooking time per inch thickness for frozen fish, plus additional cooking time for heat to penetrate foil and fish. An extra 5 minutes for fresh fish and 10 minutes for frozen fish is recommended.

C. *Baked Stuffed Fish*

1. Clean the fish by removing the viscera, scales and fins or ask your dealer to do this for you. The head and tail may be left on if desired. Wash and dry the fish.

2. Sprinkle it on the inside with salt. Stuff it loosely with the stuffing of your choice, allowing about ¾ cup for each pound of dressed fish (if the backbone is removed, allow about 1 cup for each pound of dressed fish).

125

3. Fasten the opening with small skewers or toothpicks and loop string about them as you would lace shoes; or sew the opening with a large needle and coarse thread. Place the stuffed fish on a greased baking pan and brush with melted fat or oil.

4. Measure the stuffed fish at the thickest part. Bake in a hot oven (450° F.). Allow 10 minutes cooking time per inch of stuffed thickness.

D. *Broiling Fish*

Broiling is one of the best and easiest methods of cooking fish steaks, fillets or small whole fish.

1. Measure thickness of the fish or pieces of fish and place on a greased broiler pan.

2. Baste with melted fat or a basting sauce.

3. Place broiler pan in a preheated oven so that the fish is 2 to 4 inches from heating unit. If fish is frozen place lower in oven to prevent over-cooking surface before interior is cooked. Leave oven door ajar unless manufacturer's directions state otherwise.

4. When fish is browned on one side, season and turn. Brush with melted fat and complete cooking and seasoning. Allow 10 minutes cooking time per inch thickness for fresh fish and about 20 minutes cooking time per inch thickness for frozen fish. Cuts of fish ¾ to 1 inch thick have less tendency to dry out during broiling than thin cuts. Thin cuts of fish may be broiled without turning.

E. *In the Frying Pan*

This is a popular method for cooking fish steaks, fillets and small whole fish. For easier handling, frozen fish may be partially thawed and then cooked immediately.

1. If necessary, cut fish into serving-size pieces. Season with salt and pepper.

2. Dip fish in liquid (milk or beaten egg) and then in flour or other breading mixtures.

3. Heat ¼ inch of melted fat or oil in frying pan. Have it hot, but not smoking.

4. Fry fish until golden brown on one side, turn and brown the other side. The complete cooking time will be approximately 10 minutes per inch thickness. Drain and serve piping hot.

F. *In Deep Fat*

Fillets, smelts, fish cakes and some shellfish are delicious when fried in deep hot fat. If frozen fish is used, it is preferable to partially thaw it for even cooking throughout.

1. Cut fillets into uniform size not thicker than half an inch. If too thick, make several slits in the sides. This will help the fish to cook more evenly and quickly.

2. Sprinkle fish with salt. Dip in batter or dip in liquid (milk or beaten egg) and then in flour or other breading.

3. Place one layer of fish in frying basket. Do not attempt to fry more than one layer at a time as this lowers temperature of fat below proper cooking temperature.

4. Fry in hot deep fat at 375° F. until golden brown, about 3 or 4 minutes. Drain and serve piping hot.

G. *In Boiling Water*

Fish for salads, casseroles, fish cakes or creamed fish dishes may be cooked in water or in court bouillon.

1. Sprinkle fish with salt and place on a piece of greased aluminum foil or a sheet of dampened parchment paper.

2. Measure thickness of fish at thickest part.

3. Add some onion flakes and celery salt if you wish, and wrap securely by folding the foil over the fish and securing the open edges with double folds to make package water tight. (Or draw up corners of parchment paper, pouch fashion, and tie with string).

4. Place the package in rapidly boiling water and cover. When water returns to the boil, time the cooking period.

5. Boil 10 minutes per inch thickness for fresh fish and about 20 minutes per inch thickness for frozen fish. When removing fish from package, save the juices for use in fish sauces.

H. *In Court Bouillon*

Make a court bouillon as follows:

½ cup vinegar	½ teaspoon peppercorns
1 tablespoon salt	1 bay leaf
1 stalk celery	1 teaspoon finely chopped
¼ cup sliced onion	parsley
¼ cup sliced carrots	1 quart (5 cups) boiling
¼ teaspoon thyme	water

Combine ingredients in a saucepan. Cover and boil 10 minutes. Use this liquid, which makes about 1 quart, for poaching the fish.

1. Wrap the fish in cheesecloth before cooking it in court bouillon. Be sure to leave long ends on the cheesecloth to serve as handles when lifting the fish in or out of the liquid.

2. Allow 10 minutes cooking time per inch thickness for fresh fish and about 20 minutes cooking time per inch thickness for frozen fish.

3. When the fish is tender, lift it out of the bouillon, remove the cheesecloth and serve immediately.

I. *In Steam*

Fish may also be steamed over boiling water. If you do not have a regular steamer, improvise one by using a sieve or a colander that will fit into a deep saucepan or soup kettle.

1. Partially fill the bottom of the steamer or kettle with boiling water.

2. Add 1 teaspoon of salt to the water. Bring the water to a rapid boil.

3. Place the fish in the upper part of steamer or in the sieve or colander and place over boiling water. For ease in handling, tie fish in cheesecloth. Don't let the water touch the fish. Cover closely.

4. Allow 10 minutes cooking time per inch thickness for fresh fish and double the cooking time if fish is frozen.

J. *In Milk*

Fish may also be poached in milk. Smoked fish is especially good when cooked this way. The fish may be poached in milk on top of the stove or baked in a hot oven (450° F.). Do not overcook or milk will curdle.

1. Measure thickness of fish.

2. In a covered pan, simmer the fish fillets in milk until fish flakes easily when tested with a fork.

3. Allow 10 minutes cooking time per inch thickness for fresh fish and about 20 minutes cooking time per inch thickness for frozen fish.

4. Dot with butter and sprinkle with pepper. Serve milk (thickened or unthickened) poured over the fish.

Arctic Char

From the glacial streams of the rugged Canadian Arctic and sub-Arctic comes a fish as delicate in flavour as taste itself. Not quite a salmon and not quite a trout, it combines the best characteristics of both and yet has its own distinctive qualities. Arctic Char is scaleless, with a silvery belly and sides spotted with large pink dots. It has a dark green back and may vary in size from 5 to 20 pounds. During spawning time the male turns a brilliant orange-red colour and his lower jaw becomes protruded and hooked.

The flesh of the Arctic Char may be white, pink, or a deep salmon colour, distinguishing it from the trout which has yellowish flesh. It may be cooked in more than 20 ways, all of which are delicious.

Baked Char, Mushrooms and Eggs au Gratin

1½ pounds Arctic char
1 small tin mushroom pieces
1 tablespoon butter
4 hard boiled eggs
2 tablespoons butter
2 tablespoons flour
1 cup milk
¾ cup fine bread crumbs
1 tablespoon grated cheddar cheese
½ teaspoon salt
¼ teaspoon pepper
Paprika

1. Tie the Arctic char in a cheesecloth bag and boil until tender.

2. Drain well and flake the fish.

3. Sauté the mushroom pices in 1 tablespoon butter and set aside.

4. Melt 2 tablespoons butter in saucepan and blend in the flour and milk. Cook over low heat, stirring constantly until thickened. Season with salt and pepper.

5. Add the flaked char and sautéed mushrooms to the sauce.

6. Cut the hard boiled eggs into quarters and place in a greased casserole. Pour the sauce over the eggs.

7. Mix the grated cheese and bread crumbs together and sprinkle over the top of fish mixture.

8. Dot the top with pieces of butter and sprinkle with paprika.

9. Bake in a moderate oven 350° F. for about 50 minutes. Serves 4.

Deep Fried Arctic Char

2 pounds char fillets
4 tablespoons flour
1 teaspoon baking powder
½ teaspoon salt
½ teaspoon sugar
1 teaspoon cooking oil
½ cup water

1. Mix the flour, salt, sugar and baking powder together.

2. Blend in the water and cooking oil, beating to form a smooth batter.

3. Cut the fillets into serving portions and dip into the batter.

4. Deep fry the fillets in hot fat until golden brown, about 3-4 minutes. Drain on paper towelling. Serves 6.

Baked Stuffed Arctic Char

1 Arctic char
¾ cup stuffing per
   pound of fish
¼ cup butter
   Salt
   Pepper

1. Prepare char for baking as follows:
   If fish is frozen, thaw it slowly in the refrigerator. As soon as the flesh is thawed, slit the belly and remove the entrails (which will still be frozen) intact. Wash and dry the fish, leaving the head and tail on if desired. Sprinkle the cavity with salt. If you don't care for the eyes, remove them with a small measuring spoon and place red or green cherries in the cavities.

2. Stuff the fish, loosely, allowing about ¾ cup stuffing for each pound of fish (dressed weight.)

3. Fasten the opening with small skewers or toothpicks and loop string about them as you would lace shoes.

4. Butter the outside of the fish and sprinkle lightly with salt and pepper.

5. Wrap in greased foil, using the drug store wrap to ensure a sealed closure, but leave room for expansion of steam.

6. Measure the fish at its thickest depth and allow 10 minutes cooking time for each inch of stuffed thickness after the first 15 minutes. Bake in a hot oven at 450° F.

7. Open the foil for the last 10 minutes of baking time to crisp the skin, and brush the surface with melted butter once or twice during this period.

8. Transfer the fish whole to a large platter, or a board covered with gold or silver foil, and garnish with parsley, lemon slices, and penguins or murres made from peeled hard cooked eggs and ripe olives (see page 166). Serve with lemon butter or sour cream caper sauce. Serves two per pound of uncooked weight.

Broiled Kabobs of Arctic Char

2 pounds Arctic char steaks, 1 inch thick
1 cup chili sauce
⅓ cup olive oil
¼ cup lemon juice
2 tablespoons brown sugar
2 teaspoons celery salt
⅛ teaspoon Tabasco sauce

1. Remove the skin and bones from the char.
2. Cut into one-inch cubes. (Two pounds makes about 30 cubes).
3. Combine the remaining ingredients to make a sauce.
4. Place the cubes of fish in the sauce and marinate for several hours.
5. Drain the cubes and put on skewers.
6. Broil over embers for about 10 minutes, turning and basting with the sauce. Fish should flake easily when tested with a fork.

Curried Arctic Char

1 pound char fillets
4 tablespoons chopped onion
4 tablespoons chopped celery
2 tablespoons butter
½ teaspoon salt
Dash pepper
1 teaspoon curry powder
2 tablespoons flour
¼ cup milk

1. Cut the char fillets into serving portions and season with salt and pepper.
2. Heat 2 tablespoons butter in heavy fry pan and sauté the onions and celery until tender.
3. Stir in the curry powder.
4. Mix a paste of 2 tablespoons flour and ¼ cup milk and stir into the onions and celery. Cook until thickened.
5. Spread ⅔ of the sauce in a casserole and place the fillets on top of the sauce, then cover with the remaining sauce.
6. Bake in hot oven 500° F. for about 40 minutes or until fish flakes easily with a fork.
7. Garnish with lemon and parsley.

Steamed Char

2 pounds Arctic char fillets
1 tablespoon onion
1 tablespoon chopped celery
½ teaspoon salt
¼ teaspoon pepper

1. Wipe the fish fillets with a damp cloth.
2. Sprinkle with salt and pepper.
3. Place the fillets on a greased sheet of aluminum foil and top with chopped onion and celery.
4. Wrap the foil into a watertight pouch and boil in a covered pot, 10 minutes per inch thickness for fresh fish and 20 minutes per inch thickness for frozen fish.
5. Drain the fish and chill for serving with salads or alone with Tartar sauce.

Note
Juices from the cooked fish should be saved for sauces and casseroles.

Clams

How to Prepare Clams

Scrub shells and carefully wash free of sand using several waters. Place in steamer or sieve over rapidly boiling water and cover closely. Steam until shells open, about 10 minutes. Remove one shell from each clam and serve clams very hot with strained clam liquid, melted butter, salt and pepper. The number allowed for each serving depends on size of clams used.

Clam Chowder

1 pint clams and liquor *or* canned clams (20 oz tin)
¼ cup finely diced salt pork *or* bacon
½ cup chopped onion
1 cup diced potatoes
2 cups liquid (clam liquor plus water to make volume)
2 cups rich milk
½ teaspoon salt
⅛ teaspoon pepper
1 tablespoon chopped parsley

1. Drain the clams and save the liquor.

2. Fry the salt pork or bacon in a heavy pot until crisp. Remove the scraps and save for use as garnish.

3. Sauté the onions until tender in the bacon fat, then add the potatoes and the two cups of clam liquid and water. Cover and simmer for 10 to 15 minutes or until potatoes are tender.

4. Add the clams, chopped or whole, milk, salt and pepper and bring to simmer but do not boil.

5. When serving, add the salt pork or bacon scraps and garnish with parsley. Place a small piece of butter in each soup plate before serving the chowder. Serves 6.

Clam Pie

2 cups clams, chopped
3 cups cold boiled potatoes
1 small onion, minced
2 tablespoons finely chopped green pepper
1 teaspoon celery salt
¼ teaspoon pepper
½ teaspoon salt
2 tablespoons flour
½ cup rich milk
1 tablespoon butter
2 cups sifted flour
4 tablespoons baking powder
1 teaspoon salt
½ cup shortening
½ cup milk

1. Cover the bottom of greased baking dish with a layer of coarsely chopped clams.

2. Combine the onion, green pepper, celery salt, salt and pepper and spread half the mixture over the clams.

3. Slice the cold boiled potatoes and place a layer over the onion mixture, then dredge with flour.

4. Add another layer of clams, a layer of onion mixture and top with a layer of sliced potatoes.

5. Dredge with flour and dot with butter. Pour in the milk and any clam liquid.

6. Make a rich dough by sifting the flour, baking powder and salt. Cut in the shortening then stir in the milk.

7. Top the baking dish with rolled out pastry, making a few gashes in the crust to allow steam to escape.

8. Bake in a moderately hot oven (400° F.) for 40 minutes or until the crust is nicely browned.

Escalloped Clams

24 clams in the shell
1 egg
1 cup milk
2 tablespoons butter, melted
½ teaspoon salt
⅛ teaspoon pepper
1 tablespoon grated onion
2 cups cracker crumbs

1. Carefully open the clams and remove from the shell.

2. Scrub the shells thoroughly with a brush, using several changes of water.

3. Place two clams in each of twelve cleaned shells.

4. Beat the egg, add the milk, melted butter, salt and pepper and blend well.

5. Add the grated onion and all but 3 tablespoons cracker crumbs.

6. Spread the mixture over the clams in the shells and top with a sprinkle of cracker crumbs.

7. Bake in a moderate oven (350° F.) for 15 minutes or until nicely browned. Serve hot.

Fried Clams

2 cups clams
1 tablespoon flour
Salt and pepper
1 egg
1 tablespoon water
1 cup cracker crumbs

1. Clean the clams carefully and dry between paper towels.

2. Sprinkle with flour, salt and pepper.

3. Beat the egg well and blend with the cold water.

4. Dip the clams in the egg-water liquid, then roll in the cracker crumbs.

5. Fry in deep hot fat until golden brown. Drain and serve with a slice of lemon.

Cod

Fish and Brewis

¼ pound fat back pork
1 medium size fresh cod
½ pound hard tack

1. Cut pork into ¼-inch cubes and cook in a heavy iron pot until the fat is rendered out, leaving the fat and "scrunchions" in the bottom of the pot.

2. Remove head, tail, skin and entrails from a medium sized fresh cod, cut into 4 pieces and cook with fat and scrunchions until tender. (about 15 to 20 minutes).

3. Remove bones from the fish and return the fish to the pot.

4. Break hard tack into powdery crumbs and mix thoroughly with the fish, fat and scrunchions in the pot.

5. Serve piping hot.

133

Fluffy Codfish Pie

½ pound dry salt cod *or* 1 cup
    freshened, cooked salt cod
4 slices bacon, diced
⅔ cup chopped onion
¼ cup chopped green pepper
¼ cup chopped pimiento *or*
    sweet red pepper
1 tablespoon flour
1¼ cups milk
¼ teaspoon dried thyme
¼ teaspoon pepper
2 eggs, separated
1 cooked pie shell
    (9 inches)

1. Soak salt cod in cold water overnight and bring to boiling point in fresh water.

2. Fry bacon until crisp; remove from pan and add onion, green pepper, and pimiento and cook until tender.

3. Sprinkle with flour and add 1 cup of milk, stirring until thickened and smooth.

4. Add flaked fish, bacon, thyme and pepper.

5. Beat egg yolks with remaining milk, add to fish mixture.

6. Fill the pie shell and bake in a moderate oven (350° F.) for 20 minutes or until lightly browned. Makes 4 to 6 servings.

Variation
TUNA PIE—Substitute 1 can (6 or 7 ounces) tuna and 2 tablespoons butter or margarine for the salt cod and bacon. Make the pie according to directions given above.

Salt Cod and Rice Casserole

2 cups salt cod
1½ cups cooked rice
2 tablespoons chopped onion
2 tablespoons diced green
    pepper
1½ cups thin white sauce
¼ cup chopped tomatoes
1 cup soft bread crumbs,
    buttered

1. Soak the cod overnight in cold water to cover.

2. Drain and add fresh water. Simmer over low heat, then drain. If the fish is still too salty, add fresh water and simmer once more, then drain.

3. Flake the fish.

4. Place half of the cooked rice in the bottom of greased casserole.

5. Lay the flaked fish over the rice, then sprinkle with a layer of onions and green pepper.

6. Pour ¾ cup of white sauce over the onions and pepper, followed by the remainder of the rice.

7. Pour the remainder of the sauce over rice then top with the chopped tomatoes.

8. Spread the buttered crumbs over the whole mixture and bake in a moderate oven (350° F.) for 20-30 minutes or until bubbling hot and the crumbs are nicely browned. Serves 6.

Crab

How to Prepare Live Crab

Plunge live crab into boiling salted water. Use ¼ cup salt to each quart of water. Cover and simmer 15 to 20 minutes. Pull off the top shell and remove gills. Turn crab on its back and break off mouth parts, tail or apron and scrape out yellow fat and viscera. Rinse with cold water. Break body shell in two and pick or shake out body meat. Twist off and crack the legs and claws. Then shake out meat. Rinse meat in salted water and drain. To serve cracked crab, put the body meat back in the top shell and place it on a platter of crushed ice. Arrange cracked legs attractively around it.

Crab Meat Patties

1 tablespoon butter
2 tablespoons flour
1 cup milk
2 egg yolks
2 cups crab meat, flaked
1 tablespoon minced parsley
¼ teaspoon mace
½ teaspoon salt
¼ teaspoon cayenne
1 cup bread crumbs

1. Melt the butter in saucepan over hot water and blend in the flour. Add the milk, stirring constantly until thick and smooth.

2. Beat the egg yolks and blend into the sauce.

3. Add the flaked crab meat, parsley, mace, salt and cayenne. If not thick enough add a few of the bread crumbs.

4. Shape into small round patties, about one-half inch thick.

5. Roll in bread crumbs and deep fry in hot fat until golden brown. Serve with Tartar sauce.

Barbecued Crab

1 onion, chopped
2 cloves garlic, minced
1 cup diced celery
4 tablespoons vegetable oil
   or olive oil
1 bay leaf, crushed
½ teaspoon peppercorns
2 tablespoons Worcestershire
   sauce
1 cup tomato juice
2 cups chicken broth *or* beef
   broth
4 tablespoons soy sauce
3 cups flaked crab meat
   Cooked rice

1. Heat the oil in heavy fry pan and cook the chopped onion, garlic and celery until tender but not brown.

2. Add the crushed bay leaf, peppercorns and Worcestershire sauce, then pour in the tomato juice and chicken or beef broth.

3. Cover and let simmer over low heat for forty minutes.

4. Add the soy sauce and strain.

5. Cook the flaked crab meat in the sauce for twenty minutes. Serve hot with cooked rice.

Grayling

The Arctic Grayling is a freshwater fish distantly related to the salmon, having a large high dorsal fin and a weak mouth. It is highly esteemed by fly fishermen who like to work the icy streams and rivers of the Northwest Territories. It may reach two pounds in size and the flash of silver when it strikes affords a real thrill to the sportsman. Freshly caught and pan fried in butter over the glowing coals of a campfire, its flavour is hard to equal.

Pan Fried Grayling

2   grayling
½ cup flour
½ teaspoon salt
⅛ teaspoon pepper
½ cup milk
¼ to ½ cup fat

1. Clean and wash the fish, then wipe with a clean damp cloth.

2. Dip the fish in seasoned flour, then in milk and then in flour.

3. Heat the fat in a heavy fry pan and brown the fish on both sides, turning once.

Halibut

Fried Halibut Fillets

2   chicken halibut
½ teaspoon salt
¼ teaspoon pepper
1   cup dry bread crumbs
1   egg, beaten
½ cup cold water

1. Clean, wash and fillet the halibut.

2. Cut the fillets in two crosswise, to make shorter fillets.

3. Roll the fillets and fasten with a skewer or toothpicks.

4. Mix the beaten egg and the cold water.

5. Sprinkle the rolls with salt and pepper.

6. Dip the rolls in sifted bread crumbs, then in the egg mixture and again in the bread crumbs.

7. Fry in deep hot fat until golden brown. Serve with tartar sauce or lemon slices.

Island Loaf

1   cup flaked leftover cooked halibut
3   tablespoons butter
1   tablespoon Worcestershire sauce
1   slightly beaten egg
Salt and pepper to taste
¼ cup soft bread crumbs
½ cup milk *or* fish stock
2½ cups cooked rice
1   sliced hard-cooked egg
2   tablespoons butter

1. Combine fish with butter, Worcestershire sauce, egg, salt, pepper, bread crumbs and milk.

2. Line buttered loaf pan with 2 cups rice.

3. Add fish mixture.

4. Top with layer of sliced egg.

5. Cover with remaining rice.

6. Dot generously with butter.

7. Place in shallow pan of hot water.

8. Bake at 350° F. for 40 minutes.

9. Serve with buttered peas and carrots, olives, celery and relishes plus hot cross buns. Serves 2-3.

Baked Halibut

4 thin slices of salt pork
   or strips of bacon
2 pounds sliced halibut
1 small onion, sliced
1 bay leaf
½ cup buttered bread crumbs

1. Place the slices of salt pork or bacon in the bottom of baking dish.

2. Add the onion, thinly sliced, and the bay leaf.

3. Lay the slices of halibut over the onions and cover with the buttered bread crumbs.

4. Bake in a 400° F. oven for 40 minutes.

5. Sprinkle with paprika and lemon juice and garnish with parsley. Serves 4-6.

Orange Broiled Halibut Steaks

2 pounds fresh halibut steaks
   (1 inch thick)
½ teaspoon salt
⅛ teaspoon pepper
1 orange
1 tablespoon butter

1. Season the steaks with salt and pepper.

2. Blend the juice of one half orange with the butter.

3. Brush the steaks with one half of the orange butter. Set them on greased broiler 3 or 4 inches from heat. Broil for 5 minutes, or until steak is browned. Turn, brush with remaining butter and broil five more minutes.

4. Slice the remaining half orange and top the steaks with the slices, broil a few more minutes until fish flakes easily with a fork. Serves 6.

Herring

Herring in Sour Cream

10 salted herring
2 onions
1 lemon
12 whole peppercorns
1 cup white vinegar
1½ cups sour cream

1. Soak the salted herring in clear cold water for two days, changing the water at least three times.

2. Drain and remove the heads and tails and split in two lengthwise, removing the bones.

3. Put a layer of herring halves in a deep earthenware dish or large glass jar.

4. Slice the onions very thin and place a layer over the herring.

5. Cut the lemon in paper thin slices and place a layer over the onions.

6. Add a few bruised peppercorns.

7. Repeat the layers until all herring are used.

8. Pour the vinegar over the fish, then the sour cream, entirely covering the fish.

9. Cover the jar or crock and let marinate for one or two days.

Kippered Herring Casserole

2 cans (7 ounces each)
    kippered herring
4 cups uncooked noodles
1 tin cream of celery soup
½ soup tin of milk
1 cup soft bread crumbs,
    buttered

1. Remove the skin from the kippers and break into bite-size pieces.

2. Cook the noodles in boiling water until tender. Drain.

3. Combine the noodles and kippers and place in a greased casserole.

4. Mix the celery soup and the milk together and pour over the noodle mixture.

5. Top with buttered bread crumbs and bake in moderate oven (350° F.) for 20 to 30 minutes or until hot. Serves 6.

Jansson's Temptation

½ cup marinated herring tidbits
3 medium potatoes
2 medium onions, sliced
3 tablespoons butter
½ teaspoon salt
1 cup heavy cream

1. Drain herring tidbits.

2. Peel potatoes and cut lengthwise into thin strips to make shoestring potatoes.

3. Pan fry sliced onions in 2 tablespoons butter until golden.

4. Place half the potatoes in the bottom of a greased one-quart casserole.

5. Add the herring, onions and the remaining potatoes in layers.

6. Sprinkle with salt.

7. Pour the cream over the top and dot with 1 tablespoon butter.

8. Bake in moderate oven (350° F.) for 1 hour, or until potatoes are tender. Serves 4.

Inconnu

The Inconnu, meaning "unknown," has long been considered a northern delicacy. Caught in the icy waters of the rivers in the late fall it is firm-fleshed and delicious, with a taste somewhat comparable to rich cream. Its size may vary from 8 to 80 pounds, and a large roasted cony head will provide a generous meal for several persons. It is covered with dime-sized silver scales, its fins are colourless and its back an olive green shade. It almost appears to glow as it slices its way through the green waters, and the Russians have long referred to it as the Nelma or White Salmon. It is a game fish, and "jigging" through the ice for cony is a favourite pastime of many families throughout the winter.

Pan Fried Inconnu

1 medium or small Inconnu
1½ teaspoons salt
¼ teaspoon pepper
2 tablespoons vegetable oil
  or olive oil
2 tablespoons butter

1. Clean, wash and fillet the fish.
2. Cut the fillets in serving pieces or in rounds with a biscuit cutter.
3. Season with salt and pepper.
4. Heat the oil in a heavy fry pan and when hot add the butter.
5. Fry the fish on one side until nicely browned, then turn and brown the other side.

Poached Inconnu

1 small Inconnu (8-10 lb)
2 tablespoons butter
1 teaspoon salt
4 cups water
¼ cup vinegar

1. Clean the fish and tie it into a cheesecloth bag.
2. Place the bag on a rack in a large pot.
3. Melt the butter, add the salt, water and vinegar and pour this over the fish.
4. Cover tightly and cook about 20 minutes or until tender, or reduce the heat and simmer until the liquid has almost evaporated. Serve with lemon juice or a tart sauce.

Loche

The Loche or Ling cod is the only fresh water cod. An ugly fish, with a big head and upper body, it is valued by the northerners mainly for its liver and roe. The loche are caught in the small streams of the Mackenzie Delta in October, slit open, the liver and roe removed, and the remainder of the fish used mainly for dog food. The liver is large and a real delicacy and is sometimes mixed with ground ptarmigan gizzard for a camp treat.

Loche Liver and Roe

Loche liver
Loche roe (eggs)
Lard or butter

1. Remove the liver and roe from freshly caught loche.

2. Cut or chop the liver into small pieces and mix with the roe.

3. Melt lard or butter in a frying pan and cook liver and eggs together until the liver is lightly browned. Serve hot.

Perch

Barbecued Perch Fillets

2 pounds fresh perch fillets
½ cup melted butter
2 tablespoons lemon juice
¼ cup tomato catsup
1 teaspoon Worcestershire sauce
¼ teaspoon dry mustard
2 tablespoons minced onion
Parsley

1. Place fillets on a greased broiler pan.

2. Combine butter, lemon juice, catsup, Worcestershire sauce, mustard, salt and onion.

3. Heat the mixture and pour over the fillets.

4. Place under pre-heated broiler 2 to 4 inches from the source of heat.

5. Broil fish on one side only, allowing 10 minutes broiling time per inch thickness of fish.

6. Garnish with parsley. Serves 6.

Broiled Perch Fillets

2 pounds perch fillets
½ cup dry white wine
1 cup water
½ bay leaf
1 teaspoon cornstarch mixed with ¼ cup cold water
2 egg yolks, beaten
1 lemon, sliced thin
½ cup slivered almonds (if desired)
4 tablespoons butter
Salt and pepper

1. Arrange the fillets in a large shallow baking dish.

2. Add the wine, water and bay leaf and simmer 20-25 minutes in a hot oven.

3. Pour the juice from the fillets into a saucepan. Discard the bay leaf.

4. Beat the egg yolks and mix in 1 tablespoon of water, then stir into the juice.

5. Mix cornstarch with cold water, then add slowly to the hot liquid, stirring constantly.

6. Stir over low heat until sauce reaches consistency of thick cream, then remove from heat.

7. Pour the sauce over the fish in the baking dish, arrange lemon slices around it and sprinkle with slivered almonds, if desired.

8. Dot with butter and season with salt and pepper.

9. Place under a pre-heated broiler until the perch fillets become hot and the sauce is a rich golden colour. Serves 4-6.

Pickerel

The Pickerel, Walleye or Dore lives in clear, cold lakes throughout Canada. It is a fighting game fish and may reach 25 pounds in size, though most pickerel caught will vary from 2 to 10 pounds. It is olive brown in colour with brassy yellowish mottlings, and must be handled with care because of its spiny dorsal fins and sharp teeth. It is an active swimmer and tagged pickerel have been known to travel 175 miles in less than two months.

Pickerel Broiled with Mint

2 pounds fresh pickerel fillets
½ teaspoon salt
⅛ teaspoon pepper
2 tablespoons melted butter *or* salad oil
2 tablespoons lemon juice
1 tablespoon chopped fresh mint

1. Season fish with salt and pepper.

2. Mix melted butter or oil, lemon juice and chopped mint.

3. Brush fish with marinade and broil about 5 inches from the heat for 5 minutes.

4. Turn, brush again with marinade and broil 5 minutes longer or until cooked.

5. Serve decorated with extra sprigs of mint. Serves 8.

Baked Stuffed Pickerel

1   2½-pound pickerel
1½ cups 3-day-old bread crumbs
¼   cup finely diced celery
2   teaspoons finely diced green
    peppers
1   tablespoon chopped onion
½   teaspoon salt
¼   teaspoon marjoram
    Pinch of thyme
2   tablespoons butter

1. Scale and clean pickerel, leaving head on.

2. Wipe with a damp cloth, inside and out.

3. Make dressing as follows:
   a. Sauté celery, green pepper and onion in butter, just until the onion becomes transparent.
   b. Add seasonings and bread crumbs; mix well.

4. Stuff fish and place in a shallow greased baking dish.

5. Brush with melted butter and bake at 450° F. for 15 minutes for each inch of thickness. Serves 4.

Pike

The Pike or Jackfish, as it is sometimes called, is a fighting game fish that may reach 40 pounds in size. It has been treated with contempt by some fishermen, but those who have tasted a Great Northern Pike, freshly caught in clean cold waters, filleted and fried in butter, have realized a taste thrill that is hard to equal.

The skin of the pike has large scales and a heavy mucous, so filleting the fish is the easiest method of preparing it for cooking. It may also be drawn, then stuffed without scaling it. Wrap the prepared fish in heavy brown paper and bake it in a hot oven. When you unwrap the cooked fish, the scales and skin cling to the paper, leaving the tender meat intact.

Baked Whole Pike

1   dressed pike (2-3 pounds)
    Salt
    Monosodium glutamate
1   medium onion, sliced
2   tablespoons butter
2   tablespoons fresh lemon juice
¼   teaspoon tarragon

1. Wipe with a damp cloth, and sprinkle flesh with salt and monosodium glutamate.

2. Place slices of onion inside of fish.

3. Combine butter, lemon juice, tarragon and sprinkle 1 tablespoon of this mixture on the onion.

4. Close fish and lace with string.

5. Place in a greased baking dish.

6. Pour remaining liquid over fish and bake at 450° F. for 20 minutes.

Broiled Salmon Steaks

4 fresh salmon steaks
2 tablespoons melted butter
1 teaspoon salt
¼ teaspoon pepper
1 tablespoon chopped parsley, fresh *or* dried
2 tablespoons melted butter
2 tablespoons lemon juice, frozen *or* canned

Salmon

1. Wipe steaks with a clean damp cloth.

2. Place steaks on a greased broiler pan, brush with melted butter, sprinkle with salt and pepper.

3. Place in pre-heated broiler and broil one side until evenly browned. Turn steaks over carefully, brush again with melted butter, salt and pepper, then broil other side till fish is cooked through. This usually takes 6-10 minutes, depending on the thickness of the steak.

4. Add chopped parsley to melted butter then add the lemon juice. Serve hot with the steaks. Serves 4.

Baked Salmon

1 small salmon
1 teaspoon minced onion
1 teaspoon minced dill pickle
½ teaspoon minced parsley
1 cup bread crumbs
¼ cup evaporated milk
½ cup water
2 tablespoons butter
1 teaspoon salt
⅛ teaspoon pepper
1 lemon

1. Clean, wash and dry the fish.

2. Combine the onion, pickle and parsley with the bread crumbs, then add the milk.

3. Place the fish in an open roaster, and stuff with the dressing. Dot the surface with butter and sprinkle with salt and pepper.

4. Add ½ cup water to the roaster and place in a 350° F. oven. Bake approximately one hour, basting the fish with the liquid from the bottom of the roaster.

5. Serve hot with wedges of fresh lemon.

Salmon Burgers

1 can (15 ounces) salmon
½ cup chopped onion
¼ cup melted butter
⅓ cup salmon liquid
⅓ cup dry bread crumbs
2 eggs, beaten
¼ cup chopped parsley
1 teaspoon dry mustard
½ teaspoon salt
½ cup dry bread crumbs for rolling
6 hamburg buns, buttered
Lemon wedges

1. Drain and flake salmon, reserving liquid.

2. Cook onion in butter until tender.

3. Add salmon liquid, ⅓ cup dry bread crumbs, eggs, parsley, mustard, salt and salmon and mix well.

4. Shape into 6 cakes and roll in the ½ cup of dry bread crumbs.

5. Pan fry in ¼ inch hot fat until golden brown on both sides, about 10 minutes.

6. Place cakes in buns.

7. Serve with lemon wedges. Serves 6.

Salmon Croquettes

1 15-ounce can pink salmon
1 cup thick white sauce
1 tablespoon lemon juice
1 egg, beaten
1 cup fine bread crumbs

1. Drain salmon and flake coarsely.

2. Add white sauce and lemon juice and mix thoroughly.

3. Cool and shape into croquettes, roll in beaten egg, then in bread crumbs.

4. Package in moisture-vapour-proof material and freeze.

5. To prepare, take from freezer and let thaw 5 to 10 minutes at room temperature.

6. Cook in deep fat heated to 375° F. until croquettes are golden brown.

7. Serve hot. Serves 9.

Salmon Cups

2 cans (7¾ ounces each) salmon
½ cup liquid (salmon liquid plus milk to make volume)
1 egg
½ cup finely chopped celery
1 tablespoon grated onion
1 tablespoon lemon juice
¼ teaspoon Worcestershire sauce
1¼ teaspoons salt
Few grains pepper
1 cup coarsely crushed potato chips
Whole potato chips for garnish

1. Drain salmon and save liquid.

2. Flake salmon.

3. Mix together all ingredients except garnish.

4. Spoon into four greased custard cups.

5. Garnish edges with extra potato chips.

6. Place cups on a baking sheet.

7. Bake in a moderate oven (350° F.) for 35 to 40 minutes. Serves 4.

Salmon Loaf

1 15-ounce can salmon
½ cup salad dressing
1 tin condensed cream of celery soup
1 egg, beaten
1 cup bread crumbs
½ cup chopped onion
¼ cup chopped green pepper
1 tablespoon lemon juice
1 teaspoon salt

1. Combine salmon, drained and flaked, with salad dressing, condensed cream of celery soup, beaten egg, dry bread crumbs, chopped onion, chopped green pepper, lemon juice and salt.

2. Pour into greased 8½″ × 4½″ loaf pan.

3. Bake at 350° F. for 1 hour.

4. Serve with cucumber sauce. Serves 8.

Cucumber Sauce
Mix ¼ cup salad dressing with ½ cup dairy sour cream and ¼ cup chopped cucumber.

Salmon Casserole

1   15-ounce can salmon
1   can mushroom soup
½ cup grated cheddar cheese
1   cup cooked rice
1   cup medium white sauce
¼ cup chopped celery
½ cup chopped onion
1   tablespoon butter
¾ cup soft bread crumbs

1. Cook celery and onion in water for 5 minutes.
2. Flake salmon; grate cheese.
3. Make white sauce.
4. Add salmon, rice, cheese, soup, celery and onion to white sauce and pour into greased casserole.
5. Melt butter and mix with bread crumbs and spread on top.
6. Bake at 350° for 20 minutes. Serves 6-8.

Sardines

Sardine Croquettes

1   3¼-ounce can sardines
2   tablespoons butter
2   tablespoons flour
½ cup milk
¾ cup bread crumbs
     Salt and pepper to taste
½ teaspoon Worcestershire sauce
1   tablespoon minced parsley
1   egg, beaten
½ cup crushed corn flakes
     Fat or shortening
4   lemon wedges

1. Melt butter in saucepan; blend in flour.
2. Gradually add milk, stirring constantly until thick and smooth.
3. Mash sardines into sauce; add 4 tablespoons bread crumbs, salt, pepper, Worcestershire sauce and parsley.
4. Chill half hour or longer.
5. Shape into croquettes.
6. Roll in remaining bread crumbs, then in egg and then in corn flakes.
7. Fry in fat, ½ inch deep, until golden.
8. Serve with lemon wedges. Makes 4 good-sized croquettes.

Easy Pizza Pie

1   cup biscuit mix
¼ cup milk
2   cans (3¼ ounces each) sardines in oil
1   can (8 ounces) tomato sauce
1   cup grated cheddar cheese

1. Combine biscuit mix with milk.
2. Turn out on a lightly floured board and knead for 10 seconds.
3. Roll out into 11-inch circle and fit into a greased 9-inch pie plate.
4. Flute the edges of the dough, and brush all dough with the salad oil.
5. Drain sardines and place half of them evenly on the dough.
6. Sprinkle one-half cup of cheese over sardines.
7. Pour the tomato sauce over the sardines and cheese and sprinkle with the remaining cheese.
8. Arrange the remainder of the sardines spoke-fashion on top of the cheese.
9. Bake in a moderately hot oven (400° F.) for 20 minutes. Makes 6 servings.

Wine Poached Trout

Trout

4 rainbow trout (5 ounces each)
¼ teaspoon dill seeds
¼ teaspoon rosemary
½ teaspoon seasoning salt
½ cup dry white wine
   Lettuce *or* Romaine

1. Clean trout and remove head, tail and fins.
2. Add seasonings to wine and poach trout for 15 to 20 minutes or until done.
3. Allow fish to cool in poaching liquid.
4. Remove skin and lift meat from bones in one solid piece.
5. Serve trout on crisp lettuce, with mayonnaise. Serves 4.

Trout Stuffed with Mushrooms

2 rainbow trout, cleaned
1 cup fresh mushrooms
2 tablespoons butter
½ cup sherry
½ teaspoon salt
⅛ teaspoon pepper
   Lemon wedges

1. Sauté sliced fresh mushrooms in butter for 10 minutes.
2. Pour a good amount of sherry over them.
3. Boil until liquid has evaporated.
4. Season with salt and pepper and stuff into cleaned trout.
5. Wrap each fish with string and tie.
6. Place trout under a hot broiler or in a skillet until they are brown, then place on a hot platter and garnish with lemon.
7. In camps you may wrap trout in foil so that no juice will escape and bake them in hot coals; be sure the foil is secure. Serves 2.

Pan Fried Lake Trout

2 pounds of lake trout
½ cup flour
½ teaspoon salt
⅛ teaspoon pepper
½ cup milk
¼ to ½ cup fat

1. Wipe fish with damp cloth and cut into individual servings.
2. Dip fish in seasoned flour, then into milk and then in flour.
3. Fry in hot fat until brown, turn and brown the other side.

Lake Trout Casserole

2 cups cooked lake trout, flaked
6 tablespoons butter or other fat
6 tablespoons flour
2 cups milk
1 cup cooked peas
¼ cup sliced stuffed olives
¼ cup buttered crumbs
¼ cup blanched slivered almonds

1. Make a white sauce by combining the melted butter, flour and milk. Cook over low heat until thickened. Season to taste.
2. Add the flaked fish, peas and olives and pour into a greased casserole.
3. Top the casserole with buttered crumbs and almonds and bake in a moderate oven 350° F. for 20 or 30 minutes or until hot and bubbly. Serves 6.

Baked Trout

1 3½-pound dressed trout
1 teaspoon salt
2½ cups canned tomatoes
¼ cup diced onion
½ cup diced celery
Lemon wedges

1. Rub the trout with salt and place in a baking pan or skillet.
2. Cover the trout with 2½ cups canned tomatoes, ¼ diced onion and ½ cup diced celery.
3. Bake as for stuffed fish.
4. When trout is cooked, garnish with lemon wedges and serve hot.

Tuna

Baked Tuna-Cheese Buns

1 6½- or 7-ounce can tuna
  (1 cup)
¼ pound process cheddar
  cheese, cubed
3 hard-cooked eggs, chopped
2 tablespoons pickle relish
1 tablespoon minced green
  pepper
2 tablespoons minced onion
½ cup mayonnaise
3 tablespoons chopped stuffed
  olives
6 split hamburger buns, buttered

1. Combine all ingredients except buns.
2. Spoon mixture between bun halves.
3. Wrap in foil and refrigerate at least 1 hour.
4. Bake wrapped buns at 400° F. for 15 minutes.
5. Serve hot. Serves 6.

Kay Cardiff's Tuna-Cheese Souffle

1 cup medium white sauce
2 eggs, separated
¾ cup grated cheddar cheese
1 7-ounce can tuna fish, flaked
  Crushed potato chips or
  Corn flakes for topping

1. To 1 cup medium white sauce add the beaten egg yolks, grated cheese and flaked tuna fish.
2. Fold in the stiffly beaten egg whites.
3. Pour into greased casserole and top with crushed potato chips or corn flakes. Bake in a slow oven (350° F.) for 1 hour.

Irish Scalloped Tuna Casserole

1 7-ounce can tuna or salmon
2½ cups uncooked potatoes,
  pared and thinly sliced
3 tablespoons butter
3 tablespoons flour
1½ cups milk
1 medium minced onion
½ teaspoon salt
  Pepper to taste
1 tablespoon minced green
  pepper (optional)
1 tablespoon minced parsley
  (optional)

1. Boil potatoes in salted water 10 minutes.
2. Drain.
3. Melt butter in saucepan; blend in flour.
4. Add milk gradually, stirring constantly until thick and smooth.
5. Add onion, salt, pepper, green pepper and parsley.
6. Arrange potatoes and fish (flaked and boned) in alternate layers in buttered casserole.
7. Pour sauce over all.
8. Bake at 350° F. for 40 minutes. Serves 4.

Spanish Tuna and Olives

1 7-ounce can tuna
¾ tablespoon butter
¾ tablespoon flour
½ cup sherry *or* white wine
2 teaspoons lemon juice
   Pepper to taste
½ teaspoon lemon rind
1 can *or* jar of olives
1 tablespoon chopped parsley

1. Melt butter in saucepan; blend in the flour.
2. Add sherry, lemon juice and pepper.
3. Cook, stirring constantly until thick and smooth.
4. Add tuna, lemon rind and olives.
5. Heat thoroughly.
6. Garnish with parsley.
7. Serve with boiled rice. Serves 4.

Tuna Touchdown

1 can condensed cream of mushroom soup
½ cup milk
1 7-ounce can drained flaked tuna
1¼ cups crushed potato chips
1 cup unsalted cooked green peas, drained

1. Preheat oven to 375° F.
2. Empty soup into 1-quart casserole.
3. Add milk and mix thoroughly.
4. Add tuna, 1 cup potato chips and peas to soup; stir well.
5. Sprinkle top with rest of potato chips.
6. Bake 25 minutes or until heated through. Serves 4.

Tuna Stuffed Baked Potato

6 medium potatoes
6 tablespoons butter
   Small amount of milk
1 teaspoon salt
⅛ teaspoon pepper
1 7-ounce can white tuna
2 tablespoons onion
1 cup grated cheddar cheese

1. Bake potatoes at 400° F. until done (about 1 hour).
2. Split each potato in half.
3. Remove potato from shell.
4. Add butter, milk and seasonings.
5. Mash until smooth; add grated onion and tuna.
6. Fill shells again with the potato mixture.
7. Sprinkle cheese on top.
8. Return to oven until cheese melts. Serves 6.

Whitefish

Quick Baked Whitefish

2 large whitefish fillets *or* steaks
1 teaspoon salt
¼ cup milk
1 cup finely crushed corn flakes
2 tablespoons melted butter
   Paprika
   Milk

1. Soak the fish in milk for several hours.
2. Preheat oven to 500° F.
3. Dip fish in salted milk, then corn flake crumbs.
4. Place on greased baking sheet.
5. Drizzle the tops with melted butter.
6. Add a dash of paprika.
7. Bake 10 to 15 minutes in very hot oven or until fish flakes.

Broiled Whitefish

2 pounds whitefish fillets *or* steaks
¼ cup butter *or* other fat, melted
½ teaspoon salt
⅛ teaspoon pepper

1. Have steaks cut 1 inch thick.
2. Cut steaks or fillets into serving-size portions and place on greased broiler pan.
3. Brush with half the melted fat.
4. Place broiler pan 2 to 4 inches from heating unit.
5. If fish is frozen, place pan 6 to 8 inches from heating unit.
6. Allow 10 minutes broiling time per inch thickness for fresh fish and double that time for frozen fish.
7. At half time, season and turn fish.
8. Brush with remaining fat and complete cooking.
9. Season other side. Serves 6.

Whitefish with Crab Sauce

1 5-pound whitefish
6 tablespoons butter
2 tablespoons flour
2 cups milk
1 hard-cooked egg, chopped
1 teaspoon Worcestershire sauce
1 lemon, juice and rind
3 tablespoons chopped onion
1 7½-oz tin crab meat
Salt and pepper
Pinch of paprika
½ cup white wine
Chopped parsley
Lemon slices

1. Fillet the whitefish.
2. Melt butter, stir in flour and gradually add the milk.
3. Simmer, stirring constantly, until sauce becomes thick.
4. Add chopped hard cooked egg, Worcestershire sauce, grated rind and juice of lemon, onion and crab meat.
5. Season to taste with salt, pepper and paprika; keep hot.
6. Arrange fillets in a shallow baking dish, pour wine over them and bake in a pre-heated 400° F. oven for 15 minutes.
7. Remove from oven and pour crab sauce over whitefish.
8. Return to oven and bake 10 minutes longer.
9. Garnish with lemon slices and parsley. Serves 4-6.

Pan Fried Whitefish

2 pounds whitefish
½ cup flour
½ teaspoon salt
⅛ teaspoon pepper
¼ to ½ cup fat

1. Wipe fish with damp cloth and cut in individual servings.
2. Dip fish in seasoned flour.
3. Fry in hot fat until brown on one side; turn and brown the other side. Serves 6.

MISCELLANEOUS FISH RECIPES

Whole Baked Fish with Tarragon Dressing

1   dressed fish (9 pounds)
1   teaspoon salt
    Tarragon Dressing (See recipe
    below)
4   tablespoons fat

1. Wipe the fish with a damp cloth.

2. Sprinkle inside and out with salt.

3. Stuff fish loosely, and fasten the opening with skewers and lace with string.

4. Brush the outside of the fish with melted fat.

5. Bake in a hot oven (450 to 500° F.) about 10 minutes per inch of stuffed thickness.

Tarragon Dressing

½ cup diced onion
1   cup diced celery
½ teaspoon tarragon
½ cup butter
1   tablespoon salt
10 cups soft bread crumbs

1. Cook onion, celery and tarragon in butter until onion and celery are tender.

2. Add salt to bread crumbs.

3. Combine all ingredients and mix thoroughly.

4. This quantity will stuff a 9-pound fish.

Fish Chowder — Fresh or Smoked

1   pound fillets, fresh *or* smoked
2   tablespoons butter *or* other fat
1   medium onion, thinly sliced
½ cup diced celery
2   cups diced raw potatoes
½ cup sliced carrots
2   cups boiling water
1   teaspoon salt
⅛ teaspoon pepper
2   cups milk

1. Cut fillets into bite-size pieces.

2. Melt fat in large saucepan and cook onion and celery until tender.

3. Add potatoes, carrots, water, salt and pepper.

4. Cover and simmer 10 to 15 minutes until vegetables are tender.

5. Add fish and cook 10 minutes longer.

6. Add milk. Reheat but do not boil. Makes 8 servings.

Danish Fish Pudding

1½ pounds fish pulp
4   egg yolks
1   thick slice bread, remove crust
1½ cups milk
¼ pound butter
3   teaspoons salt
½ teaspoon pepper
1   teaspoon nutmeg
4   egg whites

1. Use any fish with few bones, mash into pulp.

2. Add egg yolks to pulp, one at a time, and stir in well.

3. Soak bread in milk and add to mixture.

4. Add butter, salt, pepper and nutmeg and stir well.

5. Fold in stiffly beaten egg whites.

6. Pour into a 2-quart greased mold, place mold in a pan of water in a 325° F. oven and oven poach for 3 hours.

7. Serve with drawn butter. Serves 6.

Smoked Fillets in Milk

2 pounds smoked fillets
1–2 cups milk
⅛ teaspoon pepper
1 tablespoon butter

1. Wipe fish with a damp cloth.
2. Simmer fillets in milk until fish flakes easily with a fork.
3. Season with pepper, dot with butter and serve immediately.
4. If desired, milk may be thickened and served as a cream sauce. Serves 6.

Smoked Fish in Tomato Sauce

2 pounds smoked fillets
¼ cup chopped onion
¼ cup butter *or* other fat
¼ cup flour
1 teaspoon sugar
⅛ teaspoon pepper
1 can (20 ounces) tomatoes
  Spice bag
6 peppercorns
1 bay leaf

1. Cut fillets into serving-size portions if desired and place in greased baking pan.
2. Cook onion in butter or other fat until tender; blend in flour and cook until bubbly.
3. Add sugar, pepper, peppercorns and bay leaf.
4. Slowly add tomatoes and cook and stir until thickened.
5. Add spice bag and cook for 5 minutes longer. Remove spice bag and bay leaf.
6. Pour sauce over fish and bake in a hot oven (450° F.).
7. Allow 10 minutes cooking time per inch thickness for fresh fish or 20 minutes cooking time per inch thickness if fish is frozen.
8. Allow an additional 5 minutes cooking time in either case because the fish is covered with a sauce. Serves 6.

Fish in Wine Sauce

1½ pounds fish fillets
1 cup white wine
2 tablespoons lemon juice
12 large mushrooms, sliced
¼ cup butter
2 egg yolks
1 cup heavy cream
1 tablespoon chopped parsley
¾ teaspoon salt
⅛ teaspoon pepper

1. Poach fish fillets in wine and lemon juice until tender.
2. Sauté mushrooms in 1 tablespoon butter.
3. Remove fish to hot platter and keep warm while making sauce. Serves 6.

Sauce
1. Heat wine in which the fish was cooked to boiling and continue cooking for 10 minutes.
2. Beat egg yolks and add cream.
3. Pour wine over mixture, stirring constantly.
4. Add remaining butter, mushrooms, salt and pepper.
5. Pour over hot fish and serve.

Fish and Pineapple Mystery Packages

2 pounds fish fillets
2 teaspoons salt
¼ teaspoon pepper
½ teaspoon ground ginger
1 can (20 ounces) pineapple chunks, drained
1 green pepper, cut in strips
6 tomato slices

1. Cut fillets into 6 portions.

2. Season with salt, pepper and ginger.

3. Cut six 12-inch squares of aluminum foil and grease them.

4. On each square place a portion of fish, 6 pineapple chunks, 4 to 6 green pepper strips and 1 tomato slice.

5. Seal the foil with double folds and pinch folds to make packages steam-tight.

6. Arrange packages in a single layer in baking pan.

7. Bake in hot oven (450° F.) for 15 to 20 minutes or until fish is cooked.

8. Serve the packages unopened on individual dinner plates. Serves 6.

Quick Fish Casserole

1 pound cooked fillets
2 cups cooked rice
¾ cup chopped onion
¼ cup chopped green pepper
2 tablespoons butter
1 can (10 ounces) cream of tomato soup
½ cup milk
2 cups potato chips, coarsely crushed

1. Flake fish and add to cooked rice.

2. Cook onion and green pepper in butter until tender.

3. Add them to the fish and rice mixture and mix lightly.

4. Blend soup and milk.

5. Place half of the potato chips in the bottom of a greased 2-quart casserole.

6. Cover with alternate layers of fish and soup mixture.

7. Top with remaining potato chips.

8. Bake in moderately hot oven (450° F.) for about 20 minutes. Makes 6 servings.

Fish Poached in Milk

1 pound fillets
½ teaspoon salt
1 cup skim milk
2 tablespoons butter *or* other fat
⅛ teaspoon pepper
2 tablespoons flour
1 teaspoon lemon juice
2 tablespoons chopped green onions *or* chives

1. Cut fillets in serving-size portions.
2. Simmer gently in salted milk for 5 to 10 minutes, or until fish flakes easily when tested with a fork.
3. Remove from heat.
4. Carefully transfer fish to heated platter, and keep warm.
5. Melt fat, blend in flour and pepper.
6. Gradually add hot milk that fish was cooked in and stir until thickened.
7. Add lemon juice and 1 tablespoon chopped green onion or chives.
8. Pour sauce over fish.
9. Sprinkle with remaining chopped greens.
10. Serve at once. Serves 4.

Poached Fish with Olive Sauce

1 pound fish fillets
½ teaspoon salt
1 cup milk
2 tablespoons melted butter
2 tablespoons flour
1 teaspoon lemon juice
¼ cup sliced stuffed olives

1. Cut fillets in serving-size portions.
2. Simmer gently in salted milk for 5 to 10 minutes, or until fish flakes easily when tested with a fork.
3. Remove from heat.
4. Carefully remove fish to heated platter and keep hot.
5. Combine melted butter and flour.
6. Add to hot milk.
7. Cook and stir over low heat until thickened.
8. Add lemon juice and olives.
9. Pour sauce over fish. Serves 3.

Savoury Fish

1 pound fresh fish fillets
1 teaspoon butter *or* other fat, melted
1 tablespoon lemon juice
½ teaspoon salt
  Few grains pepper
4 slices tomato
4 slices onion *or* 4 green pepper rings
4 bay leaves

1. Cut fillets into 4 portions and place on a large sheet of heavy duty aluminum foil or place each portion on an individual sheet of foil.

2. Combine melted fat, lemon juice, salt and pepper.

3. Pour mixture over fish portions in foil.

4. On top of each portion place a tomato slice, then an onion slice or green pepper ring and bay leaf.

5. Wrap fish in the foil.

6. Make double folds in the foil and pinch to make steam-tight.

7. Place package or packages on a baking sheet and bake in a hot oven (450° F.) for 15 minutes.

8. Packages may also be placed directly on the coals on an outdoor barbecue allowing the same cooking times. Serves 4.

Pawtucket Fish

1½ cups leftover cooked fish, flaked and boned
2 tablespoons butter
3 tablespoons flour
1½ cups milk plus fish liquid
½ teaspoon salt
1 teaspoon Worcestershire sauce
1 well-beaten egg yolk
¼ cup grated cheddar cheese
¼ cup buttered bread crumbs

1. Melt butter in saucepan; blend in flour; add milk and fish liquid.

2. Simmer, stirring until thick and smooth.

3. Add salt and Worcestershire sauce, remove from heat.

4. Stir in egg yolk; fold in fish flakes.

5. Fill 4 individual buttered baking dishes or 1 shallow one.

6. Sprinkle with grated cheese.

7. Top with buttered crumbs.

8. Bake at 375° about 20 minutes until top is brown. Serves 4.

SEA MAMMALS

Seal

There are five species of seal in the Canadian Arctic, of which the ringed or jar seal and the bearded seal or square-flipper are the most common and have been the most valuable to the Eskimo economy. Seal are marine aquatic mammals living mainly on plankton, bottom organisms and some fish. They have played a vital role in the life of the Eskimo—their skins providing material for clothing, boots and boats; their fat or blubber supplying fuel for light and heating; and the meat providing food for man and his dogs.

During the summer months, seal are hunted in the bays and inlets along the Arctic coast from canoes, whaleboats or Eskimo schooners. The small bobbing head of a ringed seal, about the size of a large grapefruit, presents one of the most difficult targets ever sighted by a hunter.

Seals may also be hunted at their breathing holes on the spring ice. Hunters travel by dog-sled over sea ice that is still solid and safe despite long hours of sunlight and temperatures above freezing. When a seal is spotted, the dog team is stopped a quarter to a half mile away, and the hunter must stalk the seal across the ice to within a shooting range of 50 to 200 yards.

Definite open season dates have not been set for seal because the season depends on ice conditions which may vary from year to year and from one part of the coast to another. The spring seal hunt generally takes place in May and June, and the summer hunt during late July and August. Sport hunting of the square-flipper seal is not allowed.

Skin and dress the seal according to directions from the Eskimo guide. Seal skins can be made into beautiful garments or wall hangings provided they are properly cared for and tanned.

Discard the liver of the bearded seal. Like polar bear, it also has a high concentration of Vitamin A which produces a toxic reaction in the body, and may cause death.

The meat from young seals is excellent but is highly flavoured in its natural state. It should be washed thoroughly and then hung in the fresh air for a few days before cooking. Blanch the meat by placing it in a pot of cold water, bring the water to a boil then remove and drain the meat. Remove all blubber (seal fat) before cooking, and use beef suet or salt pork to enhance the flavour.

Braised Seal

2 pounds seal meat
1 teaspoon soda
1 quart water
2 tablespoons butter *or* pork fat
Flour for dredging
½ cup chopped celery
1 cup diced carrots
4–5 potatoes, diced
1 lemon, juice and rind
Salt and pepper to taste

1. Soak seal meat in soda and water solution for ½ hour. Drain, then trim off all the fat.

2. Cut seal meat in small pieces and dredge in flour.

3. Heat butter or pork fat in a heavy pot and brown the pieces of meat.

4. Add the chopped celery, carrots, potatoes, and lemon juice and rind.

5. Add enough water to cover and simmer until tender and flavours are blended. Season to taste. Serves 6.

Baked Seal Flippers with Vegetables

2   seal flippers
1   teaspoon soda
1   quart cold water
3   slices salted pork fat
2   onions, chopped
2   carrots, cut up
1   turnip, cut up
1   parsnip, cut up
5   potatoes, cut up
1   teaspoon salt
¼   teaspoon pepper

Biscuit Dough

2   cups sifted flour
4   teaspoons baking powder
½   teaspoon salt
½   cup shortening
½   cup water (approx.)

1. Soak seal flippers in soda and water to cover for about ½ hour.

2. Remove the white fat from seal meat with a sharp knife. Wash the meat and cut it into serving portions.

3. Fry the slices of salt pork in a heavy pot, then remove the "scrunchions".

4. Brown the seal flipper pieces in the hot fat, add 1 cup water, reduce heat and let simmer until partly tender.

5. Add the chopped vegetables, except the potatoes, and 1 cup water. Boil about 30 minutes.

6. Add the potatoes, salt and pepper and cook another 15 minutes, adding more water if needed and cook until tender.

7. Place in a casserole and top with biscuit dough as follows:

8. Sift flour, baking powder and salt together.

9. Cut in the shortening with pastry blender or two knives.

10. Add the water and blend to make a stiff dough.

11. Roll out ½ inch thick and place on top of meat and vegetables in casserole.

12. Bake in hot oven 425° F. for 20 minutes or until lightly browned. Serves 6.

Seal and Rice Casserole

3   cups cooked rice
4   tablespoons melted butter
     Salt and pepper to taste
2   tablespoons flour
½   teaspoon salt
1   cup milk
1   cup cooked seal meat, chopped
1   tablespoon chopped parsley
1   tablespoon minced onion
     Dash of curry powder
     (optional)
1   egg, slightly beaten
½   teaspoon Worcestershire sauce

1. Grease 1½ quart casserole.

2. Combine cooked rice with 2 tablespoons melted butter, and line the casserole with it. Saving ½ cup for top.

3. Make a medium white sauce by melting 2 tablespoons butter in a saucepan, add the flour and salt and stir till smooth. Gradually add the milk, stirring constantly until sauce is thickened.

4. Add remaining ingredients to the white sauce and fill the rice mould with the mixture.

5. Spread the remaining rice on top of the casserole.

6. Place casserole in pan of water in a 350° F. oven and bake for 40 minutes. Serve with tomato or parsley sauce. Serves 6.

Seal on a Bun

1 cup cooked seal meat, chopped
1 cup grated cheddar cheese
2 tablespoons chopped sweet pickle
2 tablespoons chopped onion
2 tablespoons prepared mustard
6 hamburger *or* hot dog buns

1. Combine first five ingredients.
2. Spread mixture generously on the buns, then wrap each bun in aluminum foil.
3. Seal the ends and heat in 350° F. oven for 20 minutes.
4. Serve hot with potato chips, carrot sticks and ripe olives. Serves 6.

Casserole of Seal

2½ pounds seal meat
4 tablespoons flour
1 teaspoon salt
¼ teaspoon pepper
3 tablespoons butter
½ cup dried onion flakes
¼ teaspoon ground cloves
¼ teaspoon thyme
1½ cups water
½ cup dehydrated carrots *or*
1 cup fresh *or* canned
½ cup dehydrated turnips *or*
1 cup fresh *or* canned
2 bouillon cubes
3 tablespoons butter
3 tablespoons flour

1. Trim all fat from seal meat.
2. Cut meat into 2 inch portions and dredge in flour seasoned with salt and pepper.
3. Melt 3 tablespoons butter in heavy fry pan and brown the chunks of meat.
4. Place in casserole, add onion flakes, ground cloves, thyme and 1½ cups of water.
5. Cover and bake in 300° F. oven for 1½ hours.
6. Parboil the dehydrated carrots and turnips until almost tender.
7. Drain, then add 2 bouillon cubes to the liquid and thicken with 3 tablespoons butter and 3 tablespoons flour crumbled together, stirring until smooth.
8. Add the carrots and turnips to the meat in casserole, then pour in the gravy and blend. Serve hot. Serves 6.

Newfoundland Flippers

4 seal flippers
1 quart cold water
1 teaspoon soda
1 tablespoon fat
3 tablespoons chopped onions, *or*
2 tablespoons onion flakes
1 teaspoon salt
1 tablespoon flour
1 cup cold water
1 teaspoon Worcestershire sauce

1. Soak seal flippers in water and soda solution for about ½ hour. This solution makes the fat snow white. Take a sharp knife and remove all traces of fat.
2. Dip the seal flippers lightly in seasoned flour and brown in hot fat in heavy fry pan.
3. Add the chopped onions and brown lightly. Remove from pan and place in roaster.
4. To make gravy, combine 1 tablespoon flour and 1 cup water, pour this paste into frying pan stirring until smooth. Add Worcestershire sauce and season to taste.
5. Pour gravy over meat and onions in roaster. Cover and bake in moderate oven (350° F.) until tender. Serves 4.

Quick Seal Casserole

1 cup cooked seal meat, chopped fine
2 cups cooked rice (*or* soft bread crumbs)
¾ cup chopped onion
¼ cup chopped green pepper
2 tablespoons butter
1 10 ounce tin cream of tomato soup *or* cream of mushroom *or* celery soup
½ cup milk
2 cups potato chips, coarsely crushed

1. Add chopped seal meat to rice.
2. Cook onion and green pepper in the butter over low heat until tender.
3. Add to seal and rice and mix lightly.
4. Blend soup and milk.
5. Place half the crushed potato chips in the bottom of a greased 2 quart casserole.
6. Cover with alternate layers of seal mixture and soup, ending with soup on top.
7. Top with remaining potato chips. Bake in a moderately hot oven (375° F.) for approximately 25 minutes. Serves 6.

Note
⅓ cup dehydrated onions and 2 tablespoons pepper flakes may be used instead of fresh. Pour boiling water over them, let stand for 15 minutes, then drain and use as above.

White Whale

(Beluga)

As early as the 17th Century, the white whale of Canada's Arctic waters attracted the attention of European whalers, and for many decades it was hunted commercially for its valuable oil. While there are now no commercial whaling operations based on the beluga, it is still hunted by residents of the far north, including those on the shores and islands of Hudson and Baffin Bays, as a source of food and fuel. Sport hunting of the beluga is forbidden.

The beluga averages ten feet in length and 700 pounds in weight, but it may grow to a length of sixteen feet and weigh as much as three to four thousand pounds. Its colour ranges from the slate blue of the young, through the grey of the half grown animal, to the pure white colouring of the fully grown whale. They feed mainly on squid, shrimp, capelin and other fish.

Whale meat is boneless and free from gristle. It is very fine grained, similar in appearance and texture to liver due to its high blood content. If the blood is removed by soaking the meat in salt water, the appearance and texture of the meat becomes similar to fine grained beef, and it may be prepared by any of the methods recommended for tender cuts.

Muktuk is the outer covering of the whale. It includes the white skin, approximately 1 to 2 inches thick, plus a thin pinkish layer immediately underneath. Most Northerners prefer to eat their muktuk raw, as it has a tender-crisp texture and tastes like fresh coconut. (If the whale has been caught in swiftly running water, and the muktuk is eaten soon after the kill, there is little danger from bacterial poisoning). Between the muktuk and the whale meat is a four- to five-inch layer of fat or blubber which is valued for fuel, as it has a low melting point (180° F.) and is easily rendered.

Whale Bobotee

4 cups cooked whale meat, chopped
1 large onion, chopped fine
1½ teaspoons salt
1 teaspoon Worcestershire sauce
½ teaspoon savory
¼ teaspoon pepper
1 cup tomato juice
4 cups mashed potatoes

1. Combine the coarsely chopped whale meat and the finely chopped onion.

2. Add the Worcestershire sauce, salt, pepper, savory and tomato juice.

3. Place in a buttered casserole and cover with the mashed potatoes.

4. Bake in a moderate oven (375° F.) for about 30 minutes or until the potatoes are lightly browned. Serves 4.

Stuffed Whale Roast

5 pounds whalemeat
1 gallon water
2 tablespoons salt
1 tablespoon soda
4 tablespoons butter
1 teaspoon celery salt
1 large onion, chopped
4 cups cooked rice
1 teaspoon salt
¼ teaspoon pepper
6 slices salt pork or thick bacon

1. Slice whale meat into 6 slices (approximately 1 inch thick).

2. Soak the meat for an hour in a brine made from one gallon of cold water and 2 tablespoons salt, to remove the blood. Drain the meat.

3. Place the meat in a pot, sprinkle 1 tablespoon soda over it then cover it with fresh water.

4. Bring the water slowly to a boil and let the meat simmer for 20 minutes, skimming the surface of the liquid as necessary. Remove the meat, spread it out and pat dry.

5. While the meat is simmering, melt the butter in a heavy fry pan, add the celery salt, onion, cooked rice, salt and pepper and stir until lightly browned.

6. Divide the rice mixture into 6 equal portions and spread on the slices of meat, then roll and tie each slice.

7. Place the stuffed rolls in a roaster, putting a piece of salt pork or bacon on top of each one. Roast in a 375° F. oven until tender, (about 1 hour), basting occasionally. Serves 6 generously.

Fillet of Whale with Mushroom Sauce

2 pounds whale meat
1 gallon water
2 tablespoons salt
1 tablespoon soda
3 tablespoons butter *or* margarine
½ teaspoon salt
¼ teaspoon pepper

1. Slice the whale meat into 4 steaks.

2. Soak the meat for an hour in a brine made from one gallon of cold water and 2 tablespoons salt, to remove the blood. Drain the meat.

3. Place the meat in a pot, sprinkle 1 tablespoon soda over it then cover it with fresh water.

4. Bring the water slowly to a boil and let the meat simmer for 20 minutes, skimming the surface of the liquid as necessary. Remove the meat, spread it out and pat dry.

5. Melt the butter in a heavy fry pan, sprinkle the meat with salt and pepper then place it in the melted butter in the fry pan over lowest heat and let stand for 1 hour, turning the steaks over once during this time.

6. Pour off the butter into a saucepan and use it for making the sauce.

7. Brown the meat on both sides in fry pan over high heat. Serve hot with mushroom sauce.

Mushroom Sauce

1 tablespoon flour
1 cup water
½ pound mushrooms
2 tablespoons lemon juice
Salt and pepper

1. Add flour to melted butter poured from meat.

2. Stir until well blended, then add water and sliced mushrooms and cook until mushrooms are tender.

3. Add the lemon juice, season to taste, and pour the sauce over the meat. Serves 4.

CHAPTER VI

EGGS
CEREALS
and
BEVERAGES

EGGS

Eggs are the most versatile of all foods, and have been used by man since the dawn of civilization. There is no waste to an egg, they are easily digested, and whether they are large or small, long or round, white or brown or speckled, they are an excellent source of protein, minerals, vitamins and fat. Hen's eggs are generally the most popular choice for eating fresh, but eggs from other birds, reptiles and fish are also edible. Caviar, the eggs or roe from a sturgeon, has long been a symbol of luxurious eating. Turtle eggs in China, ostrich eggs in Arabia and plover eggs in England are all considered delicacies, and those who have eaten the roe and liver from a loche, freshly caught in October's icy streams near Aklavik claim it as an unforgettable taste treat.

Fresh hen's eggs are not always available in the north, but many birds have Arctic breeding grounds. Most notable among these are ducks, geese, golden plovers, kittiwakes, Arctic terns and the comical murres or okpas, which in spite of their short wings and upright stance, perform incredibly beautiful joy-flights and under-water dances during their mating season. The noisy return of the birds, heralding the end of the long Arctic winter, is greeted with delight by all northerners. While the nests of many birds are inaccessible and the law prohibits eating the eggs of most of them, there are occasions when some eggs are available for a fortunate few.

To compensate for the high cost, or complete lack, of fresh eggs, dried egg powder is available in most settlements. If properly prepared, it can be an acceptable substitute in most recipes which require eggs. Add 3 tablespoons of warm water to 1 tablespoon of dried egg powder for 1 "egg", preferably several hours before it is to be used. An alternative method is to sift the egg powder with the flour or dry ingredients, and add the water to the liquid ingredients. Better results can sometimes be obtained if an additional ⅛ teaspoon of baking powder is also added. Once a can of egg powder has been opened, always keep the unused part covered in a cool place.

If you happen to be in an area where fresh eggs are occasionally available, they may be stored for several months by coating them with a thin layer of lukewarm mineral oil, draining them well, then placing them in cases or cartons in a cool dark place until required. An alternative method is to store them in an earthenware crock filled with limewater. Scald 2 pounds of unslaked or hydrated lime in a little water, then stir into this, 5 gallons of water that has previously been boiled and allowed to cool. Allow the mixture to stand until the lime settles to the bottom, then use the clear liquid. Place clean, fresh eggs in a clean earthenware crock or wide-mouthed glass jar, and completely cover the eggs plus 2 inches more, with the clear limewater. Cover the crock or jar and keep it in a cool, dry place. The eggs may be removed as required.

To test an egg for freshness, put it in a small pot or bowl of cold water. If it is fresh, it will sink to the bottom of the pot. Always break an egg into a saucer or small bowl before adding it to a mixture. This will prevent ruining the mixture in case the egg has gone bad. Eggs should be cooked over low to moderate heat, never high heat. High heat hardens the protein, making the eggs tough and leathery. When adding beaten eggs to hot mixtures, always add a little of the hot mixture to the beaten eggs first. If you add the eggs to the hot mixture, the first drops poured out will cook immediately, making lumps that can't be stirred out.

French Toast or Bannock

2 tablespoons butter *or* margarine
2 tablespoons egg powder
¼ cup milk powder
1½ cups water
½ teaspoon salt
4 slices of bread *or* bannock

1. Mix powdered eggs, milk powder and water. Beat well. Add salt.

2. Heat the frying pan and melt some of the fat in it.

3. Dip the bread in the egg mixture. Put the slices into the frying pan.

4. Cook slowly until brown on one side, then turn over, adding more fat if necessary.

5. When both sides are browned, remove from heat and serve with syrup or jam.

Soft-Cooked Eggs

4 eggs warmed to room
  temperature
1 quart water

1. Add cold water to eggs in a saucepan.

2. Bring water to boiling point, then turn off the heat and cover the saucepan.

3. Let stand 3 minutes for soft-cooked eggs and 5 minutes for medium. Remove eggs from the water as soon as the time is up and serve immediately.

Hard-Cooked Eggs

4 eggs warmed to room
  temperature

1. Add cold water to eggs in a saucepan and cover.

2. Place pan on heat and bring to boiling point.

3. Reduce heat to simmer (below boiling point) and leave for 15 minutes.

4. Remove eggs immediately and plunge them into cold water to prevent the black line from forming around the yolk.

Custard Made with Egg Powder

½ cup milk powder
2 cups water
3 tablespoons egg powder
9 tablespoons water
Few grains salt
3 tablespoons sugar
½ teaspoon vanilla

1. Mix milk powder and 2 cups water in the top of a double boiler. Heat the milk in the double boiler.

2. Mix the egg and water in a bowl, add salt and sugar. Mix.

3. Pour hot milk slowly, while stirring, into the egg mixture.

4. Return mixture to double boiler and cook. Stir.

5. Cook until the custard will stick to the spoon (coats the spoon). Add vanilla. Chill.

Baked Custard

1. Make the recipe for custard following steps 1 to 3 in the above recipe. Add vanilla before cooking.

2. Put the custard in a greased baking dish.

3. Place the dish of custard in a large pan which has a little hot water in the bottom of it. Put both pans in the oven.

4. Bake at 300° F. for about 45 – 55 minutes, or until a knife comes out clean when inserted in the custard.

Devilled Eggs

6 hard cooked eggs
¼ teaspoon salt
⅔ teaspoon mustard
3 tablespoons lemon juice
1 tablespoon butter
Dash cayenne

1. Cut hard cooked eggs in half lengthwise.

2. Spoon out the yolks into a small bowl and mash.

3. Add salt, butter and dry mustard and blend well.

4. Mix in the lemon juice.

5. Refill the egg whites with the mixture and sprinkle a dash of cayenne over top of each one.

Serve on lettuce or use as a garnish on your favourite salad.

Variations
1. Minced ham or tongue with a little Worcestershire sauce may be added to the egg yolk.

2. Mayonnaise may be used in place of lemon juice.

164

Scrambled Eggs Using Egg Powder

2 tablespoons fat
1 cup *fresh* egg powder
3 cups water
1 cup milk powder
½ teaspoon salt
¼ teaspoon pepper
½ teaspoon onion salt
　(optional)

1. Melt the fat in a heavy frying pan on top of the stove, then reduce the heat to low.
2. Mix water and milk powder.
3. Very slowly add egg powder, beating constantly to prevent lumping.
4. Add salt and pepper and onion salt if desired. Mix well.
5. Pour the mixture into the frying pan and cook slowly over low heat, beating with a fork until the mixture sets. Serve scrambled eggs on toast or bannock. Serves 4-6.

Variations
1. Western Eggs—Chop 3 strips of bacon into small pieces. Brown them lightly in the fry pan, omitting the fat. Add 1 tablespoon chopped onion or onion flakes, cook 3 minutes, then add egg and milk mixture as above.
2. Cheese and Eggs—Add ½ cup grated cheddar cheese and 1 tablespoon chopped onion.
3. Ham and Egg Scramble—Add ½ cup cooked diced ham, 1 tablespoon chopped onion, 1 tablespoon parsley, fresh or dried.

Scrambled Eggs Using Fresh Eggs

2 tablespoons fat
5 eggs
¼ cup milk
½ teaspoon salt
¼ teaspoon pepper

1. Melt fat in a heavy frying pan on low heat.
2. Beat eggs, milk and seasonings.
3. Pour egg mixture into pan and cook slowly, stirring with a fork or spatula until eggs are set but not dry. Serve on buttered toast or bannock. Serves 4.

Susan's Egg and Olive Murres

4 hard cooked eggs
10 pitted, large ripe olives
1 raw carrot, scraped
8 grains cooked rice
  Toothpicks

1. Slice bottom off large end of hard cooked eggs, so eggs will stand upright. See diagram 1.

2. Fasten a ripe olive to the top with a toothpick.

3. Cut 4 olives in half lengthwise and fasten 2 halves to each egg with toothpicks to make the wings, as shown in diagram 1.

4. Cut remaining 2 olives in half lengthwise, then cut each half as shown in diagram 2, to make the feet. Fasten feet to front of murres with toothpicks as shown.

5. Cut a piece of carrot into small sticks to resemble beaks, make a slit in the olive with the tip of a sharp knife and insert the beak. See diagram 3 for shape of beak.

6. Make slits for eyes with the tip of a sharp knife and insert grains of white rice to resemble eyes.
   Use murres as a garnish for stuffed baked Arctic char, or any meat or fish salad.

Diagram 1   Diagram 2   Diagram 3

Marg Wickett's Pickled Eggs

2 dozen eggs
4 cups white wine vinegar
2 cups water
2 tablespoons salt
1 tablespoon brown sugar
½ teaspoon turmeric
2 tablespoons mixed pickling
  spice

1. Place eggs in a large saucepan with 2 quarts lukewarm water. Bring to a boil over direct heat, then reduce heat immediately, cover and keep just *under* boiling temperature for 30 minutes.

2. Remove eggs from hot water, plunge immediately in cold water until chilled, then remove shells.

3. Mix vinegar, water, salt, sugar and turmeric. Add pickling spices tied in a cheesecloth bag. Bring to a boil, then reduce heat and simmer for 10 minutes. Remove spice bag. Cool syrup.

4. Pour syrup over hard cooked eggs. Let stand 24 hours before serving.

166

Susan's Baked Eggs with Cheese

4 eggs
4 tablespoons milk *or* cream
4 tablespoons grated cheese
½ teaspoon salt
½ teaspoon pepper
1 teaspoon onion salt (optional)

1. Set oven at 300° F. Grease 4 custard cups or muffin pans (half fill unused muffin cups with water).

2. Break one egg into each cup. Add one tablespoon milk to each, sprinkle one tablespoon grated cheese on each, then season with salt, pepper and onion salt if desired.

3. Bake in 300° F. oven for 20 minutes or until eggs are set but not hard. Serve on toast.

CEREALS

Canada's Food Guide recommends that we eat one serving of whole grain cereal each day. Whole grain cereals contain the endosperm layer, the bran layer and some of the germ of the kernel of grain. They are a good source of carbohydrates, iron, the B Vitamins and cellulose, and, in addition, are usually inexpensive. The cereals most familiar to the north are oats, wheat, barley, rice and rye. Porridge is a term used by many when referring to cooked rolled oats, but it also applies to any hot cereal. Opened packages of cereal should be stored in an airtight container.

General Directions for Cooking Cereals

1. Always read the labels on the packages or containers. If you like thin porridge, use more water.

2. Bring water to a boil in the top of a double boiler over direct heat. Add salt.

3. Add the cereal slowly, stirring constantly to prevent lumps. Continue cooking for 5 minutes over direct heat.

4. Place the cereal over water boiling in the bottom of the double boiler and continue cooking for the recommended time.

5. Serve with milk, cream, white or brown sugar, or syrup as desired. Fruit, berries and raisins may also be added.

Oatmeal Topping for Fruit

1. Use any kind of canned fruit or dried cooked fruit.

2. Place the juice from the can, or the juice in which the dried fruit was cooked in a casserole.

3. Stir 1 tablespoon flour into the juice.

4. Place the fruit in the juice.

5. Mix 1 cup of rolled oats and ½ cup of brown sugar and spread it on top of the fruit.

6. Bake uncovered in a 350° F. oven for about half an hour, or until the fruit is hot and the topping lightly browned.

BEVERAGES

Milk

Milk is the baby's first food, and it is an important food for health for the rest of of his life. It is the most nearly perfect food, supplying proteins, carbohydrates, fats, many minerals and some vitamins. Canada's Food Guide recommends that young children should drink at least 2½ cups of milk a day, adolescents should drink at least 4 cups of milk a day, adults should drink at least 1½ cups of milk a day and expectant or nursing mothers should drink at least 4 cups of milk a day. Some of this milk can be mixed into cereals, sauces and puddings if desired.

Milk comes from many kinds of animals, and while most of the milk on this continent comes from cows, in other parts of the world it is obtained from such animals as llamas, sheep, goats, camels, yaks and reindeer. It is available in many forms, fresh, canned and powdered or dried, so no matter where you are, you should be able to have milk in one form or another. In northern Canada, most of the milk is powdered or canned, but these forms of milk have as many nutrients as fresh milk, and when properly prepared, taste just as good also.

To make powdered milk like fresh milk, add 1 part of milk powder to 4 parts of water, stir it well then chill it. To reconstitute canned or evaporated milk, add one can of water to one can of milk. Always keep packages of powdered milk in a dry place, and once they have been opened, cover them tightly each time after using. Opened cans of milk should also be kept covered in a cool place and used up as quickly as possible.

When heating milk, always heat it over low heat to prevent it from burning, or better still, heat it over boiling water in a double boiler. Cover the pot to help prevent a scum forming on top, but if scum does form, beat it into the milk, as it contains valuable vitamins and minerals.

Cheese, made from the protein in milk, is an excellent source of milk nutrients. It is concentrated, keeps well, and may be served in a variety of ways to add interest to meals or to snacks. Recipes using cheese are found throughout this book.

Cocoa

3 tablespoons cocoa
Few grains of salt
3 tablespoons sugar
1 cup powdered milk
4 cups water

1. Measure the cocoa, salt, sugar and ½ cup of the water and put into the top of a double boiler.

2. Put the pot on the stove, bring it slowly to a boil. Reduce the heat and simmer for 5 minutes, stirring constantly.

3. Mix milk powder with the rest of the water and add to the other ingredients in the pot.

4. Place the pot over boiling water in the bottom of the double boiler and cook for 15 minutes over low heat. Stir frequently. Serve hot. Marshmallow may be floated on top if desired.

Chocolate Syrup

¾ cup cocoa
1½ cups sugar
⅛ teaspoon salt
1½ cups boiling water
3 tablespoons butter

1. Combine cocoa, sugar and salt and mix well.

2. Add boiling water slowly, stirring constantly.

3. Bring to a boil over low heat, then reduce the heat and simmer for 5 minutes, stirring occasionally. Add butter.

4. Pour into a clean jar, cover and store in a cool place.

5. To use, mix 1 tablespoon syrup to 1 glass of hot or cold milk.

Hot Chocolate

1½ oz unsweetened chocolate
4 tablespoons sugar
¼ teaspoon salt
1 cup boiling water
3 cups milk

1. Melt the chocolate in the top of the double boiler.

2. Add sugar, salt and boiling water, stir until smooth and boil 2 minutes.

3. Add the milk. Heat.

4. Beat with an egg beater until a froth forms. Serve hot.

Coffee (kaapi)

1. Buy fresh coffee and keep it tightly covered in a cool place.

2. Always use a clean coffee pot. Wash it with soap and water after each use, then rinse it in hot water. If the coffee pot becomes stained, put 1 teaspoon of soda in the pot, then add water and let it boil until the stains disappear. Rinse well.

3. Start with fresh cold water and always measure the amount of coffee used:
For weak coffee, use 1 tablespoon per cup.
For medium coffee, use 2 tablespoons per cup.
For strong coffee, use 3-4 tablespoons per cup.

4. Place the coffee in the pot, add the water, bring it to a boil, then reduce the heat and let the coffee stand for 6 minutes over low heat.

5. Add 2 tablespoons cold water to settle the grounds.

6. Serve immediately. Add cream or sugar if desired.

7. If using a percolator, dripolator or a vacuum drip pot, follow the directions that come with the pot.

Tea (tii)

1. Always use fresh water. Bring it to a strong bubbling boil over high heat.
2. "Hot the pot"—Preheat the teapot by filling it with hot water for a few minutes, then pour the water out.
3. Measure the tea into the hot teapot. Use 1 teaspoon of tea per person and add one for the pot. (If using teabags, follow the directions on the bag).
4. Add 1 cup of boiling water for each person. The water should still be bubbling as you pour it over the tea.
5. Put the lid on the teapot and let it stand a full 5 minutes before serving.
6. Serve with milk, sugar or lemon if desired.

Instant Tea or Coffee

1. Put 1 teaspoon instant tea or coffee in the cup.
2. Add briskly boiling water and stir well.
3. Add cream or sugar if desired.

CHAPTER VII

FLOUR MIXTURES

YEAST BREADS
QUICK BREADS
CAKES
COOKIES

The worth of a wife in the wilderness is often judged by her ability to make bread, and the only good excuse for not baking bread is the lack of an oven. There are few household tasks performed which offer the sense of accomplishment felt on seeing golden loaves of crusty bread cooling in a kitchen. And for children, the smell and taste of homemade bread will forever after conjure up visions of the warmth and love and laughter of home.

Bread in its various forms has been of major importance in the life of man since the dawn of recorded time. From the sun-baked cakes of grain of the cave-man to the refined, enriched, pre-sliced bread of to-day, it has been a staple part of almost every meal. It has been fabled in story and song, used as a means of class distinction in the middle ages and even used as a form of money. The labourers who built the Great Pyramids of Egypt were paid three loaves of bread and two jugs of wine from sun to sun. Even to-day, a person who earns a living, regardless of his occupation, is called a breadwinner.

Canada is often referred to as the bread-basket of the world. The flour milled from hard wheat, sun ripened on the Canadian Prairies, is unequalled anywhere for bread-making qualities, while flour from soft wheat grown in Eastern Canada is ideal for making tender cakes and pastry. The difference between the two types of flour lies in their protein content. The flour milled from hard wheat, called bread flour, is high in protein. When the flour is moistened, the protein forms an elastic-like substance called gluten, which will stretch to twice its size without collapsing, thus allowing the bread to rise. The flour milled from soft wheat, called cake or pastry flour, is low in protein and therefore gives a tender, crumbly texture to cakes and pastry.

All-purpose flour is a mixture of bread and cake flour that can be used for all types of baking. Unless otherwise specified, the recipes in this book use all-purpose flour. If a recipe does call for cake or pastry flour, and you have only all-purpose flour on hand, use only ⅞ of a cup of all-purpose flour for each cup of cake or pastry flour called for in the recipe.

Breads

There are two main types of breads, Yeast breads and Quick breads. The difference depends on what is used to make them rise, or leaven. Yeast breads depend on the action of yeast plants for leavening. These are tiny plants, which, when moistened with warm water and fed on sugar, start to grow. As they eat they give off a gas called carbon dioxide. When yeast is mixed with warm water, sugar and flour, the tiny bubbles of carbon dioxide make the gluten in the flour stretch, and the dough rises and becomes light. Baking bread stops the action of the yeast plants and hardens the gluten, giving the bread its characteristic form.

Quick Breads are leavened by baking powder instead of yeast. When baking powder is moistened it also gives off gas, but its action is much faster than yeast, and the flavour is different. Instead of baking powder, baking soda and an acid such as sour milk, molasses or lemon juice may be used for leavening, but in all cases the batters or doughs should be stirred as little as possible to prevent toughness and tunnels.

YEAST BREADS MADE WITH GRANULAR YEAST

Note: All yeast breads have to be allowed to rise in a warm place free from drafts at some point in their preparation. If you can't find just the right place for this, place the bowl or pans of dough on the lowest rack of the *unheated* oven, and put a shallow pan of hot water on the bottom of the oven. Keep the water hot during the rising period, but otherwise keep the oven door closed.

Light Whole Wheat Bread

½ cup lukewarm water
1 teaspoon white sugar
1 package yeast
1 cup lukewarm water
2 cups sifted white flour
2 tablespoons white sugar
2 teaspoons salt
3 tablespoons shortening
½ cup firmly packed brown sugar
½ cup hot water
4 cups unsifted whole wheat flour

1. Dissolve 1 teaspoon sugar in ½ cup lukewarm water, sprinkle yeast on top, cover and let stand 10 minutes.

2. Add 1 cup lukewarm water, 2 cups sifted white flour, 2 tablespoons white sugar and 2 teaspoons salt. Beat well until smooth. (This can be done with an electric mixer if desired).

3. Let rise in a warm place until light and bubbly.

4. Measure 3 tablespoons shortening and ½ cup firmly packed brown sugar into a small bowl. Pour ½ cup hot water over them, stir till the shortening has melted and the mixture has cooled to lukewarm, then add it to the risen yeast mixture.

5. Add 4 cups unsifted whole wheat flour and mix until smooth.

6. Knead dough on a floured board for about 10 minutes.

7. Place dough in a greased bowl, cover, and let rise in a warm place about 1½ hours, or until the dough will retain the impression of two fingers.

8. Turn dough out onto a floured board. Divide in half, mold into 2 balls. Let stand, closely covered, for 15 minutes.

9. Shape balls into two loaves. Place in bread pans and cover.

10. Let rise in warm place until dough fills the pans, and the centres are well above the top of the pans, about 1-1¼ hours.

11. Bake in a 350° F. oven for one hour, or until loaf sounds hollow when tapped with the knuckles.

12. Remove from pans and cool. Makes 2 loaves.

White Bread

1 cup lukewarm water
2 teaspoons sugar
2 packages yeast
4 tablespoons shortening
6 tablespoons sugar
1 tablespoon salt
2 cups milk
12–14 cups flour
2 cups cold water

1. Dissolve 2 teaspoons sugar in 1 cup of luke-warm water in a 1-quart bowl. Sprinkle yeast on top, cover and let stand 10 minutes, then stir well.

2. Measure 4 tablespoons shortening, 6 table-spoons sugar and 1 tablespoon salt into a large mixing bowl.

3. Scald the milk by heating it in a saucepan on top of the stove until it comes to a boil and climbs the side of the pan, remove from the heat immediately and pour it over the shorten-ing, sugar and salt in the mixing bowl. Stir until shortening has melted and sugar has dissolved.

4. Add 2 cups cold water to mixing bowl to cool the liquid to lukewarm. Test the temperature by placing a few drops on the inside of the wrist—it should feel neither hot nor cold. If the liquid is too hot, the yeast plants will be killed, if it is too cold the bread will take much longer to rise.

5. When the liquid is lukewarm, add the dis-solved yeast and stir well.

6. Blend in the sifted flour, beating well after each addition. Add just enough flour so that dough will hold together and can be turned out onto a floured board.

7. Knead the remainder of the flour into the dough, adding a little at a time until the dough is just past the sticky stage and becomes satin smooth and elastic.

8. Continue kneading the dough, without adding any more flour, for at least another 5 minutes. The longer the kneading period the better the bread—you can't over-knead!

9. Grease bowl lightly then return dough to bowl. Cover with a clean cloth and let rise in a warm place, away from drafts, until double in bulk, about 2 hours.

10. With your fist, punch down dough in the middle. Fold the sides over and invert the dough in the bowl. Cover and let rise a second time until double in bulk, about 1 hour. To test when dough is ready, poke 2 fingers into it; the impression should remain without springing back.

White Bread (concluded)

11. Turn dough out onto floured board and divide into 6 equal parts. Lightly grease your hands, then form the dough into rounded balls, cover and let rest for 15 minutes. Shape into loaves as follows: Press dough out into rectangle, then fold each side into the middle, pressing down after each fold to squeeze out the air bubbles. Repeat twice, then place loaves in greased pans, seam side down. Each loaf should about half fill the bread pan.

12. Cover and let rise in a warm place until doubled in bulk, about 1 hour. Test for readiness by poking with fingers as described above, or until dough appears to be stretched above the side of the pan.

13. Bake in a 375° F. oven for 35 to 45 minutes, or until loaf sounds hollow when rapped with knuckles.

14. Remove from pans immediately and let cool on wire racks. Makes 6 loaves.

Whole Wheat Bread

4 cups water
2 packages yeast
6 tablespoons honey or brown sugar (part molasses if desired)
5 teaspoons salt
¼ cup salad oil *or* melted shortening
10 cups whole wheat flour
½–1 cup powdered milk

1. Dissolve yeast in 1 cup lukewarm water in which 2 tsp. white sugar has been dissolved. (See directions on yeast packages.)

2. In a large bowl dissolve honey, salad oil and salt in 2 cups hot water. Add another cup of water of the right temperature to make mixture lukewarm, just before adding dissolved yeast.

3. Stir yeast mixture into bowl.

4. Gradually add 9 to 10 cups flour and powdered milk. (A stiff dry dough makes a finer textured bread.)

5. Knead well and let rise in greased bowl, about 1½ hours or until double in bulk. Knead thoroughly again, divide into 3 or 4 sections (depending on size of pans,) shape into balls and let rest in bowl for 10 minutes.

6. Shape into loaves after knocking air out of dough by striking ball several times with palm of hand. (Rough treatment at this stage is good). Put in well-greased pans and cover.

7. Let rise about 1½ hours, then bake in slow oven, 300-325°, about 55 minutes.
Small deep pans seem to be best for this bread.

175

Crusty French Bread

½ cup lukewarm water
1 teaspoon sugar
1 package yeast
1 tablespoon shortening
1 tablespoon salt
2 teaspoons sugar
1 cup boiling water
1 cup cold water
6 cups flour
1 egg white, slightly beaten

1. Dissolve 1 teaspoon sugar in lukewarm water and sprinkle the yeast on top. Cover and let stand 10 minutes, then stir well.

2. Measure 1 tablespoon shortening, salt and 2 teaspoons sugar into a large mixing bowl.

3. Pour 1 cup boiling water over the shortening and stir until shortening is melted.

4. Add 1 cup cold water to cool to lukewarm, then add the dissolved yeast and stir well.

5. Fold in the flour gradually until well blended.

6. Turn the dough out on floured board and knead until dough becomes elastic.

7. Place in a greased bowl, cover and let rise in a warm place until double in bulk, about 1½ hours.

8. Punch down the dough and shape into oblong loaves. Place the loaves on a baking sheet and let rise until double in bulk, about 1 hour.

9. Brush the top of the loaves with slightly beaten egg whites and make three slashes along the top with a sharp knife.

10. Bake in hot oven (400° F.) for 15 minutes. Reduce heat to 350° F. and bake for another 45 minutes.

Italian Bread

1 package dry yeast
1 teaspoon sugar
2 cups lukewarm water
1 tablespoon salt
6 cups sifted flour

1. Dissolve 1 teaspoon sugar in ½ cup luke-warm water. Sprinkle yeast on top, cover and let stand 10 minutes.

2. Add 1½ cups lukewarm water.

3. Add flour and salt gradually, mixing until dough is well blended.

4. Turn out onto a floured board and knead for 15 minutes. Place in a greased bowl and cover.

5. Let rise in a warm place free from drafts until double in bulk, about 2 hours.

6. Turn out on board and knead for 5 minutes.

7. Divide in 2, shape into balls, cover closely and allow to rest for 10 minutes.

8. Shape into oblong loaves, pointed at each end and place on a greased baking sheet.

9. Let rise in a warm place until double in size, about 1 hour.

10. Bake in a 425° F. oven for 10 minutes, then reduce heat and bake at 350° F. for 45-50 minutes. Makes 2 loaves.

Oatmeal Casserole Bread

2 packages dry yeast
1 cup lukewarm water
2 teaspoons sugar
1 cup boiling water
1 cup rolled oats
⅓ cup shortening
½ cup light molasses
2 tablespoons egg powder
5½ cups flour
1 tablespoon salt

1. Dissolve 2 teaspoons sugar in lukewarm water. Sprinkle yeast on top. Cover and let stand 10 minutes, then stir well.

2. Sift flour and egg powder together.

3. Cream shortening in a large mixing bowl, then add 1 cup boiling water, stirring until shortening is melted. Add 1 cup rolled oats, molasses and salt. Blend well. When mixture is lukewarm, add the yeast mixture.

4. Fold in the sifted flour and egg powder and mix well. Place the dough in greased mixing bowl and store in refrigerator for at least 2 hours.

5. Turn chilled dough out on floured board and shape into 2 loaves.

6. Place in greased loaf pans and cover. Let rise in a warm place till double in bulk, about 2 hours.

7. Bake in moderate oven (350° F.) for 1 hour. Remove from pans immediately and cool on rack.

Raisin Bread

1 package yeast
½ cup lukewarm water
1 teaspoon sugar
1¼ cups milk
2 tablespoons sugar
2 cups sifted flour
¼ cup shortening, softened
3 tablespoons sugar
2 teaspoons salt
1½ cups floured raisins
2-2½ cups sifted flour

1. Dissolve 1 teaspoon sugar in ½ cup lukewarm water, add the yeast. Cover and let stand for 10 minutes, then stir well.

2. Scald 1¼ cups milk and pour into a large mixing bowl.

3. Add 2 tablespoons sugar, stir, then cool to lukewarm.

4. Add the yeast mixture to lukewarm milk.

5. Stir in 2 cups sifted flour and beat the mixture for 1 minute.

6. Cover and let rise until light and bubbly, about 45 minutes.

7. Stir the mixture and add ¼ cup soft shortening, 3 tablespoons sugar, 2 teaspoons salt and 1½ cups floured raisins.

8. Add the flour a little at a time, mixing well each time to form dough.

9. Turn dough out on a lightly floured board and knead for 5 minutes.

10. Shape into a smooth ball and place in a lightly greased bowl.

11. Grease top of dough, cover and let rise until doubled in bulk. 1-1½ hours.

12. Punch down the dough and divide into two equal parts.

13. Cover and let rest for 15 minutes.

14. Shape each part into a loaf. Place in greased loaf pan, grease the top, cover and let rise until double.

15. Bake at 400° F. for 25-30 minutes.

Crusty Rolls

½ cup lukewarm water
1 teaspoon sugar
1 package dry granular yeast
2 tablespoons shortening
1 tablespoon sugar
1 teaspoon salt
½ cup boiling water
1 cup flour
2 stiffly beaten egg whites
2¾ cups flour
  Cornmeal (about ½ cup)
1 egg yolk
2 tablespoons water

1. Dissolve 1 teaspoon sugar in ½ cup lukewarm water, sprinkle yeast on top, cover and let stand 10 minutes.

2. Measure 2 tablespoons shortening, 1 tablespoon sugar, and 1 teaspoon salt into a large bowl. Pour ½ cup boiling water over and stir till shortening is dissolved. Let cool to lukewarm.

3. Add yeast mixture, 1 cup flour and 2 stiffly beaten egg whites and beat well.

4. Blend in remainder of flour, mixing thoroughly.

5. Turn out onto a floured board and knead for 10 minutes.

6. Place in a greased bowl, cover and let rise in a warm place until doubled in bulk, about 1 hour.

7. Punch down by plunging your fist into the centre of the dough. Fold the edges toward the centre, then turn dough upside down in the bowl and cover it.

8. Let rise in a warm place until double in bulk, about ½ hour.

9. Shape into oval shaped rolls, dip bottoms of rolls into corn meal and place at least 3 inches apart on a greased cookie sheet.

10. Let rise in a warm place until double in bulk, about one hour.

11. Combine 1 slightly beaten egg yolk with 2 teaspoons of cold water, and brush over the tops of the rolls.

12. Place a shallow pan of boiling water on the lowest rack in the oven.

13. Place the rolls on the rack above the pan of water and bake at 400° F. for about 20 minutes. Makes about 2 dozen rolls.

Buns

2 packages yeast
2 teaspoons sugar
1 cup lukewarm water
2 cups milk
⅓ cup sugar
¾ cup butter *or* margarine
1½ teaspoons salt
3 eggs, beaten
8-9 cups flour

1. Dissolve yeast and 2 teaspoons sugar in 1 cup lukewarm water. Let stand for 10 minutes.

2. Scald the milk and add ⅓ cup sugar, salt and butter or margarine.

3. Cool till lukewarm then add beaten eggs.

4. Stir in the dissolved yeast.

5. Add the flour gradually then knead the dough until smooth.

6. Shape the dough into a round, then brush top of dough lightly with grease. Cover and let rise until double in bulk.

7. Shape into rolls and place on a greased cookie sheet or in muffin tins. Cover and let rise 1-1½ hours.

8. Bake in a 375° F. oven for 10-15 minutes.

Hot Cross Buns

½ cup lukewarm water
2 teaspoons sugar
2 packages dry yeast
½ cup sugar
½ cup soft butter
2 eggs, beaten
½ cup lukewarm milk
¾ cup mashed potatoes
4 cups sifted all-purpose flour
1 teaspoon cinnamon
½ teaspoon nutmeg
1 teaspoon salt
1 cup currants

1. Dissolve the yeast and 2 teaspoons sugar in ½ cup lukewarm water. Let stand for 10 minutes.

2. Cream ½ cup sugar and soft butter together, then add beaten eggs, blending thoroughly.

3. Add ½ cup lukewarm milk and ¾ cup mashed potatoes to creamed mixture. Add yeast mixture.

4. Stir together half the flour, with the cinnamon, nutmeg and salt, and fold in 1 cup currants.

5. Add the dry ingredients to the creamed mixture and mix until smooth. Add enough of the remaining flour to make dough easy to handle.

6. Turn out on lightly floured board and knead until smooth. Let rise in a warm place until double in bulk (about 1 hour).

7. Punch the dough down and divide into about 30 pieces, shaping each piece into a round bun.

8. Place on a greased cookie sheet, 2 inches apart, and let rise until double in size.

9. Brush top of buns with glaze made of 1 egg yolk and 2 tablespoons cold water, well beaten.

10. Bake in hot oven 375° F. for 20-25 minutes. Make a cross on top of the buns with quick icing made of 1 cup icing sugar and 1½ tablespoons cream blended together.

Air Buns

2 packages yeast
¼ cup lukewarm water
2 cups milk
½ cup butter
½ cup white sugar
1½ teaspoons salt
2 eggs, beaten
5 cups sifted flour

1. Dissolve 2 packages of yeast in ¼ cup luke-warm water.
2. Scald the milk, then add butter, sugar, salt and beaten eggs.
3. Blend well, then set aside to cool to luke-warm.
4. Add the dissolved yeast to lukewarm milk mixture, stirring well until blended.
5. Gradually add the sifted flour until a soft dough is formed.
6. Cover and let rise until double in bulk.
7. Stir down, then put by spoonfuls into greased muffin tins (half full).
8. Let rise again until double in bulk.
9. Bake at 400° F. for about 20 minutes.

Raised Doughnuts

½ cup lukewarm water
2 teaspoons sugar
2 envelopes granular yeast
2 tablespoons milk powder
½ cup water
½ cup sugar
1½ teaspoons salt
4 tablespoons shortening
1 tablespoon powdered egg
4 cups sifted flour
   Fat for deep frying
1 cup granulated sugar

1. Measure water and sugar into a bowl and stir until sugar is dissolved.
2. Sprinkle yeast on top of water, cover and let stand 10 minutes, then stir well.
3. Mix milk powder with water, then bring to a boil. Remove from heat immediately.
4. Pour scalded milk over sugar, salt and shorten-ing in a bowl. Cool to lukewarm.
5. Add yeast mixture.
6. Combine powdered egg with sifted flour, then add to yeast and milk mixture and beat until smooth, not sticky.
7. Sprinkle lightly with flour, cover with a clean cloth and let rise in a warm place free from drafts until double in bulk.
8. Turn out onto a floured board and roll out to 1 inch thickness with rolling pin, handling as little as possible.
9. Cut with doughnut cutter and let rise until light, about 30 minutes.
10. Fry in deep fat at 365° F., raised side down until golden brown.
11. Turn over and cook other side until golden.
12. Drain on absorbent paper. Shake in a bag with granulated sugar. Makes about 2 dozen.

181

YEAST BREADS MADE WITH SOURDOUGH STARTER

Sourdough, another word for Yukon or Alaskan oldtimer, also means a yeasty starter for leavening hotcakes, waffles, muffins, bread and even cake. To those who lived alone or in a small group of three or four, mining, trapping, or homesteading, sourdough became the basis of their "staff of life". Bread could not be made without it, so the "starter" became a precious possession.

In the early days of the north, bread making at home was a necessity. Food supplies came only once or twice a year by ship and then were transferred to small boats, barges, river steamers, dog sleds or backpacks to reach their destination. Many localities received supplies only when a steamer could navigate the rivers or the lakes during the few months of summer thaw. Orders placed the year before required careful selection with close attention to "keeping" qualities as the en-route timing proved uncertain.

Yeast became deactivated in a short time and could deteriorate entirely en route, especially if unusual ice formation and heavy wind or seas delayed the ships' entry into rivers or ports of call. Ordinary yeast plants, sensitive to the extreme cold, would often refuse to grow. However, the combination of wild or adapted yeast in the sourdough starter proved as tough as its oldtimer namesake, and some northerners still claim to use starters which originated before the turn of the century.

For best results keep the starter in glass or pottery containers. Never use a metal container or leave a spoon in the starter. A good starter contains only flour, water, and yeast. It has a clean sour-milk odour. The liquid will separate from the batter when it stands several days, but this does not matter. If replenished every few days with flour and more water, the starter keeps fresh. If the starter should turn mouldy or develop an off-odour, throw it away and start over.

The procedure for making your own starter is as follows:

Sourdough Starter

2 cups flour
2 cups warm water
1 package dry granular yeast *or*
1 yeast cake

Mix well, then place in a warm place or closed cupboard overnight. In the morning it should be bubbly or frothy, and is called a sponge. Take out ½ cup of the sponge and place it in a scalded pint jar with a tight cover and store in the refrigerator or a cool place for future use. This is Sourdough Starter. The remaining sponge is ready to be used for pancakes, waffles, muffins, bread, or cake immediately.

Sourdough Muffins

To the remaining sponge described above add:
1½ cups whole wheat flour
½ cup sugar
1 teaspoon salt
¼ cup non-fat dry milk
1 teaspoon soda
1 cup raisins (optional)
½ cup melted fat
1–2 eggs

1. Sift dry ingredients into a bowl. Make "well" in the center.

2. Mix thoroughly the egg and fat with the sponge.

3. Add this to the "well" in the flour. Stir only enough to moisten the flour. Add the raisins.

4. Fill greased muffin tins ¾ full.

5. Bake in 375° F. oven for 30 to 35 minutes.

Sourdough Hotcakes

Set the sponge for Sourdough Hotcakes the night before. Place the ½ cup of starter in a medium size mixing bowl. Add 2 cups warm water and 2 cups flour. Beat well and set it in a warm place free from draft, to develop overnight. In the morning the batter will have gained ½ again its bulk and be covered with air bubbles. It will have a pleasant yeasty odor. Set aside ½ cup of this sponge in the refrigerator jar for Sourdough Starter.

To remaining sponge add:
1–2 eggs
1 teaspoon soda
1 teaspoon salt
1 tablespoon sugar

1. Beat with a fork and blend in all ingredients.

2. Add 2 tablespoons melted fat.

3. Bake on hot griddle, turn once.

4. Serve with a mixture of hot brown-sugar syrup or honey and melted butter.
   Molasses, jelly or rose hip syrup are other tasty combinations.

Variations
Add ½ cup whole wheat flour; cornmeal; wheat germ; or branflakes to the batter. (Using two eggs will provide the needed liquid for this addition).

Sourdough Bread

To remaining sponge which should be about 2 cups add:
4 cups sifted flour
2 tablespoons sugar
1 teaspoon salt
2 tablespoons fat

Set sponge as for hotcakes and let stand in warm place overnight or for 6 to 8 hours. Save out ½ cup for next starter.

1. Sift dry ingredients in a bowl, making a well in center.

2. Add fat to the sponge and mix it well.

3. Pour into the well of flour.

4. Add enough more flour to make a soft dough.

5. Knead on floured breadboard for 10 to 15 minutes.

6. Place in greased bowl or bread pan.

7. Let rise in a warm place 2 hours until light.

8. Bake at 375° F. for 50 to 60 minutes.

Sourdough Waffles

To remaining sponge add:

1 teaspoon salt
2 tablespoons sugar
1 teaspoon soda
2 eggs
¼ cup melted fat

Set the sponge as for hotcakes. Make it slightly thicker. Let stand overnight. Remove the usual ½ cup starter for next time.

1. Mix well and add fat just before baking.

2. Bake according to directions that come with the waffle iron.

Sourdough Chocolate Cake

½ cup thick starter
1 cup water
1½ cups flour
¼ cup non-fat dry milk
Let ferment 2 to 3 hours in a warm place until bubbly and there is a clean sour-milk odour. Add:

1 cup sugar
½ cup shortening
½ teaspoon salt
1 teaspoon vanilla
1 teaspoon cinnamon
1½ teaspoons soda
2 eggs
3 squares melted chocolate

1. Cream sugar, shortening, salt, vanilla, cinnamon and soda.

2. Add eggs one at a time beating well after each addition.

3. Combine creamed mixture and melted chocolate with sourdough mixture.

4. Stir 300 strokes or mix on low speed until blended.

5. Pour into 2 layer pans or one 9 inch square pan.

6. Bake at 350° F. for 25 to 30 minutes. Cool and frost with Butterscotch-Chocolate frosting or other icing of your choice.

Butterscotch-Chocolate Frosting

3 (1 oz) squares unsweetened chocolate
¼ cup butter *or* margarine
½ cup light cream
⅔ cup brown sugar (packed)
¼ teaspoon salt
Vanilla
Confectioner's sugar

1. Combine chocolate, butter, cream, brown sugar and salt in saucepan.

2. Bring to a boil, stirring constantly; cook until chocolate is melted.

3. Remove from heat, add vanilla and enough confectioner's sugar for good spreading consistency (about 3 cups).

4. Spread over sides and top of cake.

QUICK BREADS

Included in this category are Nut and Fruit Breads, Muffins, Hotcakes, Bannock and Tea Biscuits.

Nut and Fruit Breads

These breads are best when baked ahead of time, cooled, wrapped and stored at least a day before slicing.

Banana Bran Bread

¼ cup butter
½ cup sugar
1 egg
1 teaspoon vanilla
1½ cups mashed banana
2 tablespoons water
½ teaspoon soda
½ teaspoon salt
1½ cups flour
¾ cup walnuts, chopped fine
1 cup bran
2 teaspoons baking powder

1. Cream butter, sugar and egg thoroughly, add vanilla.
2. Mix the water, soda and salt with the mashed banana and add to the creamed mixture.
3. Combine flour, bran, walnuts and baking powder.
4. Fold into the banana mixture, forming a stiff dough.
5. Pour into a loaf pan and bake in a 350° F oven for 50 minutes.

Chocolate Bread

3 cups sifted cake flour
3 teaspoons baking powder
1 teaspoon salt
1 cup brown sugar
1 egg, beaten
1¼ cups milk
4 tablespoons melted shortening
2 1-oz squares chocolate, melted

1. Sift the flour, baking powder, salt and sugar together.
2. Combine the beaten egg and milk and add gradually to the flour mixture.
3. Add the melted shortening and chocolate, blending well.
4. Pour into two 6″ × 3″ greased loaf pans and bake in moderate 350° F. oven for 1 hour.

Cranberry Nut Bread

2 cups all-purpose flour
1 cup sugar
1½ teaspoons baking powder
½ teaspoon soda
1 teaspoon salt
¼ cup shortening
¾ cup orange juice
1 tablespoon grated orange rind
1 egg, well beaten
½ cup chopped nuts
1–2 cups cranberries

1. Sift together flour, sugar, baking powder, soda and salt.
2. Cut in the shortening, until the mixture resembles coarse corn meal.
3. Combine orange juice and grated rind with well beaten egg.
4. Pour all at once into dry ingredients.
5. Mix just enough to dampen.
6. Carefully fold in chopped nuts and cranberries.
7. Spoon into a greased loaf pan 9″ × 5″ × 3″.
8. Bake in moderate oven 350° F. about 1 hour until the crust is golden brown and toothpick inserted comes out clean.
9. Remove from the pan and cool; store overnight for easy slicing.

Steamed Brown Bread

2 cups whole-wheat flour
1 cup cornmeal
1 teaspoon salt
1 teaspoon soda
1 cup seedless raisins
2 tablespoons grated orange rind
2 cups buttermilk *or* sweet milk
with
1 tablespoon vinegar added
¾ cup molasses

1. Wash, dry and grease well, three 20 oz. cans. (fruit, vegetables, tomato juice, etc., come in this size).

2. Combine whole-wheat flour, cornmeal, salt and soda in a bowl.

3. Combine buttermilk and molasses and add to the dry ingredients all at once along with orange rind and raisins.

4. Stir ingredients just enough to moisten.

5. Spoon into cans. Cover each can with aluminum foil.

6. Set cans on a rack in a kettle of boiling water. (Have water no more than half-way up the cans). Cover tightly and steam for 2 hours or until tops spring back when touched lightly.

7. Remove from kettle, loosen bread from sides of can and turn out on racks to cool. Wrap in foil to store.

Four Fruit Bread

¾ cup dried apricots, cut up
1 cup seedless raisins
1 cup sifted all-purpose flour
2 teaspoons baking powder
1 teaspoon salt
1 cup whole-wheat flour
½ cup brown sugar
½ cup chopped dates
½ cup coarsely chopped nuts
1 teaspoon grated orange rind
   or extract
1 egg *or*
3 tablespoons egg powder
1 cup orange juice
¼ cup salad oil

1. Soak apricots and raisins in cold water for 1 hour. Drain and dry well on paper towelling.

2. Sift all-purpose flour, baking powder and salt together into a bowl.

3. Add whole-wheat flour and brown sugar and blend well.

4. Add apricots, raisins, nuts, dates and orange rind, stirring the fruit with a fork until it is well coated with flour.

5. Beat egg, orange juice and oil together, add to the flour mixture and stir just to blend.

6. Spoon into greased 9″ × 5″ × 3″ loaf pan and bake in moderate oven 350° F. about 1 hour.

7. Turn out on rack and cool.

Variation
Dried peaches may be substituted for dried apricots.

Honey Prune Bread

1 cup dried prunes
1 egg
½ cup liquid honey
2 tablespoons salad oil
1 cup sour milk (*or* 1 cup sweet milk with 1 tablespoon vinegar added)
1½ cups sifted all-purpose flour
2½ teaspoons baking powder
¾ teaspoon soda
1 teaspoon salt
½ teaspoon cinnamon
1½ cups whole-wheat flour

1. Cover the prunes with cold water and let soak for at least 2 hours. Bring to a boil in the water they were soaked in, then simmer for about 10 minutes, or until tender.

2. Drain the prunes and dry thoroughly on paper towelling before chopping.

3. Combine egg, honey, salad oil and milk in a large mixing bowl and beat lightly, then add the chopped prunes.

4. Sift 1½ cups all-purpose flour, baking powder, soda, salt and cinnamon together and stir into the liquid ingredients.

5. Add 1½ cups whole-wheat flour stirring just to blend.

6. Spoon into loaf pan 13″ × 4″ × 3″.

7. Bake in moderate oven 350° F. for about 1 hour, or until toothpick stuck in centre comes out clean.

8. Remove from loaf pan and cool on cake rack. Wrap in foil and store.

Mad Hatter Fruit Bread

¾ cup sugar
1 egg
1¼ cups orange juice
1 teaspoon grated orange rind
3 cups tea bisk mixture
¾ cup chopped nuts
1 cup chopped cranberries

1. Combine sugar, egg, juice and rind.

2. Fold into tea bisk mixture and beat vigorously for 30 seconds. Batter may still be lumpy.

3. Add the chopped nuts and cranberries.

4. Bake in a well greased loaf pan in moderate oven 350° F. for about 1 hour.
   Slice and serve buttered or plain.

Variations
Fresh or frozen whole cranberries may be used, or chopped green cherries add a bit of colour for Christmas.

Partly diluted concentrated orange juice may be used instead of juice and rind.

You may also prefer individual muffins—baking time—25-30 minutes.

Fig Bread

¾ cup brown sugar
2 tablespoons soft butter
1 egg *or*
3 tablespoons powdered egg
1½ cups milk
1 teaspoon grated lemon rind *or* extract
1 cup finely chopped figs
½ cup chopped nuts
3 cups sifted all-purpose flour
3½ teaspoons baking powder
1 teaspoon salt

1. Cream butter, sugar and egg thoroughly.

2. Stir in milk, lemon rind, figs and nuts.

3. Sift flour, baking powder and salt together and add to the mixture, stirring just to blend.

4. Spon into 9″ × 5″ × 3″ greased loaf pan. Let stand at room temperature for 20 minutes.

5. Bake in moderate oven 350° F. for about 1 hour or until a toothpick stuck into centre comes out clean.

6. Turn out on rack to cool.

Muffins

2 cups sifted flour
3½ teaspoons baking powder
½ teaspoon salt
3 tablespoons sugar
3 tablespoons shortening, melted
1 egg, beaten
1 cup milk

1. Sift flour, baking powder, salt and sugar into mixing bowl.

2. Mix the beaten egg, melted shortening and milk, then pour into centre of flour mixture.

3. Stir only until dry ingredients are dampened. Do not overmix.

4. Fill muffin tins ⅔ full and bake in hot oven 400° F. to 425° F. about 20 minutes. Serve warm.

Note
¼ cup raisins or currants may be added to the dry ingredients.

Breakfast Muffins

1 cup powdered skim milk
1 cup quick rolled oats
⅓ cup whole-wheat flour
½ cup powdered whole eggs
2 teaspoons brown sugar
1 tablespoon baking powder
1 teaspoon salt
½ cup raisins or dates
¼ cup melted fat
1 cup water

1. Sift milk powder, flour, egg powder, sugar, baking powder and salt into a bowl.

2. Add rolled oats and raisins. Mix well.

3. Make a depression in the flour mixture. Add melted fat and water.

4. Stir just until ingredients are blended.

5. Spoon mixture into greased muffin pans.

6. Bake in a 425° F. oven for 20-25 minutes. The mixture can be placed in a cake pan and baked about 30-45 minutes if there are no muffin pans.

Muffins With Egg and Milk Powder

2   cups flour
4   teaspoons baking powder
2   tablespoons sugar
½   teaspoon salt
2   tablespoons egg powder
¼   cup milk powder
2   tablespoons melted fat
1½ cups water

1. Sift the dry ingredients together.
2. Make a depression (hollow) in the flour mixture.
3. Pour in the melted fat and water.
4. Stir as little as possible to blend all the ingredients.
5. Drop the batter into well greased muffin tins.
6. Bake in a 400° F. oven for 20-25 minutes.

Apple Muffins

2¼ cups flour
3½ teaspoons baking powder
½   cup sugar
½   teaspoon salt
¼   teaspoon nutmeg
¼   teaspoon cinnamon
1   cup evaporated milk
1   egg, beaten
4   tablespoons shortening, melted
1   cup chopped canned apples
2   tablespoons sugar
¼   teaspoon cinnamon
¼   teaspoon nutmeg

1. Sift dry ingredients into a bowl.
2. Combine liquid ingredients.
3. Make a well in dry ingredients and add liquid ingredients all at once, stirring just until blended.
4. Add apples.
5. Fill greased muffin tins ⅔ full.
6. Sprinkle top of muffins with mixture of 2 tablespoons sugar, ¼ teaspoon cinnamon, ¼ teaspoon nutmeg.
7. Bake at 375° F. for 25 to 30 minutes.

Cranberry Muffins

¾   cup cranberries
½   cup powdered sugar
2   cups flour
3   teaspoons baking powder
1   teaspoon salt
¼   cup sugar
1   egg, well beaten
1   cup milk
4   tablespoons shortening, melted

1. Mix cranberries with powdered sugar and let stand while preparing the muffin mixture.
2. Sift dry ingredients.
3. Add egg, milk, and melted shortening, all at once.
4. Mix only until the dry ingredients are dampened.
5. Fold in sugared cranberries.
6. Fill greased muffin tins to ⅔ full.
7. Bake in moderate oven 350° F. for 20 minutes. Makes 12 muffins.

Fluffy Corn Bread

1 cup sifted flour
3 teaspoons double-acting baking powder
1 teaspoon salt
2 tablespoons sugar
1 cup corn meal
2 tablespoons egg powder and
6 tablespoons water *or*
2 eggs, slightly beaten
1 cup milk
¼ cup melted shortening *or* salad oil

1. Combine 2 tablespoons egg powder and 6 tablespoons water and let stand at least ½ hour before using.
2. Add the egg mixture to 1 cup milk and ¼ cup melted shortening or salad oil and blend well.
3. Sift together flour, baking powder, salt and sugar, and add the corn meal to sifted ingredients.
4. Pour the liquid into the flour mixture and mix only until flour is dampened.
5. Place in a greased 8″ × 8″ × 2″ cake pan and bake in a hot oven 400° F. for 30 minutes. Serve hot with butter.

Prune Wheat Muffins

1 cup prunes
1 cup sifted all-purpose flour
2 teaspoons baking powder
1 teaspoon salt
½ teaspoon soda
½ teaspoon cinnamon
¼ teaspoon nutmeg
⅓ cup brown sugar (packed)
1 cup whole-wheat flour
1 egg
1 cup buttermilk *or* sour milk
¼ cup melted shortening

1. Cut prunes from pits into large pieces.
2. Sift together flour, baking powder, salt, soda and spices.
3. Stir in sugar and whole-wheat flour.
4. Beat egg lightly and combine with buttermilk and shortening.
5. Stir into dry mixture, blending only until all of the flour is moistened.
6. Add prunes and mix lightly.
7. Spoon into greased muffin pans and top with additional prune halves if desired.
8. Bake in hot oven (400° F.) about 20 minutes.

Snow Muffins

2 cups sifted flour
3 teaspoons baking powder
½ cup white sugar
½ teaspoon salt
¾ cup milk
3 tablespoons melted butter
½ teaspoon grated lemon *or* orange rind
½ cup *clean* white snow
½ cup raisins

1. Sift dry ingredients into a bowl.
2. Make a well in the middle and add milk, melted butter and grated rind. Stir lightly.
3. Add snow and raisins, stir with a fork just until ingredients are blended.
4. Spoon into 12 greased muffin tins.
5. Bake at 400° F. for 15-18 minutes.

Basic Pancakes

1¼ cup sifted flour
2 teaspoons baking powder
¾ teaspoon salt
3 tablespoons sugar
1 egg
1¼ cups milk
3 tablespoons melted butter

1. Sift flour and measure.

2. Measure and sift dry ingredients into a bowl.

3. Beat egg, add the milk and melted butter.

4. Add the liquids to the dry ingredients, stirring as little as possible.

5. Heat griddle or heavy fry pan until a drop of water will dance on it.

6. Pour the batter onto the hot pan to form cakes about 3 inches in diameter.

7. Cook until air bubbles appear on top.

8. Turn pancake over and cook other side till golden brown. Makes about 8 3-inch cakes.

Pancakes or Griddle Cakes

1½ cups sifted flour
3 teaspoons baking powder
2 tablespoons sugar
¾ teaspoon salt
1 tablespoon egg powder
1⅓ cups milk
3 tablespoons melted fat

1. Sift the dry ingredients together.

2. Make a depression (hollow) in the flour mixture.

3. Pour in the melted fat and liquid.

4. Stir as little as possible to blend the ingredients.

5. Heat frying pan, griddle or iron skillet until a drop of water will dance on it.

6. Pour batter in small circles onto the hot pan.

7. Cook until little air bubbles appear on the top. Turn pancake. Turn pancakes only once during cooking so they will be light.

8. When pancakes are cooked to a golden brown, serve them hot with butter and syrup or jam. Makes about 10 3-inch cakes.

Variations
Add 1 cup of fresh, frozen or canned and drained berries or fruit. Reduce milk to 1 cup.

Wendy's Waffles

2 cups flour
3 teaspoons baking powder
½ teaspoon salt
2 tablespoons sugar
1¾ cups milk
2 eggs, separated
4 tablespoons cooking oil,
   or melted butter

1. Sift the flour and measure.
2. Resift the flour with dry ingredients into a mixing bowl.
3. Beat egg yolks, then add milk and oil to the beaten egg yolks.
4. Gradually add liquid to dry ingredients and stir.
5. Fold in the stiffly beaten egg whites.
6. Heat the waffle iron, and pour in batter until about 1 inch from all sides.
7. Bake until mixture stops steaming. Don't lift the lid to peak. Serves 4-6.

Yorkshire Pudding

1 cup sifted flour
½ teaspoon salt
1 cup milk
3 eggs
   Fat drippings from roast

1. Sift flour and salt.
2. Add milk, stirring to prevent lumps.
3. Add eggs and beat for two minutes with an egg beater, then let mixture stand in a cool place for 20 minutes.
4. Heat oven to 425° F. Place 1 tablespoon of fat drippings in each cup of muffin pan. Place pan in the oven until the fat is bubbling hot.
5. Pour pudding batter into each cup of muffin pan to a depth of ½ to ¾ inch.
6. Place pan in 425° F. oven, but reduce heat immediately to 375° F. Bake for 30 minutes.
7. Serve puddings around the roast or with gravy.

Note
If desired, pudding may be baked in an 8 inch square pan. Pour ½ cup drippings in bottom of pan and proceed as above, but bake for 50 minutes. Cut in squares to serve.

Small Bannock

3 cups flour
   Dash of salt
6 teaspoons baking powder
2 tablespoons lard
   Water

1. Combine dry ingredients in a bowl.
2. Make a little well and pour the water in.
3. Mix into a dough and knead it.
4. Flatten it out and put it in the frying pan.
5. Cook on hot ashes over open fire or in the oven. Especially good fresh eaten with lard.
(Can also be made with boiled potatoes added.)

Bannock – Enriched

2½ cups flour
¼ cup skim milk powder
2 tablespoons egg powder
½ teaspoon salt
4 teaspoons baking powder
¾ cup water
1 tablespoon melted fat

1. Sift the dry ingredients. Mix them well in a bowl.
2. Add water and melted fat. Stir until the flour is wet.
3. Knead slightly, if desired.
4. Shape into mounds. Place in a greased frying pan.
5. Cook until golden brown on one side and then turn over to cook other side.

Note
1. Raisins may be added to bannock.
2. If the bannock is not stiff enough, more flour may be added.

Top-of-the-Stove Corn Bread

1 cup sifted flour
2 teaspoons double acting baking powder
3 tablespoons sugar
1 teaspoon salt
1 cup yellow corn meal
1 tablespoon egg powder and
3 tablespoons water *or*
1 egg, beaten
1 cup milk
¼ cup melted shortening *or* salad oil

1. Mix together 1 tablespoon egg powder and 3 tablespoons water and let stand for at least ½ hour before using.
2. Add the egg to the milk and melted shortening or salad oil.
3. Sift the flour, baking powder, sugar and salt, then add the corn meal.
4. Fold the egg mixture into the dry ingredients all at once and stir until the flour is just dampened.
5. Pour into a heavy fry pan that is well greased and hot. Cover tightly and bake over low heat for 25-30 minutes.

Tea Biscuits

2 cups sifted flour
4 teaspoons baking powder
½ teaspoon salt
⅓ cup cold shortening
⅔ cup milk

1. Sift flour, baking powder and salt into mixing bowl.
2. Cut in the shortening with 2 knives or pastry blender, until shortening is the size of large peas.
3. Pour milk into centre of flour mixture. Stir until all dry ingredients stick together.
4. Turn out on floured board and knead all the dough and crumbs together and pat to 1 inch thickness.
5. Cut with cookie cutter and place on ungreased pan.
6. Bake in very hot oven 450° F.–500° F. about 12 minutes.

Note
⅔ cup grated cheese may be added after cutting in the shortening.

Scotch Scones

2 cups flour
3 teaspoons double-acting baking powder
1 teaspoon salt
2 tablespoons sugar
1 tablespoon egg powder and 3 tablespoons water
¼ cup melted shortening *or* salad oil
3 tablespoons milk
½ cup sour cream
¼ teaspoon soda
Grated lemon rind
1 tablespoon sugar

1. Mix the egg powder and 3 tablespoons water and let stand ½ hour.
2. Combine egg mixture, melted shortening, 3 tablespoons milk and ½ cup sour cream to which ¼ teaspoon soda has been added.
3. Sift the flour, baking powder, salt and sugar together.
4. Pour the egg and milk mixture into the dry ingredients and stir until flour is just dampened.
5. Turn out on floured board and knead the dough 10 to 15 strokes.
6. Roll the dough to circular shape ½ inch thick and sprinkle top with sugar and grated lemon rind.
7. Cut the dough into 12 wedge-shaped pieces and place on greased baking sheet.
8. Bake in hot oven (425° F.) 15 to 20 minutes.

Note
½ cup raisins or currants, washed and dried may be added.

194

Cranberry Coffee Cake

2 cups sifted all-purpose flour
3 teaspoons baking powder
¾ teaspoon salt
½ cup sugar
5 tablespoons butter
1 egg beaten
½ cup milk
2½ cups cranberries

Topping Recipe

Mix ¼ cup all-purpose flour
with ½ cup sugar.
Cut in 3 tablespoons of chilled
butter.

1. Sift dry ingredients.
2. Cut in butter with a pastry blender until crumbly.
3. Mix beaten egg and milk.
4. Add to the flour mixture.
5. Stir slowly to mix and then beat until blended well.
6. Spread batter evenly into an 8″ × 8″ × 2″ buttered baking pan.
7. Sprinkle cranberries evenly over the top.
8. Mix the topping. It should have the consistency of coarse crumbs.
9. Sprinkle over the cranberries.
10. Bake at 375° for 30 to 35 minutes. Cut into squares and serve warm.

Apple Puffs

2 cups sifted flour
2 teaspoons double-acting baking powder
½ teaspoon salt
½ teaspoon cinnamon
1 tablespoon egg powder and 3 tablespoons water
1 cup milk
½ teaspoon vanilla
1 cup dehydrated apples
Hot fat for frying

1. Mix 1 tablespoon egg powder and 3 tablespoons water and let stand ½ hour before using.
2. Add 1 cup milk to egg mixture and ½ teaspoon vanilla.
3. Sift flour, baking powder, salt and cinnamon together.
4. Blend the milk and egg into the dry ingredients.
5. Simmer the dehydrated apples in water until tender. Drain them and add them to the batter.
6. Drop the batter by tablespoonfuls into hot deep fat (375° F.) and fry until golden brown, turning once.
7. Place on absorbent paper, then roll in granulated or confectioners sugar.

Oklahoma Squaw Bread

2 cups flour
1 tablespoon melted lard
1 teaspoon salt
2 teaspoons baking powder
1½ cups cold water

1. Roll thin, cut in squares, punch holes with knife.
2. Brown on both sides in deep fat.

CAKES

Applesauce Cake

½ cup shortening
¾ cup sugar
1 egg
1½ cups sifted all-purpose
    flour *or*
1⅔ cups pastry flour
½ cup raisins (optional)
½ teaspoon salt
1 teaspoon baking soda
2 tablespoons cocoa
1 teaspoon cinnamon
1 cup thick sweetened
    applesauce

1. Cream shortening until fluffy, add sugar gradually and cream well together.

2. Add well-beaten egg and beat thoroughly until light and creamy.

3. Mix and sift the flour, salt, baking soda, cocoa and cinnamon together.

4. Add alternately with the applesauce to the creamed mixture, combining lightly.

5. If raisins are used, sift a little of the dry ingredients over them before adding to cake mixture.

6. Bake in a greased pan 8″ × 8″ in a moderate oven (350° F.) for 45 minutes.

Dutch Apple Cake

2 tablespoons butter
1 cup sugar
1 egg
2 cups sifted all-purpose flour *or*
2¼ cups sifted pastry flour
2 teaspoons baking powder
1 teaspoon salt
¼ teaspoon nutmeg *or* cinnamon
¾ cup milk
1½ cups sliced apples
2 tablespoons sugar
1 tablespoon butter
½ cup light cream *or*
    evaporated milk

1. Cream butter and sugar, add beaten egg.

2. Sift flour, baking powder, salt and nutmeg.

3. Add alternately with milk, to creamed mixture.

4. Pour into a greased 9″ × 9″ pan.

5. Slice apples in thin even sections and arrange on batter to completely cover batter.

6. Sprinkle with sugar and dot with butter.

7. Bake in moderate oven 350° F. 35 to 40 minutes, pouring the ½ cup light cream over the apples when cake is half baked.

8. Serve with Apple Butterscotch Sauce.

Dried apples that have been pre-soaked may be substituted for fresh apples.

Applesauce Loaf

½ cup shortening
1 cup sugar
1 egg well beaten
1 can unsweetened applesauce
1¾ cups sifted flour
1¼ teaspoons cinnamon
1 teaspoon allspice
1 teaspoon nutmeg
¼ teaspoon ground cloves
½ teaspoon salt
1 teaspoon baking powder

1. Cream shortening in a mixing bowl with sugar.

2. Add egg and blend well; stir in applesauce.

3. Sift together dry ingredients and add to creamed mixture stirring only enough to blend.

4. Pour into loaf pan 9″ × 5″ × 3″ and bake at 350° F. for 50 to 60 minutes.

5. Remove from oven and cool slightly on wire rack before removing from pan; remove from pan and cool on rack.

Apricot Fruit Cake

4 cups all-purpose flour
1 tablespoon baking powder
¼ teaspoon salt
1 cup butter *or* margarine
1 cup sugar
4 eggs
   Grated rind of one orange
1 15 ounce can apricots *or*
2 cups dried apricots that
   have been pre-soaked
½ cup glacé cherries

1. Grease and line an 8-inch square pan.

2. Sift flour, baking powder and salt together.

3. Cream butter, add the sugar, add eggs, beating after each addition. Add grated orange rind.

4. Drain apricots well and cut in quarters.

5. Halve cherries.

6. Add fruit to flour mixture, then add to egg mixture. Mix well.

7. Put into prepared tin, pushing batter to the sides and corners.

8. Bake at 325° F. for 2 hours, or until a toothpick inserted in centre comes out clean.

To Glaze Cake
Boil the reserved apricot juice until thick, allow it to cool before using. Garnish with seasonal decoration. Allow cake to age for 10 days before serving for best results. To keep fresh, wrap in foil.

Gingerbread

¼ cup shortening
½ cup brown sugar
2 eggs, beaten
½ cup molasses
1½ cups sifted flour
1½ teaspoons ginger
⅛ teaspoon salt
¾ teaspoon soda
½ cup boiling water

1. Cream the shortening and add sugar, blending well.
2. Add the beaten eggs and molasses, continue beating until smooth.
3. Sift the flour, ginger, salt and soda together.
4. Add the sifted ingredients to the creamed mixture gradually.
5. Add the boiling water quickly, stirring just until blended.
6. Pour the batter into greased 9 inch square pan and bake in slow oven 300°–325° F. for 25 to 30 minutes.

Luscious Prune Cake

1 cup cooked prunes
½ cup shortening
1 cup sugar
2 eggs
1½ cups sifted all-purpose flour
2½ teaspoons baking powder
1 teaspoon salt
⅔ cup milk
1 teaspoon vanilla
1 ounce finely cut semi-sweet chocolate

1. Pit prunes and chop finely.
2. Cream shortening and sugar together thoroughly.
3. Add eggs one at a time, beating thoroughly after each addition.
4. Sift together flour, baking powder and salt.
5. Blend into creamed mixture alternately with milk.
6. Blend in vanilla, prunes and chocolate.
7. Turn into two greased 8-inch layer cake pans.
8. Bake in modern oven 350° F., about 35 minutes.
9. Let stand 5 or 10 minutes; turn out onto wire rack to cool.
10. Frost with a fluffy frosting and decorate with chocolate curls as desired.

Fluffy Frosting

1 cup brown sugar
¼ teaspoon cream of tartar
⅓ cup water
2 egg whites
1 teaspoon vanilla

1. Combine sugar, cream of tartar and ⅓ cup water.
2. Boil to 242°F.
3. Beat 2 egg whites until stiff.
4. Add hot syrup slowly, beating rapidly until frosting is of spreading consistency.
5. Stir in vanilla.

Miracle Whip Chocolate Cake

1 cup Miracle Whip salad dressing
1 cup white sugar
1 teaspoon vanilla
2 cups sifted flour
   Dash of salt
½ cup cocoa
1 teaspoon baking soda
1 teaspoon baking powder
1 cup cold water

1. Combine Miracle Whip and sugar, stirring until smooth. Add vanilla.

2. Sift flour, cocoa, soda, baking powder and salt together.

3. Add the dry ingredients to Miracle Whip mixture alternately with the water.

4. Blend well after each addition until smooth.

5. Pour into 2–8-inch layer pans and bake in a moderate oven 350° F. for 25–30 minutes. Decorate with your favorite icing.

Peach Upside-Down Cake

¼ cup soft butter *or* margarine
½ cup brown sugar (packed)
1½ cups drained canned peach slices
5 maraschino cherries
⅓ cup shortening
½ cup sugar
1 egg
1¼ cups sifted cake flour
1½ teaspoons baking powder
½ teaspoon salt
½ teaspoon grated orange rind
½ cup orange juice

1. Spread butter in bottom of 8-inch round baking dish; sprinkle with brown sugar and arrange very well-drained peaches and halved cherries on top.

2. Cream shortening and sugar together thoroughly.

3. Blend in unbeaten egg and beat well.

4. Sift together flour, baking powder and salt.

5. Add to creamed mixture alternately with orange rind and juice.

6. Pour batter carefully over peaches.

7. Bake in moderate oven 350° F. for 45 to 50 minutes, or until cake is done.

8. Allow to cool 5 to 10 minutes; invert over serving plate to remove cake, and allow syrup to drain a minute.

Butterscotch Bars

½ cup butter *or* margarine
½ cup brown sugar
1 cup sifted flour
2 eggs, unbeaten
⅛ teaspoon salt
1 cup brown sugar
1 teaspoon vanilla
2 tablespoons flour
½ teaspoon baking powder
1 cup chopped nuts
   Shredded cocoanut

1. Cream the butter and sugar thoroughly, then fold in 1 cup flour and blend well.

2. Press the mixture in an 8″ × 12″ pan and bake in moderate oven 325° F. for 10 minutes. Do not brown.

3. Combine 2 eggs, salt and 1 cup brown sugar and vanilla, then add 2 tablespoons flour and ½ teaspoon baking powder. Beat until light and creamy.

4. Add the chopped nuts, then spread the mixture over the cooked batter. Sprinkle the top with cocoanut and bake in a 325° F. oven for 10 minutes. Cut into squares while warm.

Eileen Thrower's Brownie Cake

1 cup butter
1 cup white sugar
4 tablespoons cocoa
2 eggs, unbeaten
¼ teaspoon salt
2 teaspoons vanilla
1 cup flour
1 cup chopped walnuts

1. Cream the butter, sugar and eggs together, then add the cocoa blending thoroughly. Add the vanilla.

2. Sift the flour and salt and mix into the creamed mixture, beating well, then add the chopped walnuts.

3. Spread the mixture in a cake pan and bake in a 300° F. oven for 30 minutes.

Mocha Icing

1½ cups icing sugar
3 tablespoons cocoa
3 tablespoons butter
3 tablespoons strong coffee

1. Cream the butter and add the icing sugar and cocoa alternately with the coffee, to make a thin icing.

2. Ice the cake the day before if possible.

Matrimonial Squares

1½ pounds dates
1½ cups boiling water
Grated rind of 1 lemon
Juice of 1 lemon
2 cups sifted flour
¼ teaspoon salt
1 teaspoon baking powder
½ teaspoon soda
½ cup brown sugar
2½ cups quick-cooking rolled oats
1 cup butter

1. Add the boiling water and lemon rind to the dates and cook over low heat until thickened. Remove from stove and add the lemon juice.

2. Sift the flour, salt, baking powder, soda and sugar together, then add the rolled oats.

3. Cut in the butter with two knives or pastry blender until mixture is crumbly.

4. Spread half of the flour mixture in a greased 12" x 8" x 2" pan and press down.

5. Pour the date mixture over this and spread evenly.

6. Cover the top with remaining flour mixture, patting it to make it smooth.

7. Bake in moderate oven 350° F. for 1 hour. Cool in the pan, then cut into squares.

COOKIES

Dad's Cookies

1 cup butter
1½ cups sugar
2 eggs
2 tablespoons corn syrup
2 cups rolled oats
½ cup cocoanut
2 cups flour
½ teaspoon salt
½ teaspoon allspice
2 teaspoons cinnamon
2 teaspoons ginger
3 teaspoons baking soda

1. Cream the butter and sugar together thoroughly.

2. Add the eggs and corn syrup and beat until light and creamy.

3. Sift together the flour, salt, spices and baking soda and combine with the rolled oats and cocoanut.

4. Fold the flour mixture into the creamed mixture blending well.

5. Drop by spoonful on greased baking sheet and bake in moderate oven about 15 minutes.

Drop (Fruit) Cookies

⅔ cup shortening
1 cup brown sugar
2 eggs
2 tablespoons milk
½ teaspoon vanilla
2 cups flour
1 teaspoon baking powder
¼ teaspoon baking soda
¼ teaspoon salt
1½ to 2 cups chopped
    fruit or chopped nuts

1. Cream shortening in a large bowl.
2. Slowly add sugar to shortening and beat until sugar and shortening are well mixed.
3. Add eggs and beat. (Use powdered eggs mixed with water).
4. Sift flour, baking powder, baking soda together.
5. Add sifted dry ingredients alternately with milk and vanilla.
6. Add chopped nuts and/or fruit.
7. Drop by spoonfuls onto a greased cookie sheet. Bake in a 375° F. oven for about 15 minutes.

Oatmeal Molasses Cookies

½ cup shortening
½ cup brown sugar, firmly
    packed
½ cup molasses
1 teaspoon vinegar
⅓ cup evaporated milk
2 eggs
1¾ cups sifted all-purpose flour
1 teaspoon baking soda
¼ teaspoon salt
2 teaspoons cinnamon
¾ teaspoon cloves
2 cups quick cooking oats
1 cup raisins

1. Cream shortening. Slowly add sugar. Add molasses. Beat well.
2. Add vinegar to milk and add to the above mixture.
3. Beat eggs into mixture. Use powdered eggs mixed with water.
4. Sift flour, soda, salt, cinnamon and cloves.
5. Stir in oats and add sifted dry ingredients.
6. Stir the mixture well. Add raisins.
7. Drop batter by spoonfuls onto cookie sheet and bake in a 375° F. oven for about 15 minutes. Makes 5 to 6 dozen cookies.

Rolled Oat Cookies

1 cup shortening
1 cup sugar
2 cups rolled oats
1¾ cups flour
3 teaspoons baking powder
1 teaspoon salt
2 tablespoons powdered milk
½ cup water

1. Cream shortening and sugar together.
2. Combine rolled oats, flour, baking powder, salt and powdered milk.
3. Add dry ingredients to creamed mixture alternately with water and blend well.
4. Turn out dough on floured board and roll to ¼ inch thickness.
5. Cut out circles with cookie cutter or use an ordinary drinking glass.
6. Place on cookie sheet and bake in moderate oven 350° F. for 10-12 minutes.

Jane's Peanut Butter Cookies

1 cup butter
1 cup peanut butter
1 cup white sugar
1 cup brown sugar
2 eggs
2 cups flour
1 teaspoon soda
1 teaspoon vanilla

1. Combine butter, peanut butter, sugar and eggs and beat until light and creamy. Add the vanilla.

2. Sift the flour and soda together and fold into the creamed mixture, mixing until a soft dough is formed. If too soft, sprinkle a little more flour over the dough and blend well.

3. Roll the dough into small balls and place on baking sheet about 1 inch apart.

4. With a fork, press the rolls flat. Bake in moderate oven 350° F. for about 10 minutes.

Oatmeal Cookies

1 cup butter
½ cup white sugar
½ cup brown sugar
1 egg
2½ cups oatmeal
1 cup flour
1 teaspoon soda
1 teaspoon vanilla

1. Combine the butter, white and brown sugar and egg and beat until creamy.

2. Sift the flour and soda together and fold into the creamed mixture alternately with the oatmeal, blending well after each addition.

3. Add the vanilla, then shape the dough into cookies with cooky cutter or glass. Bake in moderate oven (350° F.) for about 15 minutes.

Variation:
1 cup chopped walnuts may be added.

Top-of-the-Stove Cookies

2 cups white sugar
½ cup milk
½ cup shortening
1 teaspoon vanilla
Pinch of salt
2 cups oatmeal
1 cup coconut
1 square semi-sweet chocolate *or*
5 tablespoons cocoa

1. Combine the sugar, milk and shortening in a saucepan and bring to a boil. Boil for 1 minute then remove from heat.

2. Add the remaining ingredients and stir until blended.

3. Place in a greased square cake pan, let stand until firm and cut into squares.

Ethel's Jam Buns

2 cups flour
3 teaspoons baking powder
2 tablespoons sugar
¼ teaspoon salt
1 cup shortening
1 egg
½ cup milk
1 teaspoon vanilla
Jam

1. Mix the flour, baking powder, sugar and salt together.

2. Cream the shortening and egg together then add the milk and vanilla. Add dry ingredients.

4. Roll out the dough and cut in squares. Drop a little jam on centre of square and pinch the corners to seal.

5. Place in muffin tins and bake in 375° F. oven for 15 minutes.

Prune Refrigerator Cookies

1 cup brown sugar (packed)
½ cup white sugar
1 cup shortening
2 eggs
1 tablespoon vinegar
1 teaspoon vanilla
1 cup chopped cooked prunes
4 cups sifted all-purpose flour
1 teaspoon soda
1½ teaspoons salt

1. Cream sugars with shortening.

2. Add beaten eggs, vinegar, vanilla and prunes.

3. Sift flour with soda and salt; combine with first mixture.

4. Knead until smooth, shape into roll 2 inches in diameter and allow to chill in refrigerator overnight.

5. Slice as thin as possible and place on greased baking sheets.

6. Bake in hot oven (400° F.) about 10 minutes.

Joyce's Rolled Oat Cookies

3 cups rolled oats
3 cups flour
1 cup sugar
2 teaspoons salt
1 teaspoon soda
1½ cups lard
¾ cup cold water

1. Combine rolled oats, flour, sugar, salt and soda.

2. Work in the lard as for pastry.

3. Moisten with cold water.

4. Roll thin on board sprinkled with rolled oats, and cut into rounds with cooky cutter or glass.

5. Bake in moderate oven 350° F. for 15 minutes.

Note
Try making a sandwich of two cookies with cooked dates spread between them.

Sugar Cookies

½ cup shortening *or* rendered bear fat
½ cup sugar
1 tablespoon powdered milk
1½ cups flour
1½ teaspoons baking powder
¼ teaspoon salt
¼ cup water

1. Cream shortening or fat and sugar together.

2. Combine flour, powdered milk, baking powder and salt.

3. Add flour mixture alternately with water to the creamed mixture.

4. Turn out on floured board and roll lightly to about ¼ inch thickness.

5. Cut into desired shapes with cookie cutter.

6. Place on cookie sheet and bake in moderate oven 350° F. for 10-12 minutes.

CHAPTER VIII

VEGETABLES, SALADS
and
SALAD DRESSINGS

VEGETABLES

Vegetables add interest and excitement to a meal. They provide contrast in colour, flavour, texture, temperature and form. They are a valuable source of minerals and vitamins which are needed for proper growth and development of the body. They also provide cellulose which acts as an intestinal broom to keep the digestive tract clean and healthy. Canada's Food Guide recommends that we eat one serving of potatoes and at least two servings of other vegetables daily, preferably green or yellow vegetables, and often the vegetables chosen should be raw.

Until fairly recently, our choice of vegetables depended on the climate in which we lived. In the high Arctic, the only fresh vegetables available were the wild greens which carpeted the tundra

during the short Arctic summer. North of the tree-line, the long hours of sunlight help to hasten plant growth, but locating suitable soil for vegetable seeds was often a problem. Now, however, Provincial Departments of Agriculture can analyse soil samples, and recommend suitable compounds to improve the fertility of the soil, so that with ingenuity and perseverance, fresh vegetables can be grown almost any-where in the world. Even in areas where no soil is available, seeds can be planted in a mixture of decayed seaweed and fish waste or household refuse. By building or improvising greenhouses, hot beds, cold frames, window boxes or seed flats, vegetables can be given a head start while the nights are still cool but the days are lengthening. The results will be well worth the extra effort involved, for vegetables grown in the north can be without equal for size, colour and flavour.

Choosing Vegetables for the Family

By growing our own gardens and by developing wise shopping habits, it is pos-sible to have peak-of-the-season freshness in vegetables for most of the year. When purchasing fresh vegetables, buy the ones that are currently in season in order to obtain the best value for your money. The vegetables will be fresher, more attractive, have higher nutritive value and a better flavour. When choosing green leafy vege-tables, pick out the ones with the brightest colours, but examine them for wilted leaves, cuts, bruises and soft spots. Root vegetables should be firm, of medium size, and feel heavy for their size. They too, should be free of bruises or soft spots. If necessary, ask the store clerk to open sealed bags, so you can make sure that the quality of the vegetables is in keeping with the price you are paying. Don't be afraid to experiment with dried vegetables. Modern drying methods are such that long soaking and cooking is no longer necessary, and quite often the quality of the vege-tables may even be superior to that of the available fresh ones. Potatoes, onions, carrots, cabbage, parsley, red and green peppers, sweet potatoes and herbs can all be dried successfully, and the list is growing longer every year. Canned vegetables are generally more expensive and more imagination is required in their preparation. On the other hand, there is little or no waste, they can be kept for a long time without deteriorating, and if you buy by the grade, you can get good value for your money. Fresh frozen vegetables must be kept frozen until used and may also be a little more expensive. But little preparation is required, there is no waste, and the colour, flavour and nutritive value is comparable to fresh vegetables.

Preparing and Cooking Vegetables

Vegetables are excellent sources of vitamins and minerals, and if they can be eaten raw when freshly picked, very little of the nutrients are lost. Some vegetables require cooking to make them edible, however, and in order to prevent the loss of the valuable minerals and vitamins a good general rule to follow is to cook the vegetables as quickly as possible in as small an amount of water as possible, and do not over-cook them. Save the water drained from the vegetables for use in soups, gravies, stews and sauces. Always prepare the vegetables as close to meal-time as possible. Do not leave vegetables soaking in water that is later discarded, as the water-soluble vitamins will be lost. Cook vegetables in as large pieces as possible to avoid loss of nutrients through the exposed surface.

Cook vegetables with the skins on, whenever possible. If they must be peeled, peel them thinly, or preferably, simply brush or scrape them. Have the water boil-ing in the pot before adding the vegetables and cover the pot tightly. This not only reduces the cooking time but cuts down on the loss of Vitamin C through oxidation. Serve the vegetables as quickly as possible after they are cooked, to prevent loss of both flavour and nutritive value.

When cooking mild-flavoured green vegetables, wash them thoroughly, rinse them well, and cook them only in the water that clings to the leaves. The green colour may be preserved if the lid is left off the pot for the first two or three minutes of cooking. This allows the volatile acids to escape before they can destroy the colour. Cover the pot tightly for the remainder of the cooking time.

The strong flavour of turnip, onion, parsnip, cabbage, cauliflower and brussel sprouts can be reduced if they are cooked in a large amount of rapidly boiling water with the lid off. Drain them well when tender, but remember not to discard the cooking water, as it will contain the water-soluble vitamins and minerals! Again, do not over-cook.

To cook frozen vegetables, follow the directions given on the package. Freezing softens the tissues and generally cuts the cooking time in half.

When serving canned vegetables, the flavour may be improved if the liquid is drained from the vegetables and simmered on the stove until its volume is reduced by half. Then add the drained vegetables and quickly heat them through. If any liquid remains after heating, save it for using in soups and sauces etc.

Salad greens should be clean, crisp, cold and dry. Wash them thoroughly, rinse them, drain them, and, if they are not to be used immediately, store them in a plastic bag in the refrigerator so they will remain crisp until needed.

Storing Vegetables

Fresh Vegetables—Store in a clean, cool, dark, well-ventilated area. The temperature in the storage area should be as low as possible without freezing. Potatoes and root crops (with the exception of onions) require high humidity to prevent shrivelling, while vine crops such as squash, pumpkin and vegetable marrow keep longer if the humidity is low. Onions also should be kept dry. Make sure that the vegetables selected for storage are fully mature, free from damage and thoroughly dry. Remove tops and stems so moisture will not be drawn out to the leaves. If potatoes start to sprout, remove the sprouts immediately or the potatoes will start to shrivel and will become soft. Discard the sprouts.

Dried Vegetables—Keep packages tightly sealed and store in a cool dry place. Refrigeration is not necessary. Once the package is opened, transfer the contents to a container with a tightly fitting lid, and use as soon as possible.

Canned Vegetables—Store in a cool, dry area, preferably around 50° F. If the vegetables are frozen accidentally, keep them frozen until used. Opened cans of vegetables should be covered and kept in the refrigerator and used up as quickly as possible.

Frozen Vegetables—Frozen vegetables should be stored at 0° F. and the temperature should remain constant at that point to avoid deterioration.

Note: If root vegetables such as potatoes, carrots and beets, accidentally become frozen, keep them frozen until needed, then cook them without thawing them first. Peel after cooking. Add approximately ½ hour to the boiling or baking time for potatoes.

EDIBLE WILD PLANTS

No northern cookbook would be complete without some mention of edible wild plants. Even though most of them are available only during the short summer months, they can provide delicious variety to the menu, and some of them are excellent sources of vitamin C. No poisonous plants, berries or mushrooms have been reported from north of the tree-line, and old-timers will insist that nothing poisonous grows in the Northwest Territories.

Caution: If you are south of the tree-line however, and want to investigate the flavour of wild plants, be sure you are thoroughly familiar with the appearance of Water Hemlock, the Death Cup Mushroom and the Baneberry. These three are poisonous and can cause death.

GREENS

Wild Greens

Bracken or Brake-Fern
Dandelion
Lamb's Quarters or Pigweed
Scurvy Grass
Sourdock
Strawberry Blight or Red Flowering Pigweed
Wild Mustard

1. Choose only tender young leaves.
2. Wash well, rinse, then cook in a small amount of water just until tender.
3. Drain and serve with butter, salt and pepper.

Variations:
Use the tender young leaves as salad greens. They should be clean, cold and crisp.

Fireweed or Willow Herb

This prolific perennial plant with the beautiful purple flowers grows throughout the north, on the tundra in isolated semi-sheltered locations, and on the barrens in sandy, gravelly soils. The new shoots that poke through the soil in the springtime can be picked and used as a substitute for asparagus. Later on, the fleshy leaves can be picked and prepared as any other green. They resemble spinach in flavour and are delicious served with butter, salt, pepper and a sprinkle of vinegar.

Fiddleheads

These are the young curled-up bracken or fern fronds. Pick them just after they appear above the surface of the ground, before they straighten out. Wash and cook in a very small amount of water. Drain and serve with butter and seasonings. Later on, the tender growing portion at the base of the fern stem is delicious either boiled or raw. The rootstalks are also good, although rather woody. Try cleaning and trimming them, then cooking them around a roast for the last 30 to 45 minutes of cooking time.

Labrador Tea

Dry fresh leaves of this shrubby plant, which is found in muskeg areas all across Canada (including boggy or peaty soils throughout the Arctic). Place them in a shallow pan in the oven or on top of the stove at low heat. When dry, crumble them and use as a substitute for tea.

The infusion is reminiscent of an oriental tea and is high in Vitamin C.

Mountain Sorrel

This perennial herb is found throughout the barren lands, and produces fresh growth and green leaves all summer. Both the leaves and stems are juicy and edible and have a flavour similar to rhubarb. They may be used chopped up in a salad, cooked as a green, or puréed to make a cream soup. In some areas mountain sorrel is picked and fermented as a sauerkraut.

Scurvy Grass

This is a fleshy herb with crisp tender leaves and stems, and a flavour similar to water-cress. Excellent served raw in salads or sandwiches and, as the name implies, it is high in Vitamin C.

Spruce Tips

Pick young twigs and leaves from the black or white spruce. Wash, then steep in boiling water for a drink high in Vitamin C.

Poplar and Jack Pine

Another excellent source of vitamin C is the new growth found between the wood and the bark of poplar or jack pine. Scrape the pulp into a bowl and eat with a spoon.

Willow Tips

Pick the willow leaf buds, just after they show green in the springtime. Serve in a bowl with milk and sugar. Peter Murdoch says they taste like a crunchy breakfast cereal (and are a good source of Vitamin C).

Wild Rhubarb

This reddish-stemmed perennial grows 3 to 6 feet high in the Yukon and along the banks of the Mackenzie River and its tributaries. Pick the young, bright red, juicy stems shortly after the snow disappears. Cut them up and simmer them gently in a small amount of water. Add butter, salt and pepper and serve as a vegetable or add sugar to taste and a dash of cinnamon for a refreshing dessert.

ROOTS

Alpine Bistort

This low perennial herb is common north of the tree-line on the tundra. Its root is about the size of a pecan and tastes best when cooked. The spike of the plant bears quantities of small bulbs which become reddish when ripe and, when stripped from the spike, make a sweet, nut-like nibble with an almond flavour.

Dandelion Roots

Trim the roots, wash and peel. Dry thoroughly in a shallow pan over a low heat, or in a 200° F. oven. When dried, grind them, and use them as a substitute for coffee.

Liquorice Root (Masu)

This perennial herb belongs to the pea family, and the root resembles the carrot in flavour. Dig the roots in August or in the springtime before the new growth starts. Wash, peel, boil till tender and serve with butter, salt and pepper.

Woolly Lousewort

Called Ussusaq by the Eskimo, this perennial herb grows up to 8 inches in height and is common throughout the Arctic tundra. In June the flowering stems may be used raw in salads, or boiled as greens. The roots taste like sweet young carrots and may be eaten raw or boiled and served as a hot vegetable with butter, salt and pepper.

Fresh Asparagus

12 stalks asparagus
½ teaspoon salt
1 tablespoon butter
¼ teaspoon pepper

1. Clean the asparagus and remove the scales from the stalks. Tie in a bundle.
2. Place the bundles with the tips up in boiling water, to which ½ teaspoon salt has been added. The water should cover the stalks but not the tips. Cover.
3. Cook until stalks are tender.
4. Remove the bundle from the water, taking care not to break the tips.
5. Put in serving dish, coat lightly with butter, sprinkle with pepper. Serves 3.

Variations
1. Serve with white sauce, garnished with a sprinkle of paprika.
2. Serve on hot buttered toast with a cheese sauce.
3. Cut the asparagus in pieces. Cook the stalks first until almost tender, then add the tips for the last few minutes of cooking. Add to 1 cup of medium white sauce. Serve hot on toast, garnished with hard cooked eggs, peeled and sliced.
4. Canned asparagus may be used in place of the fresh cooked asparagus.

Company Beans

1 15-ounce can green beans
1 tablespoon chopped red pepper
1 tablespoon chopped green pepper
1 tablespoon chopped onion
1 tablespoon butter
½ teaspoon salt
¼ teaspoon pepper

1. Drain the liquid from the beans and let it simmer on top of the stove until half of it has evaporated.
2. Add chopped pepper and onions and simmer till tender.
3. Add drained beans, mix and heat through.
4. Drain any remaining liquid and season to taste.
5. Place vegetables in hot serving dish, dot with butter and serve.

Variations
1. Substitute dried onions and red and green pepper flakes for the fresh ones. Add to the liquid and simmer as in step 1 above.
2. Use fresh or canned button mushrooms in place of the onion and green peppers. Add a dash of garlic salt, and sprinkle with slivered almonds before serving.

Baked Beans, Western Style

1   pound navy or pea beans
1   large onion, sliced
2   tablespoons oil
¼   cup vinegar
½   cup catsup
1½ cups canned tomatoes
2   tablespoons molasses
4   tablespoons brown sugar
2   teaspoons salt
¼   teaspoon pepper
¼   teaspoon dry mustard
½   pound salt pork, diced

1. Wash beans thoroughly, then drain well.

2. Cover with water and soak overnight.

3. In the morning, add 1 teaspoon salt to the beans and simmer them over low heat until they can be pierced with a toothpick, about ½ hour.

4. Heat the oil in a heavy pot, add the thinly sliced onion and sauté for 3 minutes.

5. Add vinegar, catsup, tomatoes, molasses, brown sugar, remaining salt, pepper and dry mustard. Bring to a boil, reduce heat and simmer for 5 minutes.

6. Drain the beans, saving the liquid, and place them in the bean pot in layers with the diced salt pork.

7. Add the sauce, and enough liquid drained from the beans to cover.

8. Cover and bake in a 300° F. oven for 6-8 hours, adding more liquid as needed.

Note: Sweet pickle juice may be used in place of the vinegar and fresh side pork (fried and drained) in place of the salt pork, for a tasty variation.

Dilly Beans

1 15-ounce can wax beans
1 tablespoon fresh *or*
   dried dill leaves
1 tablespoon butter
½ teaspoon salt
¼ teaspoon pepper

1. Drain liquid from can of wax beans and simmer on top of stove until half of it has evaporated. (If using dried dill, add it to the liquid before simmering).

2. Add beans and heat through, then drain.

3. Wash the dill thoroughly.

4. Toss beans with fresh dill and butter.

5. Season to taste and serve.

Variations
If you have your own garden, freshly picked wax beans and dill are delicious. Cook the beans in a small amount of water just until tender, then drain them. Add the washed dill, and the butter and season to taste. Toss lightly and serve hot.

Spanish Green Beans

2½ cups cooked green beans *or*
1 15-ounce can green string beans
1 teaspoon salt
¼ teaspoon pepper
1 teaspoon mustard
1 teaspoon sugar
I cup tomato soup
2 slices bacon
½ cup grated cheese

1. Dice the bacon and fry it crisp. Drain the beans.

2. Remove bacon and add rest of ingredients to the fat.

3. Add drained beans and crisp bacon and reheat.

Beet Greens

2 pounds fresh beet greens
1 tablespoon butter
½ teaspoon salt
¼ teaspoon pepper

1. Use the tops from young beets, or the beets thinned from the vegetable garden.

2. Wash thoroughly in at least two waters and rinse well. Trim and discard coarse stems and roots.

3. Place in a heavy pot with a tightly fitting lid. Do not add water, the water that clings to the leaves after rinsing should be enough to prevent the greens from burning. Cook until tender.

4. Drain, chop coarsely, dot with butter, season to taste and serve. Serves 4.

Variations
1. Sprinkle with white wine vinegar before serving.

2. Add 2 slices of cooked, crumbled bacon and sprinkle with nutmeg just before serving.

Harvard Beets

1 tablespoon cornstarch *or*
2 tablespoons flour
½ cup sugar
½ tablespoon salt
½ cup vinegar
2 teaspoons margarine *or* butter
3 cups cooked beets, sliced *or*
   diced

1. Mix the cornstarch or flour, sugar and salt.

2. Add the vinegar and boil 5 minutes, stirring constantly.

3. Add the margarine and beets and let stand 10 minutes to blend flavours.

4. Reheat if necessary before serving.

Bracken or Brake Fern

1 pound of bracken
1 egg, well beaten
1 cup fine bread crumbs
½ teaspoon salt
   Few grains of pepper

1. Wash the shoots carefully, tie in small bunches and stand upright in boiling salted water.

2. Cook about twenty minutes or just until tender.

3. Remove from water and drain thoroughly.

4. Beat the egg until light and foamy.

5. Add salt and pepper and beat again.

6. Dip the bracken in the beaten egg, then in the bread crumbs and fry in butter until a lovely golden brown. Serves 2.

Broccoli

1½ pounds fresh
   broccoli
1 teaspoon salt
2 tablespoons butter
½ teaspoon salt
¼ teaspoon pepper

1. Rinse broccoli well, then soak in 1 quart cold water to which 1 teaspoon of salt has been added for 10 minutes.

2. Drain from water, separate flowerets from main stalk, and split the stalks. Discard any woody portions.

3. Boil until tender in enough boiling water to cover, leaving the lid off.

4. Drain, coat with butter, add salt and pepper and serve. Serves 4.

Variations

1. Serve with a white sauce made from 1 cup milk, 2 tablespoons butter and 2 tablespoons flour, ½ teaspoon salt, ¼ teaspoon pepper. Melt the butter, add the flour and seasonings and stir until the flour has absorbed the butter. Gradually add the cold milk, stirring constantly until thick and smooth. Reduce heat and simmer 7 minutes.

2. Serve with cheese sauce. Use recipe for white sauce above, but add ¼ cup grated cheese at the last and simmer until cheese has melted. Sprinkle a dash of paprika over the sauce for added colour.

Brussel Sprouts

1 pound fresh brussel sprouts
2 tablespoons butter
½ teaspoon salt
¼ teaspoon pepper

1. Wash brussel sprouts, remove outer leaves if discolored or wilted.

2. Place in enough boiling water to cover and boil just until tender, leaving the lid off. Do not overcook, as this reduces the colour and strengthens the flavour.

3. Drain well, coat with butter, salt and pepper. Serve hot. Serves 4.

Variations

1. Serve with white sauce or cheese sauce (see broccoli, for recipe).

2. Cook brussel sprouts as above, then place in a buttered baking dish. Mix 1 tin condensed cream of mushroom sauce with ¼ cup of milk and pour over the sprouts. Top with ½ cup grated cheddar cheese mixed with 1 cup buttered bread crumbs. Bake in 350° F. oven till contents are well heated and the top is nicely browned (about 30 to 40 minutes). Serve hot.

Cabbage Custard Ring

4¼ cups finely shredded
    raw cabbage
2½ cups rich milk
6 slices bacon
3 eggs
1 teaspoon salt
¼ teaspoon pepper
⅛ teaspoon nutmeg
1 cup fine dry bread crumbs

1. Scald the milk in the top of a double boiler, then set aside to cool.
2. Fry the bacon until crisp, drain on paper, then crumble it.
3. Beat the eggs until light and foamy, add salt and pepper and nutmeg.
4. Add the raw cabbage, the crumbled bacon and the bacon fat.
5. Add the bread crumbs.
6. Butter generously a two-quart ring mold and pour in the mixture.
7. Place the mold in a pan of hot water. Bake in a 350° F. oven for 40 minutes.
8. Unmold on a large platter and fill center with creamed peas, carrots or hard-cooked eggs. Serves 8.

Glorified Cabbage

4 cups cabbage, coarsely cut
1 cup medium white sauce
1 cup peanuts, chopped
1 teaspoon salt
⅛ teaspoon white pepper
¼ teaspoon celery salt
1 cup buttered bread crumbs
½ cup grated Cheddar cheese

1. Butter a quart size casserole well.
2. Place 1 cup of cabbage in bottom and then sprinkle over it ¼ cup peanuts.
3. Fill casserole in like manner until all cabbage and peanuts are used.
4. Add seasonings to white sauce, then pour over the cabbage.
5. Bake in a 350° oven for 30 to 40 minutes.
6. Remove from oven, cover with grated cheese and top with buttered bread crumbs.
7. Return to oven to melt the cheese and toast the bread crumbs.

Cabbage, Rice and Tomato Casserole

2 cups shredded cabbage
¾ cup cooked rice
2 cups tomatoes
1 cup grated cheddar cheese
2 strips crisp bacon, crumbled
1 cup buttered crumbs
2 teaspoons sugar
½ teaspoon salt
⅛ teaspoon pepper

1. Mix grated cabbage, rice, tomatoes and crumbled bacon with seasonings in a 2 quart casserole.
2. Cover with a layer of grated cheese.
3. Top with buttered crumbs.
4. Bake at 350° F. for 35 minutes. Serves 4.

Braised Cabbage

1 medium-size cabbage
1 onion sliced thin
1 diced carrot
1 diced turnip (small)
1 diced stalk of celery
3 sprigs chopped parsley
1 tablespoon minced sweet green pepper
⅛ teaspoon of savory seasoning
1 pinch of thyme
2 cups water drained from cabbage
  Salt and pepper to taste
  Few grains cayenne
1 bouillon cube
1 tablespoon cornstarch
2 tablespoons butter

1. Wash cabbage, trim and cut out the core.

2. Cover with salted boiling water and cook rapidly uncovered, until wilted (about 5 minutes).

3. Drain in a sieve.

4. Add chopped vegetables and seasonings to 2 cups cabbage water in deep saucepan.

5. Lay the cabbage on top.

6. Boil until all the vegetables are tender (about 10 minutes).

7. Lift out cabbage, drain and cut into neat serving pieces and put in a hot serving dish.

8. Dissolve a bouillon cube in the hot vegetable stock.

9. Add 1 tablespoon cornstarch rubbed into 2 tablespoons butter; stir constantly until thickened.

10. Reduce heat, simmer for 7 minutes, then pour over the cabbage. Serves 6.

Honey Carrots

6 medium carrots
1 tablespoon honey
1 tablespoon butter
  Salt and pepper

1. Scrape and slice the carrots in 4 lengthwise sections 2 inches long.

2. Cook about 10 minutes in a small amount of water.

3. Drain and add the honey and butter.

4. Salt and pepper to taste.

Carrots with Orange Sauce

4　tablespoons sugar
1　tablespoon flour
1　cup boiling water
¼　cup orange juice
1　tablespoon grated orange rind
1　tablespoon butter
6　medium carrots, cooked and sliced, *or*
1　tin of canned carrots, drained

1. Mix sugar and flour in saucepan.

2. Add boiling water and cook until clear, stirring constantly.

3. Cook and stir for 1 minute longer.

4. Add orange juice, rind, and fat to sugar mixture.

5. Add carrots, and heat until carrots are hot. Serves 4.

Glazed Carrots

4　medium-sized carrots
1½ tablespoons butter
½　cup sugar
½　teaspoon salt
　　Dash of pepper
½　cup vegetable water

1. Wash and scrape carrots; cut in slices, strips or cubes.

2. Cook in boiling, salted water 15 minutes; drain; reserve ½ cup of the vegetable water.

3. Add butter, sugar, vegetable water and seasonings to the partially cooked carrots, continue cooking until carrots are tender and glazed, turning them carefully in the syrup. Serves 4.

Pickled Carrots

12　small carrots
2　cups vinegar
2　cups water
2　tablespoons sugar

1. Choose small carrots uniform in size. Scald them and rub off the skins.

2. Boil in salted water until tender.

3. Drain, place in clean jars.

4. Combine vinegar, water and sugar; boil five minutes and pour over the carrots.

5. Seal jars, let stand for 2 days before using.

Sweet and Pungent Carrots

4　cups carrots
2　tablespoons fat
1　cup boiling water
3　tablespoons sugar
1　teaspoon salt
2　tablespoons cornstarch
¼　cup water
¼　teaspoon soy sauce

1. Slice carrots diagonally and cook in 2 tablespoons fat for 3 minutes.

2. Add 1 cup boiling water, sugar and salt and cook until tender (about 10 minutes).

3. Blend cornstarch and cold water and soy sauce.

4. Add to carrots and cook until thickened.

Cauliflower with Parsley Sauce

1 small cauliflower
½ teaspoon salt
1 cup milk
1 tablespoon butter
1 tablespoon flour
½ teaspoon salt
¼ teaspoon pepper
1 tablespoon chopped fresh *or* dried parsley

1. Choose a firm white cauliflower, remove outer leaves. Soak, top down, in cold water for 20 minutes. Drain.

2. Place whole head in enough boiling salted water to cover. Cook rapidly just until tender, leaving the lid off the pot.

3. In a small pot, make the parsley sauce as follows: Melt the butter, add the flour, salt and pepper and stir till smooth. Gradually add the cup of cold milk, stirring constantly until thick. Reduce the heat, add the parsley, cover and keep hot until needed.

4. When the cauliflower is tender, carefully remove it to a hot serving dish. Pour the parsley sauce over it and serve immediately.

Corn Vegetable Soufflé

2 cups canned corn, cream style (*or* use any leftover *or* freshly prepared vegetable)
1 cup thick white sauce
3 eggs, separated
¼ cup melted butter
½ teaspoon salt
⅛ teaspoon nutmeg
⅛ teaspoon pepper
3 tablespoons bread crumbs
2 teaspoons butter

1. Mash corn; combine with white sauce.

2. Beat yolks until thick. Add butter and corn stirring until well mixed.

3. Add salt to egg whites; beat to form softly rounded peaks. Fold into corn mixture. Season to taste.

4. Pour corn mixture into a 6- to 8-inch baking dish; sprinkle with crumbs and dot with butter. Set in a shallow pan of hot water.

5. Bake soufflé at 350° F. for 30 to 35 minutes; serve immediately. Serves 6.

Scalloped Corn and Oysters

1 10-ounce can oysters
2 cups cream style corn
1½ cups cracker crumbs
2 tablespoons dehydrated onion flakes
¼ cup milk powder
¼ teaspoon salt
Dash pepper
1 tablespoon egg powder mixed with 3 tablespoons warm water
1 cup water
1 teaspoon Worcestershire sauce
2 tablespoons melted butter
½ cup cracker crumbs

1. Mix 1½ cups cracker crumbs, onion flakes, milk powder, salt and pepper.

2. Combine the egg powder mixed with 3 tablespoons warm water, 1 cup water and Worcestershire sauce with the cracker crumbs.

3. Add the oysters and the corn to the mixture, then pour into a greased casserole.

4. Mix ½ cup cracker crumbs and 2 tablespoons melted butter and spread over top of casserole.

5. Bake in moderate oven 350° F. for 1 hour. Serves 6.

Corn Fritters

1 can corn niblets
1 cup flour
1 teaspoon salt
1 teaspoon baking powder
2 eggs
¼ cup milk
1 pound shortening *or*
2 cups vegetable oil
   for deep fat frying

1. Sift flour, salt and baking powder.

2. Beat eggs, add milk and corn.

3. Add liquid and corn to sifted dry ingredients and mix well.

4. Heat shortening or oil in a deep pot to 360° F. or until a 1-inch cube of bread will brown in 60 seconds.

5. Drop batter by tablespoonsful into hot fat and fry till golden brown, about 4 to 5 minutes, turning once.

6. Drain on absorbent paper. Serves 4-6.

Note
Egg powder may be used instead of fresh eggs. Use 2 tablespoons egg powder blended with 6 tablespoons water to equal 2 eggs. Add ¼ teaspoon more baking powder to the flour.

Casserole of Canned Corn

1   12-ounce can creamed corn
1   large onion thinly sliced *or*
2   tablespoons dehydrated
    onion flakes
¼ cup butter
1½ cups dry bread crumbs
½ teaspoon salt
¼ teaspoon pepper
1   tablespoon Worcestershire
    sauce

1. Melt the butter in a small pan, remove from heat and add the bread crumbs, salt, pepper and Worcestershire sauce. Stir till well mixed.

2. In a greased baking dish, put a layer of creamed corn, a layer of onion rings then a layer of bread crumbs and continue alternating the layers until full, ending with crumbs on top.

3. Bake in a shallow pan of water in a 350° F. oven for 45 minutes.

Variations
1. Substitute thinly sliced green pepper rings for the sliced onions.

2. Add 2 tablespoons chopped red pimiento to the corn and crumbs.

3. For a special occasion, add layers of fresh oysters to the casserole.

Creamed Mushrooms

1   pound fresh mushrooms
2   tablespoons butter
¼   teaspoon salt
¼   teaspoon pepper
2   tablespoons flour
1   cup milk

1. Clean mushrooms by scraping stem and peeling membrane from cap if necessary. Slice.
2. Melt butter in small fry pan, add cut-up mushrooms and sauté over medium heat till lightly browned, about 3-4 minutes.
3. Add flour and seasonings, stirring until the flour absorbs the butter.
4. Add the milk gradually, stirring constantly until mixture is thick and creamy.
5. Serve hot on toast. Serves 2.

Variations
1. Add 1 cup canned peas. Heat before serving.
2. Add 2 or 3 diced, hard cooked eggs, 2 tablespoons chopped green pepper, ½ teaspoon curry powder and a dash of garlic salt. Serve with rice cooked in bouillon or beef stock.

Amber Onions

6   large onions
2   tablespoons butter
2   tablespoons honey
2   tablespoons lemon juice
½   teaspoon salt
¼   teaspoon pepper
¼   teaspoon paprika

1. Peel onions (under water, if they make you weep!). Cut in half crosswise.
2. Place onions in a buttered baking dish.
3. Melt the butter, add the honey, lemon juice, salt and pepper and heat just until the honey is liquified and the ingredients are blended.
4. Pour the sauce over the onions, sprinkle with paprika, cover and bake at 350° F. for 1 hour.
5. Serve with wild game, or on hot buttered toast with sausages for a quick supper dish. Serves 6.

Fresh Onion Pickles

4   medium onions
1   cup white wine vinegar
1   cup sugar
¼   teaspoon ground cloves
1   cinnamon stick *or*
½   teaspoon ground cinnamon
1   teaspoon celery seed
½   teaspoon salt

1. Simmer vinegar, sugar and spices for 10 minutes. Let cool.
2. Slice fresh onions into a clean jar or narrow bowl. Add syrup. Chill at least 12 hours before using. Delicious with egg sandwiches.

Variation
Save the pickle juice (and the jar) when you use sweet pickles, then slice the fresh onions directly into the pickle jar. Cover and chill for at least 12 hours. These pickles will keep well for 4 or 5 days.

Onions

1 pound cooking onions
2 tablespoons butter
½ teaspoon salt
¼ teaspoon pepper

1. Peel the onions under water. Cut up or leave whole as desired.

2. Place the onions in rapidly boiling water and cook with the lid off, just until tender. There should be enough water in the pot to cover the onions.

3. Drain, add butter and seasonings and serve. Serves 6.

Variations
1. Serve with a medium white sauce made from 2 tablespoons butter, 2 tablespoons flour and 1 cup of milk.

2. Serve with a cheese sauce (made by adding ½ cup grated cheese to the white sauce).

3. Serve with a mushroom sauce. Use 1 can cream of mushroom soup. Heat until smooth and creamy, stirring constantly. Do not dilute. Cream of celery soup or cream of green pea soup may also be used.

4. Canned whole onions may be substituted if desired.

French Fried Onion Rings

3 large onions
½ cup flour
½ teaspoon salt
½ teaspoon baking powder
2 teaspoons vegetable oil
1 egg, beaten
¼ tablespoon milk
2 pounds shortening *or*
4 cups vegetable oil
  for frying

1. Peel onions under water. Separate into rings.

2. Sift the flour, salt and baking powder.

3. Add the vegetable oil and stir till smooth.

4. Add the milk to the beaten egg.

5. Add the milk and egg mixture to the flour mixture and beat till thick and smooth.

6. Dip onion rings into the batter.

7. Heat the oil in a deep kettle to 365° F., or until a 1-inch cube of bread will brown in 60 seconds. (The oil should be at least 3 inches deep, with at least 3 inches between the level of the fat and the top of the kettle, to prevent the fat from boiling over when the food is added).

8. Remove onion rings from the batter and fry 3 or 4 at a time until golden brown. Drain on absorbent paper. Keep hot until needed. Be sure to bring the fat back up to 365° F. after each batch of rings is fried before adding the next batch. This prevents the food from absorbing more fat than is necessary.

Cucumbers and Onions in Sour Cream

1 medium cucumber
2 spanish onions
2 cups cream
1 tablespoon sugar
2 tablespoons vinegar *or* sweet pickle juice
½ teaspoon salt
¼ teaspoon black pepper

1. Wash, peel if desired, and slice the cucumber in thin slices in a glass or pottery (not metal) serving dish.

2. Add thinly sliced onions.

3. Add vinegar, sugar and seasonings to the cream and pour over cucumber and onion slices.

4. Chill for at least ½ hour before serving.

Variations

1. Commercial sour cream may be substituted for the sweet cream and vinegar. Dilute with milk to make it of pouring consistency.

2. Add ¼ teaspoon celery seed to the sour cream.

3. Add 2 tablespoons chopped fresh dill fern.

Pan Fried Onions

4 medium cooking onions
2 tablespoons butter
½ teaspoon salt
¼ teaspoon pepper

1. Peel onions under water. Slice or dice.

2. Melt butter in heavy fry pan.

3. Add onions and seasonings.

4. Reduce heat and simmer until onions are translucent. Do not burn.

5. Serve hot. Serves 2.

Pan Fried Onion Rings

4 medium onions
3 tablespoons butter
¾ cup milk
½ cup flour
½ teaspoon salt
¼ teaspoon pepper

1. Peel onions under water. Slice crosswise in ¼ inch thick slices. Separate into rings. Soak rings in milk in a bowl.

2. Add salt and pepper to flour and mix well.

3. Remove rings from milk, drain well, then dredge in seasoned flour.

4. Melt butter in heavy fry pan.

5. Pan fry onion rings till golden brown. Serves 4.

Scalloped Onions

4 cups thinly sliced onions
3 tablespoons butter
½ teaspoon salt
⅛ teaspoon pepper
¾ cup thick white sauce
¼ cup soft bread crumbs
3 tablespoons grated cheese
⅛ teaspoon paprika

1. Wash and peel onions; slice ¼-inch thick.

2. Heat butter in saucepan; add onions, cover, and cook until golden, stirring two or three times.

3. Place onoins in shallow, 6 to 8-inch baking dish; add seasonings and white sauce.

4. Sprinkle top with crumbs, cheese, and paprika. Bake at 375° F. for 20 minutes.

Stuffed Onions

12 medium size onions
2 cups cooked salmon
2 tablespoons minced green pepper
½ teaspoon salt
¼ teaspoon pepper
¼ cup flour
2 eggs, well beaten
¾ cup fine bread crumbs

1. Peel the onions and cook in boiling salted water thirty minutes or until just tender.
2. Drain, cool, cut a slice from top of each onion, remove center leaving 2 or 3 layers of onion to make a firm shell.
3. Flake the salmon, add green pepper, the chopped onion centers, salt and pepper.
4. Sprinkle each onion lightly with flour, dip in the well beaten eggs, then roll in crumbs.
5. Fill onion centers with the salmon, sprinkle a few crumbs over the top, place close together in a well greased baking dish.
6. Bake in a 400° F. oven for 45 minutes until tender and nicely browned.

Parsnip Fritters

1 pound fresh parsnips
1 tablespoon butter
½ teaspoon salt
½ cup flour
½ teaspoon baking powder
1 egg
2 tablespoons milk
1 pound shortening *or*
2 cups vegetable oil
for deep fat frying

1. Wash parsnips, peel or scrape and cut up, removing any woody core.
2. Cook until tender in rapidly boiling water, leaving the lid off the pot.
3. Drain and mash well with butter and salt.
4. Sift flour and baking powder, add beaten egg and milk, then combine with mashed parsnip.
5. Heat shortening or vegetable oil in a deep kettle to 360° F. (or until a 1-inch cube of bread will brown in 60 seconds).
6. Drop parsnip batter by tablespoons into hot fat. Fry till golden brown, about 3 to 5 minutes, turning once.
7. Drain on absorbent paper. Keep hot till needed. Serves 4.
   Note
   These may be made the day before and reheated in the oven before serving.

Peas and Mushrooms

1 cup cooked or canned mushrooms
½ cup sliced onion
2 tablespoons cooking fat
¼ teaspoon salt
¼ teaspoon nutmeg
⅛ teaspoon dried marjoram
2 cups cooked drained peas

1. Cook onions in the fat until tender.
2. Add rest of ingredients and blend well.
3. Reheat and serve.

Creamed Peas

1 15-ounce can peas
1 tablespoon butter
2 tablespoons flour
1 cup milk
½ teaspoon salt
¼ teaspoon pepper
¼ teaspoon paprika

1. Drain peas from liquid in the can, then simmer the liquid on top of the stove until half of it has evaporated.

2. Add the peas and heat through, reduce heat.

3. Make a white sauce as follows: Melt the butter, add flour and seasonings and stir until flour absorbs the butter. Gradually add the milk, stirring constantly till mixture is smooth and has thickened.

4. Drain the hot peas from the liquid and add them to the white sauce. Sprinkle with paprika before serving.

Variations
1. Add 12 tiny white cooked onions to the creamed peas before serving.

2. Add 1 tablespoon dried onion flakes to the liquid drained from the can of peas before simmering.

3. Add ½ teaspoon onion salt, 1 teaspoon Worcestershire sauce and 1 tablespoon chopped pimiento to the creamed peas before serving.

4. Add 2 chopped hard boiled eggs and 1 tablespoon chopped ripe olives to the creamed peas before serving.

Stuffed Green Peppers

6 sweet green peppers
2 tablespoons flour
½ teaspoon salt
2 tablespoons butter
1 cup top milk or evaporated milk
1½ cups ground meat
¼ teaspoon grated onion
½ cup buttered crumbs

1. Select peppers of suitable size and shape for stuffing; cut slice from end; remove tongue and seeds.

2. Make white sauce from the next 4 ingredients; add meat and grated onion.

3. Fill peppers with the mixture; cover with buttered crumbs.

4. Place in baking-pan, add a little hot water, to a depth of about ½ inch.

5. Bake in moderate oven 30 minutes. Serves 6.

Baked Potatoes

4 large baking potatoes
4 teaspoons butter
½ teaspoon salt
¼ teaspoon pepper

1. Scrub potatoes thoroughly, cut out any blemishes with a sharp knife.

2. Pierce the potato skins with the tines of a fork in one or two places.

3. Place the potatoes on a rack in the oven and bake at 400° F. until tender, about 45 minutes to 1 hour, depending on the size of the potato.

4. When tender, make a lengthwise and a crosswise slash through the skin at the top of each potato thus, +. Press gently on the sections with the thumb and forefinger of both hands, gently forcing the potato pulp up to the opening. Place a teaspoon of butter in the opening, sprinkle with salt and pepper and serve immediately. Serves 4.

Variations
1. Serve with commercial sour cream, crisp crumbled bacon, chopped chives, or more butter!

2. The potatoes skins may be buttered before baking if desired.

3. The potatoes may be wrapped in a double thickness of foil and buried in campfire coals or cooked on the back of a barbecue.

4. A clean tin can makes a good oven for a potato baked in campfire coals.

Baked Stuffed Potatoes

4 medium sized potatoes
2 tablespoons butter
¼ cup milk
½ teaspoon salt
¼ teaspoon pepper
4 tablespoons grated cheddar cheese

1. Scrub potatoes, pierce skins with a fork and bake in a 400° F. oven until tender, about 45 minutes.

2. Remove from oven, cut potatoes in half lengthwise and remove the pulp from the skins, being careful not to tear the skins.

3. Put the potato pulp in a bowl, add butter, salt, pepper and milk, then mash until smooth and fluffy.

4. Pile the mashed potatoes back into the potato skins. Top each half with 1 tablespoon of grated cheese.

5. Place stuffed potatoes on a baking sheet, and return them to the oven until the potatoes are hot and the cheese has melted to a golden brown. Serves 4.

Variations
1. Steps 1 to 4 may be done ahead of time. Return potatoes to the oven and heat thoroughly just before serving time.

2. Add 1 teaspoon of peanut butter for each potato when mashing them. Top with crumbled bacon instead of grated cheese.

Cheezie Potatoes

4 medium potatoes
1 teaspoon onion salt
1 teaspoon celery salt
½ teaspoon pepper
4 tablespoons grated Parmesan cheese
8 teaspoons butter
Foil

1. Wash and peel potatoes and cut in lengthwise strips as for french fries (about ½″ x ½″ x 3″ long).

2. Cut 4 7-inch squares of baking foil and butter a 4-inch circle in the centre.

3. On each square of foil, place 1 cut-up potato, sprinkle with onion salt, celery salt, pepper, 1 tablespoon of grated parmesan. Dot with 2 teaspoons butter.

4. Seal the potatoes in the foil in loose packages.

5. Bake at 375° F. for approximately 30 minutes. Serves 4.

Variation
Use canned potatoes, or dehydrated potatoes (reconstituted), in place of fresh potatoes.

Clean-Up Day Potatoes

2 cups leftover mashed potatoes
1 egg, separated
1 cup leftover cooked vegetables
4 eggs
4 tablespoons milk *or* cream
4 tablespoons grated cheese

1. Thoroughly mix cold mashed potatoes with the well beaten yolk of 1 egg and then form the mixture into 4 nests on a greased pie plate or baking sheet.

2. Brush the nests with slightly beaten egg white, then place ¼ cup leftover vegetables in each nest.

3. Place in preheated 375° F. oven for 15 minutes, then remove and add 1 tablespoon milk or cream to each nest.

4. Break 1 egg into each nest, top with 1 tablespoon of grated cheese and return to the oven for 10 to 15 minutes until the eggs are set and the cheese has melted. Serves 4.

Foil Baked Potatoes

4 medium sized potatoes
2 medium sized onions
2 tablespoons butter
½ teaspoon salt
¼ teaspoon pepper
¼ teaspoon paprika

1. Wash potatoes, peel, then slash crosswise in ½-inch slices.

2. Peel and slice onions thinly.

3. Insert a slice of onion in each slash in the potato. Sprinkle with salt and pepper.

4. Butter 4 pieces of foil, each large enough to hold a potato.

5. Wrap potatoes in the buttered foil, sealing carefully. Allow a small amount for expansion.

6. Bake 1 hour at 400° F. until tender. Fold back the foil, sprinkle each potato with paprika and serve in the foil cup. Serves 4.

Variations
1. Substitute dehydrated vegetable or onion soup for the fresh onions and sprinkle ½ teaspoon of dried milk between each 2 slices of potato.

2. Spread the slices of potato with condensed cream of mushroom soup, then reassemble the slices in order and wrap in buttered foil.

Note:
These potatoes may be buried in campfire coals. but use a double thickness of foil and reduce the cooking time. Check for doneness after ½ hour.

Potatoes and Onions au Gratin

6 cups diced boiled potatoes
1½ pounds small white onions *or*
1 15-ounce can whole onions
4 tablespoons butter
4 tablespoons flour
3 cups milk
½ cup chicken broth
½ pound cheddar cheese, grated
½ cup finely grated Parmesan cheese
¼ teaspoon pepper
½ teaspoon seasoned salt
¼ teaspoon garlic salt

1. Peel and cook onions just until tender in enough boiling salted water to cover. Leave lid off while cooking. Drain.

2. Put diced potatoes and onions in a large shallow casserole and set aside.

3. Melt the butter in a heavy saucepan. Add the flour and stir until smooth.

4. Gradually add the milk and the chicken broth, stirring until mixture comes to a boil and is thickened.

5. Add the cheeses and the seasonings, reduce the heat and simmer until the cheese melts, stirring constantly.

6. Pour the sauce over the potatoes and onions in the casserole. Bake in a 350° F. oven until bubbly and golden brown, about 45 minutes. Serves 6.

Duchess Potatoes

2 cups mashed potatoes
1 egg *or* 2 egg yolks
½ teaspoon salt
¼ teaspoon pepper

1. Prepare mashed potatoes, (or use leftover mashed potatoes, or instant mashed potatoes prepared according to directions on the package).

2. Beat 1 whole egg or 2 egg yolks well.

3. Add egg, salt and pepper to the mashed potatoes and beat till smooth.

4. Pile the potatoes in a buttered baking dish and heat thoroughly in a 400° F. oven. Serves 4.

Variations
1. Use egg powder in place of fresh eggs if desired. Add 3 tablespoons warm water to 1 tablespoon egg powder and let stand for ½ hour, then beat well and add to potatoes.

2. Top with grated cheese if desired.

3. Add 1 tablespoon dehydrated or fresh grated onion to the potatoes before baking.

French Fried Potatoes

4 large potatoes
1 teaspoon salt
2 pounds cooking oil, lard,
   or vegetable shortening

1. Wash and peel potatoes, then cut them into strips approximately ½″ x ½″ x 3″ long.

2. Soak the potatoes in cold water for at least 10 minutes. Drain and dry well.

3. Place the oil or shortening in a deep kettle and heat slowly to 365° F. or until a ½-inch cube of bread will brown in 60 seconds.

4. When fat is hot, add the potatoes, a serving at a time, and fry until golden brown, about 5 to 10 minutes.

5. Drain the potatoes well, salt lightly and serve. Serves 4.

Note
The fat should be at least 3 inches deep in the kettle for frying and should not be above 3 inches from the top of the kettle. Lower the potatoes gently into the hot fat, being careful not to splash, use a wire basket preferably, or a long-handled, slotted spoon. After frying, allow the fat to cool, then strain and refrigerate until next use.

Hash Brown Potatoes

4 medium sized cold boiled
   potatoes *or*
1 15-ounce can potatoes
2 tablespoons butter
1 medium onion *or*
1 tablespoon onion flakes
½ teaspoon salt
¼ teaspoon pepper

1. Dice the potatoes and the onion.

2. Melt the butter in a heavy fry pan.

3. Add the potatoes, onions and seasonings and cook over medium heat until browned and crisp on the bottom.

4. Using a spatula or pancake turner, flip the potatoes over and brown on other side. Serves 4.

Home Fried Potatoes

4 medium potatoes
¼ cup butter
½ teaspoon salt
¼ teaspoon onion
   salt
¼ teaspoon pepper

1. Wash and peel potatoes. Slice ⅛ inch thick.

2. Soak slices for 10 minutes in cold water, drain and dry.

3. Melt butter in heavy fry pan.

4. Add potatoes and seasonings and pan fry until tender and nicely browned. Be careful not to break up the potato slices while cooking. Serves 4.

Scalloped Potatoes

3 medium potatoes
1 large onion
3 tablespoons flour
½ teaspoon pepper
1 tablespoon butter
2 cups milk

1. Wash and peel potatoes. Slice thinly, or grate, using a grater with large openings.

2. Peel and slice onion thinly.

3. In a buttered baking dish, place a layer of potatoes, then a layer of onions. Sprinkle with 1 tablespoon of flour and a dash of pepper. Dot with butter.

4. Continue the layers in this manner until baking dish is ¾ full.

5. Heat the milk to boiling point, then pour it over the potatoes, until they are barely covered.

6. Cover the baking dish and bake the potatoes in a 375° F. oven for 1 hour. Remove the cover for the last 15 minutes if desired. Serves 4.

Note
Be sure to pass the salt! Not adding the salt to the casserole results in a smoother sauce.

Variations
1. Sprinkle the potatoes with grated cheese before baking.

2. Or top the casserole with buttered crumbs.

3. Dried onions and dehydrated sliced potatoes may be used instead of fresh ones.

4. Use dehydrated vegetable soup in place of the onions for a pleasant change.

Mock French Fried Potatoes

6 medium potatoes
2 teaspoons salt
2 quarts cold water
½ cup cooking oil
1 teaspoon salt

1. Wash and peel potatoes, cut in lengthwise strips as for french fries.

2. Soak potatoes for ½ hour in 2 quarts of cold water in which 2 teaspoons of salt have been dissolved.

3. Preheat oven to 400° F.

4. Drain potatoes and dry thoroughly with absorbent paper or a clean tea towel.

5. Place potatoes in a shallow roaster or the bottom of the broiler pan, pour cooking oil over them, and bake in the oven until tender, turning frequently (about 30 to 40 minutes).

6. Remove from oven, season with salt and serve. Serves 4.

   Note

   The potatoes may be cooked under the broiler if desired. This will cut the cooking time in half, but be careful not to let them burn!

Joe's Fried Tomatoes

3 medium-sized green tomatoes
4 tablespoons butter
3 tablespoons flour
½ teaspoon salt
¼ teaspoon pepper

1. Wash firm green tomatoes, then slice in ½ inch thick slices.

2. Add salt and pepper to the flour. Mix well.

3. Dip tomato slices in the seasoned flour.

4. Melt butter in heavy frying pan. Add tomato slices, cooking one layer at a time.

5. Cover pan, reduce heat and cook 10 minutes.

6. Remove cover, increase heat and brown the slices on both sides. Serve hot.

   Note

   Frozen tomato slices may be cooked the same way.

1. Choose green tomatoes free from blemish. Wash and wipe dry.

2. Slice as above, and freeze slices individually on a tray.

3. When frozen, wrap enough slices for one meal in foil, placing waxed paper between the slices. Seal edges of foil securely.

4. Use as above. No pre-thawing is necessary, but allow 15 minutes cooking time before browning.

Scalloped Tomatoes

2 cups sliced fresh *or* canned tomatoes
2 tablespoons finely chopped fresh onion *or* dried onion flakes
1–2 teaspoons sugar
1 tablespoon finely chopped green pepper *or* green pepper flakes
½ teaspoon salt
¾ cup soft bread crumbs
2 tablespoons butter
¼ cup grated cheese

1. Combine tomatoes, onion, green peppers, seasonings, and sugar.
2. Place alternate layers of tomato mixture and crumbs in 6- to 8-inch baking dish, ending with crumbs on top.
3. Dot crumbs with butter; bake at 365° F. for 25 minutes.
4. Add cheese to top last 10 minutes of baking. Serves 4.

Fresh Tomatoes in Vinegar

3 large red tomatoes
½ cup vinegar
¼ cup water
1 tablespoon sugar
1½ tablespoons minced green onion *or* dried onion soaked in boiling water 15 minutes, then drained
¼ teaspoon black pepper

1. Wash tomatoes, then slice in thick slices or in wedges. Place in bowl.
2. Mix water, vinegar, sugar and minced onion and pour over the tomatoes. Let stand 15 to 20 minutes.
3. Sprinkle with black pepper and serve immediately. Serves 6.

Tomato Surprise

1 28 ounce can tomatoes
2 ounces dehydrated mixed vegetables
6 slices cooked bacon, *or* equivalent amount of any cooked meat
1 cup grated cheddar cheese
1 cup bread *or* cracker crumbs
½ teaspoon salt
¼ teaspoon pepper

1. Mix tomatoes, vegetables, meat in a buttered baking dish.
2. Season to taste.
3. Top with grated cheese and bread crumbs.
4. Bake in a 325° F. oven for 45 minutes.

Mashed Turnip

1–2 pounds turnip
3 tablespoons white sugar
2 tablespoons butter
½ teaspoon salt
¼ teaspoon pepper

1. Wash turnip, slice and peel.

2. Cut into cubes.

3. Put cubes into rapidly boiling water, add the sugar and boil quickly just until tender. Leave the lid off the pot and do *not* over-cook as this develops the strong flavour that many people find objectionable.

4. When the turnip cubes are tender, drain, add butter, salt and pepper and mash until smooth. Serve hot. Serves 4–6.

Turnips au Gratin

4 tablespoons butter
3 tablespoons flour
1 cup canned milk
1 cup water *or* vegetable juice
¼ cup grated cheddar cheese
5 cups (2 pounds) diced cooked turnips
Salt and pepper to taste
Buttered bread crumbs

1. Make 2 cups of white sauce with butter, flour, milk and water or vegetable juice.

2. Add cheese, turnips, salt and pepper.

3. Cover with buttered bread crumbs and bake in oven 375° F. for 30 minutes.

Candied Squash

1 small Hubbard squash
1 cup sugar (white *or* brown)
¼ cup butter
½ teaspoon salt
1 cup water

1. Wash the squash and cut into suitable pieces for serving, about 3″ × 4″; remove the seeds and membrane.

2. Make a thin syrup of the sugar, butter, salt and water.

3. Pour into a large shallow baking pan.

4. Arrange the pieces of squash yellow side down in the pan.

5. Bake in a moderate oven 350°–375° F. until squash is very tender. It may also be cooked slowly on top of the stove if tightly covered in a heavy pan.

6. Serve the pieces yellow side up with any remaining syrup placed in the center of each piece.

Squash

1 medium Buttercup squash
1½ teaspoons salt
4 tablespoons butter
½ teaspoon salt
   few grains pepper

1. Choose a fully ripe squash (sounds hollow when tapped with knuckles).

2. Cut in half, remove seeds and pulp, pare, then dice.

3. Cook quickly in a small amount of rapidly boiling salted water. By the time the squash is cooked, the water should have disappeared. Watch it closely, because it burns quickly.

4. When the squash is tender, drain it well, then mash with butter and season to taste.

Note
Other varieties of squash may be used, especially hubbard squash, but be sure the squash is fully mature, in order to preserve the dryness and the nut-like flavour.

Baked Vegetable Marrow

2–3 pounds vegetable marrow
¼ cup butter
½ teaspoon salt
¼ teaspoon pepper

1. Cut marrow in half, remove seeds and stringy fibres, then cut into 2 inch squares. Peel tough outer skin from the squares.

2. Place the squares in a buttered baking dish, dot well with butter, season with salt and pepper and bake at 350° F. until tender, about ¾ of an hour. Serves 4–6.

Company's Coming Bean Salad

1 15 ounce can green beans
1 15 ounce can wax beans
1 15 ounce can lima beans
1 15 ounce can kidney beans
1 15 ounce can chick peas
2 sweet green peppers
2 medium onions
¾ cup white sugar
⅓ cup salad oil
⅔ cup white wine vinegar
    Salt and pepper to taste
    Garlic salt (optional)

1. Open the cans of beans and peas and drain well, placing the kidney beans in the bottom of the seive or colander.

2. Wash the green peppers, cut out the stem and pulp. Cut into pieces.

3. Wash the onions, peel under water, and slice thinly.

4. Add the green peppers and the onions to the drained beans.

5. Put the sugar, salad oil and vinegar in a jar and shake until the sugar is dissolved. Pour over the beans and mix well.

6. Season to taste with salt and pepper (and garlic salt, if desired).

7. Let stand 24 hours before serving, stirring occasionally to ensure that the vegetables are well marinated. Serves 12 generously.

Hot Bean Salad

4 tablespoons fat or oil
1 teaspoon mustard
1 tablespoon Worcestershire
    Salt
    Cayenne

1. Mix and pour over 2 cups hot cooked or canned beans.

Potato Salad

4 cups cold diced potatoes
3 tablespoons sweet *or* dill pickles, chopped
¾ cup mayonnaise
¼ cup onion, diced
¼ teaspoon celery salt
¼ teaspoon paprika
1 teaspoon salt

1. Potatoes may be cooked in their skins, allowed to cool, then peeled and diced.

2. Combine potatoes and pickles.

3. Add the diced onion, celery salt, paprika and salt to the mayonnaise.

4. Blend the mayonnaise into the potatoes and pickles, tossing lightly until potatoes are coated with the mixture.

5. Chill and serve.

Note
The salad may be garnished with sliced hard boiled egg and sprigs of fresh parsley.

Cabbage and Apple Salad

2 cups finely shredded,
    crisp cabbage
2 cups chopped, unpeeled
    red apples
½ cup seedless raisins
  Salad dressing
  Salt to taste

1. Combine apples, cabbage and raisins. Add salad dressing and salt.
2. Toss lightly together and serve immediately.

Hot Cabbage Slaw

½ minced peeled clove of
    garlic
3 teaspoons salad oil *or* butter
8 cups finely shredded cabbage,
    well packed
¼ cup water
1 egg
⅓ cup canned milk *or* cream
    (sweet *or* sour)
1 tablespoon lemon juice
1 tablespoon sugar
1 teaspoon salt
½ teaspoon celery seed

1. Brown the garlic in the fat at low heat for 5 minutes.
2. Add cabbage and water and cover.
3. Simmer 8 to 10 minutes.
4. Mix the egg, milk, lemon juice, sugar, salt and celery seed.
5. Pour over hot cabbage and toss lightly.
6. Serve at once.

FISH SALADS

Salmon Salad

2 cups salmon
3 hard-cooked eggs
½ cup diced cheese
3 medium tomatoes, diced
1½ cups macaroni
¼ cup diced sweet pickles
2 tablespoons sweet pickle juice
½ cup diced celery
  Salt to taste
¾ cup mayonnaise

1. Mix thoroughly and chill.
2. Serve on crisp salad greens. Serves 4.

Shrimp Salad

1 7¾ ounce can large shrimp
¼ cup diced celery
2 tablespoons chopped olives
1 tablespoon chopped green
    pepper
2 tablespoons mayonnaise
1 teaspoon Worcestershire sauce

1. Drain the shrimp and let stand in salted water for a few minutes, then rinse with cold water and dry.
2. Leave shrimp whole or break into pieces.
3. Combine the shrimp, celery, olives and green pepper and mix together with the blended mayonnaise and Worcestershire sauce.
4. Serve on lettuce and garnish with celery hearts, gherkins, olives, water cress, sliced cucumber or peas as desired.

Salmon Apple Salad

1 can (7¾ ounces) salmon
  (sockeye *or* cohoe)
1 cup chopped unpeeled apple
1 tablespoon lemon juice
2 cups chopped celery
½ cup whole peanuts (optional)
¼ cup salad dressing

1. Drain and flake salmon.
2. Sprinkle apple with lemon juice and add to salmon.
3. Add celery, peanuts and salad dressing.
4. Toss ingredients lightly.
5. Serve on lettuce cups. Makes 6 servings.

Favourite Fish Salad

1½ cups leftover cooked
  fish, boned
¼ cup mayonnaise
¼ cup French dressing
¼ cup paper-thin onion rings
½ cup diced, pared cucumber
½ cup chopped tomato
2 tablespoons diced celery
1 diced, peeled avocado
  Salt and pepper to taste
  Mixed salad greens
2 chopped hard-cooked eggs

1. Combine mayonnaise, French dressing, onion rings, cucumber, tomato, celery, avocado, salt, pepper and fish.
2. Chill well.
3. Serve on mixed greens; garnish with eggs. Serves 3-4.

Crunchy Tuna Salad

1 cup canned tuna *or* salmon
¼ cup mayonnaise
2 tablespoons diced sweet pickle
1 tablespoon pickle juice
½ cup sliced celery
½ cup chilled cooked *or*
  canned peas
1 cup coarsely crushed corn
  flakes *or* potato chips
  Salad greens

1. Toss mayonnaise with pickle, pickle juice, tuna, celery, peas.
2. Add chips.
3. Serve at once on greens. Serves 4.

Curried Rice and Fish Flake Salad

1½ cups cooked fish, boned
  and flaked
2½ cups cooked rice
  French dressing
⅓ cup parsley
½ cup mayonnaise
1 tablespoon lemon juice
1½ teaspoons curry powder
½ cup peas (optional)
½ cup chopped celery
½ tablespoon chutney

1. Chill rice in French dressing with 2 tablespoons parsley.
2. Blend mayonnaise with lemon juice, curry powder and rest of parsley.
3. Add fish, peas and celery.
4. Chill.
5. Just before serving, place rice on serving platter; top with fish mixture; garnish with chutney.
6. This is an appetizer or side dish for 4—as a main course, serves 2.

JELLIED SALADS

Cranberry Gelatin Salad

2 cups cranberries
¾ cup sugar
1¼ cups water
1 package lemon *or* lime gelatin
1 cup diced celery
½ cup sliced pecans *or* walnuts
   if desired

1. Boil cranberries, sugar and water for 3 minutes.
2. Add gelatin and stir to dissolve.
3. Cool.
4. When syrupy, add celery and pecans or walnuts.
5. Pour into a mold and chill.

Lemon Sour Cream Mold

1 envelope unflavoured gelatin
2 tablespoons lemon juice
1 package lemon jelly powder
1 cup hot water
½ cup cold water
½ pint (1¼ cups) sour cream
1½ cups cottage cheese
1 tablespoon sugar
¼ teaspoon salt
¼ cup finely chopped celery
2 tablespoons finely chopped
   green onion
¼ cup mayonnaise

1. Soften gelatin in lemon juice. Add jelly powder and hot water. Stir until dissolved.
2. Add cold water and sour cream to jelly mixture. Chill until partly set. Blend in remaining ingredients.
3. Turn mixture into a mold which has been rinsed in cold water. Chill until set.

Marie Brown's Pimiento Salad

1 lemon jelly powder
1 cup pimiento, chopped
   Cream cheese
   Walnuts, finely chopped

1. Make the lemon jelly, following directions on package.
2. Fold in the chopped pimientos, and let the mixture cool.
3. Make balls of cream cheese and roll them in chopped walnuts.
4. Place the cream cheese balls in the bottom of individual molds, then fill the molds with jello and pimiento mix.
5. Chill until set firmly. Unmold and set on a lettuce leaf with your favorite garnish.

Quick Tomato Aspic

1 package lemon jelly powder
2 cups tomato juice
¼ teaspoon ground cloves
1 tablespoon chopped onion
¼ teaspoon celery salt

1. Heat tomato juice with cloves, onion and celery salt. Simmer for 5 minutes.
2. Add hot juice to jelly powder. Stir till powder is dissolved.
3. Pour into moistened molds and chill until set.

DESSERT SALADS

Grace Spencer's 24 Hour Salad

1 large can sliced pineapple
½ pound marshmallows
½ pound blanched almonds
4 egg yolks
1 cup cream *or* top milk
Few grains salt
2 tablespoons sugar
1 cup cream, whipped
1 tablespoon lemon juice

1. Combine beaten egg yolks, cream or top milk, salt and sugar in top of double boiler and cook, stirring constantly until mixture thickness and coats the spoon. Remove from heat.

2. When cool, add pineapple, cut-up marshmallows and almonds.

3. Fold in the whipped cream, then add 1 tablespoon lemon juice. Chill 24 hours.

Frozen Delight

1 tablespoon lemon juice
¼ cup mayonnaise *or* salad dressing
1 8-ounce package cream cheese
½ teaspoon salt
¼ cup crushed pineapple
½ cup canned peaches, chopped
½ cup chopped dates
½ cup maraschino cherries, cut up
½ cup toasted almonds
1 cup heavy cream, whipped

1. Gradually add the lemon juice and mayonnaise to the cream cheese, blending until smooth.

2. Add the salt, pineapple, dates, cherries, almonds and peaches. Fold in the whipped cream.

3. Pour into 6 or 8 individual moulds. Freeze until firm. Serves 6–8.

SALAD DRESSINGS

Boiled Salad Dressing

½ cup sugar
1 teaspoon salt
1 tablespoon flour
1 teaspoon dry mustard
2 eggs, beaten
½ cup vinegar
½ cup water

1. Combine all ingredients in a heavy saucepan.

2. Cook over low heat until thickened, stirring constantly.

3. Place in a clean jar and store in a cool place.

French Dressing

¼ cup vinegar
2 tablespoons water
⅔ cup salad oil
1 teaspoon salt
½ teaspoon dry mustard
¼ teaspoon garlic salt
1 tablespoon grated onion *or* dried onion flakes
1 tablespoon catsup
½ teaspoon sugar
¼ teaspoon pepper
½ teaspoon paprika

1. Measure all ingredients into a jar which has a close fitting top.

2. Cover and shake vigorously or blend in electric mixer.

3. Place in a clean jar and store in a cool place. Shake well each time before using.

Mrs. Hatting's Salad Dressing

1½ cups sweetened condensed milk
½ cup vinegar
2 teaspoons dry mustard
½ cup salad oil

1. Mix ingredients in order given.
2. Beat well together until thick.
3. Place in clean covered jar. Store in cool place.

Hot Bacon Dressing For Greens

1 teaspoon sugar
1 teaspoon salt
1 teaspoon grated onion
Vinegar
Grated yolk of hard-cooked egg
Crisp bacon
Select young dandelion greens,
endive, lettuce, spinach *or*
cabbage leaves *or* a
combination of these

1. Wash, drain and cut the greens into 1 inch sections.
2. Season with 1 teaspoon sugar, salt and grated onion.
3. Fry bacon, allowing ½ strip to each serving.
4. Remove bacon, drain. Add twice as much vinegar as fat to the fry pan.
5. Bring to a boil, then pour it over the greens and toss lightly.
6. Garnish with grated egg yolk and crumbled bacon.

No Egg Mayonnaise

2 tablespoons sugar
½ teaspoon paprika
½ teaspoon dry mustard
½ teaspoon salt
½ cup undiluted evaporated milk
2½ tablespoons vinegar *or*
   lemon juice
1¼ cups salad oil

1. Combine sugar, paprika, salt and mustard with ½ cup evaporated milk.
2. Add vinegar or lemon juice beating constantly.
3. Add salad oil gradually and continue beating until blended.
4. Place in a clean jar and store in a cool place.

Potato Mayonnaise

2 medium baked potatoes
2 teaspoons dry mustard
1½ teaspoons salt
2 teaspoons white sugar
¼ cup vinegar
1½ cups salad oil

1. Wash potatoes, prick with a fork and bake at 425° F. until tender.
2. Cut potatoes in half, remove pulp and mash well until no lumps remain.
3. Add the mustard, salt and sugar and blend well with the potatoes.
4. Add the vinegar and oil alternately, beating after each addition, until mixture is thick and smooth.
5. Place in a clean jar, cover tightly and store in a cool place.

Quick Mayonnaise

1 can evaporated milk
1 cup vinegar
2 eggs
2 teaspoons sugar
1 teaspoon salt
1 teaspoon prepared mustard
2 tablespoons melted butter

1. Place all ingredients in a bowl.

2. Beat with an egg beater until smooth.

3. Place in a clean jar, cover tightly and store in a cool place.

Variation
Sweet pickle juice may be substituted for the vinegar and sugar.

Sour Cream Dressing

1 cup thick sour cream
2 tablespoons sweet pickle juice
½ tablespoon minced onion
½ teaspoon sugar
¼ teaspoon salt

1. Combine all ingredients and mix thoroughly.

2. Place in clean jar. Store in a cool place.

CHAPTER IX

DESSERTS, JAM, JELLY, CANDY, PASTRY and PIE

Desserts are generally described as a delicious taste of sweetness at the end of a meal, and berries and fruit whether fresh, frozen, dried or canned, make an ideal dessert. But they may also be served at other times as an appetizer, salad, a sauce or a between-meal snack. Canada's Food Guide recommends that we eat fruit at least twice a day, and at least one of the servings should be a satisfactory source of vitamin C, the vitamin that prevents scurvy. While fresh fruit is not always available in all parts of the north, dried, canned and (sometimes) frozen fruits are, and during the short Arctic summer almost everybody can enjoy the captivating taste of fresh berries.

The names of the berries are as appealing as their flavour. High bush cranberry, lingenberry or mountain cranberry, partridge or twin berry, mossberry, blueberry, salmonberry, thimbleberry, wild raspberry, wild strawberry, nagoonberry, bogberry, bilberry, bearberry, crowberry, cloudberry, rose-berry, pincherry, chokecherry and saskatoons are abundant in many localities in northern Canada. By picking and preserving the berries at their peak-of-the-season best, you can enjoy a taste of summer all year round.

Good quality dried fruits include apples, pears, peaches, prunes, apricots, raisins, currants, dates and figs. If prepared properly, they will have good colour and flavour and be plump and juicy. With modern methods of drying, long pre-soaking is no longer needed. Wash them well, drain them, then soak them for an hour in enough lukewarm water to cover them well and plump them up. Cook them in the water in which they were soaked, simmering them just until tender. This will usually take 5 to 10 minutes, although apples and prunes may take up to 30 minutes. If you need to sweeten them, add the sugar *after* cooking them to prevent toughness.

Canned fruits are graded "Canada Fancy", "Canada Choice" and "Canada Standard". All have excellent flavour and are equally nutritious, but the standard grade is not as perfect in appearance and is therefore lower in price.

Always keep fruit and berries in a cool place to preserve their freshness, except for bananas which should be stored at room temperature. All fruit should be washed before eating. Wash only the berries that will be eaten at the next meal, as they do not keep as well after washing.

Uncooked Blueberry Jelly

3 cups berry juice
4½ cups sugar
1 box powdered pectin
½ cup water

1. Add the sugar to 1½ cups of the berry juice and stir thoroughly.

2. Add the powdered pectin slowly to the ½ cup of water and heat almost to boiling stirring constantly.

3. Pour the pectin mixture into the remaining 1½ cups of berry juice and stir until the pectin is completely dissolved.

4. Let the pectin mixture stand 15 minutes and stir it occasionally.

5. Mix the juice mixture with the pectin mixture and stir until all the sugar is dissolved.

6. Pour into containers and let stand at room temperature until set which will be from 6 hours to overnight.

7. Store in refrigerator or freezer.

Spiced Blueberry Jam

4½ cups blueberries
½ teaspoon cinnamon
½ teaspoon cloves
7 cups sugar
  Grated rind and
  Juice of 1 lemon
1 bottle commercial pectin

1. Simmer all ingredients except pectin for 5 minutes.

2. Remove from heat and add 1 bottle commercial pectin.

3. Stir and skim.

4. Spoon into sterilized jars and seal. Makes 3 pints.

Blueberry Jam Uncooked or Frozen

2 cups of berries, crushed
4 cups sugar
1 cup water
1 package powdered pectin

1. Mix berries and sugar; let stand 20 minutes, stirring occasionally.

2. Combine the pectin with the water and bring to a boil and boil 1 minute, stirring constantly.

3. Add pectin to the berries and the sugar and stir about 2 minutes more.

4. Pour into clean sterilized jars and cover with a lid or aluminum foil.

5. Let stand at room temperature for 24 hours until jam congeals slightly; then refrigerate until set.

6. Store in the refrigerator or the freezer until used.

Cranberry and Carrot Jam

1 quart cranberry pulp
1½ quarts diced carrots
5 cups sugar

1. Combine ingredients in a preserving kettle and cook, stirring frequently, for 20 minutes or until the mixture reaches the thickness desired.

2. Remove from heat, pour into sterilized jars and seal.

High Bush Cranberry Jelly

2 cups berries
3 cups water
⅔ cup sugar for each cup of juice

1. Simmer berries and water for 10 minutes to start the juice extraction then let boil rapidly from 3 to 5 minutes.

2. Strain through a jelly bag.

3. Measure strained juice.

4. Add ⅔ cup sugar for each cup of juice.

5. Bring juice and sugar to a boil, stirring constantly, then boil rapidly until liquid will sheet from the side of a spoon (not drip off in separate drops).

6. Pour into sterilized glasses and seal.

Cranberry Raw Relish

2 cups cranberries
1 cup sugar

1. Grind cranberries.

2. Add sugar.

3. Stir well.

4. Serve cold with meat.

Variations

1. Add 1 orange, ½ lemon and 1 apple to the above recipe. Wash and grind the orange peel and apple. Slice pulp of orange with sharp knife. Mix well.

2. Spiced—add 1 teaspoon cinnamon, ½ teaspoon cloves and 2 teaspoons grated orange peel.

Cranberry Catsup

1 pound onions chopped fine
4 pounds cranberries
2 cups water
2 cups vinegar
4 cups sugar
1 tablespoon ground cloves
1 tablespoon cinnamon
1 tablespoon allspice
1 tablespoon salt
1 tablespoon celery seed
1 teaspoon pepper

1. Cook onions and cranberries in water until soft.

2. Rub through food sieve.

3. Add remainder of ingredients and boil until thick. Pour into sterilized jars and seal. (Makes about 3 pints.)

Serve with poultry, meat, or on baked beans. Other berries may be substituted in the above recipe.

Cranberry Apple Butter

1 pound dried apples
2 quarts water
2 quarts cranberries
6 cups sugar
1 teaspoon cinnamon
½ teaspoon cloves
¼ teaspoon salt
Grated rind and
Juice of 1 lemon

1. Soak 1 pound dried apples in 2 quarts water for 1 hour.

2. Add the 2 quarts cranberries and cook until soft.

3. Put the pulp through a sieve or food mill.

4. Reheat and add the sugar, salt and spices.

5. Cook until clear.

6. Remove from the heat and add the lemon juice and grated rind.

7. Spoon into jars and seal.

Ways of Using Cranberries

1. Use cranberry sauce or a combination of cranberry sauce and applesuace as a filling for sweet rolls and coffee cake.

2. Cranberry icing — add whipped cranberry sauce to standard recipe for butter icing and mix to a spreading consistency. Cut cookies in interesting shapes. Bake and cool. Decorate with the cranberry icing.

3. Add chopped fresh cranberries to Waldorf salad.

4. Place drained pear or peach half on lettuce and fill the center with whole cranberry sauce.

5. Add sweetened, chopped cranberries to vanilla pudding.

6. Cranberry-Apple Pie—use equal amounts of apples and cranberries; proceed as with regular apple pie.

7. Cranberry Upside-Down Cake — substitute whole cranberry sauce for pineapple slices and proceed as usual.

8. Cherry-Cranberry Cobbler—use cherry cobbler recipe but substitute cranberries for half of the cherries.

9. Applesauce-Cranberry Cake—use applesauce cake recipe but substitute cranberry sauce for all or at least ⅔ of the applesauce.

10. In a meat loaf, substitute cranberry sauce for the liquid called for in the recipe.

Stewed Prunes

2 cups prunes
2½ cups cold water
¼ cup sugar
1 tablespoon lemon juice

1. Wash the prunes thoroughly in warm water.

2. Cover with cold water and let soak for one hour.

3. Simmer the prunes in the water in which they were soaked, in a covered saucepan until tender, about 10 minutes.

4. Add the sugar, stir until sugar is dissolved then add 1 tablespoon lemon juice.

5. If a thicker juice is required, the prunes may be cooked a little longer with the lid off to evaporate some of the liquid.

6. Chill and serve. Serves 4.

Tropical Baked Peaches

6–8 canned peach halves
1 banana
⅓ cup brown sugar (packed)
⅓ cup orange juice
¼ cup shredded coconut
¼ cup fine dry bread crumbs

1. Place peaches in flat baking dish, slice banana over them.
2. Combine brown sugar and orange juice and boil 3 minutes until slightly thickened and pour over peaches.
3. Top with coconut and crumbs blended together.
4. Bake in a moderate oven 350° F. about 25 minutes.
5. Serve warm with cream.

Frozen Raspberry Jam

3 cups crushed raspberries
5 cups fine white sugar
2 tablespoons lemon juice
½ bottle liquid pectin *or*
¾ cup water and
1 package pectin crystals

1. Crush the berries and add the sugar and lemon juice. Let stand for 20 minutes, stirring occasionally.
2. Add the liquid pectin, or mix ¾ cup water and 1 package pectin crystals and boil for 1 minute, then stir into the fruit, blending well.
3. Let stand overnight in room temperature.
4. Pour into freezer cartons and store in freezer. Will keep for 6 months.

Wild Raspberry Jam

8 cups crushed raspberries
6 cups sugar

(If the berries seem to be exceedingly seedy, part of the pulp may be put through a sieve.)
1. Heat berries thoroughly in a large kettle.
2. Add sugar to the heated berries.
3. Cook, stirring continuously until the mixture has a thick jelly-like consistency.
4. Pour into hot sterilized jars and seal immediately.

Raspberry and Red Currant Jam

3 cups crushed red currants
¾ cup water
4 cups raspberries
7 cups sugar
½ cup liquid pectin

1. Cook the crushed red currants and water together for 10 minutes.
2. Strain through a sieve or a jelly bag.
3. Return to kettle and add raspberries and sugar.
4. Boil hard 1 minute and remove from the heat.
5. Add liquid pectin.
6. Pour into clean sterilized jars and seal with paraffin.

250

Raspberry Punch

2 cups raspberry juice
1 teaspoon cornstarch
¼ cup sugar
5 cloves
1 2" stick cinnamon
1 cup orange juice
¾ cup grape juice

1. Boil raspberry juice with sugar, cornstarch and spices.
2. When cool add orange and grape juice.
3. Serve over cracked ice or freeze and serve as sherbet.

Raspberry Shrub

Raspberries
White wine vinegar

1. Fill a jar with ripe raspberries and press them down slightly.
2. Fill the jar with vinegar.
3. After a month, strain the juice and seal in sterilized bottles.
4. Dilute with cold water and sweeten to taste to make a refreshing drink.

Rose Hip Syrup

4 cups rose hip fruit
2 cups water
2 cups sugar

1. Wash rose hips thoroughly.
2. Remove stems and the flower remnants.
3. Boil rose hips and water 20 minutes in covered saucepan.
4. Strain through a jelly bag or with 1 cup cellulose pulp to clear the sediment from the mixture.
5. Return the clear juice to the kettle.
6. Add the sugar to the juice and boil the mixture for 5 minutes.
7. Store in a refrigerator jar until you use it; this syrup keeps indefinitely.

Applesauce Fortified With Rose Hip Syrup

1 quart applesauce
¾ cup rose hip syrup

1. To 1 quart of applesauce, add ¾ cup rose hip syrup.
2. This applesauce, frozen in ice cube trays, then cut into squares for a frozen salad and topped with your favourite salad dressing, makes an excellent accompaniment for pork roasts and game meat.

Rose Hip Jam

2 pounds rose hips
6 cups sugar
6 cups boiling water
  Grated rind and
  Juice of 2 lemons

1. Simmer rose hips in boiling water for 30 minutes.
2. Press through sieve to make a purée.
3. Slice lemon rind very thin and cook in a small amount of water for 1 minute.
4. Combine the purée, the lemon and the sugar.
5. Cook until the mixture is thick and clear.
6. Spoon into sterilized jars.

Rose Hip Cranberry Jam

2 pounds rose hips and
  cranberries
6 cups sugar
½ cup lemon juice

1. Choose slightly under-ripe rose hips and cranberries.
2. Wash and pick over if necessary.
3. Mash or put through a food grinder.
4. Add boiling water to almost cover and cook 10 minutes.
5. Put berries through a food mill or sieve to remove seeds and skins.
6. For every 8 cups rose hips and cranberry purée add   6 cups sugar and measure out ½ cup lemon juice.
7. Stir and boil rose hip and cranberry purée with the sugar for 5 minutes.
8. Add the lemon juice and stir well.
9. Pour into sterilized jars and seal.

Rose Hip Purée

1 pound rose hips
3 cups boiling water

1. Simmer rose hips in boiling water for 30 minutes.
2. Press though a sieve to make a purée.
3. Add enough water to make 4 cups of purée.

Variations
1. Apple juice (unfortified) is low in vitamin C. Add 2 tablespoons rose hip purée to a 6 ounce glass apple juice to improve vitamin C content. Stir and chill before serving.
2. Mix equal parts of rose hip purée and water. Add sugar to taste. Stir and chill before serving.

252

Candied Rose Hips

1½ cups rose hips
½ cup sugar
¼ cup water

1. Remove seeds from rose hips.

2. Combine sugar and water to make syrup.

3. Add rose hips to syrup and boil 10 minutes.

4. Lift fruit from syrup with a skimmer and drain on waxed paper.

5. Dust with sugar and dry slowly in the sun or very slow oven, adding more sugar if the fruit seems sticky.

6. Store between sheets of waxed paper in a closely covered metal container until used.

Uses of Candied Rose Hips

1. In your favourite cookie recipe in place of, or in addition to, nuts or chopped fruit as in oatmeal cookies, fruit squares or filled sugar cookies.

2. In puddings with added grated rind of lemon or in place of nuts or fruits.

Rose Hip and Prune Juice Sherbet

1 cup sugar
1 cup water
½ cup canned prune juice
½ cup light corn syrup
½ cup rose hip syrup
¼ teaspoon salt
1 egg white

1. Combine sugar and water and boil 5 minutes.
2. Add the syrups, juice and salt.
3. Freeze until almost firm in an ice cube tray.
4. Whip the egg white stiff.
5. Fold into the frozen mixture.
6. Return to ice cube trays and refreeze.
7. Keep frozen until served.

Rose Hip and Rhubarb Jam

1 cup rose hips
4 cups diced rhubarb
1 cup water
¼ teaspoon salt
2 cups sugar
1 tablespoon grated lemon rind

1. Use slightly under-ripe rose hips; cut in half and remove the seeds with the point of the knife.
2. Combine rose hips, rhubarb, water and salt.
3. Boil rapidly 1 minute.
4. Add sugar and lemon rind.
5. Boil rapidly 1 minute.
6. Seal in sterilized jars.

Rose Petal Jelly

1 cup rose petals
2 tablespoons lemon juice
Sugar

1. Pack the rose petals into the cup and press down tightly to measure.
2. Place petals in saucepan, add water to cover and lemon juice.
3. Boil until the petals have a washed-out colour.
4. Strain the liquid and measure it.
5. Add ¾ as much sugar as liquid and bring to a boil.
6. Boil rapidly for 10 minutes.
7. Skim.
8. Test on a small cold saucer to see if it will jell.
9. Cook again if it does not give the jell test.
10. Pour into sterilized glass jars.
11. Seal or cover with paraffin and store in a cool place.

Note
Rose hips may be used instead of the rose petals and the same method of jelly making can be followed.

Salmonberry Jam

1 cup salmonberries (crushed)
2 cups diced rhubarb
3 cups sugar

1. Combine in a large kettle.
2. Stir and boil rapidly until the mixture reaches the thickness you desire.
3. Pour into sterilized jars.
4. Seal with paraffin.

Salmonberry Preserves

4 cups salmonberries
4 cups sugar

1. Cook slowly for 15 minutes, equal amounts of salmonberries and sugar. Stir constantly to prevent burning.
2. Remove from fire and, with a slotted spoon, remove the berries to a separate dish.
3. Boil the remaining juice very hard for 15 more minutes.
4. Return the berries and bring to a boil, stirring constantly. Pour the preserves into sterilized jars and seal.

Note
Golden yellow salmonberries have better flavour than the red ones.

Apple Fritters

1 cup dried apple rings
  Water
1 tablespoon egg powder and
3 tablespoons water *or*
1 egg
½ cup milk
¼ cup sugar
1 cup flour
½ teaspoon baking powder
¼ teaspoon salt

1. Soak the dried apple rings in water to cover, overnight.
2. Cook the apple rings in the water they were soaked in. Simmer 10-15 minutes. Drain.
3. Combine 1 tablespoon egg powder and 3 tablespoons water with sugar and milk and blend well.
4. Sift together, flour, baking powder and salt.
5. Mix the dry ingredients into the egg and milk mixture gradually, beating well to make a smooth batter.
6. Dip the apple rings separately into the batter and drop into hot deep fat 375° F. and fry until golden brown, turning once.

Note
If you have any leftover batter it can be dropped by spoonfuls into the hot grease and served as an extra.

Apple Crisp

2 cups dried apples
½ cup sugar
1 cup flour
1 cup brown sugar
1 cup rolled oats
1 teaspoon baking powder
1 teaspoon cinnamon
¼ teaspoon salt
¾ cup butter

1. Wash the dried apples, then soak overnight in water to cover.

2. Simmer the apples in the water they were soaked in for 10 to 15 minutes, then add ½ cup sugar. Stir.

3. Pour the apples into a casserole.

4. Combine the flour, brown sugar, rolled oats, baking powder, cinnamon and salt.

5. Rub ¾ cup butter into the flour mixture to form coarse crumbs.

6. Spread crumb mixture over the apples in casserole and bake in a moderate oven, 350° F., for 30 minutes. Serve with cream.

Apple Crumble

4 cups sliced apples, or
6 medium apples
4 tablespoons sugar
Cinnamon
¼ cup shortening (part butter)
¾ cup brown sugar
½ cup flour or
¼ cup flour and
½ cup fine rolled oats
¼ teaspoon salt

1. Place sliced apples in greased baking dish and sprinkle with sugar and cinnamon.

2. Cream shortening and brown sugar well together.

3. Blend in flour, salt and rolled oats (if used) and sprinkle mixture on top of fruit.

4. Bake in moderate oven 350° F. until fruit is soft and top is golden brown, about 40 minutes. Canned or dried apples may be used if desired. Pre-soak dried apples according to directions on the package.

Apple Dumplings

2 cups sifted pastry flour or
1¾ cups sifted all-purpose flour
½ teaspoon salt
4 teaspoons baking powder
1 tablespoon sugar
½ cup shortening
½ cup milk (approximately)
6 medium apples
Sugar and cinnamon or
Mincemeat or jam

1. Mix and sift flour, salt, baking powder and sugar.

2. Cut in shortening.

3. Add milk to make a soft biscuit dough.

4. Roll to ¼ inch thickness.

5. Cut dough in 6 squares, place cored and pared apples in center of each. Fill cavity of each apple with mixture of sugar and cinnamon or mincemeat or jam.

6. Draw dough up around apples and pierce with fork.

7. Place in greased baking dish and bake in moderate oven 350° F. until apples are tender, about 40 minutes.

8. Serve with cream and sugar or hot pudding sauce.

Eve's Pudding

1–2 pounds apples (sweetened and stewed)
½ cup sugar
½ cup butter
1 egg
1 cup flour
1 teaspoon baking powder
¼ teaspoon salt
½ cup milk

1. Put apples in a deep pie dish.
2. Cream butter and sugar, add egg and beat well, add sifted dry ingredients alternately with milk.
3. Spread mixture on top of apples and bake in a moderate oven at 350° F. until firm and golden brown, about 45 minutes.
4. Serve hot with custard sauce.

Steamed Apple Pudding

3–4 cups thinly sliced, pared apples
⅓ cup sugar
1 cup sifted all-purpose flour *or*
1 cup plus 2 tablespoons sifted pastry flour
2 teaspoons baking powder
½ teaspoon salt
2 tablespoons shortening
½ cup milk

1. Place apples in 6 greased individual moulds.
2. Sprinkle with sugar.
3. Mix and sift flour, baking powder and salt.
4. Cut in shortening and add milk.
5. Spread dough over apples, filling moulds not more than ⅔ full.
6. Cover with heavy waxed paper, parchment paper or aluminum foil, letting it extend at least an inch over the edge. Tie in place tightly.
7. Place in steamer and steam 35 minutes.
8. Turn out and serve with Apple Butterscotch Sauce or Cream.

Mamie Leonard's Steamed Pudding

1 egg
1 cup finely ground suet
1 cup brown sugar
1 teaspoon baking soda
1 cup applesauce
1 cup raisins, scalded
1 cup red and green maraschino cherries, chopped (optional)
1½ cups sifted flour
1½ teaspoons baking powder
¼ teaspoon salt
1 teaspoon cinnamon
¼ teaspoon nutmeg
¼ teaspoon ground cloves

1. In a mixing bowl, beat the egg, add the suet and the brown sugar and mix well.
2. Add 1 teaspoon baking soda to 1 cup applesauce, stir well, then add to the suet mixture.
3. Scald raisins and mix with the cherries if desired.
4. Sift flour, baking powder, salt, cinnamon, nutmeg and ground cloves. Add raisins and cherries and stir until fruit is coated with flour mixture.
5. Fold flour and fruit into suet mixture. Pour into a lightly greased casserole, cover and place in a pan of water in a 350° F. oven.
6. Bake 1½ hours or until firm.
7. Serve hot with vanilla sauce.

Blueberry Buckle

½ cup sugar
2 cups flour
2½ teaspoons baking powder
¼ teaspoon salt
1 egg
½ cup milk
¼ cup melted fat
1 pint blueberries

Crumb Topping
½ cup sugar
⅓ cup flour
¼ cup butter
½ teaspoon cinnamon

1. Sift together sugar, flour, baking powder and salt.
2. Beat the egg, and the milk and melted fat and blend well.
3. Make a well in the flour mixture and add the liquid ingredients all at once. Stir quickly until flour mixture is just moistened.
4. Pour into a shallow glass baking dish, 13″ × 9″.
5. Cover with blueberries and top with the crumb mixture.
6. Bake at 350° F. for 40 to 50 minutes.

Blueberry Slump

1 quart blueberries
½ cup water
1½ cups sugar
1 teaspoon nutmeg

Batter
1 cup flour
1 teaspoon baking powder
1 tablespoon sugar
¼ teaspoon salt
1 egg
3 tablespoons milk
2 tablespoons melted fat

1. Boil blueberries, water, sugar and nutmeg in a heavy saucepan.
2. Sift dry ingredients, combine egg, milk and melted fat and add to flour mixture, stirring just until dry ingredients are moistened.
3. Drop batter mixture by spoonfuls on boiling berries.
4. Cover and cook 10 minutes.
5. Serve hot with cream.

Blueberry Kuchen

1⅓ cups crumbled shredded wheat biscuit *or*
1⅓ cups packaged corn flake crumbs
1 cup brown sugar, firmly packed
1⅓ tablespoons cinnamon
1 teaspoon salt
⅓ cup soft butter or margarine
½ cup chopped nutmeats
1 package (1 pound 4 ounces) white cake mix
1¼ cups (12 ounce package) frozen blueberries, thawed *or*
1¼ cups fresh blueberries

1. Crush cornflakes or shredded wheat biscuits into crumbs.
2. Combine sugar, cinnamon, salt and butter.
3. Mix well with pastry blender.
4. Add crumbs and nutmeats; blend thoroughly.
5. Prepare cake mix according to package directions.
6. Sprinkle 1½ cups of the crumb mixture over bottom of greased 13″ × 9″ baking pan.
7. Spread cake batter evenly over crumbs.
8. Sprinkle drained blueberries and remaining crumb mixture over cake batter.
9. Bake in moderate oven 350° F. about 40 minutes or until done.
10. Cut in squares and serve warm or cold.

Blueberry Crisp

⅓ cup sugar
2 tablespoons cornstarch
¼ teaspoon salt
⅛ teaspoon cinnamon
¼ teaspoon nutmeg
1 tablespoon lemon juice
4 cups drained sweetened
   blueberries
1 cup juice drained from fruit

Topping

⅓ cup butter *or*
   margarine
2 tablespoons flour
1 cup brown sugar, firmly
   packed
3 cups corn flakes

Make topping as follows:

1. Melt butter in heavy saucepan.
2. Combine brown sugar and flour, add to butter.
3. Cook, stirring constantly, over low heat until sugar is dissolved.
4. Add corn flakes, mixing quickly until well-coated with syrup.
5. Set aside.
6. Combine sugar, cornstarch, salt and spices in medium sized saucepan.
7. Add lemon juice and fruit juice; stir until smooth.
8. Cook over low heat, stirring constantly, until thickened and clear.
9. Stir in fruit.
10. Pour into buttered 11″ × 7″ pan.
11. Sprinkle evenly with corn flake topping.
12. Bake in moderately hot oven (400° F.) about 40 minutes.
13. Serve warm or cold with cream if desired.

Blueberry Pockets

1 cup blueberries
2 tablespoons sugar and
1 tablespoon sugar
1¾ cup sifted enriched flour
¾ teaspoon salt
2½ teaspoons baking powder
⅜ teaspoon cinnamon
⅛ teaspoon allspice
⅓ cup shortening
1 cup bite-size shredded wheat
   biscuits crushed to ½ cup
1½ teaspoons grated lemon peel
⅔ cup milk

1. Heat oven to hot (450°).
2. Butter 12 muffin cups.
3. Combine blueberries and 2 tablespoons sugar, let stand.
4. Sift together flour, 1 tablespoon sugar, salt, baking powder, cinnamon and allspice.
5. Cut in shortening until uniform.
6. Stir in cereal crumbs and lemon peel.
7. Add milk; stir until mixture holds together.
8. Knead lightly 10 times on floured board.
9. Roll or pat ¼ inch thick.
10. Cut into 3-inch squares.
11. Place dough squares in muffin cups
12. Fill with a heaping tablespoon of berries.
13. Bring corners together, press edges together lightly, letting biscuits gently fill the cups.
14. Bake 20 minutes or until brown and bubbly.

Cocoa Milk Pudding

3 tablespoons cornstarch
⅓ cup sugar
3 tablespoons cocoa
½ cup milk powder
  Few grains salt
2 cups warm water
1 teaspoon vanilla
2 teaspoons butter

1. Mix cornstarch, sugar, cocoa, milk powder and salt in the top of a double boiler.

2. Add the warm water slowly to the cornstarch mixture. Stir.

3. Put over boiling water in the bottom of the double boiler and cook until thick, about 20 minutes, stirring occasionally. There should be no taste of raw starch.

4. Remove the pudding from the heat. Add vanilla and 2 teaspoons of butter. Cool before serving. Serves 4-6.

Cornstarch Pudding

3 tablespoons cornstarch
3 tablespoons sugar
¼ teaspoon salt
½ cup milk powder
2 cups warm water
1 teaspoon vanilla
1 teaspoon butter

1. Mix cornstarch, sugar, salt and milk powder in the top of a double boiler.

2. Add the warm water slowly to the cornstarch mixture. Stir.

3. Put over boiling water in the bottom of the double boiler and cook until thick, about 20 minutes, stirring occasionally. There should be no taste of raw starch.

4. Remove the pudding from the heat. Add vanilla and 1 teaspoon of butter. Cool before serving. Serves 4-6.

Peach Crisp

1 large can sliced peaches and juice
2 tablespoons minute tapioca
¾ cup sugar
1 teaspoon grated lemon rind
½ teaspoon nutmeg
¾ cup flour
¼ cup butter

1. Combine peaches, tapioca, ¼ cup sugar, rind and nutmeg in a shallow dish.

2. Blend flour, butter and remaining sugar and cover the peach mixture.

3. Bake in 350° F. oven for 45 minutes.

4. Serve with cream (warm or cold).

Charlie Pudding

1 cup white sugar
1 cup sifted flour
2 teaspoons baking powder
½ cup milk
1 cup raisins (or any chopped fruit)
2 cups boiling water
1 cup brown sugar
2 tablespoons butter

1. Sift sugar, flour and baking powder into a small greased casserole.

2. Add milk and fruit and stir till dry ingredients are moistened.

3. Add butter and brown sugar to the boiling water and pour over the pudding in the casserole.

4. Bake in a 375° F. oven for 30 minutes.

Cranberry Pudding

2 cups bread crumbs
1 quart milk
3 eggs, separated
1½ cups sugar
2 tablespoons melted butter
2 cups cranberry sauce or jelly

Meringue

3 egg whites
¼ cup sugar
½ teaspoon cream of tartar
1 tablespoon water

1. Soak together the bread crumbs and milk.
2. Combine well beaten egg yolks, sugar and melted butter.
3. Add to the bread crumbs.
4. Turn into a baking dish.
5. Place in a pan of hot water.
6. Bake in a moderate oven at 350° F. 45 minutes or until firm.
7. Spread the 2 cups cranberry sauce or jelly over the baked custard and cover with the meringue.
8. Brown in the oven at 450° F. for 5 minutes. Serves 6.

Tapioca Cream Pudding

1 egg separated
2 cups milk
2 tablespoons rose hip syrup
¼ teaspoon salt
3 tablespoons minute tapioca
2 tablespoons sugar
¼ cup candied rose hips

1. In saucepan, mix the egg yolk with some of the milk.
2. Add the remaining milk, rose hip syrup, salt and tapioca.
3. Bring to a full boil over direct heat until it is thick.
4. Beat egg white until stiff.
5. Gradually add 2 tablespoons sugar.
6. Stir hot tapioca mixture slowly into the egg white—cool.
7. When cool, stir in the candied rose hips.
8. Chill and serve. Serves 4-5.

Monah Carley's Pineapple Squares

½ cup melted butter
2½ cups finely crushed
   graham wafer crumbs
½ cup soft butter
1½ cups sifted icing sugar
2 unbeaten eggs
1 can crushed pineapple
½ pint whipped cream

1. Mix together ½ cup melted butter and the graham wafer crumbs.

2. Press the mixture into greased cake pan and bake in moderate oven 350° F. for 15 minutes. Cool.

3. Beat together until light and creamy ½ cup soft butter, icing sugar and 2 eggs.

4. Spread this mixture over the cooled baked cracker crumbs.

5. Drain the crushed pineapple and fold into the whipped cream, then spread over the icing sugar mixture.

6. Sprinkle the top with fine wafer crumbs and chill for several hours.

Variations
Delicious made with fresh berries in season, canned fruit cocktail, or orange slices, in place of pineapple.

Apple Butterscotch Sauce

¼ cup butter
¾ cup brown sugar
3 tablespoons cornstarch
Pinch of salt
1 cup apple juice
1 cup water

1. Melt butter.

2. Blend in sugar, cornstarch and salt.

3. Cook until mixture is slightly browned.

4. Add apple juice and water and cook, stirring constantly, until sauce thickens.

5. Cook 5 minutes.

6. Serve with steamed fruit puddings or hot gingerbread.

Blueberry Syrup

2 quarts berries
1 quart sugar
¾ cup cold water

1. Pick over and mash fruit, sprinkle with sugar, cover and let stand overnight.

2. Add water, bring slowly to boiling point and cook 20 minutes.

3. Force through a double thickness of cheese-cloth.

4. Again bring to boiling point.

5. Fill small glass jars to overflowing and adjust covers. Use as foundation for beverages, ices or sauces.

Blueberry Topping for Cake or Ice Cream

1 quart blueberries
½ cup sugar
1 cup water
1 tablespoon cornstarch
2 tablespoons water
1 tablespoon lemon juice
1 cup whipped cream

1. Wash and pick over blueberries.

2. Add sugar and water.

3. Heat to boiling.

4. Make a thin paste of cornstarch and two tablespoons of water, and add slowly to blueberries.

5. Cook 15 minutes, cool, fold in whipped cream and lemon juice.

Blueberry Sauce

2 cups berries
4 cups sugar

1. Combine and stir in a crock or a pottery bowl.

2. Let stand 5 days; stir 4 to 6 times each day.

3. On the sixth day, spoon into sterile jars and seal.

4. Good on cake or ice cream; will keep several months if kept in a cool place.

Butterscotch Sauce

2 tablespoons butter
¾ cup brown sugar
½ cup corn syrup
⅓ cup evaporated milk
½ teaspoon vanilla
¼ teaspoon salt

1. Melt butter in a heavy pot on top of the stove. Add brown sugar and corn syrup and mix well, then cook over low heat without stirring to 234° F. or until a drop of the syrup will form a soft ball when dropped into cold water.

2. Remove from heat, add milk, vanilla and salt. Serve hot or cold.

Fruit Sauce on Cake or Bannock

1 can of fruit
3 tablespoons sugar
3 tablespoons flour
1 tablespoon butter

1. Drain juice from can of fruit in saucepan.

2. Heat juice to boiling.

3. Remove juice from heat and slowly add sugar and flour. Stir so flour does not form lumps.

4. Return the mixture to low heat. Cook the mixture until it becomes thick. Stir constantly.

5. Add butter to sauce.

6. Add fruit to sauce and continue cooking over low heat about 10 minutes.

7. Serve fruit sauce over cake or bannock.

8. Lemon juice (1 tablespoon) can be added to the fruit.

Caramel Sauce

¼ cup butter
1 cup brown sugar
1 tablespoon cornstarch
1 cup cold water
1 teaspoon vanilla

1. Melt butter in heavy saucepan.

2. Mix sugar and cornstarch with cold water.

3. Add sugar mixture to melted butter, bring to a boil and cook over low heat for 7 minutes, stirring constantly.

4. Remove from heat, add vanilla, stir well.

Chocolate Sauce No. 1

2 1-ounce squares unsweetened chocolate
1 tablespoon butter
¾ cup hot water
¾ cup sugar
½ teaspoon vanilla

1. Melt butter and chocolate in top of double boiler.

2. Add hot water, transfer to direct heat and stir until ingredients are well blended.

3. Add sugar, stir until sugar has dissolved, then continue cooking for 12 minutes.

4. Remove from heat, add vanilla and stir well.

Chocolate Sauce No. 2

6 tablespoons cocoa
4 tablespoons butter
¾ cup hot water
¾ cup sugar
½ teaspoon vanilla

1. Cream butter, add cocoa and blend well.

2. Add hot water and sugar, cook and stir until sugar dissolves, then continue cooking over medium heat for 12 minutes.

3. Remove from heat, add vanilla, stir well.

Lemon Sauce

½ cup white sugar
1 tablespoon cornstarch
¼ cup cold water
¾ cup boiling water
3 tablespoons butter
1 tablespoon grated lemon rind
Juice of 1 lemon

1. Mix sugar and cornstarch with ¼ cup cold water.

2. Add to ¾ cup boiling water, stir till mixture comes to a boil and is thickened.

3. Add butter, lemon juice and lemon rind and continue cooking over low heat for 7 minutes.

Note

If you are making this in an aluminum pot, always use wooden spoon for stirring. A metal spoon will darken the sauce.

Quick Dessert Sauce

1   package prepared pudding
      mix (regular size)
3   cups milk
½   teaspoon vanilla
1   tablespoon butter

1. Use vanilla, butterscotch, caramel or chocolate pudding mix.

2. Place mix in a heavy pot over medium heat, add milk and stir constantly until mixture comes to a boil and is thickened.

3. Remove from heat, add butter and vanilla and stir until smooth. Serve hot or cold over pudding, fruit, cake or ice cream.

Vanilla Sauce

½   cup white sugar
1   tablespoon cornstarch
½   teaspoon cinnamon (optional)
¼   teaspoon salt
¼   cup cold water
½   cup boiling water
1   tablespoon butter
1   teaspoon vanilla

1. Mix white sugar, cornstarch, cinnamon and salt.

2. Add cold water and mix well.

3. Add sugar and cornstarch to boiling water, stirring constantly. Bring back to a boil, reduce heat and cook 7 minutes.

4. Just before serving, add butter and vanilla. Serve hot on pudding, cake or ice cream.

Rum Sauce

1   cup sugar
1   tablespoon cornstarch
½   cup cold water
1   cup boiling water
2   tablespoons lemon juice, fresh
      frozen or canned
½   cup white rum
1   tablespoon butter

1. Mix cornstarch and sugar to a thin paste with cold water.

2. Add to boiling water, stirring constantly. Continue stirring until mixture comes to a boil and is thickened. Reduce heat and simmer for 7 minutes.

3. Remove from heat, add lemon juice, rum and butter, stir until butter melts. Serve immediately.

Butterscotch-Chocolate Frosting

3 1-ounce squares unsweetened chocolate
¼ cup butter *or* margarine
½ cup light cream
⅔ cup brown sugar (packed)
¼ teaspoon salt
Vanilla
Confectioner's sugar

1. Combine chocolate, butter, cream, brown sugar and salt in saucepan.

2. Bring to a boil, stirring constantly; cook until chocolate is melted.

3. Remove from heat, add vanilla and enough confectioner's sugar for good spreading consistency (about 3 cups).

4. Spread over sides and top of cake.

Fluffy Cake Frosting

1 cup brown sugar
¼ teaspoon cream of tartar
⅓ cup water
2 egg whites
1 teaspoon vanilla

1. Combine sugar, cream of tartar and ⅓ cup water.

2. Boil to 242° F.

3. Beat 2 egg whites until stiff.

4. Add hot syrup slowly, beating rapidly until frosting is of spreading consistency.

5. Stir in vanilla.

Quick Icing

2 cups icing sugar
¼ teaspoon salt
3 tablespoons butter
2 teaspoons vanilla *or*
2 tablespoons coffee, dry sherry, rum, lemon juice and grated rind, orange juice and grated rind, apricot brandy, crème de menthe liqueur, blueberry syrup, *or* cranberry syrup as desired.

1. Sift icing sugar, measure, then sift with the salt.

2. Cream the butter until very soft then blend the sugar into it.

3. Add vanilla or any desired flavouring.

4. If icing is too stiff, thin it with a little cream or evaporated milk. If it is too thin, add more icing sugar.

Apricot Bavarian Cake

1 envelope unflavoured gelatin
¼ cup orange juice
½ cup white sugar
1 tablespoon lemon juice
⅛ teaspoon salt
1 cup mashed, cooked dried apricots
1 cup heavy cream, whipped
1 8-ounce angel food cake

1. Soften gelatin in orange juice, then dissolve over hot water.

2. Stir in sugar, lemon juice, salt and apricots.

3. Refrigerate about 15 minutes or until thickened.

4. With egg beater, beat apricot mixture until frothy.

5. Fold in whipped cream.

6. Slice angel food cake crosswise into 3 layers.

7. Reassemble, spreading apricot mixture between layers, then over top and sides.

8. Refrigerate several hours or overnight.

Filling and Frosting for Angel Food

8 egg yolks
1 cup granulated sugar *or* fruit sugar
1 cup cream, whipped
1½ tablespoons gelatin
3 tablespoons cold water
3 tablespoons hot water
1 teaspoon vanilla
1 cup toasted shredded cocoanut

1. Prepare angel food cake according to your favorite recipe. Let cool.
2. Beat 8 egg yolks until thick and lemon colored.
3. Gradually add sifted sugar, beating well after each addition.
4. Whip one cup of whipping cream until thick, then fold it into the egg and sugar mixture.
5. Soften gelatin in cold water, then dissolve in hot water and add.
6. Add vanilla. Chill mixture in a cool place until it reaches spreading consistency.
7. Fill the hole in the centre of the angel food and spread over the entire cake.
8. Sprinkle toasted shredded cocoanut on top and sides.

Note
½ cup drained crushed pineapple, chopped peaches or any fruit or berries may be added if desired.

Marshmallows

2 tablespoons unflavored gelatin
½ cup cold water
2 cups granulated sugar
½ cup hot water
1 teaspoon vanilla

1. Sprinkle gelatin over cold water in a cup and allow to soften.
2. Combine sugar and hot water in a saucepan, place over high heat and boil for 2 minutes.
3. Remove saucepan from heat and add softened gelatin to syrup. Stir until dissolved.
4. Beat the mixture until very stiff, using an egg beater or electric mixer.
5. Add 1 teaspoon vanilla flavouring, pour into a well greased cake pan (9″ x 12″) and cover with a greased sheet of wax paper.
6. Cool and cut into squares.
7. Roll each marshmallow in sifted icing sugar.

Variations
Other flavourings and food coloring can be added to the basic mixture if desired.
Marshmallows can be rolled in toasted coconut or colored sugar.

Fondant

3 pounds icing sugar
½ pound butter (softened)
1 can Eagle Brand milk
2 tablespoons corn syrup

1. Combine all ingredients and mix thoroughly.

2. Divide the mixture into separate portions, depending on the number of different flavors you intend to make.

3. Mix in the desired flavor to each portion, shape as desired and freeze.

Flavorings

Maple Walnut—Maple flavoring and chopped walnuts.
Chocolate   —Cocoa.
Cherry   —Chopped cherries, red food coloring.
Mint   —Peppermint flavor, green food coloring.
Vanilla   —Vanilla flavoring.
Coffee   —Instant coffee.

4. As desired, remove from freezer and coat with chocolate.

Chocolate Coating

1 pound semi-sweet chocolate
1 pound sweet chocolate
¼ block paraffin

1. Melt the chocolate and paraffin over boiling water. Stir until blended.

2. Using a toothpick to pick up the candies, dip them into the chocolate until coated all over.

3. Place the dipped chocolates on waxed paper in a cool place until firm. The toothpick hole can later be filled with a swirl of chocolate.

Uncooked Chocolate Fudge

3¼ cups icing sugar
½ teaspoon salt
4 tablespoons evaporated milk
  or cream
1 egg, fresh *or* reconstituted
3 tablespoons butter
3 squares unsweetened chocolate
1 teaspoon vanilla
1 cup chopped nuts (optional)

1. Blend icing sugar, salt, milk and egg in mixing bowl.

2. Melt butter and chocolate over boiling water, then add to icing sugar mixture. Beat well.

3. Add vanilla and chopped nuts. Pour into an 8 inch buttered cake pan.

4. Chill until firm then cut into squares.

Peanut Butter Fudge

1 cup peanut butter
1 cup corn syrup
1¼ cups milk powder
1¼ cups sifted icing sugar

1. Blend ingredients in order given, knead for 3 minutes then form into balls.

2. Chill until firm.

3. Balls may be rolled in crushed corn flakes, toasted coconut, chopped peanuts, or coated with chocolate if desired.

Tasty Pastry

5 cups flour
1 pound lard *or* shortening
1 teaspoon salt
1 egg
1 tablespoon vinegar
  Water

1. Sift the flour and salt into a large mixing bowl.
2. Blend the chilled lard or shortening into the flour with a pastry blender, leaving pea-size pieces.
3. Beat the egg in a measuring cup with a fork, then add the vinegar. Continue beating and add enough water to fill the cup to the 8 oz line. Mix well.
4. Add the water and egg mixture to the flour gradually, tossing lightly until blended.
5. Press the dough together and place in a covered container in the refrigerator until needed.

This makes enough pastry for 3 pies, but need not be used all at once.

One-Crust Blueberry Pie

1 cup sugar
2 tablespoons cornstarch
⅔ cup cold water
½ cup blueberries
1 tablespoon butter
1 tablespoon lemon juice
1 teaspoon grated lemon rind
1½ cups frozen *or* fresh blueberries
1 cup whipping cream

1. Make your favourite pastry for a one-crust 9-inch pie. Bake and cool.
2. Combine sugar, cornstarch, cold water, ½ cup blueberries, butter, lemon juice and lemon rind.
3. Cook until thick.
4. Fold in frozen or fresh blueberries and cool mixture.
5. Whip the cream (sweeten to taste).
6. Spread the cream on the bottom of the pie shell.
7. When ready to serve, spoon the blueberry mixture over the whipped cream in the pie shell, leaving the cream uncovered around the edge.

Two-Crust Blueberry Pie

3 cups blueberries
3 tablespoons flour *or* minute tapioca
1 cup sugar
⅛ teaspoon salt
1 tablespoon butter

1. Make your favourite pastry recipe for a two-crust 9-inch pie.
2. Arrange ingredients in lower crust of the pie and dot with butter.
3. Cover with the second crust and bake at 450° F. for 10 minutes.
4. Lower the temperature to 350° and continue baking for 30 minutes or until the juice bubbles up and the crust is brown.

269

Mock Cherry Pie

3 cups cranberries, washed
1 cup scalded raisins
1½ cups sugar
4 tablespoons flour
½ teaspoon salt
1 cup water
½ teaspoon almond flavouring
  Pastry for 2-crust pie

1. Mix flour, sugar and salt in a saucepan, add water and bring slowly to a boil, stirring constantly.
2. Add cranberries and raisins, bring back to a boil, then reduce heat and simmer for 5 minutes, stirring constantly.
3. Remove from heat, add almond flavouring and let cool.
4. Pour into prepared pie crust, cover with top crust and bake in 425° F. oven for 15 minutes, reduce to 375° F. and continue baking for 30 minutes or until crust is lightly browned.

Cheese Pastry

¼ pound cream cheese
½ pound butter
4 tablespoons white sugar
2 cups flour

1. Cream the cheese and butter together.
2. Add the sugar, then fold in the flour and blend well.
3. Roll out the pastry into circles and put a little crabapple jelly on the circles, then fold over, press edges together.
4. Bake in 375° F. oven for about 10-12 minutes.

Maple Syrup Pie

1 tablespoon butter
2 tablespoons flour
2 egg yolks, beaten
1 cup maple syrup
½ cup water
1 baked 9-inch pie shell
1 cup whipped cream

1. Cream the flour and butter together, then add the beaten yolks and blend well.
2. Combine the maple syrup and water and add to the creamed mixture.
3. Cook in double boiler until mixture begins to thicken.
4. Pour into baked pie crust and allow to set.
5. Top with whipped cream and sprinkle with maple sugar shavings.

Pumpkin Pie

1¾ cups pumpkin
1 tin evaporated milk (tall)
2 eggs, beaten
½ cup brown sugar
¼ cup white sugar
1 teaspoon cinnamon
1 teaspoon nutmeg
¼ teaspoon ginger
¼ teaspoon cloves
½ teaspoon salt
  Pastry

1. Mix all ingredients together.
2. Pour into uncooked pie shell.
3. Bake in hot oven 400° F. for 40 minutes or until knife (metal) inserted in center comes out clean.

270

Cranberry Pie

3 cups cranberries
1 tablespoon flour
1 cup sugar
¼ teaspoon salt
3 teaspoons water
1 teaspoon vanilla
Butter
Pastry

1. Mix first six ingredients in the order given.

2. Pour into pastry-lined pie tin and dot with butter.

3. Cover with strips of pastry in a lattice design.

4. Bake in hot oven, 450° F. for 15 minutes.

5. Reduce heat to 350° F. and bake about 30 minutes longer.

Variations

Use 2 cups cranberries and 1½ cups soaked dried apples or 1½ cups soaked dried apricots in place of cranberries.

Mardy Gallagher's Saskatoon Berry Pie

3 cups saskatoon berries
2 tablespoons flour
¾ cup granulated sugar
2 teaspoons lemon juice
1 tablespoon butter
Pastry for 9-inch pie

1. Pick over saskatoons, wash and drain.

2. Line 9-inch pie plate with pastry.

3. Coat the berries with flour.

4. Alternate layers of sugar and berries in the pie plate, sprinkle lemon juice on top and dot with butter.

5. Cover top with a crust or lattice of pastry.

6. Bake at 400° F. for 10 minutes, reduce heat to 375° F. and continue baking for 25 minutes. Serve warm with whipped cream.

Joan Bellward's Mincemeat

1 pound raisins
1 pound sultanas
1 pound currants
½ pound mixed peel
½ pound blanched almonds, chopped
1 pound ground suet
12 apples, chopped
2 teaspoons cinnamon
1 teaspoon cloves
½ teaspoon nutmeg
¼ teaspoon ginger
2½ cups brown sugar
½ cup brandy
1 cup (approx.) of juice drained from fruit cocktail, canned pineapple, tropical fruit salad, *or* use any sweet fruit juice

1. Scald raisins and currants; toast almonds if desired; peel, core and chop apples.
2. Mix all ingredients in a large bowl. Let stand at room temperature for a day or two before making tarts or pies. Keep any leftover mincemeat in a clean covered jar in a cool place until needed.

Golden Peach Pie

1 can peach slices
1 cup syrup from peaches
⅓ cup sugar
1½ teaspoons cornstarch
¼ teaspoon salt
1½ teaspoons orange juice
1 teaspoon grated orange rind
1 tablespoon butter *or* margarine
Pastry for 8-inch crust and stars *or* strips for top

1. Drain peaches, reserving syrup.
2. Heat syrup to boiling.
3. Blend together sugar, cornstarch and salt and stir into hot syrup.
4. Cook until thick and clear.
5. Add orange juice, rind and butter.
6. Arrange peach slices in pastry-lined pie pan and pour thickened syrup over peaches.
7. Arrange pastry stars or strips on top.
8. Bake in hot oven 425° F. for 30 to 35 minutes.

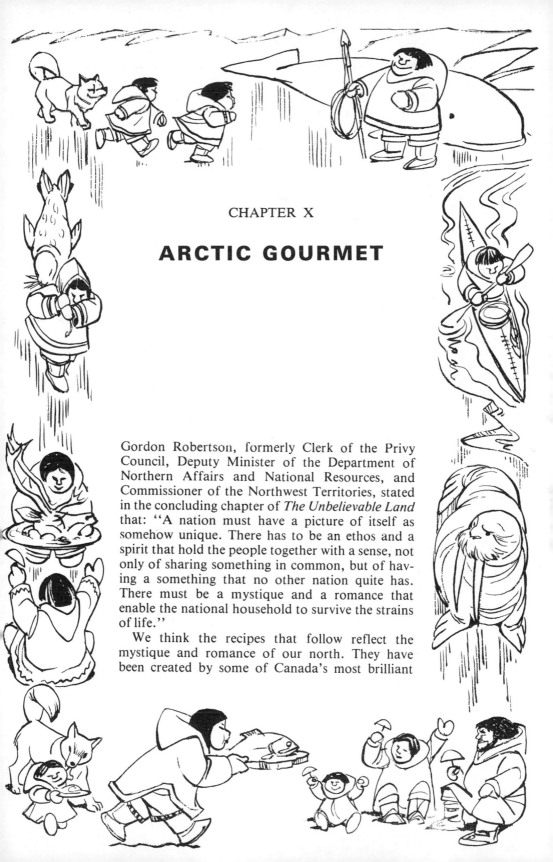

CHAPTER X

ARCTIC GOURMET

Gordon Robertson, formerly Clerk of the Privy
Council, Deputy Minister of the Department of
Northern Affairs and National Resources, and
Commissioner of the Northwest Territories, stated
in the concluding chapter of *The Unbelievable Land*
that: "A nation must have a picture of itself as
somehow unique. There has to be an ethos and a
spirit that hold the people together with a sense, not
only of sharing something in common, but of having a something that no other nation quite has.
There must be a mystique and a romance that
enable the national household to survive the strains
of life."

We think the recipes that follow reflect the
mystique and romance of our north. They have
been created by some of Canada's most brilliant

chefs, using indigenous foods, certainly "a something that no other nation quite has". By sharing these unique recipes with you, perhaps we can make a small contribution towards building up the ethos and spirit of our national household.

We are indebted to Mr. Eric Hofmann, a former Food Specialty Officer with the Industrial Division of the Department of Indian Affairs and Northern Development, for his assistance in the selection of these recipes.

Cold Whole Arctic Char Fairbanks

1 whole Arctic char (10-12 lbs. with head on)
3 small cans white asparagus tips
2 small cans red pimiento
1 cucumber
2 bunches parsley
2 bunches radishes
30 mushroom heads
20 lemon wedges
15 eggs, hard-cooked
　Black olives
　White almond pieces
15 tomatoes
　Shrimp salad

1. Wrap whole char in wet cheesecloth and simmer in court bouillon for 1½ to 2 hours.

2. Let the fish cool in stock, chill well, remove skin on both sides leaving the head on.

3. Dress hard-cooked eggs as penguins; heads made of whole black olives; white almond pieces for mouth and eyes, wings cut out of black olive skin.

4. Stuff the tomatoes with shrimp salad.

5. Place char on a large oval serving tray and garnish with the egg penguins, stuffed tomatoes, asparagus tips, parsley and lemon wedges. Decorate with mushroom heads, red pimiento, cucumber slices and radish.

6. Serve with sauce mayonnaise, sauce verte or sauce remoulade. Serves 20.

Sauce Verte

2 tablespoons parsley
2 tablespoons tarragon *or* dill
2 tablespoons chives
2 tablespoons spinach *or* chopped cucumber
2 tablespoons water cress
2 hard-cooked egg yolks
1 cup stiff mayonnaise

1. Chop parsley, tarragon, chives, spinach and watercress finely.

2. Pour boiling water over, leave for 2 minutes, then drain.

3. Rub through a sieve and mix to a paste with hard cooked egg yolks.

4. Add to mayonnaise and blend well.

Sauce Remoulade

1 cup mayonnaise
1 tablespoon chopped sweet pickle
1 tablespoon drained chopped capers
2 teaspoons mustard
1 teaspoon chopped parsley
½ teaspoon chopped tarragon
½ teaspoon chervil
½ teaspoon anchovy paste

Mix all ingredients in order given and blend well.

Baked Stuffed Arctic Char

Salt
Melted fat *or* oil
Desired stuffing
1 Arctic char, pan-dressed

1. Wash and dry fish. Sprinkle on inside with salt.

2. Stuff loosely with desired stuffing (¾ cup for each pound of stuffed fish, or 1 cup per pound of stuffed fish if backbone is removed).

3. Fasten opening with small skewers or sew with large needle.

4. Place stuffed fish on greased baking pan.

5. Brush with melted fat or oil.

6. Measure char at thickest part. Bake in hot oven 450° F. 10 minutes cooking time for each inch of thickness.

Basic Bread Stuffing

⅓ cup chopped onion
⅓ cup diced celery
3   tablespoons butter
½   teaspoon seasoning
    Pinch of ginger, savoury,
    thyme, sage *or* dried mint
3   cups dried bread crumbs

1. Cook onion and celery in fat until tender.

2. Add cooked vegetables and seasoning to bread crumbs. Toss lightly.

Broiled Arctic Char

Arctic char
Butter *or* olive oil
Parsley
Lemon slices
Anchovy Butter

1. Broil the char, sprinkling it with melted butter or olive oil, according to taste.

2. Set the broiled fish directly onto a very warm plate and garnish with fresh parsley and slices of lemon.

3. For best results serve with Anchovy Butter.

Anchovy Butter

¼ cup butter
1   teaspoon anchovy paste
⅛   teaspoon onion juice
¼   teaspoon lemon juice
    Few grains cayenne

1. Cream butter until soft.

2. Beat in remaining ingredients.

Arctic Char Fish Cakes

1 pound cooked Arctic char
2 cups freshly cooked
  floury potatoes
2 tablespoons reduced béchamel
  sauce
2 eggs, beaten
1 tablespoon fat
½ teaspoon salt
¼ teaspoon pepper
2 tablespoons chopped parsley

1. Flake the cooked char, removing all skin and bones.

2. Mix thoroughly the flaked fish and floury potatoes, salt and pepper.

3. Add the sauce and beaten eggs and blend the mixture to a smooth paste.

4. Roll the paste mixture into 2-ounce balls and place on flour covered board, then flatten each ball into a patty.

5. Heat the fat in heavy fry pan and pan fry the fish cakes till golden brown, turning once.

6. Place the cooked fish cakes on a napkin in serving dish and garnish with chopped parsley. Serves 4.

Reduced Béchamel Sauce

2 tablespoons butter
2 tablespoons flour
1 cup milk
1 small onion studded with
  3 whole cloves
½ small bay leaf
¼ cup heavy cream
1 teaspoon lemon juice
  Salt

1. Melt butter over low heat, blend in flour and cook for 5 minutes.

2. Remove from heat, add milk, stirring constantly.

3. Add onion studded with cloves, and bay leaf.

4. Cook and stir until sauce is smooth and thick, then place in a 350° F. oven and let sauce continue cooking until it is reduced to ¾ of its volume.

5. Remove onion and bay leaf. Add heavy cream, bring to a boil and add lemon juice. Salt to taste.

Golden Broiled Arctic Char Steaks

2 pounds char steaks
1 tablespoon chopped onion
2 tablespoons lemon juice
1 teaspoon salt
  Dash pepper
¼ teaspoon tarragon
¼ cup butter, melted
  Paprika
  Parsley

1. Place steaks on greased broiler pan.

2. Mix onion, lemon juice, salt, pepper and tarragon with melted butter.

3. Baste steaks with half of sauce, then broil (2 to 4 inches from heat for fresh fish, 6 to 8 inches for frozen).

4. When browned, turn over, and baste with remaining sauce.

5. Broil 10 minutes per inch for fresh char, 20 minutes per inch for frozen.

6. Sprinkle with paprika, garnish with parsley. Serves 4.

Fillets of Arctic Char Americain

2 pounds char fillets
1 tablespoon lemon juice
2 tablespoons butter
1 cup soft bread crumbs
1 teaspoon chopped parsley
½ cup Worcestershire sauce
6 oysters
  Salt and pepper

1. Season the fillets with salt and pepper.

2. Heat 1 tablespoon butter in heavy fry pan and pan fry the fillets until golden brown. Sprinkle with the lemon juice.

3. Fry the bread crumbs in the remaining butter and cover the cooked fillets with the hot bread crumbs.

4. Sprinkle the chopped parsley over the fish and serve with lemon wedges.

5. Bring the Worcestershire sauce to a boil and poach the oysters for about 5 minutes. Place the oysters around the fillets and serve hot. Serves 4.

Medaillons of Arctic Char

1 fillet Arctic char
2 tablespoons French dressing
  Olives
1 tablespoon chopped parsley
  Lemon wedges

1. Cut the fillet into small slices, about ¼ inch thick.

2. Place them on a buttered baking sheet and bake in a moderate oven 350° F. for about 10 minutes.

3. Cool them under a light weight, then trim the cooled slices neatly into round or oval shapes with a cutter.

4. Spread the French dressing over them and garnish with olives, lemon and parsley.
These make tasty hors d'houvres.

Poached Arctic Char in Bouillon

¼ teaspoon thyme
½ teaspoon peppercorns
1 bay leaf
1 teaspoon finely chopped parsley
1 quart (5 cups) water, boiling
½ cup vinegar
1 teaspoon salt
1 stalk celery
¼ cup sliced onion
¼ cup sliced carrots
1 Arctic char, pan-dressed

1. Boil all ingredients except the char, together for 10 minutes.

2. Wipe fish with damp cloth. Measure its thickness.

3. Simmer the fish in the bouillon in a covered pan until it flakes easily when tested with a fork. Allow 10 minutes cooking time per inch thickness for fresh fish and about 20 minutes per inch thickness for frozen.

4. The cooking liquid may be thickened and served as a sauce.

277

Fillets Arctic Char Bercy

2 pounds char fillets
2 shallots, finely chopped
  Salt and pepper
3 tablespoons white wine
3 tablespoons milk
1 tablespoon butter
  Lemon juice
  Fresh parsley

1. Butter the bottom of casserole dish and sprinkle the chopped shallots on the bottom.

2. Season the fillets with salt and pepper and lay them side by side over the shallots.

3. Pour the wine and milk over the fish and dot the top with butter.

4. Bake in hot oven 400° F. for about 25 minutes, basting frequently.

5. Sprinkle with lemon juice and garnish with sprigs of parsley. Serves 4.

Atlanta Special

1 beaver (8 to 10 pounds)
1 bay leaf
2 medium onions
1–2 garlic cloves
  Celery leaves (optional)
  Flour
  Fat
  Salt and pepper

1. Remove nearly all fat from beaver. Cut up as you do rabbit and soak overnight in salt water.

2. Parboil until about half-cooked in water with the bay leaf, onions, and garlic. Add celery if desired.

3. Drain, roll in flour and brown in hot fat, season with salt and pepper.

4. Bake in covered pan in a moderate oven until tender.

5. Gravy may be made from the drippings. Serves 6.

Crab à la Newburg

1 cup crab meat
1 cup button mushrooms
¼ cup sherry
¼ cup butter
1 tablespoon flour
½ teaspoon salt
¼ teaspoon cayenne
¾ cup cream
2 egg yolks
1 tablespoon brandy

1. Flake the crab meat into medium size pieces.

2. Place the crab meat and mushrooms in the top part of double boiler. Add the sherry and let stand for 30 minutes.

3. Add the butter to the meat and mushrooms and place the pot over hot water in the bottom of the double boiler. Cook for 10 minutes.

4. Sprinkle the flour, salt and cayenne over the mixture, blend well and continue cooking for 5 minutes.

5. Add the cream but do not continue cooking.

6. Beat the egg yolks and stir slowly into the meat mixture, being careful that it does not curdle.

7. Drip the brandy over all, lightly mixing. Heat through and serve on patty shells or buttered toast. Serves 2.

Hungarian Roast Duck

2 wild ducks, 2 to 2½ pounds
  (dressed weight)
  Garlic salt and pepper
2 tablespoons paprika
2 apples, quartered
2 onions, quartered
6 slices bacon
¼ cup butter, melted
3 cups sauerkraut
4 juniper berries, crushed
2 teaspoons caraway seeds
2 slices cooked bacon, crumbled

1. Sprinkle ducks inside and out with garlic salt, pepper and paprika.

2. Place apple and onion quarters in cavity of each.

3. Cover breasts with bacon and fasten with string.

4. Place ducks, breasts up, in a baking pan.

5. Roast in preheated 350° F. oven 1 to 1¼ hours, or 15 minutes per pound, basting frequently with melted butter.

6. Combine sauerkraut, crushed juniper berries, caraway seeds and crumbled bacon in shallow casserole.

7. Mix well. Place in oven 20 minutes before ducks are done.

8. When ducks are tender, remove them from oven, undo the string and discard the apple and quarters.

9. Carve ducks and arrange the slices on the hot sauerkraut. Serve with potato pancakes, plum jelly, hot biscuits and beverage. Serves 4.

Ragoût of Duck

2   5-pound ducks
½   cup brandy
3   cups dry red wine
1   small onion, chopped
1   garlic clove, minced *or*
     dash of garlic powder
¼   cup chopped parsley
½   teaspoon ground nutmeg
4   tablespoons butter
1   cup chopped celery
½   pound mushrooms, sliced
     Salt
     Pepper

1. Clean and cut up ducks in serving portions.
2. Marinate duck for 2 hours in mixture of brandy, wine, onion, garlic, parsley, nutmeg, salt and pepper and 1 cup of water. Remove duck and dry.
3. Sauté in butter until golden brown.
4. Place duck in a heavy saucepan and pour unstrained marinade over it.
5. Bring to a boil, reduce heat and simmer for 30 minutes.
6. Add celery and mushrooms and continue cooking for 25 minutes. Serves 6.

Cantonese Duck

2   wild ducks, 2 to 2½ pounds
     (dressed weight)
     Garlic salt and pepper
4   sprigs parsley
1   lemon, halved
6   slices bacon
½   cup beer
¼   cup dry mustard
½   teaspoon Accént
     (monosodium glutamate)
2   tablespoons soy sauce
1   cup apricot preserves
1   tablespoon lemon juice
1   teaspoon grated orange peel
¼   cup butter, melted

1. Sprinkle ducks inside and out with garlic salt and pepper.
2. Place 2 sprigs parsley and ½ lemon in cavity of each.
3. Cover breasts with bacon and fasten with string.
4. For Cantonese sauce, stir beer into dry mustard, add the remaining ingredients, except butter, and heat in double boiler over hot water.
5. Place ducks, breasts up, in baking pan.
6. Roast in preheated 350° F. oven 15 minutes per pound, basting frequently with butter and once with Cantonese sauce.
7. Carve the ducks. Serve with cooked rice, the remaining Cantonese sauce and a beverage. Serves 4.

Ruffed Grouse Amandine

4 ruffed grouse
Salt and pepper
4 slices bacon
½ cup butter, melted
¼ cup blanched almonds slivered
1 teaspoon lemon juice
4 slices buttered toast

1. Sprinkle grouse inside and out with salt and pepper.
2. Cover breasts with bacon and fasten with string or wooden picks.
3. Place grouse, breasts up, in baking pan. Preheat oven 350° F. and roast 40 to 50 minutes, or until tender. Baste frequently with ¼ cup butter.
4. Combine remaining butter, almonds and lemon juice.
5. Remove string or picks and bacon for the last five minutes of cooking.
6. Pour butter-almond mixture over grouse.
7. Serve on buttered toast with bacon, buttered peas, endive salad and beverage. Serves 4.

Grouse With Orange Slices

4 grouse
Salt and pepper
4 orange slices, ¼ inch thick, peeled and sliced
4 slices bacon
Chopped parsley
¼ cup butter, melted
Grated peel 1 orange
2 tablespoons orange juice
1 teaspoon lemon juice

1. Sprinkle grouse inside and out with salt and pepper.
2. Cover breast of each with an orange slice and a bacon slice, fasten with string.
3. Place grouse, breasts up, in a baking dish. Roast in preheated 350° F. oven 40 to 50 minutes, or until tender. Combine butter, orange peel, orange juice and lemon juice and baste frequently.
4. Remove string. Sprinkle with parsley.
5. Serve with roasted orange and bacon slices, baked hominy, brussel sprouts and beverage. Serves 4.

Pigeon à l'Italienne

4 pigeons
1 teaspoon garlic salt
¼ teaspoon pepper
Flour to dredge
¼ cup olive or salad oil
1 tin tomato sauce
½ cup beer
4 medium onions, sliced
¼ teaspoon oregano
3 tablespoons chopped parsley

1. Sprinkle the pigeons inside and out with garlic salt and pepper, then dredge with flour.
2. Heat olive or salad oil in a heavy pot, add the pigeons and brown on all sides.
3. Add tomato sauce, beer, sliced onions and oregano and bring to a boil.
4. Cover and cook over low heat about 45 minutes, or until tender.
5. Add the parsley. Serve with parmesan spaghetti, Italian bread and your favourite green salad. Serves 4.

Rabbit Chop Suey

2 cups cooked rabbit meat (coarsely cut)
¼ cup sliced mushrooms
2 tablespoons butter *or* margarine
1 cup celery, sliced thinly
1 small carrot, cut in thin strips
1 medium onion, thinly sliced
1½ cups rabbit broth *or* water with 3 chicken bouillon cubes
2 cups canned bean sprouts, with liquid
3 tablespoons cornstarch
3 tablespoons soy sauce
   Salt and pepper to taste
1½ cups hot cooked rice

1. Cook rabbit meat and mushrooms in the fat over low heat, until browned.
2. Add celery, carrot, onion, and broth.
3. Cover the pot and boil gently 10 to 15 minutes, or until vegetables are tender.
4. Add the bean sprouts and liquid, and heat to boiling.
5. Mix the cornstarch and soy sauce and add gradually to the boiling mixture, stirring constantly, until slightly thickened.
7. Add salt and pepper, serve over rice. Serves 6.

Rabbit Delight

1 young rabbit
1 tablespoon fat
1 cup broth *or* water with
1 chicken bouillon cube
¼ cup lemon juice
¾ cup orange juice
2 green peppers, chopped
½ cup mushrooms, chopped
1 tablespoon parsley, chopped
   Pinch of ginger
½ teaspoon salt
¼ teaspoon pepper

1. Joint the rabbit and brown pieces in fat in a heavy pot.
2. Add the broth and the other ingredients, season with salt, pepper and ginger.
3. Cover and cook slowly until tender. Serves 4.

Deep Fried Rabbit

2 wild rabbits
   Juice of 1 lemon
½ teaspoon salt
¼ teaspoon pepper
   Dash of nutmeg
1 egg, beaten
   Dry bread crumbs
   Parsley
   Green peas
6 slices of toast

1. Cut rabbits into serving pieces, wipe clean and parboil for 10 minutes in water to which the lemon juice has been added.
2. Drain well and season with salt, pepper and nutmeg.
3. Dip the pieces of meat in beaten egg, then roll in very dry bread crumbs.
4. Deep fry the pieces of meat in hot fat until golden brown.
5. Drain free of fat and garnish with parsley. Serve with green peas on buttered toast. Serves 6.

Jugged Hare

1 hare
2 ounces cognac
2 tablespoons olive oil
½ teaspoon salt
¼ teaspoon pepper
1 medium onion, thinly sliced
1 pound lean side pork
2 tablespoons butter
1 clove garlic, minced
2 medium-sized onions, quartered
1 tablespoon flour
3 ounces red wine
1 bay leaf
1 tablespoon chopped parsley
1 teaspoon thyme

1. Cut hare into serving pieces, wash and pat dry.

2. Place the pieces of hare in a large bowl or earthenware pot.

3. Mix the cognac, olive oil, salt, pepper, and sliced onion and pour over the meat. Let stand in the marinade for a few hours.

4. Cut the side pork into small pieces and boil for a few minutes. Drain, then dredge with flour.

5. Melt 2 tablespoons butter in heavy fry pan and sauté the pieces of pork and minced garlic until golden brown. Set aside.

6. Dredge the quartered onion with flour and sauté until golden brown, add to the pork.

7. Drain the pieces of hare, and sear them in hot fry pan. Pour 3 ounces of red wine over the meat and enough water to cover. Add the bay leaf, parsley and thyme and simmer until meat is tender.

8. Place the cooked pork and onions in a serving dish and lay the pieces of hare on top. Pour the sauce over all and serve hot. Serves 4.

Note
Small glazed onions and mushrooms may be used to garnish the dish.

Creole Rabbit

3 pounds rabbit (cut in serving pieces)
¼ cup milk
Flour, salt and pepper
3 tablespoons cooking fat *or* oil
Creole sauce

1. Dip rabbit in milk and roll it in mixture of flour, salt and pepper.

2. Heat fat or oil and brown rabbit on all sides lightly. Pour sauce over rabbit, cover pan.

3. Bake in 325° F. oven 1½ hours, or until meat is tender.

4. Uncover and bake 30 minutes longer to brown top. Serves 6.

Creole Sauce

2 medium onions, sliced
1 clove garlic, chopped fine
1 tablespoon chopped parsley
3 tablespoons butter, margarine *or* oil
3½ cups tomato juice
¼ teaspoon Worcestershire sauce
Salt and pepper to taste

1. Cook onions, garlic and parsley in fat or oil until onion is golden brown.

2. Add tomato juice and Worcestershire sauce and cook gently for 15 minutes.

3. Season with salt and pepper to taste.

Hassenpfeffer

1 small rabbit, cut in serving
   pieces (about 2½ pounds)
½ cup vinegar
2 cups water
2 teaspoons salt
¼ teaspoon pepper
½ teaspoon whole cloves
2 teaspoons sugar
4 bay leaves
1 medium onion, sliced
   Flour
3 tablespoons fat
2 teaspoons Worcestershire sauce
3 tablespoons flour

1. Make pickling mixture by combining the vinegar, water, salt, pepper, cloves, sugar, bay leaves, and onion in a glass or china bowl.

2. Add the pieces of rabbit and sliced giblets and cover the bowl.

3. Let stand in refrigerator 8 to 12 hours, turning the pieces occasionally to absorb the flavor evenly.

4. Remove the rabbit pieces. Save liquid and onions but discard bay leaves and cloves.

5. Roll the rabbit in flour.

6. Heat fat in heavy pan and brown rabbit, turning to brown on all sides.

7. Pour the pickling mixture over the rabbit.

8. Cover pan and cook over low heat, about 1 hour or until tender.

9. Take rabbit from pan and keep it hot.

10. Add Worcestershire sauce to liquid. Thicken with 3 tablespoons flour mixed with cold water and cook until sauce is thick and smooth, stirring constantly.

11. Pour sauce over rabbit. Serves 4.

Michigan Special

1 muskrat
1 tablespoon salt
1 quart water
1 teaspoon salt
⅛ teaspoon pepper
½ medium onion, sliced
½ cup fat
1 cup tomato catsup
½ teaspoon Worcestershire
   sauce
1 cup water

1. Skin and clean muskrat, remove fat, scent glands and the white tissue inside each leg.

2. Soak muskrat overnight in a weak brine solution of 1 tablespoon salt to 1 quart of water. Drain, disjoint and cut into desired pieces.

3. Place in a deep pan and add 1 quart water, 1 teaspon salt, pepper, sliced onion. Bring to a boil, then reduce heat and simmer 1 hour.

4. Remove meat and let drain.

5. Melt fat in skillet, sauté meat until brown on one side, turn over and immediately pour over the meat the catsup and Worcestershire sauce.

6. Almost cover with water (about 1 cup) and let simmer until gravy is thick enough to serve (about 30 minutes). Serves 4.

Reindeer Bourguignon

4 pounds reindeer meat
Red wine (burgundy)
1 clove garlic, chopped fine
Flour for dredging
½ teaspoon salt
¼ teaspoon pepper
2 tablespoons olive oil
1 tablespoon butter
2 tablespoons flour
1 cup broth *or* consommé
1 bay leaf
2 tablespoons tomato paste
½ cup diced carrots
4 small onions
1 cup mushrooms, sliced
1 green pepper, chopped

1. Cut the reindeer meat into bite size pieces.

2. Place in a bowl and cover with wine; add the garlic and let stand overnight.

3. Strain the meat and dredge with flour; season with salt and pepper.

4. Heat the olive oil and butter in a heavy pot and brown the meat on all sides. Remove the meat.

5. Brown 2 tablespoons flour in the pot, then add 1 cup broth and one cup of the wine which was drained from the meat, blend well. Add the bay leaf and tomato paste.

6. Return the meat to the pot, cover and simmer slowly for 2 hours.

7. Add the carrots, onions, mushrooms and green pepper and simmer until the vegetables are tender. Serve with boiled potatoes. Serves 6.

Sautéed Partridge in Grape Sauce

6 partridge breasts
2 teaspoons salt
¼ teaspoon white pepper
¼ teaspoon shortening
2 tablespoons butter
1 teaspoon tarragon leaves
1 tablespoon finely chopped shallots
½ cup white wine
½ cup chicken stock *or* chicken bouillon cube dissolved in ½ cup water
¼ cup light cream
2 teaspoons cornstarch
1 egg yolk, beaten
1½ cups seedless grapes

1. Season the partridge breasts with salt and pepper.
2. Heat the shortening and butter in heavy pot and sauté the partridge pieces until lightly browned.
3. Combine the tarragon, shallots, wine and chicken stock and pour over the partridge.
4. Simmer slowly for 20 minutes or until tender, basting occasionally.
5. Remove partridge from the pot and keep warm.
6. Blend together the cream, cornstarch and beaten egg yolk and add to the sauce, stirring continuously until sauce is thickened.
7. Return the partridge breasts to the sauce, add the grapes and heat thoroughly. Serve hot. Serves 3.

Braised Seal

1½ pounds seal meat
2 tablespoons beef suet
¼ cup dried carrots, reconstituted
¼ cup dried turnip, reconstituted
2 tablespoons onion flakes, softened in boiling water
1 tablespoon flour
1 cup water
1 tablespoon "Bovril"
¼ cup canned peas
1 tin tomatoes
½ teaspoon salt
¼ teaspoon pepper

1. Heat beef suet in heavy fry pan and pan fry the carrots, turnips and onions until lightly browned. Remove from pan.
2. Sprinkle flour into fry pan and cook until brown, add the water slowly, stirring to blend, then "Bovril", salt and pepper.
3. Add the peas and tomatoes and simmer slowly for a few minutes.
4. Place vegetables in bottom of casserole and place the meat on top.
5. Pour the gravy over the vegetables and meat, cover and bake in a moderate oven 350° F. about 2½ hours, or until meat is tender.
6. Half an hour before required, remove lid so that the meat will brown and crisp on top. Serves 6.

Braised Hearts of Seal

3 seal hearts
2 quarts water
1 tablespoon salt
¼ cup beef suet *or* cooking fat
½ cup dried onion, reconstituted
½ cup dried turnip, reconstituted
½ cup dried peas, reconstituted
¼ cup dried carrot, reconstituted
1 tablespoon flour
2 cups water or meat stock
1 tablespoon "Bovril"
½ teaspoon salt
¼ teaspoon pepper
6 whole tomatoes *or* 1 tin canned tomatoes

1. Wash hearts thoroughly and remove all blood.

2. Soak hearts in salted water for 2 or 3 hours, then remove and drain.

3. Melt suet in a heavy pan, add reconstituted vegetables and fry gently until tender, then remove and set aside.

4. Brown the flour in the remaining fat, add the water or stock, "Bovril," salt and pepper, stirring constantly until smooth and thickened.

5. Place vegetables in the bottom of a deep heavy pot, place hearts on top, and arrange tomatoes around them.

6. Add the gravy, cover tightly and simmer for 2 or 3 hours until tender.

7. Slice hearts for serving with the gravy. Serves 6.

Casserole of Seal

1½ pounds seal meat
½ teaspoon salt
¼ teaspoon pepper
2 tablespoons beef suet
3 tablespoons onion flakes, softened in lukewarm water
½ cup diced carrots
½ cup canned peas
½ cup diced turnip
2 tablespoons flour
1 cup water
1 tablespoon Worcestershire sauce
3 tablespoons tomato sauce
½ teaspoon salt
¼ teaspoon pepper

1. Cut the seal meat into small pieces and season with salt and pepper. Dredge with flour.

2. Heat a heavy fry pan and add 2 tablespoons of beef suet, then brown the pieces of meat with the onions.

3. Place a layer of browned meat and onions and a layer of vegetables alternately in a casserole.

4. Reheat the fry pan and brown the flour, add 1 cup water slowly, stirring constantly, then add the Worcestershire sauce and the tomato sauce, stirring until gravy is thickened. Add the salt and pepper.

5. Pour the gravy over meat and vegetables in the casserole. Cover.

6. Bake in a moderate oven 350° F. for about 2 hours. Serves 6.

287

Fried Seal Liver

1 pound seal liver
   Milk
8 slices bacon
1 cup chopped onion
2 tablespoons butter
½ teaspoon salt
¼ teaspoon pepper
   Flour to dredge
1 tablespoon chopped parsley

1. Cut the liver into thin slices and soak in milk for 2 hours.
2. Cook the bacon slices in heavy fry pan until lightly browned.
3. Drain off half of the bacon drippings from the fry pan and set aside. Sauté the chopped onions in the fry pan until clear and tender, stirring often. Set the onions aside with the bacon.
4. Add the remaining bacon drippings to the fry pan, then add 2 tablespoons butter and heat until very hot, but do not burn.
5. Drain the slices of liver and dredge with flour. Season with salt and pepper and cook quickly on both sides. Reduce heat and cook the liver slowly for about 5 more minutes.
6. Sprinkle the liver with chopped parsley and serve with bacon and onions. Serves 4.

Seal Portugaise

4 pieces seal meat, 1″ thick
3 tablespoons butter
1 tin tomatoes
1 tin green peas
2 tablespoons butter
2 tablespoons flour
1 cup milk
3 tablespoons tomato sauce *or* catsup
½ teaspoon salt
¼ teaspoon pepper
4 slices buttered toast

1. Cut meat into rounds about the size of a slice of bread.
2. Heat butter in a heavy fry pan and pan fry the seal meat until tender. Remove meat and keep hot until needed.
3. Add tomatoes and peas to the fry pan and heat thoroughly, then remove and keep hot.
4. Melt 2 tablespoons butter in fry pan, add the flour and heat until flour bubbles, stirring constantly. Remove from heat.
5. Add the milk slowly, stirring constantly, then return pan to heat and stir until thick.
6. Add tomato sauce or catsup and season to taste with salt and pepper. Bring to a boil, then reduce heat and simmer sauce for 5 minutes.
7. Place one slice of meat on each piece of buttered toast, cover with sauce, and serve with tomatoes and peas. Serves 4.

Roulades of Seal

1   pound seal meat, cut into
      4 rectangular pieces
4   slices of bacon
      Parsley or mixed herbs
4   ounces beef suet
½   cup dried onions, reconstituted
½   cup dried turnips, reconstituted
½   cup peas
3   tomatoes, sliced *or* ½
      cup tinned tomatoes
1   tablespoon flour
2   tablespoons vinegar
1   tablespoon "Bovril"
1   cup water
½   teaspoon salt
¼   teaspoon pepper

1. Season the pieces of meat with a little salt.

2. Lay a slice of bacon on each piece and sprinkle with parsley or mixed herbs.

3. Roll the pieces up and tie with cotton thread.

4. Heat beef suet in heavy fry pan and fry the rolls until lightly browned, then place in a baking dish.

5. Fry the onions, turnips, peas and tomatoes, then add to the meat in baking dish.

6. Sprinkle the flour into fry pan and stir until brown, then add 1 cup water, "Bovril", vinegar, salt and pepper. Bring mixture to a boil and pour over the meat.

7. Cover baking dish and bake in moderate oven 350° F. for about two hours. Remove thread and serve. Serves 4.

Savoury Seal Hearts

1   large seal heart
1   cup bread crumbs *or*
      cooked rice
1   teaspoon parsley
½   teaspoon sage
½   teaspoon salt
¼   teaspoon pepper
2   tablespoons onion flakes
      softened in lukewarm water
      Slices of fat bacon
2   tablespoons melted butter

1. Soak the heart in salted water overnight.

2. Wash the heart well and trim off the fat, large veins and thread-like cords.

3. Cut the heart into thick slices.

4. Grease a casserole well with butter.

5. Make a stuffing of bread crumbs or cooked rice, parsley, sage, salt, pepper and the onions. Toss lightly.

6. Place the slices of heart, stuffing and slices of fat bacon in layers, alternately in the greased casserole and top with the melted butter.

7. Cover tightly and bake in a moderate oven for at least 2 hours. Serves 4.

Seal Brain au Gratin

2 seal brains
1 tablespoon salt
1 tablespoon vinegar
Water to cover
2 tablespoons butter
1 tablespoon flour
1 cup milk
½ teaspoon salt
¼ teaspoon pepper
½ cup dry bread crumbs
2 tablespoons grated cheese
1 tablespoon butter
4 slices hot buttered
  toast

1. Wash the seal brains thoroughly in salt water, removing loose skin and any blood.

2. Soak the brains in fresh cold water for 1 hour, changing the water two or three times.

3. Place the brains in a saucepan and cover with water mixed with 1 tablespoon salt and 1 tablespoon vinegar. Bring to a boil and boil slowly for 15 minutes. Drain and pat dry with a clean cloth.

4. Cut the brains in bite-size pieces.

5. Make a sauce of 2 tablespoons butter melted in a saucepan. Add the flour and blend well, then add 1 cup of milk, cooking slowly and stirring until sauce is thickened. Add salt and pepper and one half of the grated cheese. Continue stirring until smooth.

6. Add the pieces of seal brain to the sauce, stirring lightly then pour into a casserole.

7. Sprinkle the top of the mixture with bread crumbs and remainder of the grated cheese. Dot with pieces of butter.

8. Place casserole in moderately hot oven 375° to 400° F. and brown quickly.

9. Serve on hot buttered toast. Serves 4.

Seal Brain Fritters

2 seal brains
1 tablespoon salt
1 tablespoon vinegar
Water to cover
2 tablespoons egg powder, mixed
  with
6 tablespoons lukewarm water
½ cup flour
¼ cup milk
½ teaspoon salt
¼ teaspoon pepper
¼ teaspoon mixed herbs
2 tablespoons melted butter
Fat for deep frying

1. Wash the seal brains in salted water. Remove loose skin and blood.

2. Soak the brains in fresh cold water for 1 hour, changing the water two or three times.

3. Cover with water to which 1 tablespoon salt and 1 tablespoon vinegar has been added and boil for 15 minutes. Drain and pat dry.

4. Mash the brains until soft and light.

5. Mix the flour, eggs and milk together, beating well to make a soft smooth batter.

6. Add the brains, melted butter, herbs, salt and pepper to the batter, and mix well.

7. Drop tablespoons of the mixture into hot fat and deep fry until golden brown.

8. Drain the fritters well before serving. Serves 4.

Arctic Muktuk Chowder

20-ounce can muktuk, chopped
8 tablespoons olive oil
8 tablespoons diced bacon
2 large onions, chopped
2 leeks, chopped
8 quarts water
2 teaspoons curry powder
2 teaspoons thyme
4 teaspoons salt
1 teaspoon marjoram
4 bay leaves
8 large potatoes, diced
3 large green peppers, chopped
8 tomatoes, peeled and chopped
1 tablespoon parsley, chopped
1 tablespoon chives, chopped
1 teaspoon Lee & Perrin's sauce

1. Place olive oil in a heavy pot, heat and sauté the bacon, chopped onion and leeks until golden brown.

2. Pour the water into the pot then add the curry powder, thyme, salt, marjoram and bay leaves. Bring to a boil.

3. Add the diced potatoes, peppers, tomatoes, parsley and chives and boil for about 30 minutes.

4. Add the muktuk and Lee & Perrin's sauce and let cook another 5 minutes. Serve with hot biscuits. Serves 8.

Tournedos of Seal

4 slices of seal meat
½ teaspoon salt
¼ teaspoon pepper
2 tablespoons butter
1 15-ounce can peas
½ cup vinegar
1 tablespoon dried onion flakes,
  softened in boiling water,
  then drained
¼ cup butter
2 tablespoons egg powder mixed
  with 6 tablespoons lukewarm
  water
½ teaspoon dry mustard
  Salt and pepper to taste
1 tablespoon chopped parsley
4 slices toast

1. Cut meat into hamburger-size rounds, about 1 inch thick. Season with salt and pepper.

2. Melt butter in heavy fry pan and pan fry the seal meat until lightly browned. Remove meat and keep hot until needed.

3. Heat canned peas slowly. Do not let them boil. Remove from pan and keep hot until serving time.

4. Put vinegar in the pan and add the onions; boil until vinegar is reduced by about half, then remove the onions.

5. Melt the butter in a small pan without boiling.

6. Add 2 tablespoons of the butter and the eggs to the hot vinegar and mix quickly with a wire whisk or dover egg beater.

7. Remove saucepan from heat, add the remainder of the butter slowly, beating continuously to prevent curdling.

8. Add mustard and season to taste with salt and pepper.

9. Place one piece of meat on each slice of hot buttered toast. Cover with sauce, sprinkle with parsley and serve with hot peas, crisp celery hearts. Serves 4.

Note
The sauce must be prepared shortly before use, if left to stand it thickens and becomes spoiled.

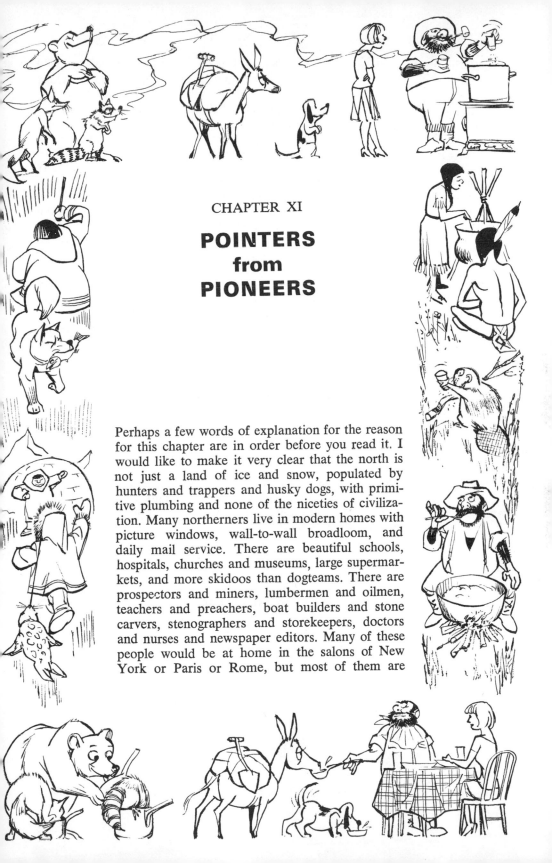

CHAPTER XI

POINTERS
from
PIONEERS

Perhaps a few words of explanation for the reason for this chapter are in order before you read it. I would like to make it very clear that the north is not just a land of ice and snow, populated by hunters and trappers and husky dogs, with primitive plumbing and none of the niceties of civilization. Many northerners live in modern homes with picture windows, wall-to-wall broadloom, and daily mail service. There are beautiful schools, hospitals, churches and museums, large supermarkets, and more skidoos than dogteams. There are prospectors and miners, lumbermen and oilmen, teachers and preachers, boat builders and stone carvers, stenographers and storekeepers, doctors and nurses and newspaper editors. Many of these people would be at home in the salons of New York or Paris or Rome, but most of them are living in the north because they like it. The north is experiencing a period of rapid development and booming economy and the smokestacks of industry are etching new silhouettes on the skyline.

But the north covers an area of a million and a half square miles, and, in spite of the expansion of the airlines and the telecommunication systems, there are still some settlements that have very little traffic. In these smaller places, travel is difficult for many months of the year, being subject to the whims and the vagaries of the weather. Their residents quite often are forced to rely on their own ingenuity for entertainment and, sometimes, their very existence.

It is for the people who will be living and working in these remote areas that this chapter is intended. The pointers have been gathered for the most part, from permanent residents of the north. Some of them came there from other parts of the world, some of them were born there, but all of them realize what it is like to be a newcomer, and all of them want to help make the first few months of adjustment a little easier.

A few old time recipes have also been included in this chapter, not as items of curiosity or amusement (many of them appear elsewhere in this book in regular form), but because the directions for preparing the foods are so delightfully direct. They have an honesty and forthrightness about them that is a true reflection of the people who originated them.

HOUSEHOLD HINTS

If cheese has started to mold, trim the mold, then wrap it in a cloth dipped in vinegar.

Fresh potatoes may be frozen for use all winter. Choose firm, clean potatoes and keep them frozen until ready to use them. Put frozen potatoes in boiling salted water without peeling and cook until tender, then peel. Or bake in a 375° F. oven, allowing an extra half hour baking time.

If mold appears on ham or bacon, wipe off with a cloth dampened in vinegar.

Always allow meat from big game animals to chill and ripen before using it. Hang animals for one week at 35° to 45° F. Liver and heart may be used at once, and the tenderloin may be used after 24 hours.

For long storage, wrap meat in moisture-proof paper, freeze and store at zero° or colder.

In cold weather, game birds may be frozen in a loaf pan of water. When frozen solid, remove from the pan and store outside or in a freezer. Be sure birds are completely covered with water before freezing.

To keep butter from becoming rancid, store it well-covered in a cool dark place.

HOUSEHOLD HINTS (continued)

Drain the liquid from canned roast beef, place beef on a rack in an uncovered roaster in a 325° F. oven until heated through. Let it stand 15 minutes before carving. Use a sharp carving knife.

To reduce the salty taste of corned beef, slice it and soak it in cold water for ½ hour before adding it to a casserole.

Soak bacon slices in cold water for 5 minutes to reduce the salt. Drain and pat dry before panfrying.

Freshen dried onion, red and green pepper or parsley flakes by soaking for 20 minutes in warm water to cover. Drain and use as fresh vegetables.

To prepare cube-style dried potatoes, soak in lukewarm water (4 cups water to 1 cup potatoes) for 20 minutes. Bring to a boil and cook 20 minutes longer.

Soak dried fruits for one hour before cooking, then bring to a boil and simmer 5 to 10 minutes until tender (apples and prunes take longer, about 30 minutes). Remove from heat, then add sugar. Use as fresh fruit.

Break sprouts off stored fresh potatoes as soon as they appear, to prevent the potatoes from becoming soft.

Soften brown sugar by storing in an air-tight container with a slice of fresh bread.

Add a bouillon cube or consommé to the water for extra flavour when cooking rice.

Add lemon juice, fresh, frozen or canned, to juice drained from canned fruit for a Vitamin C breakfast drink.

To avoid lumps when mixing milk powder, add the powder to half the water and beat with an egg beater. Then add the remaining water and stir well. Mix milk several hours ahead of time and chill thoroughly. Usual proportions are 1 part milk powder to 4 parts water.

To mix egg powder, use 1 tablespoon egg powder to 3 tablespoons water for 1 whole egg. Use warm water, add the egg powder to it and beat well. It is better if mixed several hours aread of time. When using egg powder for cakes, the powder may be added to the dry ingredients and the water added to the liquids. Add an extra ⅛ teaspoon baking powder for each egg.

To get rid of the excess moisture in canned potatoes, drain them well, then heat them slowly in a heavy covered waterless cooker for ¾ of an hour. Check to make sure they don't burn. When using them for scalloped potatoes, allow an extra ½ hour cooking time.

When using powdered milk in a recipe, you can sift the milk powder with the dry ingredients and add the water to the liquids. Batters and doughs made with powdered milk and water rise faster and are lighter than when canned milk is used.

Powdered buttermilk should be mixed and allowed to stand 24 hours before using.

To whip canned milk, chill the milk, the bowl and the egg beater. Add 1 teaspoon of lemon juice or 1 teaspoon of plain gelatin dissolved in 2 tablespoons warm water to the can of milk to make stiffer peaks.

Fresh eggs will keep longer if dipped in thin warmed mineral oil, drained, then stored in a cool place.

When using dried eggs, avoid overcooking.

If in doubt about your drinking water, boil it for 5 minutes to make it safe. Or add 1 teaspoon of a chlorine bleach to 50 gallons (oil drum) of water and let it stand 15 to 30 minutes before using.

Soften hard butter for sandwiches by inverting a warmed soup bowl over it.

When you cook eggs in the shell, a teaspoon of salt in the water prevents cracking.

To keep a shine on the oil stove, wipe it daily with crumpled wax paper or newspaper.

Wash windows with ¼ cup vinegar in 4 cups lukewarm water. Use a chamois or a soft cloth and polish with paper towels.

Add a spoon of salt to your last rinse water and your laundry won't freeze to the clothesline.

Loosen doors or windows that are frozen shut by pouring heavily salted water around the edges. Put the salt water in a clean oil can to keep the mess at a minimum.

Hard soap rubbed on drawer runners will help prevent sticking.

An old egg beater is a handy tool for mixing paint that has "settled".

Wash paint brushes in detergent and hot water. Wrap in wax paper to store. Brushes should lie flat in storage.

To remove a water ring from furniture, rub with a mixture of table salt and light oil, or cigarette ashes and butter. Wax and polish.

To remove alcohol stains, rub with a cloth saturated in ammonia, liquid wax, silver polish, linseed oil or moistened cigar ash. Wax and polish.

HOUSEHOLD HINTS (continued)

To thaw frozen pipes, wrap pipes with cloths and pour boiling water on the cloth.

Remove electrical plugs from wall fixtures by pulling on the plug, not the cord.

Clean grouting between tiles by scrubbing with a toothbrush and a solution of 3 tablespoons bleach to 1 quart water. Rinse off after 5 minutes.

Refit slip covers that have been washed, back on the furniture, before they are quite dry. Smooth out any wrinkles with an iron.

Rub the joints of the vacuum cleaner hose with waxed paper occasionally to prevent sticking.

Screen doors sometimes lock when slammed, by the hook flying in the 'eye'. To prevent this, put the hook on the door jamb and the eye on the screen door.

Use aluminum foil as a blind to foil the midnight sun if you can't sleep in sunshine. Fasten it to the window frame with strips of adhesive tape.

Remove the adhesive tape marks with alcohol or nail polish remover.

Soak a scorched pan overnight in water to which bleach has been added.

A paste of baking soda and water will take the sting out of a burn—and the burn out of a sting! A mud paste also eases insect bites.

If you don't have a bent straw for a sick-in-bed patient to use, the spout of a teapot substitutes nicely.

One or two capfuls of liquid detergent will prevent a ring from forming in the bathtub—and give your bath more bubbles.

Remove rust stains from a sink or tub with kerosene.

Keep a box of baking soda open near the stove—it smothers a small fire quickly.

Stick your sewing needles in a bar of soap in your sewing kit. They will slide easily and won't rust.

If a small amount of board, some clear plastic and a little mud (from under the moss) are available, one need not be without fresh lettuce, radishes, onions and turnip greens from July 15 to September 15. Cabbage, carrots and potatoes will also grow well.

Run rows in your garden East and West if possible.

Grow parsley in flower pots in the house. A few seeds and occasional watering will give you fresh greens all winter.

The flavour of safe but unpalatable water may be improved by adding charcoal from a campfire and allowing it to stand overnight.

If you are lost on a sunny day, put a short stick upright in the ground. Every few minutes as the sun travels across the sky, mark the end of the shadow cast by the stick. The shortest shadow will indicate north. If the day is cloudy, you may tell direction by the thickness of the bark on the willow. On the south side, the bark is thick and smooth; on the north side it is thin with spiny projections. You may also check direction by the depth of the moss on a knoll; it is thickest on the north side.

When melting snow, you need a layer of water in the bottom of the pot to prevent the pot from burning.

Let a portable gasoline or kerosene lamp stove cool before refueling it, and then fill it outdoors.

Keep flammable liquids in metal containers, never in glass bottles, in case of breakage.

A quick dry cleaning job can be done by rubbing snow into your heavy sweaters, skirts or pants, then shake them, brush them and press them with a steam iron or pressing cloth.

Rugs that are too heavy to shake can also be swept with snow outside for a quick fresh-up job.

A sheet of clear pliofilm, saran wrap, or a pane of glass helps keep a recipe book clean.

Suspend a recipe card over a work table by means of a spring clothespin.

For winter greenery, cut a 2-inch slice off the top of a carrot and set it in a shallow pan of water to grow. The greens not only look nice, they will add a tang to potato salad. This can be done with half a sweet potato, or a slice off the top of a turnip as well.

Mix apricot jam with curry for a special glaze for baked ham. Tastes good with canned roast pork too. A teaspoon of dry mustard can be added for extra tang.

When making jelly, 1 tablespoon epsom salts to 5 pounds of fruit will take the place of commercial pectin.

Freshen stale walnuts by pouring boiling water over them.

Revive tired peanuts by baking them in a 275° F. oven for one hour. Leave the shells on if you wish.

HOUSEHOLD HINTS (concluded)

Canned roast pork takes on a new flavour if you scrape the gravy off, cut it in small chunks and heat it in cream of mushroom soup. Serve hot over cooked rice.

To render animal fat, cut the suet and surface fat into cubes, heat it slowly in a heavy covered kettle, then strain it. Bring the liquid fat to a boil, reduce the heat and let simmer for 10 minutes to sterilize it. Pour fat into hot, sterilized containers, seal and store in a cool place. Rendered bear fat makes excellent pastry.

To remove small slivers of broken glass from a rug, press scotch tape against it.
To remove small slivers of glass from a smooth surface, use crumpled wet paper.

Add a teaspoon of baking soda to the rinse water when washing the inside of your refrigerator to keep it smelling fresh.

Place a damp folded cloth under the mixing bowl to keep it from sliding on the counter.

If you are going north for the first time and will be living on rations, the following items are light in weight and not always available in the north. They could be a useful supplement to add variety to your rations:

Garlic salt	Dehydrated soup mixes
Onion salt	Dehydrated sauce mixes:
Chili powder	cheese, white, sour
Poultry seasoning	cream, chili and brown
Oregano	gravy
Basil	Dehydrated chip dips
Paprika	Dehydrated fruit juices
Marjoram	Dehydrated tomato juice
Thyme	Dream Whip
Charcoal seasoning	Tomato paste
Red and Green Pepper flakes	Chocolate chips
Onion flakes	Butterscotch chips
Dried parsley	Peanut butter chips
Dried mint	Ice Cream powder
Banana flakes	Egg white powder
Banana flavoring	Meringue mix

If you have room, take along special occasion greeting cards, wrapping paper and ribbons, party favours, nylon string for an indoor clothesline, Christmas decorations, place mats and tablecloths, artificial flowers or plants, playing cards and a cribbage board, skin lotion, sun glasses (and an extra pair of your prescription glasses), garden seeds, thermal underwear, leotards and ski pants (but wait till you get north to buy your parka).

Don't forget to take along your recipe for making bread. Or better still take this book.

FISH

Roasted Fish

Clean fresh fish well, or if you are roasting frozen fish, put it in the pan with insides still in it. Roast in an oven until the fish is done. It has a good flavour when it is not opened first. When done, open the fish and clean out the insides. It is then ready to eat.

Bertha Allen

Boiled Frozen Fish

Put frozen fish into cold water on stove. Cook until the fish comes to the top. Take off skin and it is ready to eat.

Emma Arey

Fried Loche

Cut loche up and put in frying pan with a little lard and cover tightly. Cook until loche is soft. You can also add the eggs and liver of loche to it.

Bertha Allen

300

Fisherman's Style

First scale and clean the fish well. Cut up as for frying. Put lard into a good-sized roasting pan. Put in fish; then cut up a few potatoes and lay on the fish. Add 1 chopped onion, salt and pepper. Then cover with one tin of tomatoes. Roast in oven for about one hour or until done.

Bertha Allen

Smoked Fish

In springtime only, smoke fish outside using wood that is a little wet. Clean fish and cut lengthwise. Hang over a pole over the fire and smoke about 15-20 minutes. Cook by roasting in pan with onion, salt and pepper.

Sarah Tingmiak

Serving Frozen Fish

Cut frozen fish up with saw or axe. Peel the skin off and cut up with knife. This is good to eat with salt and blubber.

Fish Chowder (for any kind of fish)

Scale and clean fish well. Cut it up as for frying. Fill the pot half full of cold water. Add a few cubed potatoes, onion, salt and pepper. Boil until almost done. Mix enough flour with a little water to make a thin broth. Add this to the soup. Boil until done.

Margaret Hagen

Fish Roasted by Campfire

Clean fish thoroughly and split open. Put between a toaster and cook over medium fire for about 15 minutes.

Emily Linklater

Frozen Fish Eggs

Take fish eggs out and freeze them. They are good to eat like this.

Emma Arey

Roasted Cony Head (Inconnu)

Cut the head off the cony and split it open so that it will lie flat on the toaster. Shut the toaster well and roast over open fire very slowly. Turn when it is done on one side.

Fresh Cony Soup

Scale cony, cut up and put in a pot of cold water. Bring to boiling point and add salt and enough noodles to make a thin broth.

Fried Loche Liver and Eggs

Take liver and eggs out of the loche as soon as it is caught from fresh water. Put a small amount of lard into a frying pan and fry the liver and eggs together. This is famous in the fall when the loche family are running in the creeks. Many of the women are sitting at the mouth of the creek with their hooks and jiggle in the water hole. The best time to catch loche is at night. One has to be quiet, as they hear noise.

Bertha Allen

Fish Sauce

Cut up bacon into little pieces and fry it in frying pan. Add 2 tbsps. flour and salt and pepper to taste. Add water. This is good with boiled fish.

Emily Linklater

Fish Boiled on Open Fire

Scale fish and clean out insides. Put in an open pot with cold water and put to boil on an open fire outside in the summer. The smoke gives it a good flavour. Also put some fish eggs to boil with it.

Bertha Allen

Shrimp Salad

Dissolve 1 envelope gelatin in ½ cup tomato juice. Heat 2 cups tomato juice. Add dissolved gelatin and 4 tbsp. vinegar, ½ tsp. salt, 1 can shrimps (drained and washed), chopped celery and onion. Allow to set. Serve on lettuce and garnish as desired.

Betty Oancia

Whitefish Soup

Cut whitefish and wash it. Then put in into a pot and add water and salt. Boil it and then take off the bones. Make the fish into little pieces. Mix a little flour and water together, and add this to the fish. Add curry powder as much as you want.

MEAT

Steamed Muskrat Legs

Cut off the muskrat's legs and dip in a bowl of flour with salt, pepper and other strong seasoning. Mix with a small amount of water. Put grease into a large frying pan and put in the muskrat's legs which have been dipped in the flour mixture. Cover tightly and cook for a long time as they take long to become tender. The strong seasoning takes away the actual taste of the muskrat and turns into gravy as it steams.

Bertha Allen

Stuffed Muskrat

Clean the rats well. Put in a roaster and put bread stuffing on the top of it. Roast in an oven until the muskrats are soft.

Boiled Muskrat

Clean and wash the muskrats. Cover with cold water and add salt. Boil for an hour or until they are soft and will fall apart easily. H.P. sauce is good to eat with this.

Fried Muskrat

Clean and wash the muskrat thoroughly, taking the fat off. Cut it up and dip in a bowl with some flour, salt, pepper and a little water. Fry in deep grease until done.

Bertha Allen

Muskrat Tails

Cut off the tails and dip them into very hot water. Pull off the fur. One can either cook them on the top of the stove, turning them after a few minutes, or boil them. This is the same method as for beaver tails. Both tails are very sticky to eat.

Muskrat — Open Fire

Get a "Y" shaped stick and put the rat on it and roast slowly over open fire. This is the best lunch when one is out shooting muskrats—tea and roasted muskrat.

Campfire Muskrat

Another way of cooking muskrats on the open fire is to leave the cleaned rats on the charcoals of an open fire for a few minutes. Take out and finish cooking by boiling in an open pot on the fire. This has a good smoked taste to it.

Dried Muskrats

Clean the muskrats well and take out all the bones. Cut it up in thin pieces so it will dry easily. Put it to dry in a smoke house. Keep turning every day so that it will dry thoroughly.

Bertha Allen

Muskrat Soup

Clean and wash the rats and take all the fat off. Cover with cold water, add salt and bring to boiling point. Add dried onions, rice and continue boiling until the muskrats are soft.

Roast Muskrat

Clean and wash the muskrat with salt. Put in a roasting pan with a little water. Cook about one hour.

Caroline Moses

Boiled Porcupine

Make a fire outside and put porcupine in the fire to burn off the quills. Wash and clean well. Cut up and boil until done.

Lydia Frances

Eskimo Dry Meat (moose, caribou, muskrats, etc.)

Cut up the meat in slices 1″ thick and hang over a pole. Be sure that the two halves do not touch. Keep turning it every day and keep a fire burning for smoke to keep the flies away.

Sarah Tingmiak

Baked Skunk

Clean, skin, wash. Bake in oven with salt and pepper. Tastes like rabbit. (No smell). Skunk fat very good for whooping cough.

Indian Dry Meat

Cut up fresh meat in thin slices. Dry above stove in tent. Keep turning once a day. Do not have the fire too hot or meat too close to stove. When it is dried well, one may eat pounded bone grease with it.

Bertha Allen

305

Pounded Dry Meat

Pound up dry meat for meat balls. One may pound all day to get it soft. Add bone grease and sugar, and mix up. Roll into meat balls with hands. Keep in a cool place to keep from drying out. One may take this out camping.

Rowena Edwards

Boiled Bear Meat

Cut up the brisket and boil until soft in a large pot with salt and water.

Grizzly Bear Steaks

Cut up meat as for frying and fry in deep grease in frying pan.

Fried Meat With Left-over Porridge

Fry the meat and when done add left-over porridge. Cook a little longer.

Indian Meat Stew

Fry cubed meat in frying pan. Add onions, salt and pepper. When almost done mix ½ cup flour in with meat until meat is covered. Fill pan with cold water. Keep steaming until gravy is cooked well. Good with potatoes and vegetables.

Boiled Reindeer Head

Skin and wash the head well. Then chop it in quarters, splitting it between the eyes with an axe. Cover with cold water and boil until soft. One can also roast in an open pan in an oven very slowly.

Pemmican

Pound dried moose or deer meat on a piece of clean canvas or stone, to fine crumbs. Pour hot melted moose fat over in pan. Let freeze. Serve cold. Very rich.

Boiled Rabbit Soup

Skin the rabbit, cut it up and put in a pot of cold salted water. Bring to the boiling point. Add rice and dried vegetable mix to make a thin broth. One can also add dumplings when the soup is almost done.

Roasted Rabbit

Cut up the rabbit and put in a pan with grease and a little water. Add salt and about a handful of dried vegetable or onion flakes. Roast in the oven for an hour or until done. Mix a little flour with salt, pepper and enough water to make a thin mixture. Pour this over the rabbit and mix well together. Roast a little longer until flour is cooked. This makes good gravy. Cooked rice is good to eat with this.

Oven Roasted Lynx

Wash and clean the hind legs of the lynx and roast in a roaster with lard and a little water.

Boiled Lynx

Cut up the lynx and boil it until it is soft and well cooked. This is good to eat with muktuk.

Boiled Reindeer Tongues

Put tongues in boiling water and boil until thoroughly cooked. Potatoes and vegetables are good with this.

Boiled Smoked Beaver

Smoke the beaver for a day or so. Then cut up the meat and boil in salted water until it is done.

Duck — Open Fire

Clean duck and cut up as for frying. Fry in deep grease with onions, salt and pepper.

Boiled Reindeer or Caribou Hoofs

Put the hoofs with skin still on them in a large pot. Cover with hot water and boil for a couple of hours. The skin peels off easily then. The muscles are soft and very good to eat. The toe nails also have some soft sweet meat inside them.

Bertha Allen

Ptarmigan Soup

Clean and cut up two ptarmigan. Put into pot and cover with cold water and put on to boil. Add dried onions, 1 cup of rice and salt.

Boiled Bone Grease

Boil all the legs and whatever bones are left after the meat has been cut off. Boil them all in a big pot for two hours. Then let the grease get cold in the pot. It is easy to pick the grease off. Put the grease in a pot and keep to eat with dry meat or add to pounded dry meat.

Mipku

Cut black whale meat into thin strips, about 8 inches wide by 2½ inches long by ½ inch thick. Hang the strips over poles to dry in the sun, or cure the strips over a driftwood fire in a log smoke house. When the meat is ready it is hard and brittle. Break it off in small pieces and chew well. You must have strong teeth.

Roasted Whale Meat

Cut up the meat and some fat of a freshly caught whale. Add onions, salt and pepper. Roast in an oven for a long period until it is done.

Fried Whale Meat

Cut up freshly caught whale. Fry in grease with onions.

Bertha Allen

Muktuk   (meat inside skin and fat of whale)

After taken from whale leave 2 days hanging up to dry. Cut into pieces 6″ x 6″. Have water ready to boil. Cook until tender with a fork. Keep in oil in a 45 gal. drum after cooked, in a cool place, in order to have muktuk all year.

Rosie Peeloolook

SUPPER DISHES

Cabbage in Blubber Fat

Cut up the cabbage and put with blubber fat in a pot. Cook. This is good to eat with meat or fish.

Boiled Roots

Wash roots and boil until soft. This is good to put in a pot of blubber and to eat with meat or fish.

Bertha Allen

BREAD AND ROLLS

Sour Dough Hotcakes

Mix dough as for bread but leave thin. Leave overnight.

Add 2 eggs, ½ tsp. salt, 4 tbsp. sugar and 1 tsp. soda (mix with a little water) Stir. Let rise and cook as for pancakes. Save some of the dough for the next time, providing you have a home where it can be kept cool but not frozen.

Rosie Peeloolook

Bread

½ mixing pan flour
1 "quick rising" yeast
3 tbsp. sugar
1 tbsp. salt
½ cup lard

Mix with a liquid of half milk and water. Knead and let rise. Shape into loaves or rolls. Cook either in oven or flatten into frying pan on top of stove. In cooking on top of stove, fire must be very slow. Turn over to cook on the other side.

Winnie Elanik

PRESERVES

Cranberry Jam

Fill the saucepan with cranberries. Add about 2 cups of sugar and just enough water so berries will not stick to pot. Put on to boil and boil until all the berries have burst. It will then be thick. Cool. Put into jars.

Bertha Allen

Salmonberries

First we pick the salmonberries in dippers or pots. After the pot or dipper is full, put them into amouk (Eskimo bag for carrying berries made of seal skin). When the amouk is full of salmonberries, take home and put in a big pan ready for putting in a seal poke. When the poke is full, tie the poke with string. Save for winter in any cold place.

DESSERTS

Donuts

When baking bread, save some of the dough. Make into small rolls. Put hole through centre with finger and mark edges. Cook in hot grease.

Sarah Tingmiak

Eskimo Ice Cream

Grind up cooked meat. Melt tallow and while still warm mix well by hand. Keep adding meat until not able to stir anymore. This is good to eat with meat and bread.

Sadie Simon

Blueberry Pie

Line the pie plate with crust. Clean the berries well and fill the plate. Add 1 cup sugar or enough to make it really sweet. Sprinkle some flour on the berries. This will make a sauce. Put on the top crust and bake in oven.

Bertha Allen

Rice and Raisin Pudding

Boil 3 cups of rice in water. Add ½ cup raisins. Cook well. Eat with cream or milk.

Old Fashioned Rice Pudding

1   cup of rice
2   tbsps. moist sugar
1   quart of milk
½   oz. chopped butter or suet
½   tsp. grated nutmeg or cinnamon
    Vanilla

Put rice, milk and sugar in a pie dish. Stir. Add the butter. Grate the nutmeg on top. Bake 1½ to 2 hours.

From Mrs. Beeton's Cook Book—1850

Indian Pudding

2   cups flour
3   tsps. baking powder
1   cup raisins
1   cup cut-up fat
    Pinch of salt

Add enough water to mix ingredients. Put in a small sugar sack and boil in water for 2 hours or more.

Loche Liver

Put liver in frying pan and cook until done. Then add cranberries. Mix well. This makes a good dessert.

Blueberry Pudding

Cook 1 fish by cutting it up into boiling water with salt added. After fish is cooked, take all the bones from it and the skin. Mix this with blueberries. Stir, and it is ready to eat.

Bertha Allen

Pounded Dry Fish Pudding

Pound up 5 to 6 dry fish and throw away the skin. Add sugar to taste, a small amount of grease, and cranberries.

Bertha Allen

Wild Cranberry Pudding

Put three cups of cranberries into a saucepan and cover with water. Add ½ cup sugar and boil until the berries have all burst. Add enough custard to make it thick.

Rhubarb

Cut up the rhubarb and put into a pot. Add sugar and boil. Mix flour in water and add to boiling rhubarb. Cook a little longer.

Bear Fat Pastry

1½ cups flour
½ tsp. salt
⅓ cup Bear fat

(From a little black bear that was eating berries). Makes rich white pastry.

SOUP

Acorn Soup

Make in the fall when acorns are ripe. Grind the acorns between rocks. Fan the acorns with a fanning basket. The fine parts will stick to the basket. Put the fine meal in a wooden bin. Pour warm water over it three or four times to take out the bitter taste. Put acorn meal and water in a cooking basket (made with roots). Drop in a very hot rock. Keep turning the rock with a wooden spoon. Sometimes one rock will cook the soup.

CHAPTER XII

Hunting in the Northwest Territories
and
A Summary of the Current
Northwest Territories
Game Regulations

The Northwest Territories offer a variety of game species for sportsmen, as indicated in the "Summary of Sport Hunting Seasons" on page 321, and with the introduction of the Non-Resident Big Game licence, exciting opportunities for sport hunting are available to all. The Non-Resident Big Game Licence covers moose, black bear, grizzly bear, woodland caribou, mountain goat and Dall sheep. All offer excellent sport for hunters, but the Dall sheep present a special challenge. There has been relatively little hunting in the remote sheep ranges for two or three decades and there are good possibilities that record heads await sportsmen in the Mackenzie Mountains.

Sea mammal hunting offers unique experiences. It is different from any other type of hunting in North America—different, in fact, from hunting in any other part of the world, except possibly in other Arctic areas. There are summer seasons for seal hunting by boat, and late spring hunting by dogteam on the Arctic ice.

The Northwest Territories is one of the world's greatest waterfowl nesting grounds, but sport hunting of ducks and geese is generally limited to areas along the southern boundary and to a few more northerly locations along the Mackenzie River. For further information on game-bird hunting, please write to the appropriate agency listed under "Sources of Information" on page 325.

How To Arrange a Trip

Parts of the Great Slave Lake area can be reached by road over the Mackenzie Highway System, running northward from Grimshaw, Alberta (320 road miles northwest of Edmonton). For visitors, this road system provides access only to areas open for sport hunting of waterfowl and upland game birds.

As a general rule, visiting sportsmen fly into the Territories on scheduled airlines operating out of Edmonton, Alberta; Winnipeg, Manitoba; and Montreal, Quebec. Connections with these northern carriers can be made through any of the transcontinental or transoceanic airlines.

Anyone interested should first write to the Northwest Territories Tourist Office (Travel Arctic) for general information. This information package will include an outline of the location, services, and attractions offered by each outfitter, information on road or air travel, and answers to any questions raised.

What To Take

The type of clothing and equipment required will vary to some extent with the type of hunting and the season. Regardless of the season or type of hunting, there are certain staple items that each sportsman should bring, including cameras, sunglasses and skin lotion, a safety razor or battery-operated shaver, and a raincoat or rainproof clothing.

A heavy-calibre rifle such as the 30.06 or .303 British is recommended for moose hunting. The inexperienced moose hunter should remember that one of the major problems that will most certainly confront him is the removal of several hundred pounds of meat from the wilderness to his home. Game meat may not be left in the field or allowed to spoil. Therefore, arrangements should be made in advance for use of a boat, horse, or vehicle.

Even during early September, hunters of Dall sheep will find freezing temperatures in the high mountain meadows and will have to dress for a late fall, or, during October, for a winter hunt. Tough, non-slip, waterproof boots are a must for the long hours of climbing and stalking. A scope-sighted, high-power rifle with a flat trajectory, such as the .270, is recommended.

Sportsmen planning a hunt for seal should take special care in selecting clothing and equipment. Winter clothing, including parkas, long underwear, and warm, waterproof footgear, is required for the spring seal hunt. Although temperatures are above freezing during the summer season, the cold Arctic waters add a chill to the air that demands the equivalent of winter hunting clothes. Hunters can benefit from the experience of the Eskimo, who have designed clothing suited to their country. Eskimo parkas and footgear may be ordered in advance.

A rifle with a flat trajectory and solid hitting power, such as the .270, is recommended for spring seal hunting. Seal hunting during the summer season may require the use of two rifles. The common .22 calibre rifle is frequently used by the Eskimo during the chase, to force the seal to submerge. A heavier-calibre rifle, such as the 30.06 or .303 British, is required for the killing shot. Metal-jacketed bullets should be used on sea mammals to ensure penetration to a vital organ. (Full metal-cased, non-expanding bullets are not permitted for hunting other big-game animals.)

Sport hunters visiting the Arctic for sea mammals during the summer season should also bring along their angling equipment. Fishing for the spectacular Arctic char, lake trout, and Arctic grayling will provide hunters with a pleasant and exciting change of pace.

Summary of Current Wildlife Regulations

The following are a few of the major regulations that apply to hunting in the Northwest Territories. Please note that this summary does NOT constitute a legal document. Full information concerning hunting in both the Northwest Territories and the Yukon may be obtained by writing to the appropriate agency listed under "Sources of Information" on page 325.

1. Closed Areas

All game sanctuaries except the Mackenzie Bison Sanctuary, and all game preserves are closed to the sport hunting of game birds, small game, and big game, including: Bowman Bay Game Sanctuary, James Bay Preserve, Norah Willis Michener Territorial Park Game Preserve, Peel River Preserve, Thelon Game Sanctuary, and Twin Island Game Sanctuary.

All migratory bird sanctuaries are closed to the hunting of migratory birds. No person shall hunt, disturb, or possess a migratory bird in these areas, including: Akimiski Island, Anderson River Delta, Banks Island #1, Banks Island #2, Boatswain Bay, Bylot Island, Cape Dorset, Cape Parry, Dewey Soper, East Bay, Hannah Bay, Harry Gibbons, Kendall Island, McConnell River, Queen Maude Gulf, and Seymour Island.

Hunting by non-natives is not permitted in Auyuittuq, Nahanni, or Wood Buffalo National Parks.

2. Game Meat

Wastage of game meat is illegal, except for that of bears, wolves, and wolverines. If meat cannot be used by the hunters, it can be turned over to residents of the area if appropriate tags are completed. Sport hunters can keep game birds or big-game meat (land animals) up to the legal limit for their own use.

3. Export Permits

Export permits are required for any wildlife or part thereof, including meat, hide, and horns or antlers, that is removed from the Northwest Territories. Please consult a Wildlife officer for details.

4. Type of Firearms

No one may hunt waterfowl except with a long-bow and arrow, or shotgun of 10 gauge or smaller and with magazine plugged to limit chamber and magazine capacity to not more than three shells.

The following regulations apply to "land" species of big game. Fully automatic rifles may not be used. Any land animal may be hunted with any rifle of .23 calibre or larger. No full metal-cased, non-expanding bullets, or tracer may be used.

There are no specific regulations governing type or calibre of rifle to be used in sea-mammal hunting. The use of semi-automatic rifles is discouraged for safety reasons. Recommended calibres are listed under "What to Take."

5. Hunting from Vehicles

No hunting of game birds or land animals is allowed from a motor vehicle, including aircraft or moving powerboats. Hunting of sea mammals from powerboats is permissible.

6. Outfitters and Guides

All non-resident big-game hunters must obtain the services of a licensed outfitter or guide. All sea-mammal hunters must use Eskimo guides and crewmen. Guides are not compulsory for residents or for visitors hunting game birds, but are highly recommended for all sportsmen hunting in remote areas.

7. Safety

No one is allowed to discharge a firearm from a motor vehicle, or have a firearm that contains ammunition in the chamber, in or on a motor vehicle. No one is allowed to discharge a firearm on or across any public road or highway. While not specifically required by the regulations, hunters travelling in remote areas should file an itinerary with a Wildlife officer, or with a member of the Royal Canadian Mounted Police.

8. Reporting Kill

As soon as possible after a licence expires or before a visiting hunter leaves the Territories, the affidavit on the back of the licence should be completed and the licence forwarded to a Wildlife officer. In the case of sea-mammal licences, the filing of a formal report is not required.

9. Licences

Some fees are listed in the summary of sport-hunting seasons. See note 1, p. 323.

Licences for land-game species are available at Yellowknife, Northwest Territories, or from Wildlife officers in the major settlements.

Sea-mammal hunting licences may be purchased at the community that serves as the base for the hunting operation.

10. Use of Dogs

The use of dogs in hunting land animals, other than polar bears or wolverines, is prohibited.

Please Note

Hunting regulations in the Territories have been simplified as much as possible for the benefit of sportsmen. They are designed to ensure that surplus game can be harvested without depleting the game population. Your co-operation in observing the regulations will be appreciated. (For the non-sportsman, the Wildlife Ordinance provides penalties of up to $1,000 in fines and a year in jail.)

Please observe safety rules when handling firearms. This is particularly important in wilderness areas, where medical attention may be hours away.

Wildlife lives off the land. There is very little food in burned-out forests. Please be careful with fire.

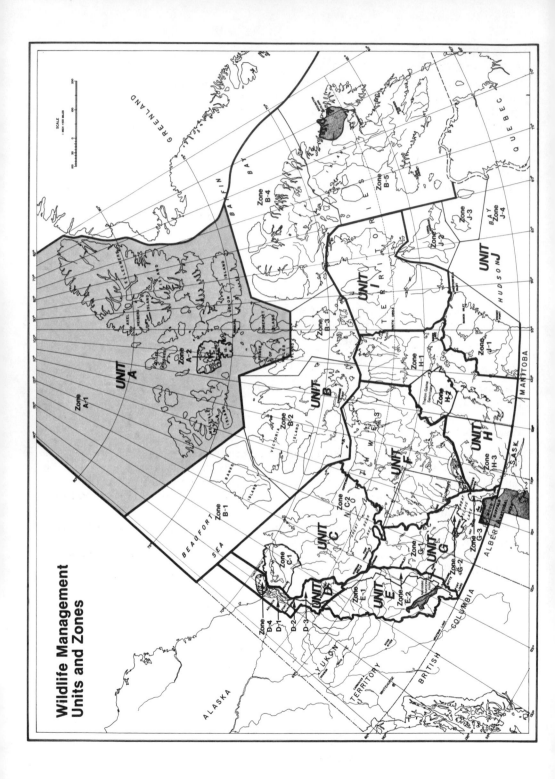

Wildlife Management
Units and Zones

Small Game

	OPEN AREAS	SEASON DATES	BAG LIMITS	STAMP AND TROPHY FEES[1]
Hare (all species)				
Resident[2]	All	1 July	No limit	$ 5
Non-resident	the	to	5 per day	$ 10
Non-resident alien	Territories[3]	30 June	5 per day	$ 25
Marmots (woodchucks or groundhogs)				
Resident		1 July	No limit	$ 5
Non-resident	As above	to	5 per day	$ 10
Non-resident alien		30 June	5 per day	$ 25
Ptarmigan or grouse				
Resident			10 per day of each species	$ 5
		1 Sept.		
Non-resident	As above	to	5 in total per day	$ 10
Non-resident alien		30 April	5 in total per day	$ 25

Big Game

	OPEN Units/Zones/Areas[1]	SEASON DATES	BAG LIMITS	STAMP AND TROPHY FEES[1]
Black bear				
Resident	C-1, D-1, D-3, F, G-1, G-3, H-1, H-3, E	15 Aug. to 30 June	1, not	$ 5
Non-resident	C-1, D-1, D-3, F, G-1, G-3, H-1, H-3, E	15 Aug. to 30 June	accompanied by cub	$ 60
Non-resident alien	E-1	15 Aug. to 30 Oct.		$ 75
Grizzly bear				
Resident	G, E, D-1, D-3	15 Aug.	1, not	$ 5
Non-resident	E-1	to	accompanied	$260
Non-resident alien	E-1	30 Oct.	by cub	$275
Polar bear				
Resident	All	1 Feb.	1, not	$ 5
Non-resident	the	to	accompanied	$510
Non-resident alien	Territories[3]	31 May	by cub	$525
Barren-ground caribou				
Resident	All the Territories, except E, G, D, J-2, C-2	15 Aug.	5[1]	$ 10[1]
Non-resident	C-1, F, H-1, I, H-3	to 30 April	1, male	$110
Non-resident alien	C-1, F, H-1, I, H-3		1, male	$125
Woodland caribou				
Resident	E, C-1, D-3, G-1	15 July to 30 Jan.		$ 5
Non-resident	E, C-1, D-3, G-1	25 July to 30 Jan.	1	$110
Non-resident alien	E-1	25 July to 30 Oct.		$125

Moose

Resident	C-1, D-1, D-3, E, F, G, H-3	1 Sept. to 30 Jan.[4]	1	$ 5
Non-resident	C-1, D-1, D-3, E, F, G, H-3	1 Sept. to 30 Jan.[4]	1, male[5]	$110
Non-resident alien	E-1	1 Sept. to 30 Oct.	1, male[5]	$125

Mountain goat

Resident		15 July		$ 5
Non-resident	E-1	to	1	$110
Non-resident alien		30 Oct.		$125

Muskox

Resident		1 Oct.		$ 5
Non-resident	To be decided	to	1, male	$510
Non-resident alien		31 Mar.		$525

Dall sheep

Resident	E	15 July		$ 5
Non-resident	E-1	to	1, male[6]	$110
Non-resident alien	E-1	30 Oct.		$125

Wolf

Resident	All	25 July	No limit	$ 5
Non-resident	the	to	1	$ 60
Non-resident alien	Territories[3]	30 April	1	$ 75

Wolverine

Resident	All the Territories[3]	25 July to 30 April	No limit	$ 5
Non-resident	All the Territories[3]	25 July to 30 April	1	$ 60
Non-resident alien	E-1	25 July to 30 Oct.	1	$ 75

Sea Mammals

	OPEN AREAS	SEASON DATES	BAG LIMITS	FEES
Seal (all except bearded or square-flipper seal)				
Resident				
Non-resident	Various areas	Spring or	Request	Request
Non-resident alien		summer[7]	bulletin	bulletin

Legend

1. Trophy fees are payable only upon export of wildlife out of the Territories. For complete information regarding types of licences available, schedule of fees, application forms, and further regulations regarding Wildlife Management Units and Zones, guides and outfitters, and the hunting and trapping of animals, please write to:

   The Superintendent
   Wildlife Service
   Department of Natural and Cultural Affairs
   Government of the Northwest Territories
   Yellowknife
   Northwest Territories X1A 2L9

2. A resident is a Canadian citizen or landed immigrant who has lived in the Northwest Territories for two years. A non-resident is also a Canadian citizen or landed immigrant, but one who lives outside of the Northwest Territories, or has not resided in the Northwest Territories for a full two years. A non-resident alien is someone from outside of Canada.

3. "All the Territories" means the whole of the Northwest Territories except those portions thereof that lie within a game sanctuary, a game preserve, a licensed trapping area, or a national park.

4. Excluding all islands in the Mackenzie River from 1 December to 30 January.

5. For purposes of the regulations, a male moose is considered to be one year old if there are visible antlers.

6. A trophy sheep means a male mountain sheep bearing at least one horn that is ¾ curl in size. A horn with ¾ curl is defined as a horn that can be intercepted at both the front of the horn base and the tip of the horn by a straight line drawn through the eye (see illustration).

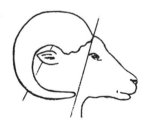

7. No specific, open-season dates are set for sea mammals. The season depends primarily on ice conditions. Please refer to the text for further explanation.

Changes in Regulations

The following changes in the regulations apply across Canada:

1. It is now mandatory that hunting be discontinued after the daily bag limit has been reached.

2. A hunter may not possess or transport a migratory bird unless one wing and the wing plumage remain attached to the bird. The wing and plumage may be removed if the bird is prepared for immediate cooking, or after the bird has been taken to the hunter's residence or to a commercial freezer locker. Migratory birds may not be exported from any province unless one wing and the wing plumage remain attached.

3. Hunters may not use recorded bird calls or sounds, or mechanically or electrically operated calling devices.

4. A hunter who cripples or wounds a migratory game bird must now make all reasonable efforts to retrieve the bird; if a wounded bird is recovered, the hunter must kill it immediately.

5. Special permits may now be obtained by managers of civilian airports or the commanding officers of military airports to take migratory birds that are endangering the safe operation of aircraft.

Customs and Entry

No passport is required for entry into Canada by British subjects or by U.S. citizens, but identifying documents should be carried. There are no special entry regulations which apply to the Northwest Territories; however, anyone planning to travel in wilderness areas should leave an itinerary with the nearest R.C.M.P. office.

Visitors from other countries can bring clothing, personal effects, hunting and fishing equipment, boats, motors, cameras, etc., but must declare major items at the Canadian border. Visitors may not bring handguns or fully automatic firearms across the border into Canada. Up to 200 cigarettes, 50 cigars, 40 ounces of alcohol, and 200 rounds of ammunition may be brought in duty free.

Visitors should check with customs officials in their own country for information on regulations governing importing of game meat.

Sources of Information

1. In the Northwest Territories and in the Yukon, administration and management of big-game animals and upland game birds is a responsibility of the territorial governments. For complete information on regulations and game conditions, please write to:

   The Superintendent
   Wildlife Service
   Department of Natural and Cultural Affairs
   Government of the Northwest Territories
   Yellowknife
   Northwest Territories X1A 2L9

   The Director of Wildlife
   Box 2703
   Whitehorse
   Yukon Y1A 2C6

   or contact the Wildlife officers in the following locations (all in the Northwest Territories): Aklavik, Inuvik, Fort Franklin, Fort Good Hope, Fort McPherson, or Norman Wells in the Inuvik area; Fort Smith, Fort Rac, Hay River, Fort Simpson, Fort Resolution, Yellowknife, Cambridge Bay, or Spence Bay in the Fort Smith area; Frobisher Bay, Resolute Bay, Broughton Island, Pond Inlet, Pangnirtung, or Cape Dorset in the Baffin Island area; Rankin Inlet, Coral Harbour, Baker Lake, Eskimo Point, or Sanikiluaq in the western Hudson Bay area.

2. In addition to the above sources, local sources of information include outfitters, Boards of Trade in the larger towns and settlements, and officers of the Royal Canadian Mounted Police.

Calorie Values of Some Common Foods
(from the Nutrition Division,
Department of National Health and Welfare)

Food	Portion	Calories
Milk		
Buttermilk	1 cup	85
Evaporated	½ cup	165
Powdered, skim	¼ cup	102
Fluid, whole	1 cup	153
Cream, 32%	2 tbs.	89
Ice Cream, plain	½ cup	163
Citrus Fruits and Tomatoes		
Grapefruit Juice, canned	½ cup	45
Lemon	1 medium	25
Orange	1 medium	44
Orange Juice, frozen	½ cup	44
Orange Juice, canned	½ cup	64
Tomato, fresh	1 medium	21
Tomato, canned	½ cup	23
Tomato Juice	½ cup	25
Other Fruits		
Apple	1 large	76
Apple Juice	½ cup	60
Apricots, dried	4–6 halves	79
Blueberries, fresh	½ cup	43
Cherries, canned	½ cup	121
Cranberries, fresh	½ cup	48
Dates	3–4 pitted	85
Grape Juice	½ cup	80
Peaches, canned	½ cup	78
Pears, canned	½ cup	78
Plums, canned	2–3	83
Prunes, dried	6 medium	137
Raisins	¼ cup	81
Raspberries, fresh	¾ cup	52
Raspberries, canned	½ cup	123
Rhubarb, fresh	1 cup	16
Salmonberries, fresh	½ cup	67
Strawberries, fresh	½ cup	36

Food	Portion	Calories
Vegetables		
Asparagus, canned	½ cup	20
Beans, green	½ cup	19
Beans, dried	1½ oz.	152
Beans, yellow, canned	½ cup	14
Beets, canned	½ cup	34
Cabbage, fresh	½ cup	13
Carrots, fresh	½ cup	45
Carrots, canned	½ cup	28
Celery, fresh	½ cup	12
Corn, creamed	½ cup	86
Dandelion greens	½ cup	49
Lettuce leaves	2	6
Mushrooms, fresh	½ cup	26
Onions, fresh	½ cup	47
Parsnips, fresh	½ cup	73
Peas, canned	½ cup	88
Potatoes, fresh	1 medium	105
Sourdock, fresh	½ cup	59
Spinach, canned	½ cup	25
Squash	5¼ oz.	47
Turnip, fresh	½ cup	40
Willow Herb	½ cup	77
Cereals, Whole Grain		
Oats, rolled	¼ cup	98
Rice, brown	2 tbs.	103
Wheat, flakes	⅔ cup	107
Wheat, shredded	1 biscuit	108
Wheat, whole	⅓ cup	102
Cereals, Refined		
Cornflakes	1 cup	77
Cornmeal	3 tbs.	102
Cream of Wheat	3 tbs.	111
Macaroni	¼ cup	108
Rice, White	2 tbs.	102
Wheat, puffed	1 cup	47
Bread		
White, enriched	1 slice	83
Whole Wheat	1 slice	72
Raisin	1 slice	85
Rye	1 slice	73
Crackers, graham	1	39
Crackers, soda	1	25

Food	Portion	Calories
Meat		
Bear, Polar	3½ oz.	130
Beaver	3½ oz.	408
Beef, hamburg	4 oz.	364
Caribou	3½ oz.	120
Chicken	4 oz.	227
Duck, Eider	3½ oz.	128
Goose	3½ oz.	210
Lamb chop	3 oz.	230
Moose	3½ oz.	110
Murre	3½ oz.	172
Muskrat	3½ oz.	65
Pork, bacon, side	2 oz.	378
Pork, chop, loin	5¾ oz.	380
Pork, ham	2 oz.	171
Ptarmigan	3½ oz.	116
Seal	3½ oz.	125
Whale, meat	3½ oz.	105
Whale, muktuk	3½ oz.	140
Fish		
Cod	4 oz.	86
Grayling	3½ oz.	108
Halibut	4 oz.	162
Lobster, canned	½ cup	60
Loche	3½ oz.	90
Pike	3½ oz.	82
Rainbow trout	3½ oz.	112
Salmon, fresh	½ cup	257
Salmon, canned	½ cup	196
Whitefish	½ cup	178
Fats		
Butter	1 tbs.	108
Lard	1 tbs.	128
Margarine	1 tbs.	109
Mayonnaise	1 tbs.	106
Salad Dressing	1 tbs.	25
Seal Blubber	1 tbs.	120
Seal Oil	1 tbs.	125
Whale Blubber	1 tbs.	112
Cheese		
Cheese, cheddar	1″ cube	80
Cheese, cream	2 tbs.	106

Food	Portion	Calories
Eggs		
Eggs, fresh	1 medium	72
Eggs, loche	3½ oz.	120
Eggs, dried	1 tbs.	84
Miscellaneous		
Beer	1 glass	114
Pop	1 bottle	78
Whiskey	1½ oz.	120
Wine	½ cup	114
Cake, plain	2 oz.	180
Candy	2 oz.	271
Cookies	1–3″ diameter	109
Pie, 2 crust, fruit	1/6 pie	393
Pancakes	2–4½″ diam.	218
Pickles, dill	1 medium	6
Peanut Butter	1 tbs.	81
Sugar, brown	1 tbs.	33
Sugar, white	1 tbs.	48
Syrup, corn	1 tbs.	57
Syrup, maple	1 tbs.	50

APPENDIX II

Standard Measures and Proportions

Abbreviations

tsp. = teaspoon
tbs. = tablespoon
c. = cup
pt. = pint
qt. = quart
oz. = ounce
lb. = pound
B.P. = baking powder
f.g. = few grains

Measures

3 tsp.	= 1 tbs.
16 tbs.	= 1 c. = 8 oz.
2½ c.	= 1 pt. = 20 oz. (Imperial)
5 c.	= 2 pt. = 40 oz. = 1 qt.
4 qts.	= 1 gal. = 160 oz.
1 oz.	= 130 grams = 2 tbs.
16 oz.	= 1 lb.
1 pound fat	= 2 cups
1 pound flour	= 4 cups, sifted
1 pound white sugar	= 2 cups

Batters and Doughs

Type	Liquid	Flour	Use
Thin or pour batter	1 cup	1 cup	Griddle cakes, popovers
Thick or drop batter	1 cup	2 cups	Cakes, muffins
Soft dough	1 cup	3 cups	Tea biscuits, bread
Stiff dough	1 cup	4 cups	Pastry, cookies

White Sauce

Type	Milk	Flour	Fat	Salt	Use
Thin	1 cup	1 tbs.	1 tbs.	½ tsp.	Soups
Medium	1 cup	2 tbs.	2 tbs.	½ tsp.	Gravies, vegetables, casseroles
Thick	1 cup	3 tbs.	3 tbs.	½ tsp.	Croquettes

APPENDIX III

Substitution Values

1 tbs. flour for thickening	=	½ tbs. starch
	=	½ tbs. tapioca
	=	2 tbs. rice
	=	1 egg
	=	1 tbs. egg powder
1 egg in a recipe	=	1 tbs. egg powder, plus 3 tbs. water.
1 c. milk	=	¼ c. milk powder plus 1 c. water.
	=	½ c. evaporated milk plus ½ c. water.
1 c. sour milk	=	1 c. milk plus 1 tbs. lemon juice or vinegar.
1 c. pastry or cake flour	=	⅞ c. all-purpose flour.
1 c. white sugar	=	1 c. brown sugar, packed
	=	1 c. corn syrup (but reduce other liquids ¼ c.)
	=	1 c. honey (but reduce other liquids ¼ c.)

1 oz. or 1 square chocolate = 3 tbs. cocoa plus ¾ tbs. butter.

1 tbs. gelatin will jell 2 c. liquid when making jelly.

Note

If no wild game is available, domestic meats may be used in the recipes as follows:

Beef may be used in place of:	Buffalo
	Caribou
	Deer
	Elk
	Moose
	Reindeer or
	Venison
Veal may be used in place of:	Lynx
Lamb or Mutton may be used in place of:	Dall Sheep
Pork may be used in place of:	Bear or
	Beaver
Chicken may be used in place of:	Muskrat
	Rabbit
	Squirrel or
	Woodchuck

Domestic meats do not have to be pre-soaked to eliminate the gamey flavour, but marinating helps to tenderize tough cuts.

INDEX

ABBREVIATIONS, 331

ACORN SOUP, 313

ALPINE BISTORT (SEE ROOTS), 211

AMANDINE, RUFFED GROUSE, 281

AMBER ONIONS, 222

AMERICAN, FILLETS OF ARCTIC
CHAR, 277

ANCHOVY BUTTER, 275

ANGEL FOOD
Apricot Bavarian, 266
Filling and Frosting for, 267

APPETIZERS
Bread Sticks, 37
Egg and Olive Murres, Susan's, 166
Party Crackers, 37
Pear and Cream Cheese Hors d'Oeûvres, 37
TV Snacks, 38

APPLE
Butter with Cranberries, 248
Butterscotch Sauce, 262
and Cabbage Salad, 238
Cranberry Butter, 248
Crisp, 256
Crumble, 256
Dumpling, 256
Dutch Cake, 196
Eve's Pudding, 257
Fritters, 255
Muffins, 189
Pudding, Steamed, 257
Puffs, 195

APPLESAUCE
Cake, 196
Fortified with Rose Hip Syrup, 251
Loaf, 196
and Rose Hips, 251
with Rose Hip Syrup, 251

APRICOT
Bavarian Cake, 266
Fruit Cake, 197

ARCTIC CHAR, 129
Baked, Stuffed, 130, 275
Baked, Mushrooms and Eggs au Gratin, 129
Broiled, 275
Broiled Kabobs, 131
Curried, 131
Cold, Whole, Fairbanks with Sauce
Verte, 274
Deep Fried, 129

ARCTIC CHAR—continued
Fillets of, Americain, 277
Fillets of, Bercy, 278
Fish Cakes, with Béchamel Sauce, 276
Medaillons of, 277
Poached, in Court Bouillon, 277
Steaks, Golden Broiled, 276
Steamed, 131

ARCTIC HARE, 89
Muktuk Chowder, 291
Ragoût of, 88

ASPARAGUS, 212

ASPIC, TOMATO QUICK, 240

ATLANTA SPECIAL, 278

AU GRATIN
Arctic Char, 129
Potatoes with Onions, 230
Seal Brain, 290
Turnip, 235

AVOCADO AND SHRIMP DIP, 39

BACON DRESSING FOR GREENS, 242

BAKED
Arctic Char
with Mushrooms and Eggs au Gratin, 129
Stuffed, 130, 275
Beans, Western Style, 213
Caribou Heart, Stuffed, 55
Custard, with Egg Powder, 164
Eggs with Cheese, Susan's, 167
Fish
Cheese Stuffing for, 27
Stuffed, 125
with Tarragon Dressing, 150
Halibut, 137
Partridge in Sherry, 109
Peaches, Tropical, 250
Pickerel, Stuffed, 142
Pike, Whole, 142
Pork Chops, Oven, 93
Potatoes, 227
in Foil, 229
Stuffed, 228
Tuna-Stuffed, 148
with Variations, 228
Rabbit
Hash, 86
Stuffed with Carrots, 82
Salmon, 143
Seal Flippers with Vegetables, 156

335

BAKED—*continued*
Skunk, 305
Squash, 235
Trout, 147
Tuna-Cheese Buns, 147
Whitefish, Quick, 148
Vegetable Marrow, 236

BANANA BRAN BREAD, 185

BANNOCK
Enriched, 193
French Toast, 162
Fruit Sauce on, 263
Small, 192

BARBECUE
Bear, 49
Caribou, Ribs of, 54
Crab, 135
Duck, 99
Perch, Fillets of, 140
Sauce, 30
for Partridge, 106
for Rabbit, 83

BASIC
Bread Stuffing, 275
Meal Pattern, 3, 4
Nutrition and Meal Planning, 1-18
Pancakes, 191
White Sauce, 30, 331

BATTERS, PROPORTIONS FOR, 331

BEAN, NAVY, SOUP, 22

BEANS
Baked, Western Style, 213
Company, 212
Dilly, 214
Salad
Hot, 237
Company's Coming, 237
Spanish Green, 214

BEAR, 48
Barbecued, 49
Boiled, 306
Fat
Pastry, 313
To Render, 48
Liver, Warning, 48
Roast, Polar, 50
Steaks
Grizzly, 306
Pan Broiled, 49
Stew, à l'Espagnole, 50

BEAVER, 76
Atlanta Special, 278
Boiled, Smoked, 307
Roast, 76
Skinning of, 76
in Sour Cream, 78
Sweet Pickled, 77
Tail, Fried, 78

BÉCHAMEL SAUCE REDUCED, 276

BEEF
Steak in Foil, 96
Stroganoff, 95
Stroganoff, Elsie Rancier's, 95
Tenderloin, Scalloped Dick's, 94
Swiss Steak in Foil, 96

BEETS
Greens, 214
Harvard, 215

BÉRCY, FILLETS OF ARCTIC CHAR, 278

BERRIES, 245-272

BEVERAGES, 168
Chocolate
Hot, 169
Syrup, 169
Cocoa, 168
Coffee
Fresh, 169
Instant, 170
Milk
Fresh, 168
Evaporated, 168
Reconstituting, 168
Tea
Fresh, 170
Instant, 170
Labrador, 209

BIG GAME HUNTING, 41-44, 315-325
Back to Camp or Car, 43
Bleeding, 42
Cutting, 44
Field Dressing, 42
Skinning, 44
Transportation, 43, 318, 325

BIRDS, GAME, 97
Care and Preparation, 97
Cleaning, 98
Plucking, 98
To Prevent Drying, 99

BISCUIT
Roll, Venison, 71
Tea (See Breads, Quick), 194
Topping, 92
Topping, for Squirrel Casserole, 90

BLEEDING ANIMALS, 42

BLUBBER, CABBAGE IN, 310

BLUEBERRIES
Buckle, 258
Crisp, 259
Jam, Spiced, 246
Jam, Uncooked or Frozen, 247
Jelly, Uncooked, 246
Kuchen, 258
Pie, 311
Pie, One-Crust, 269

BLUEBERRIES—*continued*
  Pie, Two-Crust, 269
  Pockets, 259
  Pudding, 312
  Sauce, 263
  Slump, 258
  Syrup, 262
  Topping, 259, 263

BOBOTEE OF WHALE, 159

BOB'S DIP, 40

BOILED
  Bear, 306
  Beaver, Smoked, 307
  Boiling Method, 47
  Bone Grease, 308
  Fish on Open Fire, 302
  Frozen Fish, 300
  Lynx, 307
  Muskrat, 304
  Porcupine, 305
  Rabbit Soup, 307
  Roots, 310
  Reindeer
    Head, 306
    Hoofs, 308
    Tongue, 307
  Salad Dressing, 241

BONE GREASE, BOILED, 308

BOUILLON
  Arctic Char Poached in, 277
  Court, 127

BOURGUIGNON, REINDEER, 285

BRACKEN (see Greens), 208, 215

BRAN BREAD, BANANA, 185

BRAIN
  Seal
    Au Gratin, 290
    Fritters, 290

BRAISED
  Braising Method, 46
  Buffalo Steak, Carbonade, 51
  Cabbage, 218
  Caribou, 55
  Grouse, Breast of, 105
  Heart
    Seal, 287
    Venison, 74
  Moose, 63
  Moose, Savoury Steaks, 65
  Partridge, 106
  Seal, 155, 286
  Venison in Sour Cream, 72

BRAKE FERN, 208, 215

BREAD
  Basic Bread Stuffing, 275
  Sticks, 37

BREAD—*continued*
  Stuffing for Baked Fish, 27
  To Save On, 12

BREADED BREAST OF PTARMIGAN, 115

BREADS, QUICK, 184-195
  MUFFINS, 188
    Apple, 189
    Breakfast, 188
    Cranberry, 189
    Fluffy Corn Bread, 190
    Muffins, 188
    Prune Wheat, 190
    Snow, 190
    Top-of-the-Stove, Corn Bread, 193
    with Egg and Milk Powder, 189
  NUT AND FRUIT BREADS, 184
    Banana Bran, 185
    Chocolate, 185
    Cranberry Nut, 185
    Fig, 188
    Four Fruit, 186
    Honey Prune, 187
    Mad Hatter Fruit, 187
    Steamed Brown, 186
  PANCAKES, 191
    Basic Pancakes, 191
    Pancakes or Griddlecakes, 191
    Wendy's Waffles, 192
  TEA BISCUITS, 194
    Apple Puffs, 195
    Bannock
      Enriched, 193
      French Toast, 162
      Small, 192
    Cranberry Coffee Cake, 195
    Oklahoma Squaw, 195
    Scotch Scones, 194
    Tea Biscuits, 194
  YORKSHIRE PUDDING, 192

BREADS, YEAST, 173
  WITH GRANULAR YEAST, 173
    Air Buns, 181
    Buns, 180
    Crusty French, 176
    Crusty Rolls, 179
    Donuts, Sara Tingmiak, 311
    Doughnuts, Raised, 181
    Hot Cross Buns, 180
    Italian, 177
    Oatmeal Casserole, 177
    Raisin, 178
    White, 174, 175
    Whole Wheat, 175
    Whole Wheat Light, 173
    Winnie Elanik, 310

  WITH SOURDOUGH STARTER, 182
    Sourdough
      Starter, 182
      Bread, 183

BREADS, YEAST—*continued*
    Chocolate Cake, 184
    Hotcakes, 183
    Hotcakes, Rosie Peeloolook, 310
    Muffins, 182
    Waffles, 184

BREAKFAST MENUS, 3, 8

BREAKFAST MUFFINS, 188

BROCCOLI, 216

BROILED
    Arctic Char, 275
    Broiling Method, 46
    Fish, 126
    Kabobs, Arctic Char, 131
    Mooseburgers, 62
    Pan-Broiling, 46
    Perch Fillets, 141
    Pickerel, with Mint, 141
    Steaks
        Golden, Arctic Char, 276
        Halibut, Orange, 137
        Salmon, 143
    Squirrel, 89
    Whitefish, 149
    Woodcock, 119

BROWNIES, EILEEN THROWER'S, 200

BRUNSWICK STEW, 90

BRUSSEL SPROUTS, 216

BUCKLE, BLUEBERRY, 258

BUFFALO, 50
    Cutlets, Chopped, 53
    Paupiettes, 51
    Prime Rib Roast of, 52
    Steak, Braised, Carbonade, 51

BUNS
    Air, 181
    Buns, 180
    Hot Cross, 180
    Crusty Rolls, 179
    Tuna-Cheese, Baked, 147

BUTTER
    Anchovy, 275
    Cranberry Apple, 248
    Maître d'Hôtel, 34

BUTTERSCOTCH
    Apple, Sauce, 262
    Bars, 199
    Chocolate Frosting, 184, 266
    Sauce, 263

CABBAGE
    and Apple Salad, 238
    in Blubber Fat, 310
    Braised, 218

CABBAGE—*continued*
    Casserole with Rice and Tomato, 217
    Custard Ring, 217
    Glorified, 217
    Hot, Slaw, 238

CAKES
    Applesauce Cake, 196
    Applesauce Loaf, 196
    Apricot Bavarian, 266
    Apricot Fruit, 197
    Blueberry Topping for, 263
    Brownie Cake, Eileen Thrower's, 200
    Butterscotch Bars, 199
    Dutch Apple Cake, 196
    Fruit Sauce on, 263
    Gingerbread, 198
    Luscious Prune, 198
    Miracle Whip Chocolate, 199
    Peach Upside-Down, 199
    Sourdough Chocolate, 184

CALIFORNIA DIP, 39

CALORIES, 6
    Values of Foods, 327-330

CAMPFIRE MUSKRAT, 304

CANADA GOOSE, 103

CANADA'S FOOD GUIDE, 3

CANDIED
    Squash, 235
    Rose. Hips, 253

CANDY
    Chocolate Coating for, 268
    Fondant, 268
    Marshmallows, 267
    Peanut Butter Fudge, 268
    Uncooked Chocolate Fudge, 268

CANTONESE
    Duck, 280
    Sauce, 31

CAPER SAUCE, SOUR CREAM, 35

CARAMEL SAUCE, 264

CARBOHYDRATES
    Function of, 2
    Sources of, 2

CARIBOU, 53
    Braised, 55
    Eskimo Dry Meat, 305
    Hash with Eggs, 54
    Hawaiian, 54
    Head Cheese, 67
    Heart, Baked Stuffed, 55
    Hoof, Boiled, 308
    Ribs, Barbecued, of, 54
    Standing Rib Roast of, 53
    Tongue, Fresh, 56

CARROTS
and Cranberry Jam, 247
Glazed, 219
Honey, 218
with Orange Sauce, 219
Pickled, 219
Sweet and Pungent, 219
Soup, Quick, 23

CASSEROLE
Bread, Oatmeal, 177
Cabbage, Rice and Tomato, 217
Cod, Salt and Rice, 134
of Canned Corn, 221
Corn and Oysters, Scalloped, 220
Ham, 93
Kippered Herring, 138
Lake Trout, 146
of Partridge, 106
Pork and Rice, 94
Quick
Fish, 152
Seal, 158
Salmon, 145
of Seal, 157, 287
Seal and Rice, 156
Squirrel, with Biscuit Topping, 90
Tuna, Scalloped, Irish, 147

CATSUP, CRANBERRY, 248

CAULIFLOWER, with Parsley Sauce, 220

CELLULOSE, FUNCTION OF, 2

CEREALS, 167
Cooking Methods, General, 167
In Meal Planning, 5
Oatmeal Topping for Fruit, 167
to Save on, 12
Storage of, 167

CHAR, ARCTIC
(see Arctic Char), 129

CHARLIE PUDDING, 260

CHEESE
and Onion Dip, 38
Baked Eggs with, Susan's, 167
Baked Tuna and, Buns, 147
Dip, Daisy Jensen's, 38
Head, 67
Pastry, 270
Pear and Cream Cheese Hors d'Oeûvres, 37
Sauce, 31
to Save on, 12, 13
Scrambled Eggs with, 165
Stuffing for Baked Fish, 27
Tuna-, Soufflé, 147

CHEEZIE POTATOES, 228

CHERRY, MOCK, PIE, 270

CHICKEN
Ginger, Prairie, 114
Gumbo Soup, 24
Prairie, 113, 114

CHILI CON CARNE
Moose, 63
Venison, 75

CHOCOLATE
Brownies, Eileen Thrower's, 200
Butterscotch Frosting, 184
Cake
Miracle Whip, 199
Sourdough, 184
Coating, 268
Fudge, Uncooked, 268
Hot, 169
Quick Bread, 185
Sauce
No. 1, 264
No. 2, 264
Syrup, 169

CHOPS
Mackenzie Mountain (Lamb), 56
Oven Baked, Pork, 93

CHOP SUEY, RABBIT, 282

CHOWDER
Arctic Muktuk, 291
Clam, 132
Fish, 301
Fish, Fresh or Smoked, 150

CLAMS, 132
Chowder, 132
Fried, 133
Preparation of, 132
Pie, 132
Scalloped, 133
Soup, 24

CLEANING OF GAME BIRDS, 98

CLEAN-UP DAY POTATOES, 229

COATING, CHOCOLATE, 268

COCKTAIL SAUCE, 31

COCOA, 168
Milk Pudding, 260

COD
Fish and Brewis, 133
Fluffy Codfish Pie, 134
Salt Cod and Rice Casserole, 134

COFFEE
Cake, Cranberry, 195
Fresh, 169
Instant, 170

COMPANY BEANS, 212

COMPANY'S COMING BEAN SALAD, 237

CONY
(see Inconnu), 138

COOKIES
Dad's, 200
Drop Fruit, 201
Ethel's Jam Buns, 202

COOKIES—*continued*
  Matrimonial Squares, 200
  Oatmeal, 202
  Oatmeal Molasses, 201
  Peanut Butter, Jane's, 202
  Prune Refrigerator, 203
  Rolled Oat, 201
  Rolled Oat, Joyce's, 203
  Sugar, 203
  Top-of-the-Stove, 202
COOKING METHODS, GENERAL
  CEREALS, 167
  FISH, 125-127
    Baked Stuffed Fish, 125
    Boiling Fish, 127
    in Aluminum Foil in the Oven, 125
    Boiling Water, 127
    Court Bouillon, 127
    Deep Fat, 126
    the Frying Pan, 126
    Milk, 128
    the Oven, 125
    Steam, 127
  GAME, 45-47
    DRY HEAT
      Broiling, 46
      Deep Fat Frying, 46
      Pan-Broiling, 46
      Pan-Frying, 46
      Roasting, 46
    MOIST HEAT
      Braising, 46
      Boiling, 47
      Pot Roasting, 46
      Stewing, 46
  GAME BIRDS, 97-99
  VEGETABLES, 206

COOKING TERMS, 13-18

COOKING WILD GAME, 45-47

CORN
  Bread
    Fluffy, 190
    Top-of-the-Stove, 193
  Casserole of Canned, 221
  Fritters, 221
  Scalloped, with Oysters, 220
  Vegetable Soufflé, 220

CORNSTARCH PUDDING, 260

COURT BOUILLON, 127

CRAB, 135
  à la Newburg, 279
  Barbecued, 135
  Dip, 38
  Patties, 135
  Preparation of, 135
  Sauce for Whitefish, 149

CRACKERS, PARTY, 37

CRANBERRY
  Apple Butter, 248
  Catsup, 248
  Coffee Cake, 195
  Gelatin Salad, 240
  Jam, 311
  Jam, and Carrot, 247
  Jam, and Rose Hip, 252
  Jelly, High Bush, 247
  Low Bush, Sauce, 32
  Muffins, 189
  Nut Bread, 185
  Pie, 271
  Pie, Mock Cherry, 270
  Pudding, 261
  Pudding, Wild, 313
  Raw Relish, 248
  Spiced, Sauce, 34
  Stuffing, 27
  Ways of Using, 249

CREAM CHEESE AND PEAR, HORS
  d'OEÛVRES, 37

CREAMED
  Mushrooms, 222
  Peas, 226
  Peas with Mushrooms, 225
  Rabbit on Toast, 85

CREOLE SAUCE, 31
  Rabbit in, 283

CRISP
  Apple, 256
  Blueberry, 259
  Peach, 260

CROQUETTES
  Rabbit-Ham, 88
  Salmon, 144
  Sardine, 145

CRUMBLE, APPLE, 256

CRUNCHY TUNA SALAD, 239

CRUSTY
  French Bread, 176
  Rolls, 179

CUCUMBERS
  and Onion in Sour Cream, 224
  Sauce, 224

CURRIED
  Arctic Char, 131
  Deer, 58
  Elk, 58
  Game, 58
  Pheasant, 111
  Rabbit, 85
  Rice and Fish Flakes, 239

CUSTARD
  Baked, 164
  Cabbage Ring, 217
  made with Egg Powder, 164

CUSTOMS AND ENTRY
  (see Hunting in N.W.T.)
CUTLETS, CHOPPED SWEETGRASS
  BUFFALO, 53

DAD'S COOKIES, 200
DALL SHEEP, 56
  Golden Lamb Patties, 57
  Mackenzie Mountain Chops, 56
  Roast Leg of, 57
  Roast Stuffed Shoulder of, 57
DANDELION
  Greens, 208
  Roots, 211
DANISH FISH PUDDING, 150
DEEP FAT FRYING
  Arctic Char, 129
  Fish, 126
  Rabbit, 282
DEER
  Curried, 58
  Liver, Frozen, 59
  Pemmican, 307
  Sweet and Sour Ribs, 60
DESSERTS, 241, 245-272, 311-313
DEVILLED EGGS, 164
DICK'S SCALLOPED BEEF
  TENDERLOIN, 94
DILLY BEANS, 214
DINNER MENUS, 4, 8, 9
DIPS
  Bob's, 40
  California, 39
  Cheese, Daisy Jensen's, 38
  Cheese and Onion, 38
  Crab, 38
  Shrimp, 39
  Shrimp Avocado, 39
DIRECTIONS, HOW TO FIND, 298
DOGS, HUNTING WITH, 319
DOUGH, PROPORTIONS FOR, 331
DOUGHNUTS
  Donuts, Sara Tingmiak, 311
  Raised, 181
DRESSINGS
  (see Salad Dressings), 241-243
DRIED EGG POWDER
  Custard with, 164
  Reconstituting of, 162, 296
  Scrambled Eggs, Using, 165

DRIED FISH PUDDING, POUNDED, 312
DRIED MEAT
  Eskimo, 305
  Indian, 305
  Muskrat, 304
  Pemmican, 307
  Pounded, 306
    (see also Jerky)
DRIED VEGETABLES, 207
DROP COOKIES, 201
DRY HEAT COOKING METHOD, 46
DUCHESS POTATOES, 230
DUCK
  Barbecued, 99
  Cantonese, 280
  Duckling with Onions, 101
  Ducklings, Purple-Plum, 100
  Fricassée, 101
  Hungarian, Roast, 279
  Open Fire, 307
  Ragoût of, 280
  Smothered, 99
  Wild, à l'Orange, 99
  Wild Rice Stuffing for, 29
DUMPLING
  Apple, 256
  Ptarmigan Stew with, 116
  Rabbit Stew with, 81
DUTCH APPLE CAKE, 196

EDIBLE WILD PLANTS
  (see Greens, Edible Wild
    and Roots, Edible Wild), 208-211
EGGS, 161
  Baked with Cheese, Susan's, 167
  Caribou Hash with, 54
  Custard
    Baked, 164
    made with Egg Powder, 164
  Devilled, 164
  Dried or Powdered, 162
    Reconstituting of, 162
  Fish, Frozen, 302
  Fresh
    Storing of, 162
    Testing of, 162
  French
    Bannock, 162
    Toast, 162
  Hard-Cooked, 163
  Loche Liver and, 302
  and Olive Murres, Susan's, 166
  Pickled, Marg Wickett's, 166
  and Rice Stuffing, 29
  to Save on, 12, 13

EGGS—*continued*
  Scrambled
    Fresh, 165
    Powdered, 165
    with Cheese, 165
      Ham, 165
      Western, 165
  Soft-Cooked, 163
ELK
  Curried Game, 58
  Elkburgers, 58
  English Brown Stew, 60
  Head Cheese, 67
  Meat Loaf, 58
  Steak 'N Gravy, 59
  Steak in Wine, 59
ELSIE RANCIER'S BEEF
  STROGANOFF, 95
ENGLISH BROWN STEW, 60
ESKIMO
  Dry Meat, 305
  Ice Cream, 311
EVAPORATED MILK, 6
EVE'S PUDDING, 257

FAT
  Function of, 2
  Pastry, Bear, 313
  or Suet, to Render, 48, 299
  Sources of, 2
FAISANT AUX CHOUX, 111
FAVOURITE FISH SALAD, 239
FIDDLEHEADS, 209
FIELD DRESSING OF GAME, 42
FIG BREAD, 188
FILLETS, ARCTIC CHAR
  Americain, 277
  Bercy, 278
FILLINGS AND FROSTINGS
  for Angel Food, 267
  Apricot Bavarian, 266
  Butterscotch Chocolate, 266
  Fluffy Cake, 266
  Mocha Icing, 200
  Quick Icing, 266
FIREWEED, 208
FISH AND SEA MAMMALS, 121-160
FISH AND BREWIS, 133
FISH CAKES, ARCTIC CHAR, 276
FISH, COOKING METHODS GENERAL
  in Aluminum Foil in the Oven, 125
  Baked Stuffed, 125
  in Boiling Water, 127

FISH, COOKING METHODS—*continued*
  Broiling, 126
  in Court Bouillon, 127
  in Deep Fat, 126
  in the Frying Pan, 126
  in Milk, 128
  in the Oven, 125
  in Steam, 127
FISH
  Cuts of, 122
  Dressed, 122
  Fillets, 123
  Filleting, 124
  Pan-Dressed, 122
  Preparation of, 124
  Purchasing of, 123
  to Save on, 12
  Scaling, 124
  Steaks, 123
  Whole or Round, 122
FISH, RECIPES FOR
  Arctic Char, 129-131, 274-278
  Clams, 132, 133
  Cod, 133, 134
  Crab, 135, 279
  Grayling, 136
  Halibut, 136, 137
  Herring, 137, 138
  Inconnu, 138, 139, 302
  Loche, 140, 300, 302, 312
  Perch, 140, 141
  Pickerel, 141, 142
  Pike, 142
  Salmon, 143-145
  Sardines, 145
  Shrimp, 303
  Seal, 155-158, 286-290
  Trout, 146, 147
  Tuna, 147, 148
  Whale, 158-160, 291, 309
  Whitefish, 148, 149, 303
FISH RECIPES, GENERAL
  Baked, Whole with Tarragon Dressing, 150
  Boiled, Frozen, 300
  Boiled, on Open Fire, 302
  Chowder, 301
  Chowder, Fresh or Smoked, 150
  Danish Pudding, 150
  Fish Sauce, 302
  Fisherman's Style, 301
  Frozen, 301
  Frozen Fish Eggs, 302
  Pawtucket Fish, 154
  Pineapple Mystery Package, 152
  Poached in Milk, 153
  Poached with Olive Sauce, 153
  Pounded Dry Fish Pudding, 312
  Quick Fish Casserole, 152
  Roasted, 300
  Roasted by Campfire, 302

FISH RECIPES, GENERAL—*continued*
  Savoury Fish, 154
  Smoked, 301
  Smoked Fillets in Milk, 151
  Smoked Fillets in Tomato Sauce, 151
  in Wine Sauce, 151

FISH SALADS
  (see Salads), 238-239

FISH SAUCE, 302

FLIPPER, SEAL, 156, 157

FLOUR, 171, 172
  All-Purpose, 172
  Bread, 172
  Cake or Pastry, 172

FLOUR MIXTURES, 171-203
  Cakes, 196-200
  Cookies, 200-203
  Quick Breads, 184-195
  Yeast Breads, 172-184

FOIL
  Baked Potatoes, 229
  Beef Steak in, 96
  Fish in, 125
  Swiss Steak in, 96
  Use of, in Cooking Game Birds, 99

FONDANT, 268

FOOD
  Costs, 9-13
  Purchasing, 9-13
  Requirements, 3-6
  Storage, 294-296, 298, 299

FOUR FRUIT BREAD, 186

FRENCH
  Bread, Crusty, 176
  Dressing, 241
  Fried
    Onion Rings, 223
    Potatoes, 231
    Potatoes, Mock, 233
    Rabbit, 84
  Toast or Bannock, 162

FRICASSÉE
  Duck, 101
  Rabbit, 85
  Squirrel, 91

FRIED
  Beaver Tail, 78
  Clams, 133
  Grayling, 136
  Grouse and Onions, 104
  Halibut Fillets, 136
  Inconnu, 139
  Lake Trout, 146
  Loche, 300

FRIED—*continued*
  Loche Liver and Eggs, 302
  Meat with Left Over Porridge, 306
  Muskrat, 80, 304
  Onions, 224
  Potatoes, 231, 233
  Prairie Chicken, 113
  Ptarmigan Breasts, 116
  Rabbit, 282
  Seal Liver, 288
  Southern, Pheasant, 112
  Tomatoes, 233
  Whale Meat, 309
  Whitefish, 149
  Woodchuck, 91

FRITTERS
  Apple, 255
  Corn, 221
  Parsnip, 225
  Seal Brain, 290

FROSTING
  Chocolate Butterscotch, 184
  for Angel Food, 267

FROZEN
  Blueberry Jam, 247
  Fish
    Boiled, 300
    Eggs, 302
    Serving, 301
  Raspberry Jam, 250

FROZEN DELIGHT, 241

FRUIT BREAD
  Banana Bran, 185
  Cranberry Nut, 185
  Fig, 188
  Four Fruit, 186
  Honey Prune, 187
  Mad Hatter, 187

FRUIT CAKE, APRICOT, 197

FRUIT COOKIES, DROP, 201

FRUIT
  Dried, 246
  Grades of, 246
  in Meal Planning, 5
  Preparation of, 246
  Sauce for Cake or Bannock, 263
  to Save on, 11
  Stuffing for Goose, 27

FRYING
  Deep Fat Method, 126
  Pan, Method, 46

FUDGE
  Peanut Butter, 268
  Uncooked Chocolate, 268

FUEL, to Save on, 11

GAME
  Bleeding of, 42
  Cooking of, 45-47
  Curried, 58
  Cuts of, 44
  Hunting of, 41-44, 315-325
  Larding of, 45
  Marinade for, 34, 46, 48
  Skinning of, 44

GAME ANIMALS, WILD, 41-92
  BIG GAME
    Bear, 48-50, 306
    Buffalo, 50-53
    Caribou, 53-56, 308
    Dall Sheep, 56, 57
    Deer, 58-60
    Elk, 58-60
    Lynx, 61, 307
    Moose, 62-68
    Reindeer, 69-71, 285, 306-308
    Venison, 42, 72-75
  SMALL GAME
    Beaver, 76-78, 278, 307
    Hare, 88, 89
    Muskrat, 79, 80, 284, 303-305
    Porcupine, 305
    Rabbit, 81-88, 282-284, 307
    Skunk, 305
    Squirrel, 89-91
    Woodchuck or Groundhog, 91-92

GAME BIRDS
  (see also Birds), 97-119, 279-281
  Duck, 99-101, 279, 280, 307
  Goose, 102, 103
  Grouse, 104, 105, 281
  Partridge, 105-109, 286
  Pheasant, 110-112
  Pigeon, 113, 281
  Prairie Chicken, 113, 114
  Ptarmigan, 115-117, 308
  Quail, 117, 118
  Woodcock, 119

GAME REGULATIONS
  (see Hunting in the Northwest
    Territories), 315-325

GAME ZONES, 320-323

GARDENING IN THE NORTH, 206,
  297, 298

GELATIN, CRANBERRY, 240

GINGER
  Bread, 198
  Prairie Chicken, 114

GLAZED
  Carrots, 219

GLORIFIED CABBAGE, 217

GOLDEN
  Broiled Arctic Char Steaks, 276
  Lamb Patties, 57
  Peach Pie, 272

GOOSE
  Canada, 103
  Fruit Stuffing for, 27
  Roast
    Irish, with Potato Stuffing, 103
    Wild, No. 1, 102
    Wild, No. 2, 102
  Stuffing for Wild, 102

GOULASH, REINDEER, 70

GRACE SPENCER'S 24-HOUR SALAD, 241

GRANULAR YEAST
  (see Breads, Yeast), 173

GRAPES
  Green with Quail, 118
  Sautéed Partridge in, Sauce, 286

GRASS, SCURVY, 209

GRAYLING, 136
  Pan-Fried, 136

GREASE, BONE, 308

GREEN BEANS, SPANISH, 214

GREEN PEPPERS, 226

GREENS, BEET, 214

GREENS, EDIBLE WILD
  Bracken, 208
  Brake Fern, 208
  Dandelion, 208
  Fiddleheads, 209
  Fireweed or Willow Herb, 208
  Labrador Tea, 209
  Lamb's Quarters, 208
  Mountain Sorrel, 209
  Mustard, Wild, 208
  Pigweed, 208
  Pigweed, Red Flowering, 208
  Poplar and Jack Pine, 210
  Scurvy Grass, 209
  Sourdock, 208
  Spruce Tips, 209
  Strawberry Blight, 208
  Wild Rhubarb, 211
  Willow Herb, 208
  Willow Tips, 210

GREENS, HOT BACON DRESSING
  FOR, 242

GRIDDLE CAKES, 191

GRIZZLY BEAR, 306

GROUNDHOG, 91, 92

GROUSE
  Braised Breast of, 105
  Fried, and Onions, 104
  with Orange Slices, 281

GROUSE—*continued*
  Roast, 105
  Ruffed, Amandine, 281
  in Sherry, 104
GUIDES FOR HUNTING
  (see Hunting in the Northwest
    Territories), 318

HALIBUT
  Baked, 137
  Fried Fillets, 136
  Island Loaf, 136
  Steaks, Orange Broiled, 137
HAM
  Casserole, 93
  Croquettes, with Rabbit, 88
  Eggs Scrambled with, 165
  Hot Mustard Sauce for, 33
HARD-COOKED EGGS, 163
HARE
  Arctic, 89
  Jugged, 283
  Ragoût of, Arctic, 89
HARVARD BEETS, 215
HASH
  Brown Potatoes, 231
  Caribou, with Eggs, 54
  Rabbit, Baked, 86
HASSENPFEFFER, 284
HAWAIIAN CARIBOU, 54
HEAD, REINDEER, BOILED, 306
HEAD CHEESE
  Caribou, 67
  Elk, 67
  Moose, 67
  Reindeer, 67
  Venison, 67
HEART
  Caribou, Baked, Stuffed, 55
  Moose, Stuffed, 68
  Seal, Braised, 287
  Seal, Savoury, 289
  Venison, Braised, 74
HERB, WILLOW
  (see Fireweed), 208
HERRING
  Casserole of, Kippered, 138
  Jansson's Temptation, 138
  in Sour Cream, 137
HIGH BUSH CRANBERRY JELLY, 247
HINTS FOR COOKING WITH RATIONS,
  294-300

HOLLANDAISE SAUCE
  No. 1, 32
  No. 2, 32
HOME FRIED POTATOES, 231
HOMEMADE SOUR CREAM, 32
HONEY
  Carrots, 218
  Prune Bread, 187
HOOFS, REINDEER OR CARIBOU,
    BOILED, 308
HOUSEHOLD HINTS, 294-300
HORS d'OEÛVRES, PEAR AND CREAM
    CHEESE, 37
HOT
  Bacon Dressing for Greens, 242
  Bean Salad, 237
  Cabbage Slaw, 238
  Chocolate, 169
  Cross Buns, 180
  Mustard Sauce for Ham, 33
HOTCAKES, SOURDOUGH, 183, 310
HUNGARIAN ROAST DUCK, 279
HUNTER'S STYLE PARTRIDGE, 108
HUNTING IN THE NORTHWEST
    TERRITORIES, 315-325
  Changes in Regulations, 324
  Closed Areas, 317
  Customs and Entry, 325
  Firearms, 318
  Game Meat, 318
  Game Regulations, 317-325
  Game Zones, 320-323
  Guides, 318
  How to Arrange a Trip, 316
  Hunting from Vehicles, 318
  Licenses, 319
  Reporting Kill, 319
  Safety, 319
  Sources of Information, 325
  Use of Dogs, 319

ICE CREAM
  Eskimo, 311
  Blueberry Topping for, 263
ICINGS
  Angel Food, 267
  Butterscotch Chocolate, 184
  Fluffy Cake, 198, 266
  Mocha, 200
  Quick, 266
INCONNU, 138
  Fresh Cony Soup, 302
  Pan Fried, 139

INCONNU—*continued*
  Poached, 139
  Roasted Cony Head, 302
INDIAN
  Dry Meat, 305
  Meat Stew, 306
  Pudding, 312
INSTANT
  Coffee, 170
  Tea, 170
IRISH
  Roast Goose with Potato Stuffing, 103
  Scalloped Tuna Casserole, 147
ISLAND LOAF, HALIBUT, 136
ITALIAN BREAD, 177
ITALIENNE, PIGEON, 281

JACK PINE, 210
JANE'S PEANUT BUTTER COOKIES, 202
JAM
  Blueberry, 246
    Spiced, 246
    Uncooked or Frozen, 247
  Buns, Ethel's, 202
  Cranberry, 311
  Cranberry and Carrot, 247
  Raspberry,
    Frozen, 250
    and Red Currant, 250
    Wild, 250
  Salmonberry, 255
  Rosehip, 252
    and Cranberry, 252
    and Rhubarb, 254
JANSSON'S TEMPTATION, 138
JELLIED
  Moose Nose, 66
  Rabbit Salad, 87
  Salads, 87, 240
JELLY
  Blueberry, Uncooked, 246
  Cranberry High Bush, 247
  Rose Petal, 254
JERKY
  Cold Brined, 47
  Hot Brined, 47
  Sun Dried, 47
JOAN BELLWARD'S MINCEMEAT, 272
JOE'S FRIED TOMATOES, 233
JUGGED HARE, 283
JUICE, PRUNE, AND ROSE HIP
  SHERBET, 254

KAAPI, 169
KABOBS OF ARCTIC CHAR, 131
KIPPERED HERRING CASSEROLE, 138
KUCHEN, BLUEBERRY, 258

LABRADOR TEA, 209
LAKE TROUT
  Casserole, 146
  Pan Fried, 146
LAMB
  (see Dall Sheep), 56
LAMBSQUARTERS, 208
LARDING VENISON, 45
LEMON
  Sauce, 264
  Sour Cream Mold, Jellied, 240
LICENSES
  (see Game Regulations), 319
LIQUORICE ROOT, 211
LIVER
  Bear, Warning, 48
  Deer, Frozen, 59
  Loche
    with Eggs, 302
    Pudding, 312
    and Roe, 140
  Polar Bear, 48
  Seal
    Fried, 288
    Bearded, Warning, 155
  Venison, and Onions, 75
LOCHE, 140
  Fried, 300
  Liver
    and Eggs, 302
    Pudding, 312
    and Roe, 140
LOUSEWORT, WOOLLY, 211
LOW BUSH CRANBERRY SAUCE, 32
LUNCH MENUS, 4, 9
LUSCIOUS PRUNE CAKE, 198
LYNX, 61
  Boiled, 307
  Canadian, Stew, 61
  Oven Roasted, 307
  Skinning of, 61

MACKENZIE MOUNTAIN CHOPS, 56
MAD HATTER FRUIT BREAD, 187
MAÎTRE d'HÔTEL BUTTER, 34

MAMIE LEONARD'S STEAMED
PUDDING, 257
MAPLE SYRUP PIE, 270
MARDY GALLAGHER'S SASKATOON
PIE, 271
MARIE BROWN'S PIMIENTO SALAD, 240
MARINADE, 34
for Moose, 64
for Steak, 73
for Wild Game, 48
MARSHMALLOWS, 267
MARROW, VEGETABLE, 236
MASHED TURNIP, 235
MASU, 211
MATRIMONIAL SQUARES, 200
MAYONNAISE
No Egg, 242
Potato, 242
Quick, 242
MEASURES, 331
MEAL PLANNING, 3-7
Basic Meal Pattern, 3
Bread, 6
Cereals, 5
Fruit, 5
Meat and Meat Alternatives, 6
Milk, 6
Vegetables, 5
MEAT
(see also Game)
Dry, 305
in Meal Planning, 6
to Save on, 12
Miscellaneous Recipes, 93-96
MEAT, FRIED WITH LEFT-OVER
PORRIDGE, 306
MEAT LOAF
Elk, 58
Muskrat, 80
Venison, 74
MEAT STEW
Brunswick, 90
Dorothy Macintosh's, 65
English Brown, 60
Indian, 306
à l'Espagnole, 50
Rabbit, with Dumplings, 81
MEDAILLONS OF ARCTIC CHAR, 277
MEDIUM WHITE SAUCE, 30, 331
MENUS
Breakfast, 8, 3
Dinner, 8, 9, 4
Lunch, 9, 4
Supper, 9, 4

MICHIGAN SPECIAL, 284
MILK
Cooking Fish in, 128
Evaporated, 6
Fish Poached in, 153
Fresh, 6
in Meal Planning, 6
Pudding, Cocoa, 260
Reconstituting, 6, 296
Smoked Fillets in, 151
to Save on, 11
MINCEMEAT
Joan Bellward's, 272
Moose, 67
Venison, 74
MINERALS
Function of, 2
Sources of, 2
MINT, BROILED PICKEREL WITH, 141
MIPKU, 309
MIRACLE WHIP CHOCOLATE CAKE, 199
MOCHA ICING, 200
MOCK
Cherry Pie, 270
French Fried Potatoes, 233
MOLASSES OATMEAL COOKIES, 201
MONAH CARLEY'S PINEAPPLE
SQUARES, 262
MONGOLE SOUP, 25
MOOSE, 62
Braised, 63
Broiled Mooseburgers, 62
Chili Con Carne, 63
Eskimo Dry Meat, 305
Head Cheese, 67
Heart, Stuffed, 68
Marinated, 64
Mincemeat, 67
Nose, Jellied, 66
Pemmican, 307
Savoury Steaks, 65
Soup, 64
Stew, Dorothy Macintosh's, 65
Sukiyaki, 68
Swiss Steak, 68
MOUNTAIN SORREL, 209
MRS. HATTING'S SALAD DRESSING, 242
MUFFINS
Apple, 189
Breakfast, 188
Cranberry, 189
Fluffy Corn Bread, 190
Muffins, 188
Prune Wheat, 190
Snow, 190

MUFFINS—*continued*
Sourdough, 182
Top-of-the-Stove Corn Bread, 193
with Egg and Milk Powder, 189
MUKTUK, 309
Arctic Chowder, 291
MURRES, SUSAN'S EGG AND OLIVE, 166
MUSHROOMS
Creamed, 222
Baked Char with, and Eggs au Gratin, 129
and Peas, 225
and Rice Stuffing, 28
Fillet of Whale with, Sauce, 160
Pheasant with, 112
Quail with, Sauce, in Toast Cups, 118
Sauce, 33, 160
Trout, Stuffed with, 146
MUSKRAT, 79
Boiled, 304
Campfire, 304
Dried, 304
Eskimo Dry Meat, 305
Fried, 80, 304
Meat Loaf, 80
Michigan Special, 284
Open Fire, 304
Roasted, 305
Skinning of, 79
Smothered, and Onions, 79
Soup, 304
Steamed, 303
Stuffed, 303
Tails, 304
MUSTARD
Sauce, Hot for Ham, 33
Wild, 208

NAVY BEAN SOUP, 22
NEWBURG, CRAB à la, 279
NEWFOUNDLAND SEAL FLIPPERS, 157
NO-EGG MAYONNAISE, 242
NOSE, JELLIED MOOSE, 66
NUT
Fruit Breads, 184
and Raisin Stuffing, 28
NUTRIENTS
Carbohydrates, 2
Cellulose, 2
Fat, 2
Function of, 2
Minerals, 2
Proteins, 2
Sources of, 2
Vitamins, 2
Vitamin C, 4
Water, 2

OATMEAL
Casserole Bread, 177
Cookies, 202
Cookies, Molasses, 201
Porridge, (see Cereals), 167
Topping for Fruit, 167
OATS ROLLED
Cookies, 201
Joyce's Cookies, 203
OKLAHOMA SQUAW BREAD, 195
OLD FASHIONED RICE PUDDING, 312
ONE DISH MEAL, VENISON, 73
ONIONS
Amber, 222
and Cheese Dip, 38
and Cucumber in Sour Cream, 224
French Fried, 223
Fresh, Pickles, 222
Pan Fried, 224
Pan Fried, Rings, 224
with Potatoes au Gratin, 230
Scalloped, 224
Stuffed, 225
with Variations, 223
OPEN FIRE
Duck, 307
Fish, 302
Muskrat, 304
ORANGE
Broiled Halibut Steaks, 137
Grouse with, Slices, 281
Ptarmigan with, Rice, 116
Sauce, with Carrots, 219
Wild Duck à l'Orange, 99
OVEN
Baked Pork Chops, 93
Broiled Woodcock, 119
Cooking Fish in, 125
Roasted Lynx, 307
Temperature, How to test, 300
OYSTER
Scalloped, with Corn, 220
Stew, 24

PAN BROILED
Bear Steaks, 49
Venison, 73
PAN BROILING METHOD, 46
PANCAKES
Basic Pancakes, 191
Griddlecakes, 191
Waffles, Sourdough, 184
Wendy's Waffles, 192
PAN FRIED
Grayling, 136
Inconnu, 139

PAN FRIED—*continued*
   Onions, 224
   Onion Rings, 224
   Trout, 146
   Whitefish, 149
PAN FRYING METHOD, 46
PAPRIKA, PARTRIDGE, 107
PARSNIP FRITTERS, 225
PARSLEY
   Cauliflower with, Sauce, 220
   Sauce, 33
PARTRIDGE
   Baked, in Sherry, 109
   Barbecue Sauce, 106
   Braised, 106
   Casserole of, 106
   Hunter's Style, 108
   Paprika, 107
   Pie, 109
   Pineapple Stuffing, 28
   Roast, 107
   Roast, Stuffed, 107
   Sautéed in Grape Sauce, 286
   Stew, 105
   with Sour Cream, 109
PARTY CRACKERS, 37
PASTRY
   Bear Fat, 313
   Cheese, 270
   Tasty, 269
PATTIES
   Crab, 135
   Groundhog, 92
   Lamb, Golden, 57
   Woodchuck, 92
PAUPIETTES, NORTHERN BUFFALO, 51
PAWTUCKET FISH, 154
PEACH
   Baked, Tropical, 250
   Cake, Upside-Down, 199
   Crisp, 260
   Pie, Golden, 272
   and Cream with Ptarmigan, 117
PEANUT BUTTER
   Cookies, Jane's, 202
   Fudge, 268
   Soup, Cream of, 26
PEAR AND CREAM CHEESE HORS
   D'OEUVRES, 37
PEAS
   Creamed, with Variations, 226
   and Mushrooms, 225
   Soup, Puree of Split Pea, 26
PEMMICAN, 307
PEPPER SAUCE, 34

PEPPERS, GREEN, STUFFED, 226
PERCH
   Fillets
      Barbecued, 140
      Broiled, 141
PETAL, ROSE, JELLY, 254
PHEASANT
   Curried, 111
   Faisant Aux Choux, 111
   with Mushroom Sauce, 112
   Pie, 110
   Roast, 110
   Southern Fried, 112
PICKEREL, 141
   Baked, Stuffed, 142
   Broiled, with Mint, 141
PICKLED
   Beaver, Sweet, 77
   Carrots, 219
   Eggs, Marg Wickett's, 166
PICKLES
   Onion, Fresh, 222
   Sauce, Brown's Red, 35
PIE
   Blueberry, 311
      One-Crust, 269
      Two-Crust, 269
   Cherry, Mock, 270
   Clam, 132
   Cranberry, 271
   Codfish, Fluffy, 134
   Maple Syrup, 270
   Mincemeat
      Joan Bellward's, 272
      Moose, 67
      Venison, 74
   Partridge, 109
   Pastry
      Bear Fat, 313
      Cheese, 270
      Tasty, 269
   Peach, Golden, 272
   Pheasant, 110
   Pizza, 145
   Ptarmigan, 117
   Pumpkin, 270
   Rabbit, 87
   Saskatoon Berry, Mardy Gallagher's, 271
PIGEON
   Italienne, 281
   Roast, 113
PIGWEED, 208
   Red Flowering, 208
PIKE, 142
   Baked Whole, 142
PIMIENTO SALAD, JELLIED, MARIE
   BROWN'S, 240

PINE, POPLAR OR JACK, 210

PINEAPPLE
Mystery Fish Packages, 152
Partridge Stuffing, 28
Squares, Monah Carley's, 262

PIZZA PIE, EASY SARDINE, 145

PLANTS, EDIBLE WILD
(see Greens and Roots)

PLUCKING OF GAME BIRDS, 98

POACHED
Arctic Char, in Court Bouillon, 277
Fish in Milk, 153
Fish with Olive Sauce, 153
Inconnu, 139
Trout in Wine, 146

POCKETS, BLUEBERRY, 259

POINTERS FROM PIONEERS, 293-300

POLAR BEAR
Roast, 50
Liver (Warning), 48

POPLAR OR JACK PINE, 210

PORCUPINE, BOILED, 305

PORK
Chops, Oven Baked, Joan Wilson's, 93
Ham Casserole, 94
and Rice Casserole, 94
Wieners, Heather Clayton's, 93

PORTUGAISE SEAL, 288

POSITANESE FISH SOUP, 25

POT ROAST
Reindeer, with Vegetables, 69
Venison, Spicy, 75

POT ROASTING METHOD, 46

POTATOES,
Baked
Foil, 229
Stuffed, 227
Tuna-Stuffed, 148
with Variations, 227
Cheezie, 228
Clean-up Day, 229
Duchess, 230
French Fried, 231
Hash Brown, 231
Home Fried, 231
Mayonnaise, 242
Mock French Fried, 233
with Onions au Gratin, 230
Salad, 237
Scalloped, 232
Soup, Cream of, 26
Sprouts, 207
Stuffing, 28
Stuffing for Goose, 103

POUNDED
Dry Fish Pudding, 312
Dry Meat, 306

POWDERED
Eggs, 162, 164, 165
Milk, 6, 11, 296

PRAIRIE CHICKEN
in Cream, 114
Fried, 113
Ginger, 114
Roast, 114

PRESERVES, SALMONBERRY, 255, 311

PROPORTIONS FOR
Batters, 331
Doughs, 331
White Sauce, 331

PROTEINS
Function of, 2
Sources of, 2

PRUNE
Bread, Honey, 187
Cake, Luscious, 198
Cookies, Refrigerator, 203
Muffins,—Wheat, 190
Sherbet, Rose Hips and, Juice, 254
Stewed, 249

PTARMIGAN
Breast of, Breaded, 115
Breasts, Fried, 116
Pie, 117
Roast, 115
Soup, 308
Stew with Dumplings, 116
Stuffing for, 115
with Orange Rice, 116
with Peaches and Cream, 117

PUDDING SAUCE
(see Sauces, Dessert)

PUDDINGS
Apple
Crisp, 256
Crumble, 256
Dumplings, 256
Fritters, 255
Steamed, 257
Blueberry, 312
Buckle, 258
Crisp, 259
Kuchen, 258
Pockets, 259
Slump, 258
Charlie, 260
Cocoa Milk, 260
Cornstarch, 260
Cranberry, 261
Wild, 313
Danish Fish, 150
Dry Fish, Pounded, 312

PUDDINGS—*continued*
    Eve's, 257
    Indian, 312
    Loche Liver, 312
    Peach Crisp, 260
    Pineapple Squares, Monah Carley's, 262
    Rice, Old Fashioned, 312
    Rice and Raisin, 311
    Steamed, Mamie Leonard's, 257
    Tapioca Cream, 261

PUFFS, APPLE, 195

PUMPKIN PIE, 270

PUNCH, RASPBERRY, 251

PURCHASING FOOD, 9-13

PURÉE
    Rose Hip, 252
    Split Pea Soup, 26

PURPLE PLUM DUCKLINGS, 100

QUAIL
    With Green Grapes, 118
    in Toast Cups with Mushroom Sauce, 118
    in Wine Sauce, 117

QUICK
    Baked Whitefish, 148
    Carrot Soup, 23
    Dessert Sauce, 265
    Fish Casserole, 152
    Icing, 266
    Mayonnaise, 243
    Salad Dressing, 243
    Seal Casserole, 158
    Tomato Aspic, 240
    White Sauce, 30

QUICK BREADS
    (see Breads, Quick)

RABBIT
    Arctic Hare, 89
    Baked, Stuffed with Carrots, 82
    in Barbecue Sauce, 83
    Chop Suey, 282
    Creamed, on Toast, 85
    Creole, Sauce, 283
    Croquettes,—Ham, 88
    Curried, 85
    Deep Fried, 282
    Delight, 282
    French Fried, 84
    Fricassée, 85
    Hassenpfeffer, 284
    Hash, Baked, 86
    Jugged Hare, 283
    à la King, 86

RABBIT—*continued*
    à la Mode, 84
    Pie, 87
    Ragoût of Arctic Hare, 89
    Roasted, 307
    Salad, Jellied, 87
    Sandwich Spread, 86
    Skinning of, 81
    Soup, Boiled, 307
    Stew, with Dumplings, 81
    Sweet-Sour, 83

RAGOÛT
    Arctic Hare, 88
    Duck, 280

RAISIN
    Sauce, 35
    Bread, 178
    and Nut Stuffing, 28
    and Rice Pudding, 311

RASPBERRIES
    Jam, Frozen, 250
    Jam, and Red Currant, 250
    Jam, Wild, 250
    Punch, 251
    Shrub, 251

RATIONS, HINTS FOR COOKING
    WITH, 294-300

RED
    Flowering Pigweed, 208
    Sauce, Brown's, 35

REDUCED BÉCHAMEL SAUCE, 276

REGULATIONS, GAME, 315-325

REINDEER
    Bourguignon, 285
    Goulash, 70
    Head, Boiled, 306
    Head Cheese, 67
    Hoof, Boiled, 308
    Pot Roast, with Vegetables, 69
    Rib Roast of, Stuffed, 70
    Roast, Round of, 69
    Steak Rolls, Stuffed, 71
    Swiss Steak, 70
    Tongue, Boiled, 307

RELISH, RAW CRANBERRY, 248

RÉMOULADE SAUCE, 274

RENDERING
    Bone Grease, 308
    Fat or Suet, 48, 299

RHUBARB
    Dessert, 313
    and Rose Hip Jam, 254
    Wild, 211

RICE
    Curried, and Fish Flake Salad, 239
    and Egg Stuffing, 29

RICE—*continued*
  and Mushroom Stuffing, 28
  Old Fashioned, Pudding, 312
  Pork and, Casserole, 94
  Ptarmigan with Orange, 116
  and Raisin Pudding, 311
  Salt Cod and, Casserole, 134
  Seal and, Casserole, 156
  Stuffing, 29
  and Tomato with Cabbage Casserole, 217
  Wild, Stuffing for Duck, 29
RINGS
  French Fried Onion, 223
  Pan Fried, Onion, 224
ROAST
  Bear, Polar, 50
  Beaver, 76
  Buffalo, Prime Rib, 52
  Caribou, Standing Rib, 53
  Cony Head, 302
  Dall Sheep
    Leg of, 57
    Shoulder of, Stuffed, 57
  Duck, Hungarian, 279
  Fish, 300
  Fish by Campfire, 302
  Goose
    Wild, No. 1, 102
    Wild, No. 2, 102
    with Potato Stuffing, 103
  Grouse, 105
  Lynx, Oven, 307
  Muskrat, 305
  Partridge, 107
  Partridge, Stuffed, 107
  Pheasant, 110
  Pigeon, 113
  Prairie Chicken, 114
  Ptarmigan, 115
  Rabbit, 307
  Reindeer
    Pot, with Vegetables, 69
    Round of, 69
    Stuffed Rib of, 70
  Squirrel, 91
  Venison
    with Herbs, 72
    Spicy Pot, of, 75
  Whale, 309
    Stuffed, 159
ROASTING METHOD, 46
ROE, LOCHE LIVER AND, 140
ROLLED OAT
  Cookies, 201
  Cookies, Joyce's, 203
ROLLS, CRUSTY, 179
ROOTS
  Boiled, 310
  Edible Wild, 211

ROOTS—*continued*
  Alpine Bistort, 211
  Dandelion, 211
  Liquorice (Masu), 211
  Woolly Lousewort, 211
ROSE HIPS
  Applesauce Fortified with, Syrup, 251
  Candied, 253
  and Cranberry Jam, 252
  Jam, 252
  and Prune Juice Sherbert, 254
  Purée, 252
  and Rhubarb Jam, 254
  Syrup, 251
ROSE PETAL JELLY, 254
ROULADES OF SEAL, 289
ROUND
  Cut of Meat, 45
  Roast of Reindeer, 69
RUFFED GROUSE AMANDINE, 281
RUM SAUCE, 265

SAFETY
  (see Hunting in the NWT), 319
SALADS
  DESSERT
    Applesauce and Rose Hip, 251
    Frozen Delight, 241
    Pineapple Squares, Monah Carley's, 262
    Rose Hip and Prune Juice Sherbet, 254
    24-Hour, Grace Spencer's, 241
  FISH
    Curried Rice and Fish Flake, 239
    Crunchy Tuna, 239
    Favourite Fish, 239
    Salmon, 238
    Salmon Apple, 239
    Shrimp, 238
    Shrimp, Betty Oancia, 303
  JELLIED
    Cranberry Gelatin, 240
    Lemon Sour Cream Mold, 240
    Pimiento, Marie Brown's, 240
    Rabbit, 87
    Tomato Aspic, Quick, 240
  VEGETABLE
    Bean, Hot, 237
    Cabbage, and Apple, 238
    Cabbage, Slaw, Hot, 238
    Company's Coming Bean, 237
    Potato, 237
    Tomato Aspic, Quick, 240
SALAD DRESSING
  Boiled, 241
  French, 241

SALAD DRESSING—*continued*
Mrs. Hatting's, 242
Hot Bacon, for Greens, 242
Mayonnaise
No Egg, 242
Potato, 242
Quick, 243
Sour Cream, 243

SALMON
Baked, 143
Bisque, 25
Burgers, 143
Casserole, 145
Croquettes, 144
Cups, 144
Salad, 238
Salad, Apple, 239
Steaks, 143
Loaf, 144

SALMONBERRIES
Jam, 255
Preserves, 255, 311

SANDWICH SPREAD, RABBIT, 86

SARDINES
Croquettes, 145
Easy Pizza, 145

SASKATOON BERRY PIE, MARDY
GALLAGHER'S, 271

SAUCES
Anchovy Butter, 275
Barbecue, 30
Barbecue
for Partridge, 106
for Rabbitt, 83
Basic White, 30
Béchamel, Reduced, 276
Brown's Red, 35
Cantonese, 31
Cheese, 31
Cocktail, 31
Crab, for Whitefish, 149
Cranberry
Catsup, 248
Low-Bush, 32
Raw Relish, 248
Spiced, 34
Creole, 31, 283
Cucumber, 224
Fish Sauce, 302
Grape, 286
Hollandaise
No. 1, 32
No. 2, 32
Maître d'Hôtel Butter, 34
Marinade, 34
Mushroom, 33, 112, 118, 160
Mustard, Hot for Ham, 33
Olive for Fish, 153

SAUCES—*continued*
Orange for Carrots, 219
Parsley, 33, 220
Pepper, 34
Quick White, 30
Raisin, 35
Remoulade, 274
Rum, 265
Sour Cream Caper, 35
Sour Cream, Homemade, 32
Spanish, 35
Sweet and Sour, 36
Tartar, 36
Tomato, 36, 151
Venison, 36
Verte, 274
White Sauce
Basic, 30
Medium, 30, 331
Thick, 331
Thin, 30, 331
Wine
Fish in, 151
Quail in, 117

SAUCES, DESSERT OR PUDDING
Apple Butterscotch, 262
Blueberry, 263
Blueberry Syrup, 262
Blueberry Topping, 263
Butterscotch, 263
Caramel, 264
Chocolate
No. 1, 264
No. 2, 264
Fruit, 263
Lemon, 264
Quick Dessert, 265
Rum, 265
Vanilla, 265

SAUTÉED PARTRIDGE IN GRAPE
SAUCE, 286

SAVING ON
Bread and Cereal, 12
Cheese, 12, 13
Eggs, 12, 13
Fish, 12
Fruit, 11
Fuel, 11
Meat, 12
Milk, 11
Vegetables, 12
Vitamin D, 13

SAVOURY
Fish, 154
Seal Hearts, 289

SCALING FISH, 124

SCALLOPED
Beef Tenderloin, Dick's, 94

SCALLOPED—*continued*
Clams, 133
Corn, with Oysters, 220
Onions, 224
Potatoes, 232
Tomatoes, 234
Tuna, Irish Casserole, 147

SCONES, SCOTCH, 194

SCRAMBLED
Eggs
Fresh, 165
Powdered, 165

SCURVY GRASS
(see Greens), 208, 209

SEAL
Baked, Flippers with Vegetables, 156
Bearded, Liver, 155
Brain
Au Gratin, 290
Fritters, 290
Braised, 155, 286
Casserole, of, 157, 287
Quick, 158
and Rice, 156
Heart, Savoury, 289
Hearts, Braised, 87
Liver, Fried, 288
Newfoundland Flippers, 157
on a Bun, 157
Portugaise, 288
Roulades of, 289
Tournedos of, 292

SEA MAMMALS, 155-160, 286-290, 309,
315-317, 322

SERVING FROZEN FISH, 301

SHEEP, 56

SHERBET, ROSE HIP AND PRUNE
JUICE, 254

SHERRY
Grouse in, 104
Partridge Baked in, 109

SHRIMP
and Avocado Dip, 39
Dip, 39
Salad, 238
Salad, Betty Oancia, 303

SHRUB, RASPBERRY, 251

SKINNING OF ANIMALS
Beaver, 76
Big Game, 44
Lynx, 61
Muskrat, 79
Rabbit, 81
Squirrel, 89

SKUNK, BAKED, 305

SLAW, CABBAGE, HOT, 238

SLUMP, BLUEBERRY, 258

SMALL GAME ANIMALS,
(see Game Animals, Small)

SMOKED
Beaver, 307
Fish, 301
Chowder, 150
Fillets in Milk, 151
in Tomato Sauce, 151
in Wine Sauce, 151

SMOTHERED
Duck, 99
Muskrat and Onions, 79

SNACKS, TV, 38

SNOW MUFFINS, 190

SOFT-COOKED EGGS, 163

SORREL, MOUNTAIN, 209

SOUFFLÉ
Corn Vegetable, 220
Tuna Cheese, Kay Cardiff's, 147

SOUPS
Acorn, 313
Bean, Navy, 22
Cabbage, 21
Carrot, Quick, 23
Chicken Gumbo, 24
Clam, 24
Court Bouillon, 23
Fish, Fresh Cony, 302
Fish, Positanese, 25
Mongole, 25
Moosemeat, 64
Muskrat, 304
Onion, 21
Oyster Stew, 24
Peanut Butter, Cream of, 26
Potato, Cream of, 26
Ptarmigan, 308
Rabbit, 307
Salmon Bisque, 25
Split Pea, Purée of, 26
Tomato
Clear, 22
Cream of, 26
Vegetable, 22
Whitefish, 303

SOUP STOCK, 19, 20
Clear, 20
Brown, 20

SOUR CREAM
Beaver in, 78
Caper Sauce, 35
Cucumbers and Onions in, 224
Dressing, Salad, 243
Herring in, 137

SOUR CREAM—*continued*
    Home-Made, 32
    Mold, Lemon, Jellied, 240
    Partridge with, 109
    Venison Braised in, 72

SOURDOCK, 208

SOURDOUGH
    Starter, 182
    Bread, 183
    Chocolate Cake, 184
    Hotcakes, 183
    Hotcakes, Rosie Peeloolook, 310
    Muffins, 182
    Waffles, 184

SOUTHERN FRIED PHEASANT, 112

SPANISH
    Green Beans, 214
    Sauce, 35
    Tuna and Olives, 148

SPICED BLUEBERRY JAM, 246

SPICY POT ROAST OF VENISON, 75

SPROUTS
    Bean, for Vitamin C, 4
    Brussel, 216
    Potato, Use of, 207

SPRUCE TIPS
    (see Greens), 209

SQUARES
    Matrimonial, 200
    Pineapple, Monah Carley's, 262

SQUASH
    Baked, 236
    Candied, 235

SQUAW BREAD, OKLAHOMA, 195

SQUIRREL
    Broiled, 89
    Brunswick Stew, 90
    Casserole, with Biscuit Topping, 90
    Fricassée, 91
    Roast, 91
    Skinning of, 89

STAIN REMOVAL, 296-298

STANDING RIB ROAST OF CARIBOU, 53

STANDARD MEASURES AND
    PROPORTIONS, 331

STEAKS
    Arctic Char, 276
    Boiled Bear, 306
    Braised, of Sweet Grass Buffalo
        Carbonade, 51
    Elk 'N Gravy, 59
    Elk in Wine, 59
    in Foil, 96
    Grizzly Bear, 306

STEAKS—*continued*
    Halibut, Orange Broiled, 137
    Marinade for, 73
    Moose, Savoury, 65
    Pan Broiled, 49
    Reindeer, Rolls, Stuffed, 71
    Salmon, Broiled, 143
    Swiss
        Beef, in Foil, 96
        Moose, 68
        Reindeer, 70
    Venison, Pan Broiled, 73

STEAMED
    Arctic Char, 131
    Brown Bread, 186
    Cooking in Steam, 127
    Muskrat, 303
    Pudding, Apple, 257
    Pudding, Mamie Leonard's, 257

STEW
    Bear, à l'Espagnole, 50
    Canadian Lynx, 61
    English Brown, 60
    Indian Meat, 306
    Moose, Dorothy Macintosh's, 65
    Oyster, 24
    Partridge, 105
    Ptarmigan, with Dumplings, 116
    Rabbit, with Dumplings, 81

STEWED
    Prunes, 249
    Rhubarb, 313

STEWING METHOD, 46

STICKS, BREAD, 37

STORING OF
    Eggs, 162
    Vegetables, 207

STRAWBERRY BLIGHT, 208

STROGANOFF
    Beef, 95
    Elsie Rancier's, 95

STUFFED
    Arctic Char, Baked, 130, 275
    Caribou Heart, Baked, 55
    Dall Sheep, Shoulder of, 57
    Fish, Baked, Cooking Method, 125
    Green Peppers, 226
    Moose Heart, 68
    Muskrat, 303
    Onions, 225
    Partridge, Roast, 107
    Pickerel, Baked, 142
    Potatoes, Baked, 227
    Potatoes, with Tuna, Baked, 148
    Rabbit, with Carrots, Baked, 82
    Reindeer
        Rib Roast of, 70

STUFFED—*continued*
    Steak Rolls, 71
    Trout, with Mushrooms, 146
    Whale, Roast, 159
    Wieners, Heather Clayton's, 93
STUFFINGS
    Basic Bread, 275
    Bread, for Baked Fish, 27
    Cheese for Baked Fish, 27
    Cranberry, 27
    Egg Rice, 29
    Fruit, for Goose, 27
    Nut and Raisin, 28
    Partridge Pineapple, 28
    Potato, 28, 103
    Ptarmigan, 115
    for Rabbit, 82
    Rice, 29
    Rice and Mushroom, 28
    Tarragon Dressing, 27, 150
    Wild Goose, 102
    Wild Rice, for Duck, 29
SUBSTITUTION VALUES, 333
SUET OR FAT, TO RENDER, 48, 299
SUGAR COOKIES, 203
SUKIYAKI, MOOSE, 68
SUPPER MENUS, 4, 9
SUSAN'S BAKED EGGS AND
    CHEESE, 167
SUSAN'S EGG AND OLIVE MURRES, 166
SWEET
    Pickled Beaver, 77
    and Pungent Carrots, 219
    and Sour
        Deer Ribs, 60
        Rabbit, 83
        Sauce, 36
SWISS STEAK
    In Foil, 96
    Moose, 68
    Reindeer, 70
SYRUP
    Blueberry, 262
    Chocolate, 169
    Maple, Pie, 270
    Rose Hip, 251

TAILS
    Beaver, Fried, 78
    Muskrat, 304
TARRAGON DRESSING FOR
    FISH, 27, 150
TARTAR SAUCE, 36
TAPIOCA CREAM PUDDING, 261

TEA
    Fresh, 170
    Instant, 170
    Labrador, 209
TEA BISCUITS
    Apple Puffs, 195
    Bannock
        Enriched, 193
        French Toast, 162
        Small, 192
    Cranberry Coffee Cake, 195
    Oklahoma Squaw Bread, 195
    Scotch Scones, 194
    Tea Biscuits, 194
TENDERLOIN, BEEF, SCALLOPED
    DICK'S, 94
THICK WHITE SAUCE, 331
TII, 170
TOAST
    French, 162
    Quail with Mushroom Sauce in, Cups, 118
    Rabbit, Creamed on, 85
TOMATO
    Aspic, Quick, 240
    Casserole, with Rice and Cabbage, 217
    Fresh, in Vinegar, 234
    Joe's Fried, 233
    Sauce, 36
    Scalloped, 234
    Smoked Fish in, Sauce, 151
    Soup, Clear, 22
    Soup, Cream of, 26
    Surprise, 234
    Woodchuck Meat Patties with, Sauce, 92
TONGUE
    Caribou, Fresh, 56
    Reindeer, Boiled, 307
TOP-OF-THE-STOVE
    Cookies, 202
    Corn Bread, 193
TOPPING
    Blueberry, 263
    Squirrel Casserole with Biscuit, 90
    Oatmeal, for Fruit, 167
TOURNEDOS OF SEAL, 292
TRANSPORTING GAME, 324
TROPICAL BAKED PEACHES, 250
TROUT
    Baked, 147
    Casserole of Lake, 146
    Pan Fried, Lake, 146
    Stuffed with Mushrooms, 146
    Wine Poached, 146
TUNA
    Baked Tuna-Cheese Buns, 147

TUNA—*continued*
Crunchy, Salad, 239
Irish, Scalloped, Casserole, 147
Soufflé, Kay Cardiff's, -Cheese, 147
Spanish, and Olives, 148
Stuffed Baked Potato, 148
Touchdown, 148

TURNIP
Au Gratin, 235
Mashed, 235

TV SNACKS, 38

TWENTY-FOUR HOUR SALAD, GRACE
SPENCER'S, 241

UNCOOKED
Blueberry
Jam, 247
Jelly, 246
Chocolate Fudge, 268

UPSIDE-DOWN CAKE, PEACH, 199

VALUES
Calorie, of Foods, 327-330
Substitution, 333

VANILLA SAUCE, 265

VEGETABLE MARROW, BAKED, 236

VEGETABLES, 205-244
Choosing of, 206
Cooking of, 206
in Meal Planning, 5
Preparation of, 5
Storage of, 207
To Save on, 12

VEGETABLE SALADS
Bean, Hot, 237
Cabbage and Apple, 238
Cabbage Slaw, Hot, 238
Company's Coming Bean, 237
Potato, 237
Tomato Aspic, Quick, 240

VEGETABLE SOUFFLÉ, CORN, 220

VEGETABLE SOUP, 22

VENISON
Biscuit Roll, 71
Boiled Bone Grease, 308
Braised in Sour Cream, 72
Chili, 75
Cooking of, 45-57
Cuts of, 45
Definition of, 42
English Brown Stew, 60
Fried Meat with Left Over Porridge, 306
Head Cheese, 67

VENISON—*continued*
Heart of, Braised, 74
Indian Meat Stew, 306
Larding of, 45
Liver and Onions, 75
Marinade for, Steak, 73
Meat Loaf, 74
Mincemeat, 74
One Dish Meal, 73
Roast, with Herbs, 72
Sauce, 36
Spicy Pot Roast of, 75
Steaks, Pan Broiled, 73

VERTE, SAUCE, 274

VINEGAR, FRESH TOMATOES IN, 234

VITAMINS
Function of, 2
Requirements
Vitamin C, 4
Vitamin D, 3
To Save on, 13
Sources of, 2

WAFFLES
Sourdough, 184
Wendy's, 192

WATER
Body's Use of, 6
Cooking Fish in, 127

WAYS OF USING CRANBERRIES, 249

WESTERN STYLE
Baked Beans, 213
Scrambled Eggs, 165

WHALE
Bobotee of, 159
Fillet of, with Mushroom Sauce, 160
Fried, 309
Hunting of, 158, 315-317, 322
Mipku, 309
Muktuk, 309
Chowder, Arctic, 291
Preparation of, 159
Roasted, 309
Roast, Stuffed, 159

WHEAT MUFFINS, PRUNE—, 190

WHITE BREAD, 174

WHITEFISH
Baked, Quick, 148
Broiled, 149
with Crab Sauce, 149
Pan-Fried, 149
Soup, 303

WHITE SAUCE, BASIC
Thin, 30, 331
Medium, 30, 331

WHITE SAUCE, BASIC—*continued*
  Thick, 331
  Proportions for, 331
  Quick, 30

WHOLE WHEAT
  Bread, 175
  Light Bread, 173

WIENERS, HEATHER CLAYTON'S, 93

WILD
  Cranberry Pudding, 313
  Duck à l'Orange, 99
  Game Marinade, 48
  Goose
    Roast No. 1, 102
    Roast No. 2, 102
    Stuffing for, 103
  Greens, Edible, 208
  Mustard, 208
  Plants, Edible, 208
  Raspberry Jam, 250
  Rhubarb, 211
  Rice Stuffing for Duck, 29
  Roots, Edible, 211
  Smothered, Duck, 99

WILD GAME
  (see Game)

WILLOW
  Herb, 208

WILLOW—*continued*
  Tips, 210

WINE
  Elk Steak in, 59
  Fish in, Sauce, 151
  Quail in, Sauce, 117
  Trout Poached in, 146

WOODCHUCK OR GROUNDHOG
  with Biscuits, 92
  Fried, 91
  Meat Patties with Tomato Sauce, 92
  Skinning of, 91

WOODCOCK
  Broiled, 119
  in Cream, 119
  Oven Broiled, 119

WOOLLY LOUSEWORT, 211

YEAST BREADS
  (see Breads, Yeast), 173
  with Granular Yeast, 173
  with Sourdough Starter, 182

YORKSHIRE PUDDING, 192

ZONES, GAME, 320-325